Sing the song that's in your hearts,
Sing of the great Southwest.
Thank God, for Arizona
In splendid sunshine dressed,
For thy beauty and thy grandeur,
For thy regal robes so sheen,
We hail thee Arizona
Our Goddess and our queen.

PHOTOGRAPHY BY CAROL M. HIGHSMITH

FEATURING IMAGES FROM THE CRAIG & BARBARA BARRETT
ARIZONA COLLECTION, LIBRARY OF CONGRESS

WELCOME BY CARLA HAYDEN, LIBRARIAN OF CONGRESS

REFLECTIONS ON SANDRA DAY O'CONNOR
BY SCOTT O'CONNOR, WITH BOB BOZE BELL

INTRODUCTION BY LATTIE F. COOR

CHELSEA PUBLISHING, INC.,
IN ASSOCIATION WITH THE LIBRARY OF CONGRESS

Arizona

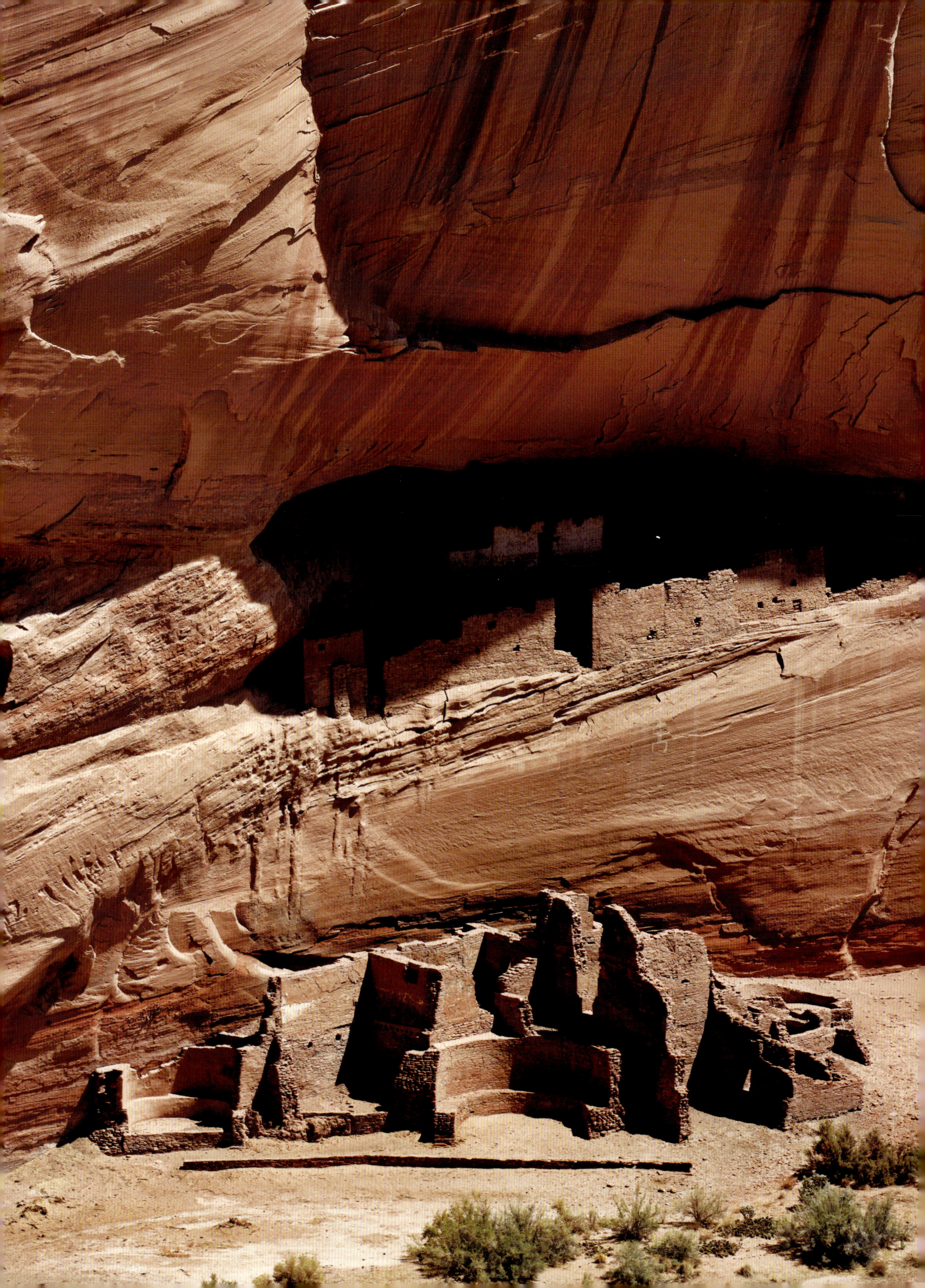

WELCOME

Carla Hayden

IN THE CLASSIC 1940 guide to their state, the Federal Writers' Project authors in Arizona cataloged its assets: "Indians, Mexicans, pioneers, engineers, cowpunchers, ranchers, miners, tourists; ruins that crumbled when Rome was young, mighty dams not yet complete; forests, deserts, mountains, mesas; mines, farms, orchards. These are Arizona, land of contrasts and contradictions, never to be fully understood by the most understanding, always to be loved by those who know the state." Carol M. Highsmith has photographed all of these, including the long-since-completed dams, and added compelling new subjects to the list. Many of them appear in this splendid volume.

Since 1980 Highsmith has followed in the footsteps and the tripod indentations of the pioneering landscape photographer Frances Benjamin Johnston (1864–1952) and the photojournalist Dorothea Lange (1895–1965). Each crisscrossed the United States and created thousands of images that are held at the Library of Congress. Johnston, who donated her life's work to the Library, and Lange, who documented rural America, prompted Highsmith to do both as well. She has methodically recorded the nation's architecture, landscapes, and its people, and in 1992 she began giving her photographs to the Library, generously permitting the public free use of them. The Highsmith Archive now holds more than fifty-two thousand images.

Thirty years into her career, Highsmith launched her ambitious This Is America project, spending months at a time in a state photographing places and people. With the publication of *Arizona*, the Library of Congress is pleased to share a beautiful sampling from the Craig & Barbara Barrett Arizona Collection, which forms a part of the This Is America project and the Highsmith Archive. The Barretts sponsored Highsmith's work in the Grand Canyon State, resulting in twenty-five hundred photographs.

I encourage you to visit the Library of Congress online at www.loc.gov, where you can access the Highsmith Archive, or drop by our Prints and Photographs Reading Room in person and see some of the other fourteen million images in our collections.

Above: Carla D. Hayden is the fourteenth Librarian of Congress. Opposite: Remains of the homes of ancient cliff dwellers in Canyon de Chelly (pronounced duh-SHAY) are part of a vast national monument on Navajo tribal lands.

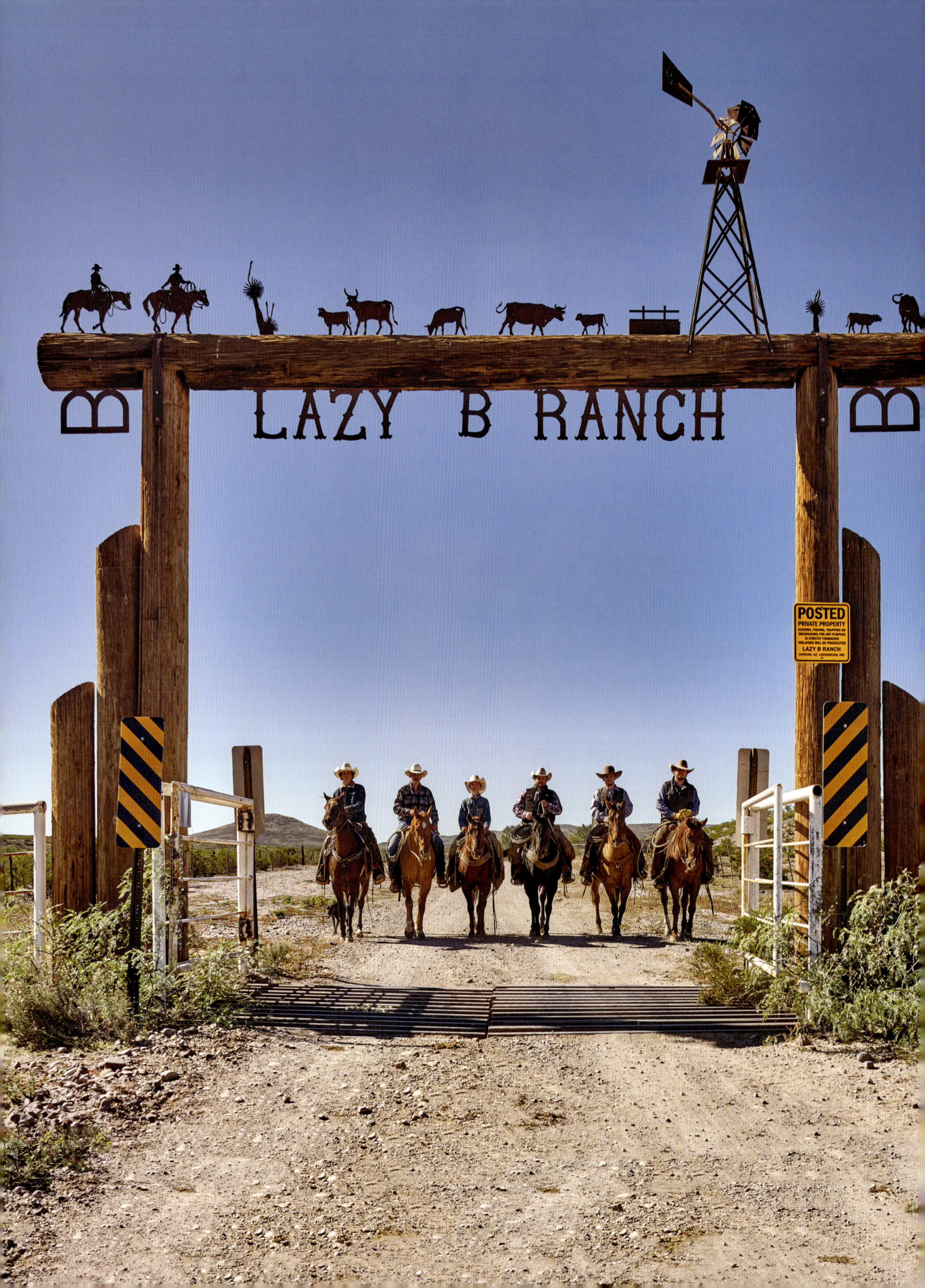

REFLECTIONS ON SANDRA DAY O'CONNOR

Scott O'Connor, with Bob Boze Bell

Whether they were wrangling ornery kids or dispatching hogs, chickens, scorpions, and rattlesnakes, the women who lived in Arizona Territory had to be tough. We, their offspring, admire and thank them for their grit. —Bob Boze Bell

OUR FOREBEARS were hardy stock. Despite the privations of Arizona pioneer life, a sense of humor was essential survival gear. We have it in our DNA.

HC Day—the family didn't take to putting periods in abbreviated names—left a poor farm in upstate Vermont to seek his fortune. He found it in Wichita, Kansas, during its cowtown boom decade from 1870 to 1880. Taking advice from his brother-in-law, recently returned from war with the Chiricahua Apache tribe, HC moved to Arizona in 1880 and brought in a herd of cattle from Mexico. He named his ranch the Lazy B after its cattle brand, modifying the sideways *B* mark with a horizontal line. No fences, no railroads, no law. It was daring. The Gunfight at the OK Corral was a year into the future. Arizona would not be a state for another thirty-two years.

Harry Alfred Day was born in 1889 to HC and Alice Hilton Day at their Franklin, Arizona, home along the Gila River, a couple of miles from the New Mexico line. DA, as he was later known, was the youngest of five children. He had a brief taste of ranch life in Arizona before HC packed up and moved again, to Pasadena, California, so his young family could receive a proper education.

DA enjoyed California, becoming a state swimming champion and a lifeguard in Long Beach. But before he could matriculate at Stanford, HC passed away; DA was sent back to Arizona to run the Lazy B Ranch for the family. He bought some bulls from Willis Wilkey and married Wilkey's attractive daughter, Ada Mae, joking that Ada Mae was part of the deal.

In 1934 Congress passed the Taylor Grazing Act, requiring fences on ranch land. With fencing came disputes over who got what. DA was appointed to the Federal Grazing Commission and had to settle those. One neighbor got thousands of acres from DA before he was willing to put away his shotgun. It was all right, as the Lazy B retained almost two hundred thousand acres, mostly federal land.

Another addition to the Lazy B in 1930 was Sandra, the first child of DA and Ada Mae. A precocious student, she lived with her grandmother Wilkey in El Paso, two hundred miles away, during the school year. On July 16, 1945, she was up early helping with breakfast at the ranch house at 5:30 A.M. and witnessed the

Above: Sandra Day O'Connor, photographed here by Yousef Khanfar in her United States Supreme Court chambers, overcame a hardscrabble childhood to become the first woman named to the Court as well as a Presidential Medal of Freedom recipient. Opposite: Formative years on her family's arid Lazy B Ranch, where she rode and roped cattle and shot with the cowhands, toughened her for life's challenges. "No one learns more about a problem than the person at the bottom," she later wrote of the experience.

flash from the world's first nuclear bomb test at White Sands, New Mexico, 175 miles away. The following year, at just sixteen, she entered Stanford.

Young Sandra shared the Lazy B with her best friends from El Paso and Stanford. Three of her college beaus made the trip to meet the parents. The first, Andy Campbell, a mechanical engineer and a Navy vet, repaired a balky pump motor, impressing the cowboys who tested him with the assignment. The second, a young Bill Rehnquist, would one day become chief justice of the United States. The third and last such guest, John O'Connor, was offered sizzling testicles straight out of the branding box as he met DA for the first time. "Mmmmm. Very good, Mr. Day. Thank you!" he exclaimed. He passed the test and married Sandra.

The newlyweds settled in Phoenix, John's choice. He was from San Francisco, her choice, but he persuaded Sandra that Phoenix was about to be a boomtown as Wichita had been for her grandfather. They each had a chance to make a difference there, he told her. Wise words.

Sandra had studied creative writing at Stanford with Wallace Stegner, who became a powerful influence. His writing about the West wove into her experience growing up on her family's beloved ranch. The connection helped shape her views on Arizona's economic development when she later found herself majority leader of the state senate and a state judge.

Beginning both their legal and community-oriented volunteer careers in Phoenix exposed the young couple to Arizona's incredible diversity of cultures, climates, flora, and fauna. Sandra joined the Heard Museum board of trustees, later serving as its president. She learned about Arizona's native tribes, taking the family to visit their communities as well as sites built by their ancestors. Having loved the outdoors since her childhood, Sandra organized family trips that involved backpacking, whitewater rafting, and skiing in snow and water.

Fifteen miles down the Gila from the Lazy B Ranch, in York, Arizona, lived Louise Guess, two years older than Harry Day. We are not sure if Harry ever met Louise, but we suspect that they did because Louise and Bob Guess were married on the Lazy B. A ten-foot-tall *Not-So-Gentle Tamer* bronze of Louise Guess stands at the civic center of Prescott Valley, representing Arizona pioneer women. Sandra has her own towering bronze statue in the Sandra Day O'Connor Federal Courthouse in Phoenix, sculpted with a law book under one arm. Louise holds a shovel, used for both gardening and killing rattlesnakes, one of which dangles helplessly from her free hand.

Sandra's law books taught her to kill veritable snakes in the legislative and litigation arenas, while Louise's hoe was used more prosaically. Both knew when and how to use their tools to best effect.

Scott, Brian, and Jay O'Connor, the sons of Sandra Day O'Connor—the first woman appointed to the United States Supreme Court—are proud of their family heritage. Bob Boze Bell is an artist, a humorist, and a raconteur, as well as editor and publisher of True West Magazine.

H. Alan Day, a rancher and a writer, is dwarfed by one of the Lazy B's two 1915-vintage wooden windmills. When he and his sisters Sandra and Ann grew up on the dusty spread along the New Mexico border, the nearest paved road was nine miles away, and the bus route to school ran thirty-two miles one way. "This was no country for sissies, then or now," Day and O'Connor wrote in a memoir of the siblings' childhoods here.

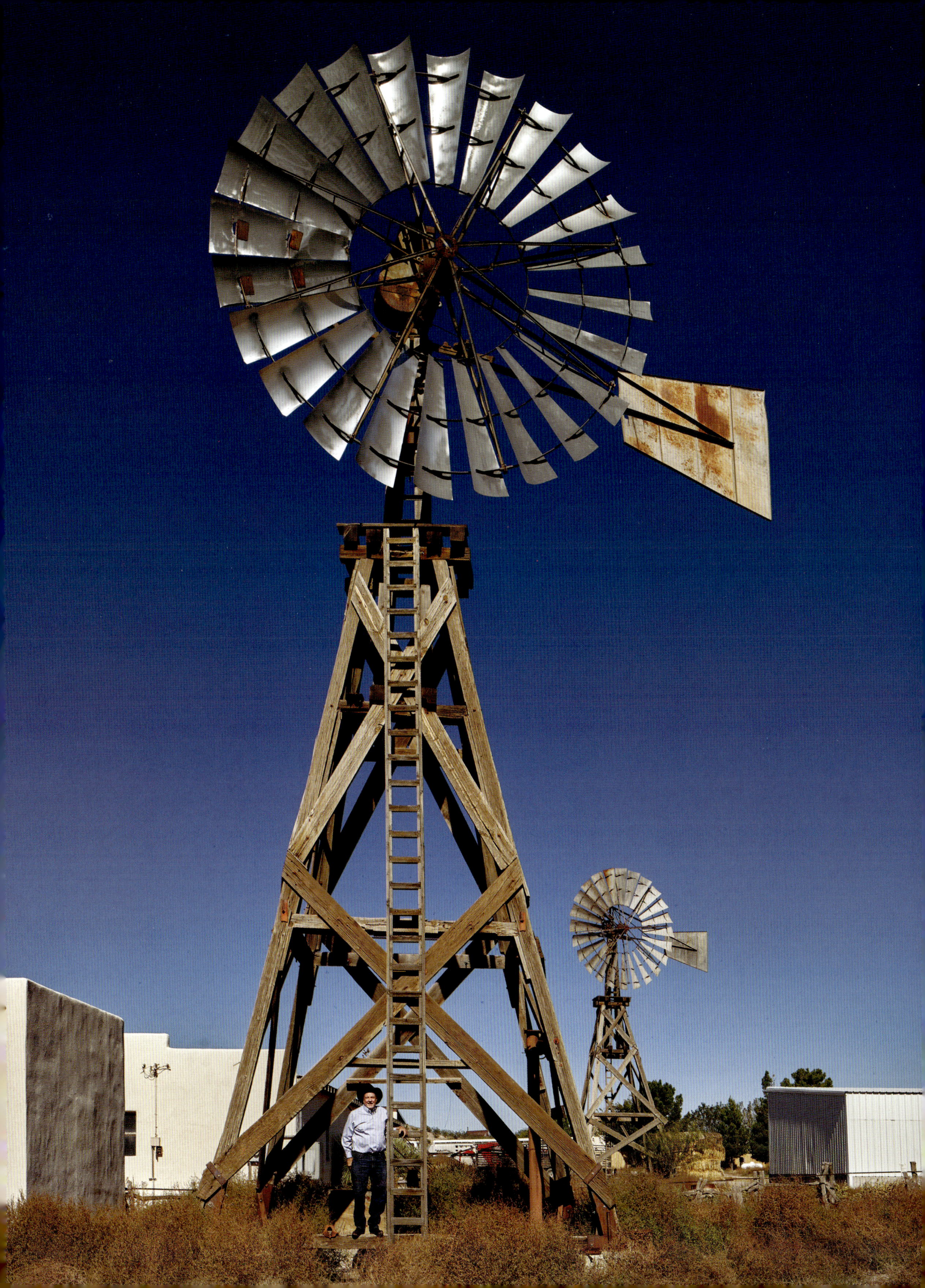

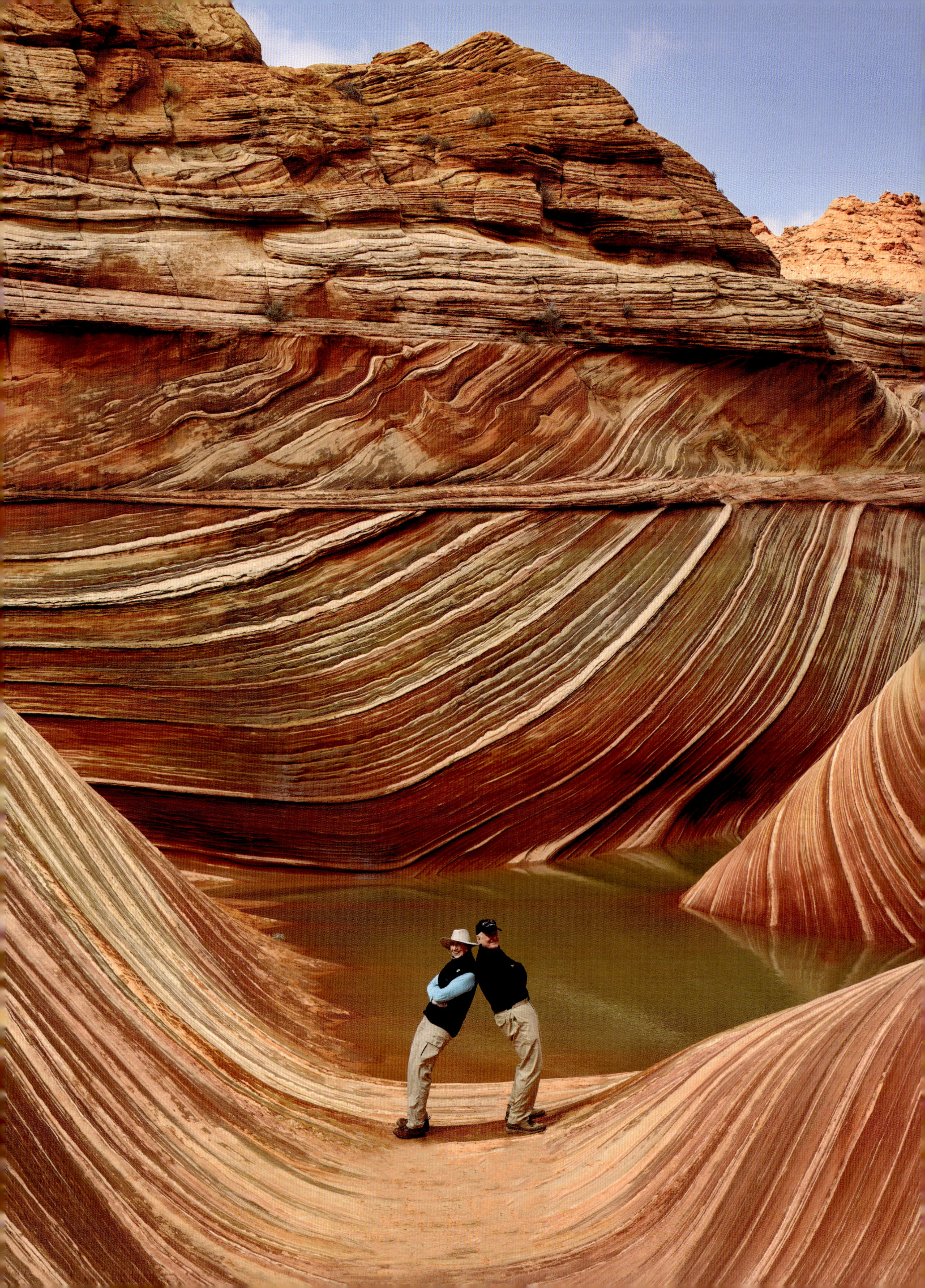

INTRODUCTION

Lattie F. Coor

THIS BOOK, with its magnificent set of images by Carol M. Highsmith, celebrates the Arizona we love and portrays who we are and what marvels we enjoy as Arizonans. My wife, Elva, and I are Arizona natives, having had the good fortune to be born into families who arrived when Arizona was still a territory. Her ancestors were ranchers and farmers who showed up in the Verde Valley in 1875, and mine came as educators to Phoenix in 1907. In every census since 1900, two-thirds of Arizona respondents have consistently indicated that they were born elsewhere. We take great pride in welcoming our newcomers, who can use this book to understand the wonderful state in which they have chosen to live.

In undertaking this project, Highsmith has captured the sheer beauty of Arizona. She has given center stage to the Grand Canyon, from its magnificent presence to the intimacy one can find in the lives of the Havasupai in their village and in the hidden crevices that cannot be seen from the rim. Here also is the steam engine of the Grand Canyon Railway that brings visitors from Williams to the canyon, just as it did a hundred years ago when the national park opened. Today's visitors can still walk through the Hopi House, where items made by Hopi artists are in full array. At Mary Colter's Lookout Studio, they can still behold a view of the canyon that continues to awe tourists and Arizonans alike.

But the Grand Canyon is just an appetizer for a universe of stunning geological sculptures, of which the Wave, west of Lake Powell in the Coyote Buttes, is, in my opinion, the most beautiful. The undulating formation shown in these pages captures a visit by Craig and Barbara Barrett, generous supporters of this photography project. Nearby—in relative Arizona terms—are Buckskin Gulch, the longest slot canyon in America, and its companion in the Paria Canyon–Vermillion Cliffs Wilderness Area. Another visitor favorite is Antelope Canyon, an accessible slot canyon near the town of Page. Even more popular is the Monument Valley Navajo Tribal Park, straddling the Utah border. Among these and other images in the book are additional manifestations of nature at its exquisite best, from Canyon de Chelly to the Painted Desert and its bewitching companion, the Petrified Forest.

Beyond these wonders, Arizona holds other exemplars of sheer beauty. Our mountains, lakes, and forests constitute a third of state land. The Colorado Plateau, from the Mogollon Rim escarpment north to the Utah border and east to the New Mexico line, incorporates roughly another third of Arizona. Ranging

Barbara and Craig Barrett have each other's backs at the Wave, an awe-inspiring but rarely beheld wonder on the Utah border. Barbara, a former astronaut and U.S. ambassador to Finland, and Craig, the retired chairman and chief executive officer of the Intel Corporation, underwrote Carol Highsmith's sweeping study of Arizona, from which the images in this book are taken. Glimpses of the Wave are rare because the Bureau of Land Management issues only twenty daily permits for visits to this highly fragile natural marvel.

from three to eight thousand feet high, it features America's largest contiguous ponderosa pine forest. Here aspen, juniper, spruce, oak, pinyon, and fir trees proliferate, sheltering the bears, antelope, deer, and elk that are at home in these dense woods.

Arizona's two tallest mountains tower nearby. One is Humphreys Peak, which soars to 12,633 feet; the other, Mount Baldy, rises 11,421 feet high southwest of Springerville. Both have ski areas. The chairlift at Arizona Snow Bowl in the San Francisco Peaks (home to Humphreys Peak) reaches 11,500 feet. Sunrise Ski Resort's lift attains 11,100 feet. Down below, Arizona's greatest lakes are a product of the Colorado River, impounded above the Grand Canyon by Lake Powell; confined below is Lake Mead. Far downstream, Lake Havasu's claim to fame is its own London Bridge. In central Arizona four lakes from reservoirs on the Salt and Verde Rivers are used actively by nearby neighbors in Metro Phoenix.

Twenty-five percent of Arizona's territory is grassland. Prairies stretch from the lowest desert to state forests and mountain valleys. Highsmith has done a fine job of capturing the range and variety of these grasses. A true story, told with amusement among Arizonans, is that the movie *Oklahoma* was filmed not on the Great Plains but in our own San Rafael Valley. Even though that area lies near the harsh Sonoran Desert, it affirms that a substantial savannah can thrive almost anywhere.

This seemingly endless desert constitutes 42 percent of state land and extends beyond Arizona into the Mexican states of Sonora and Baja California. Biologically it is one of the most diverse deserts in the world. Its signature plants are saguaro, barrel, organ pipe, prickly pear, and cholla cacti; ocotillo and yucca shrubs; spiky century plants; creosote bushes; and elephant, desert ironwood, mesquite, and palo verde trees. Animals of note include desert bighorn sheep, mule deer, mountain lions, gray foxes, coyotes, and disagreeable, boarlike javelinas. Gila monsters, tarantulas, scorpions, and a rogue's gallery of lizards and snakes—including diamondback rattlers, for which Arizona's Major League Baseball team is named—are denizens of the desert, avoided where possible by jackrabbits, kangaroo rats, and human beings. Owls, hawks, roadrunners, Gila woodpeckers, and Gambel's quail are a few of the remarkable bird species present.

The most agreeable and spectacular time in the desert is early spring, from late February, as the groundhog cholla reveal their hot-pink blooms, through March, with its riot of color from the blossoms of other chollas, ocotillos, poppies, lupines, penstemon, brittlebush, and fairy dusters. Mid-April brings the saguaro's white crown of flowers, then the ancient ironwood trees close out the season with their delicate lavender display. Some years, depending on the monsoon season—Arizona indeed has significant seasonal downpours—the flower show will be modest but still enchanting; at other times, the vibrant spectacle is almost overwhelming. The desert's magnificent sunrises, sunsets, and bountiful sunshine and blue skies are also part of Arizona's magic. Several world-class architects—Frank Lloyd Wright and Paolo Soleri among them—made the Arizona desert their home and inspiration, as you will see on several pages of this book.

Native peoples have traversed Arizona's lands since antiquity. The Hohokam lived in the low country of the Salt River valley, now the locus of Metro Phoenix. They were an agricultural people who dug a network of canals to harness and tap the water from one of the region's two major rivers, the Salt and the Gila. The Hohokam grew corn, cotton, beans, tobacco, and squash. For meat, they hunted deer, bighorn sheep, antelope, squirrels, and even mice. For reasons still unclear—perhaps drought, disease, or fear of enemies—they vacated the Salt River valley in the fourteenth century, some likely moving toward higher ground. Other indigenous peoples are represented in the desert communities of the Pima, Maricopa, Ak-Chin, and Tohono O'odom tribes that live today on vast reservations from Phoenix to the Mexican border.

Native presence in our high country is represented by Puebloan people, currently the Hopi, Zuni, and Apache, along with the Navajos who migrated

Navajo tribal members Loretta Atene, her daughter Eula, and their infant grandson and son Leon Clark offer scale and a human dimension to the immense and windswept Monument Valley (*Ooljéé'tó* in Navajo). This red-sand desert wonderland is part of the Navajo Tribal Park straddling the Arizona-Utah border. The valley's isolated, towering sandstone buttes—a popular backdrop for Western movies even before John Wayne starred in *Stagecoach* here in 1939—are eroded remains of Rocky Mountain foothills, whittled and shaped by water and wind.

Isolated at dusk, a towering saguaro is the namesake of a national park in two sections bookending Tucson. This cactus species can sprout twenty-five or more charmingly uplifted arms, but the first does not usually pop for seventy-five years or so. Although Arizona picks no official cactus among its more than fifty varieties, the saguaro's spring blooms are its state flower. In this place where water is a scare surface commodity, the saguaro's roots typically burrow just six inches into the desert sand.

from Canada and the Pacific Coast, spilling into Utah and New Mexico. At twenty-seven thousand square miles, with more than 350,000 enrolled members, the Navajo Nation is the largest native settlement in the country. Twenty-one Indian reservations occupy 27 percent of Arizona's soil. Many Native Americans regularly move into urban areas, where they attend college and establish a life off the reservation.

The panoply of evocative photographs in this book illustrate the cultural and artistic contributions of Arizona's Native Americans, as well as those of its Latino population. Spanish conquistadors first explored the Southwest more than two hundred years before the United States was founded. Francisco Vázquez de Coronado led his expedition through what are now Arizona and New Mexico eighty years before the *Mayflower* landed in Plymouth.

Many Indians follow practices with a long history, such as the Apaches' ritual of celebrating each girl's entry into womanhood through a multiday community ceremony. For boys, the Hopi have their own transition to manhood. The Heard Museum, which is dedicated to the advancement of American Indian art, annually sponsors a World Championship Hoop Dance Contest that draws dancers from tribes throughout the nation. Native peoples' artistic artifacts—from dazzling turquoise jewelry to woven goods, katsina dolls, and vivid paintings—significantly enrich our society. Inspiring, too, is the substantial number of Latino, Native American, African American, and Asian American festivals that enliven event calendars across Arizona.

At the end of the nineteenth century and the beginning of the twentieth, when Arizona was preparing its case to join the Union as the forty-eighth state, an influx of treasure seekers descended. They launched a hunt for veins of gold, copper, lead, and silver. By the 1940s Arizona was producing 70 percent of the nation's copper. Copper mines soon became such a financial force that Arizona was dubbed the Copper State until homage to the Grand Canyon replaced that nickname.

When Arizona entered the Union in February 1912, more than two hundred thousand people lived here. Many were farmers and ranchers, thanks to the Homestead Act of 1862, as well as to the completion, a year after statehood, of the Theodore Roosevelt Dam to channel the Salt River into a modern version of the canals left by the Hohokam. A significant number of Arizonans worked in the mines—many then, as now, Latinos and Native Americans. Other lures in addition to mining jobs contributed to a significant population influx. One was a national tuberculosis scare that made Arizona's dry, hot climate a magnet. Dozens of sanitariums were built in Phoenix and Tucson to accommodate those seeking treatment.

Tourism took off in the 1920s, thanks to a substantial spike in railroad and automobile traffic. Route 66 became the road of choice for romantic trips to the breathtaking West, including the increasingly accessible Grand Canyon. Fred

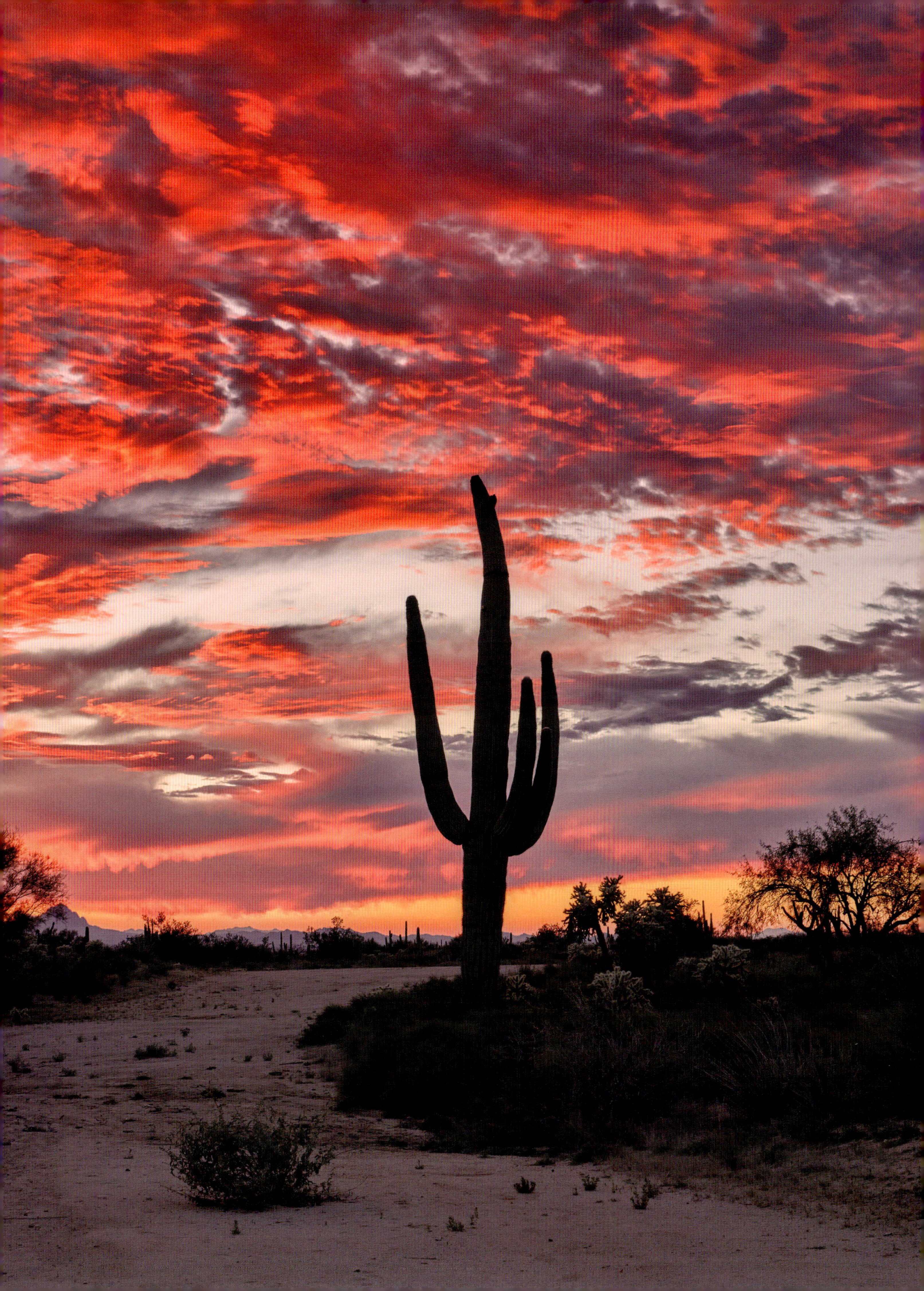

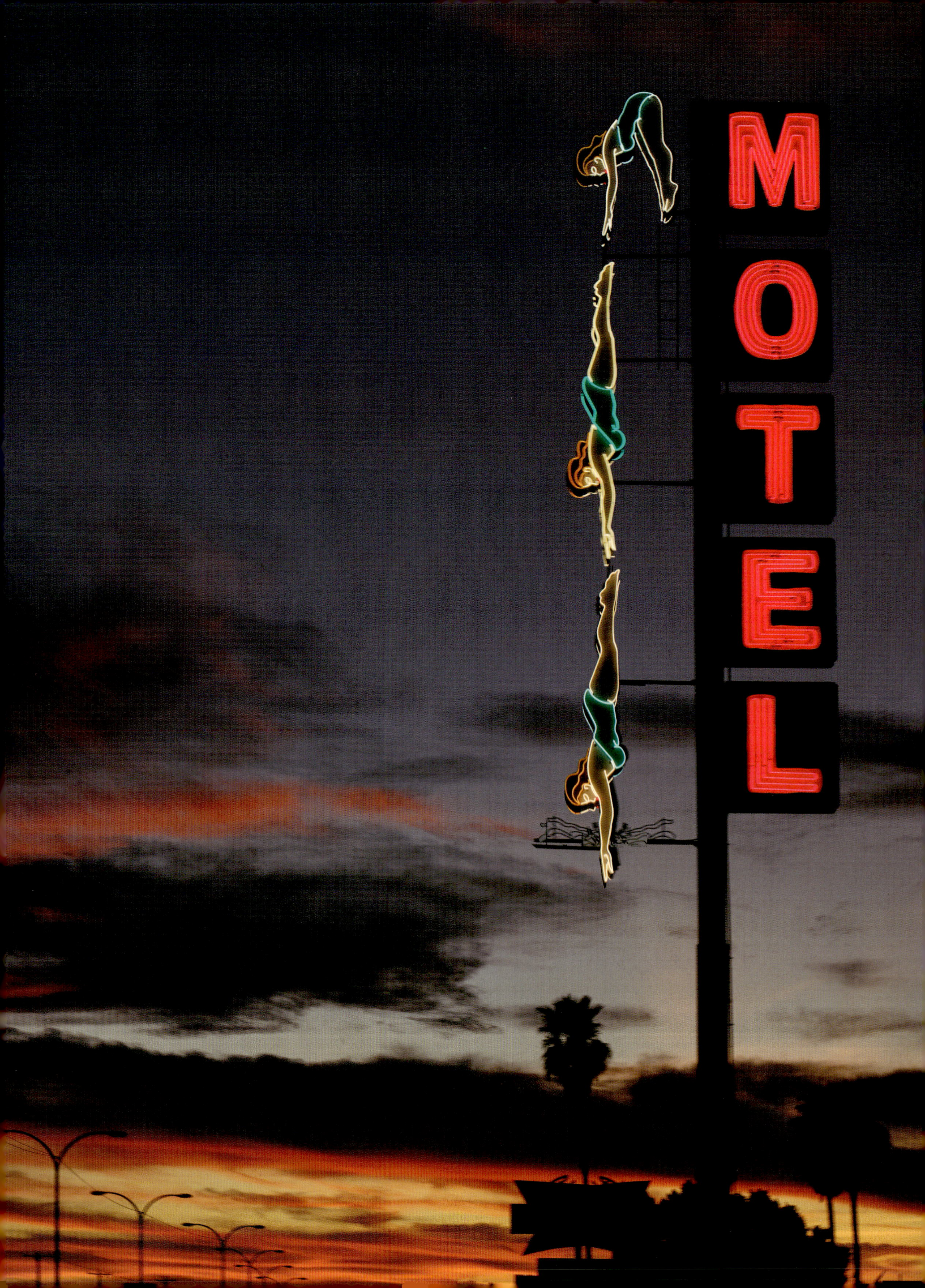
MOTEL

Harvey created classy Harvey Houses for the Atchison, Topeka and Santa Fe Railway along a line that drew tourists for meals, a glimpse of the Harvey Girls, and overnight accommodations en route to their destination, including Arizona's wondrous canyon. In the warmer parts of the state—people are often surprised by winter's icy grasp on our north country—dude ranches, resorts, mineral baths, and elegant hotels sprang up to cater to a wealthy clientele. Several superb photographs of these oases, a number of which still welcome winter guests in 1920s style, adorn this book.

Arizona's response to the two world wars also played a significant role in shaping this young state. Take the Goodyear Tire and Rubber Company's contribution during World War I. At that time, the only known material for the sidewalls of pneumatic tires was extra-long staple cotton. (A staple is a measurement for cotton fiber. Extra-long fibers from a boll exceed 1⅜ inches.) Such reinforced tires were essential for the U.S. Army's motor vehicles in the European theater. Early in the war, the Central Powers, Germany and Italy, conquered Egypt, cutting off the supply of extra-long staple cotton for which Egypt was the world's primary source. Paul W. Litchfield, then a young Goodyear executive in Akron, Ohio, challenged his staff to find a place stateside where this essential type of cotton would grow. The chosen site was a square mile in Gilbert, Arizona. There Goodyear found a way to domestically cultivate the fiber, called pima cotton in honor of the Indian tribe that largely farmed the crop. The operation prompted Goodyear to buy substantial acreage in Phoenix's West Valley in which to grow the proper cotton needed for the war effort.

At the inception of World War II, the Litchfield Naval Air Station was built just south of the Goodyear Farms to make high-tensile envelopes used as the skin of blimps. The U.S. Navy not only used the new air station for conventional military aircraft, it also dramatically expanded the blimp force to aid antisubmarine warfare off the West Coast. The air station and the blimp factory created so many jobs that an entire town, appreciatively named Goodyear, was created to house the workers. With a multitude of air bases and associated sites popping up across Arizona, entire aviation and manufacturing industries were born. After the war's conclusion in 1945, thousands of veterans returned to Arizona, laying the foundation for Phoenix and Tucson to balloon into sprawling metropolises.

The advent of domestic air conditioning led to an explosive, sustained housing boom as well. Developers such as John F. Long wooed returning veterans and erected 125 or more houses a week. His spanking-new planned community of Maryvale became Arizona's Levittown. Residential swimming pools and a spate of new golf courses attracted still more newcomers to the state's metropolitan areas.

Arizona remains one of the nation's fastest-growing states. Its population mushroomed from 750,000 in 1950 to 3.7 million in 1990 and to 6.8 million in 2015. About eight million people will call Arizona home in 2020—80 percent of

It was 1960, a tad past the heyday of two-lane highway travel but a time when Phoenix-area hoteliers were scrambling for customers during the region's first population explosion. That year the Diving Lady neon sign debuted outside Mesa's Starlite Motel. In the gloom of night, three divers became one, plunging in stages into a blue electric pool. Fifty years later, a vicious storm smashed the sign to shards, but preservationists rushed to the Diving Lady's rescue. She was revived and returned to her jackknifing descents.

them in the Phoenix and Tucson metropolitan areas. Who would have thought that Arizona would become one of the most urban states in America, albeit with a desert-themed distribution of homes and businesses?

The Sonoran Desert does indeed surround, and somewhat define, Phoenix and Tucson. But so do substantial mountains—the result of the juxtaposition of what the author John McPhee calls their "basin and range." Over millions of years, mountains form as a result of volcanic activity or uplifts, while they shed particles that provide tillable soil to otherwise arid valleys. To the north and east of Tucson, the Catalinas and the Rincons line their basin. The Santa Rita range rises to the south, with the Tortolita and Tucson Mountains encroaching on the city's western side. These ranges provide miles of trails for hiking, horseback riding, cycling, and saguaro sighting. Just south of the Rincons is a trailhead for the 814-mile Arizona Trail, a National Scenic Trail between Utah and Mexico.

Phoenix has a similar configuration of mountains and relatively flat terrain. To the south lies South Mountain Park, the largest city park in the country. Continuing the ring of hills, the Estrellas command the southwestern skyline, and the White Tanks to the west look down on Luke Air Force Base. To the east are the San Tans, the Superstitions, Usery Park, and several trails in the McDowell Mountains within Scottsdale. Even teeming Phoenix itself contains low mountains, including Piestewa Peak, the Phoenix Mountain Preserve, Mummy and Camelback Mountains, and outcroppings in Papago Park.

Look closely in this book, and you will see how our cities have snuggled up to the mountains, or vice versa. This makes possible a significant range of recreational options. In Phoenix alone, the Central Arizona Conservation Alliance unifies sixty organizations dedicated to using, preserving, and expanding open space. And Maricopa County has created a 315-mile trail that links all of the mountains surrounding the central city. Pathways along the canals that cut through Greater Phoenix are a lasting example of how to create and protect recreational opportunities. Their use as hiking and cycling trails has an interesting lineage. The canals currently used for transporting water from the Salt River and the Central Arizona Project, which carries water to both Phoenix and Tucson, are modern versions of the crude but effective network developed by the Hohokam and used for a thousand years until the 1400s.

An ample menu of other activities for relaxation is available here as well. Golfing remains so fashionable that 185 courses offer tee times in Phoenix alone. High school and collegiate athletics are robust. Arizona State University has nine men's and eleven women's varsity sports. Both ASU and the University of Arizona compete in the Pac-12 Conference, with large and enthusiastic fan bases at home and away. Most Arizonans are not a sedentary lot, but there is a strong following for professional football, basketball, baseball, and ice hockey—not to mention support for big league baseball such that half of the majors' thirty teams now train in Cactus League sites here.

Wedged into the southwestern corner of Arizona, seven miles from Mexico, Yuma seems an odd spot for an Ocean-to-Ocean Bridge. But as the first highway crossing of the lower Colorado River at its opening in 1915, it was the sole connection between East and West for automobile traffic for hundreds of miles.

As a relatively young state, Arizona has played a significant role in the nation's affairs. Henry Fountain Ashurst served as Arizona's first U.S. senator in 1912 and Carl Hayden as the new state's initial U.S. representative, continuing in office for fifty-seven years from statehood until 1969. U.S. Senator Barry Goldwater made history for Arizona in 1964 when he became the Republican nominee for president of the United States. Sandra Day O'Connor, the United States Supreme Court's first woman justice, is warmly profiled in the preceding reflections; she served from 1981 to 2006, joining her fellow Arizonan William Rehnquist during his service as chief justice. In the Arizona election of 1998, every one of the statewide elective offices was filled by a woman, a group that came to be known as the Fab Five. To date Arizona has had four female governors—Rose Mofford, Jane Dee Hull, Janet Napolitano, and Jan Brewer—the most in the nation; the last three served consecutively from 1997 to 2015.

So we are a land of achievers as well as wonders. I gladly invite you to see and read about both in this commendable book. My thanks go to Carol Highsmith, Craig and Barbara Barrett, and the Library of Congress for including Arizona as one of the early subjects of the project to celebrate America on a state-by-state basis. It encourages all Arizonans to commit ourselves to be stewards responsible for protecting and enhancing our treasures for the future.

Arizona

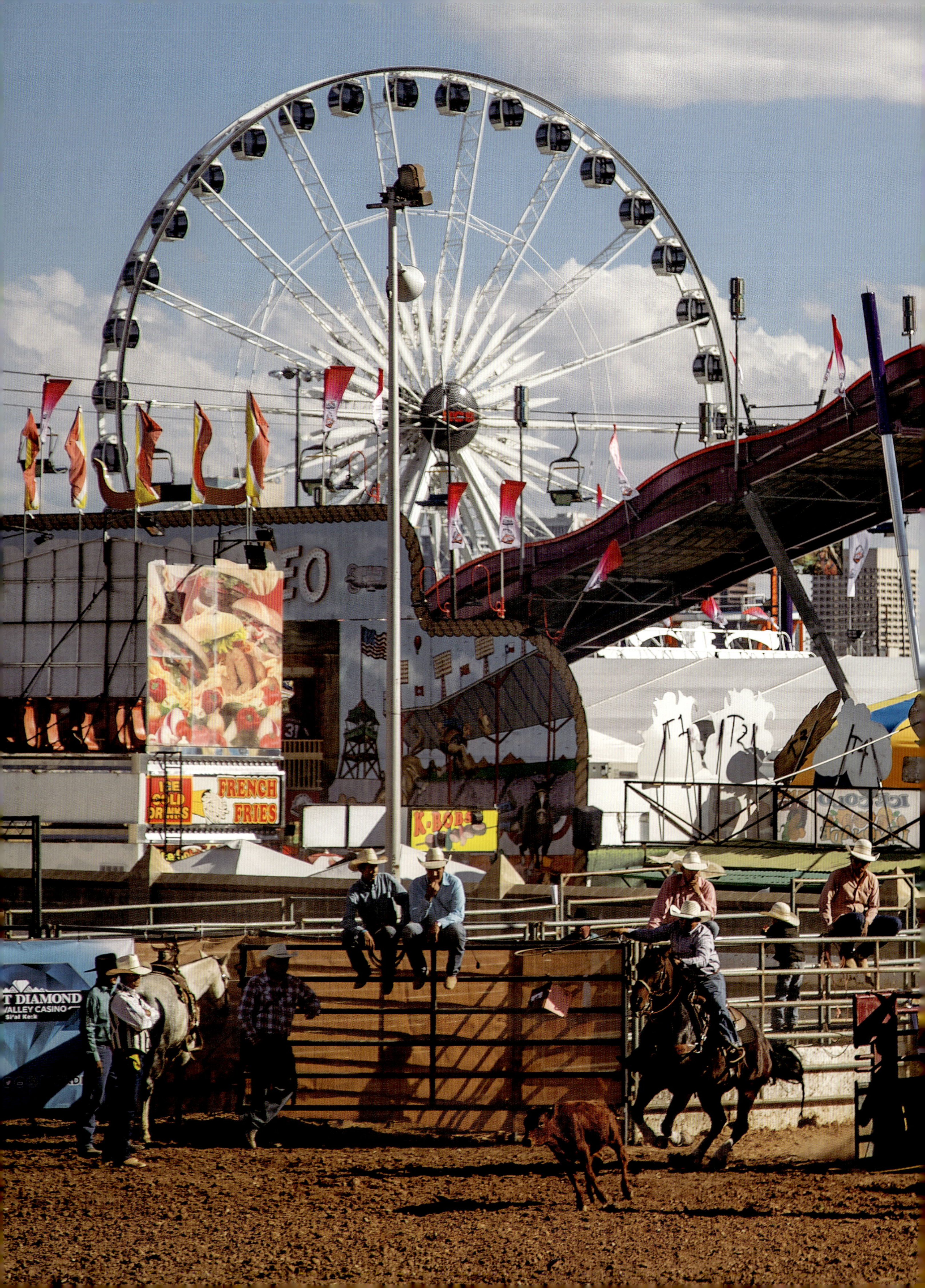
ICE
COLD
DRINKS
FRENCH
FRIES
K-BOBS
T DIAMOND
VALLEY CASINO

CRAZY COASTER
ICE COLD LEMONADE
TURKEY LEGS SMOKED & BBQ
ICE COLD BEER BEER ICE COLD
S-65
Rentals

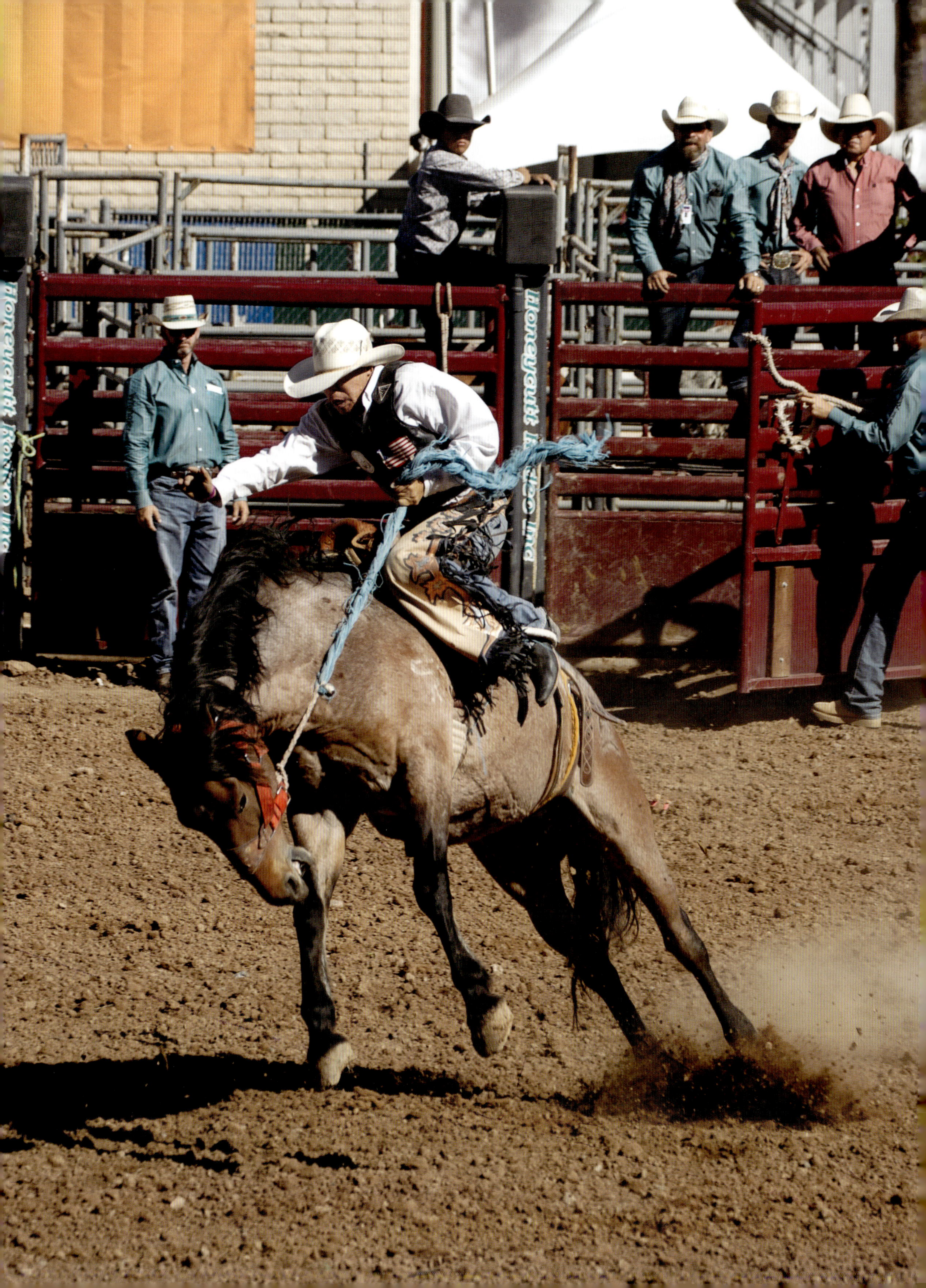

Preceding pages, opposite, and above: About one million people attend the Arizona State Fair in Phoenix, sensibly staged in temperate October. They arrive in the mood for wholesome fun and games, including rides of escalating scare levels; reliably sinful fair food; midway tests with elusive stuffed prizes; oddball events such as the Flying Meatball Circus (you'd have to be there); contests for cooks and grillers, voracious eaters, e-sport whizzes, monster-truck drivers, and proud owners and their farm animals; free concerts for all with paid tickets; and something unusual: eight events in an all-Indian rodeo.

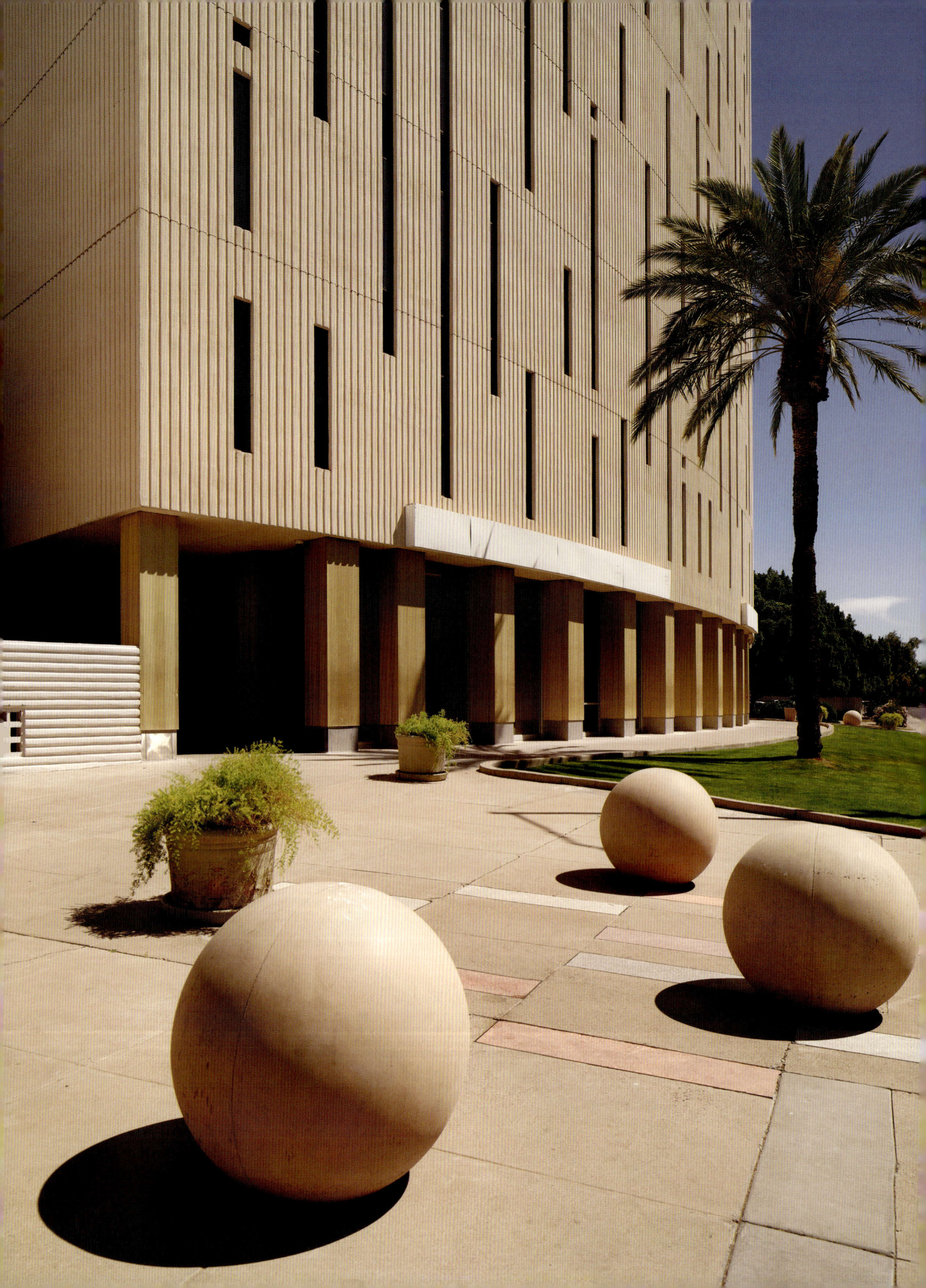

Opposite: Locals affectionately call the downtown Phoenix Financial Center the Punchcard Building. Designed by Wenceslaus Sarmiento, the 1964 high-rise recalls pieces of stiff paper, fed into mechanical readers, that coded digital information by the presence or absence of holes. Above: This replica of an adobe compound of the Hohokam people from about 1300 is displayed at the Pueblo Grande Museum and Archaeological Park across town. The site also includes a historic mound and early irrigation canals. Overleaf: The view past this modern home's infinity pool provides a panoramic view of the Valley of the Sun. And sunsets.

Valley of the Sun · 27

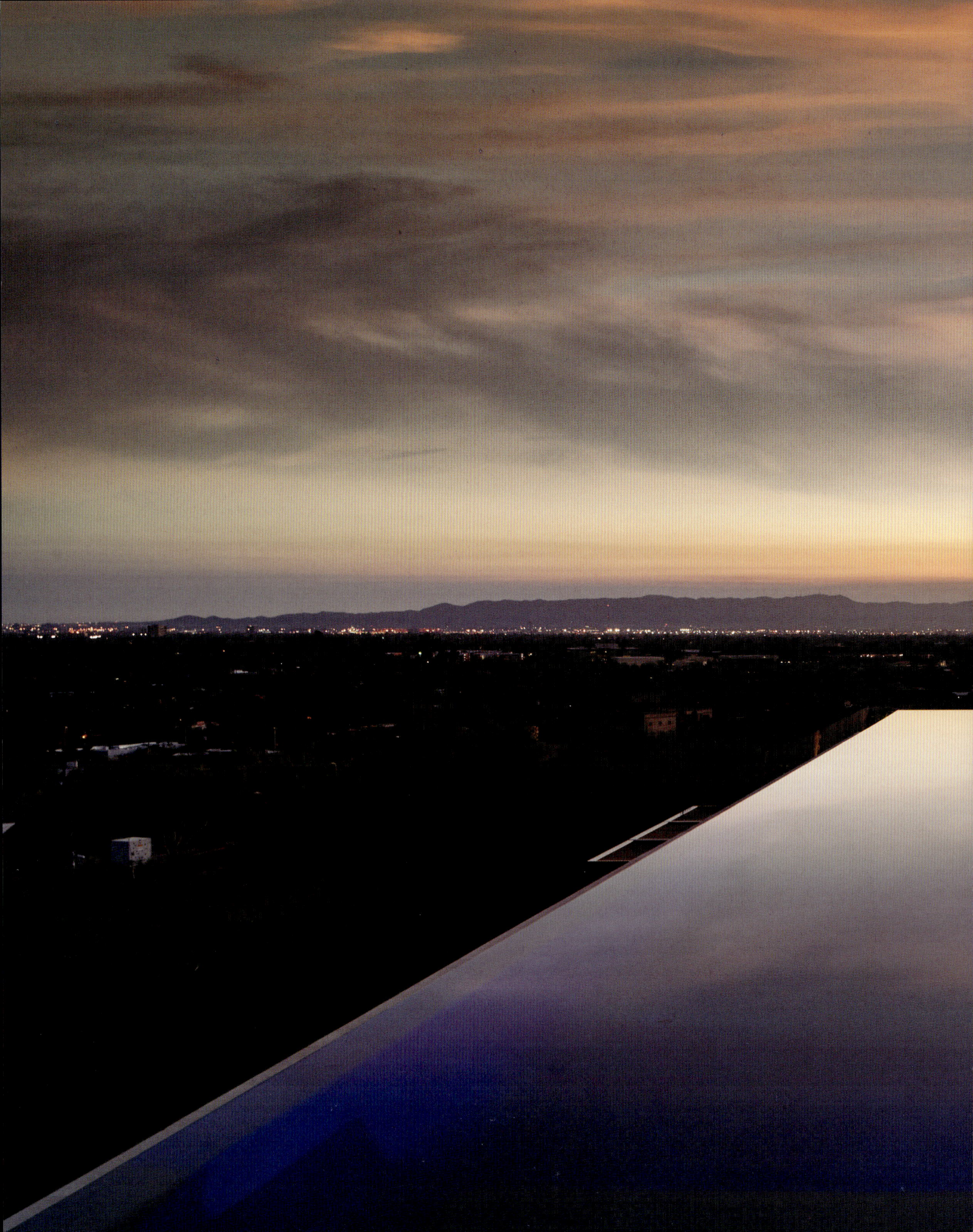

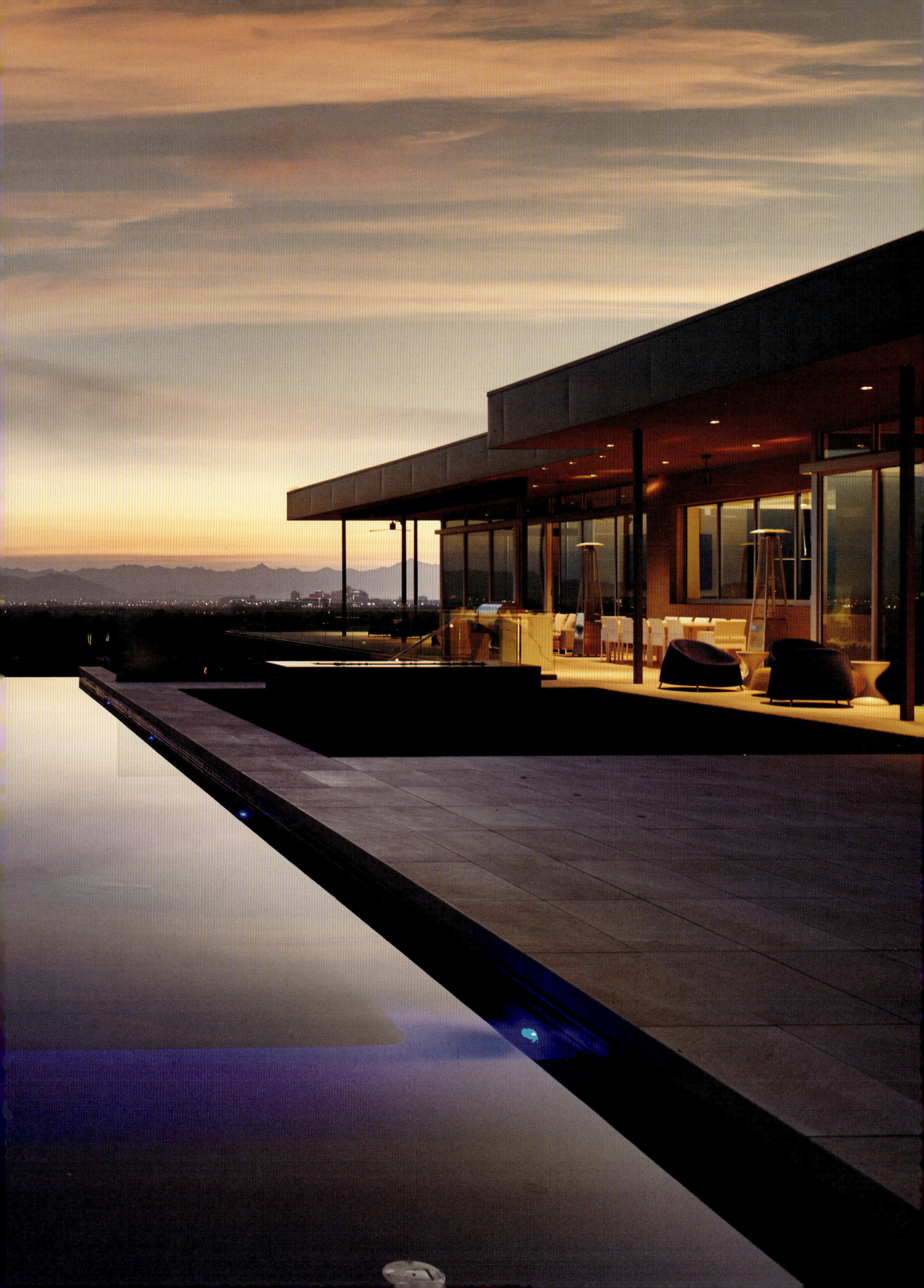

MARICOPA COVNTY COVRT HOVSE

125 W. WASHINGTON

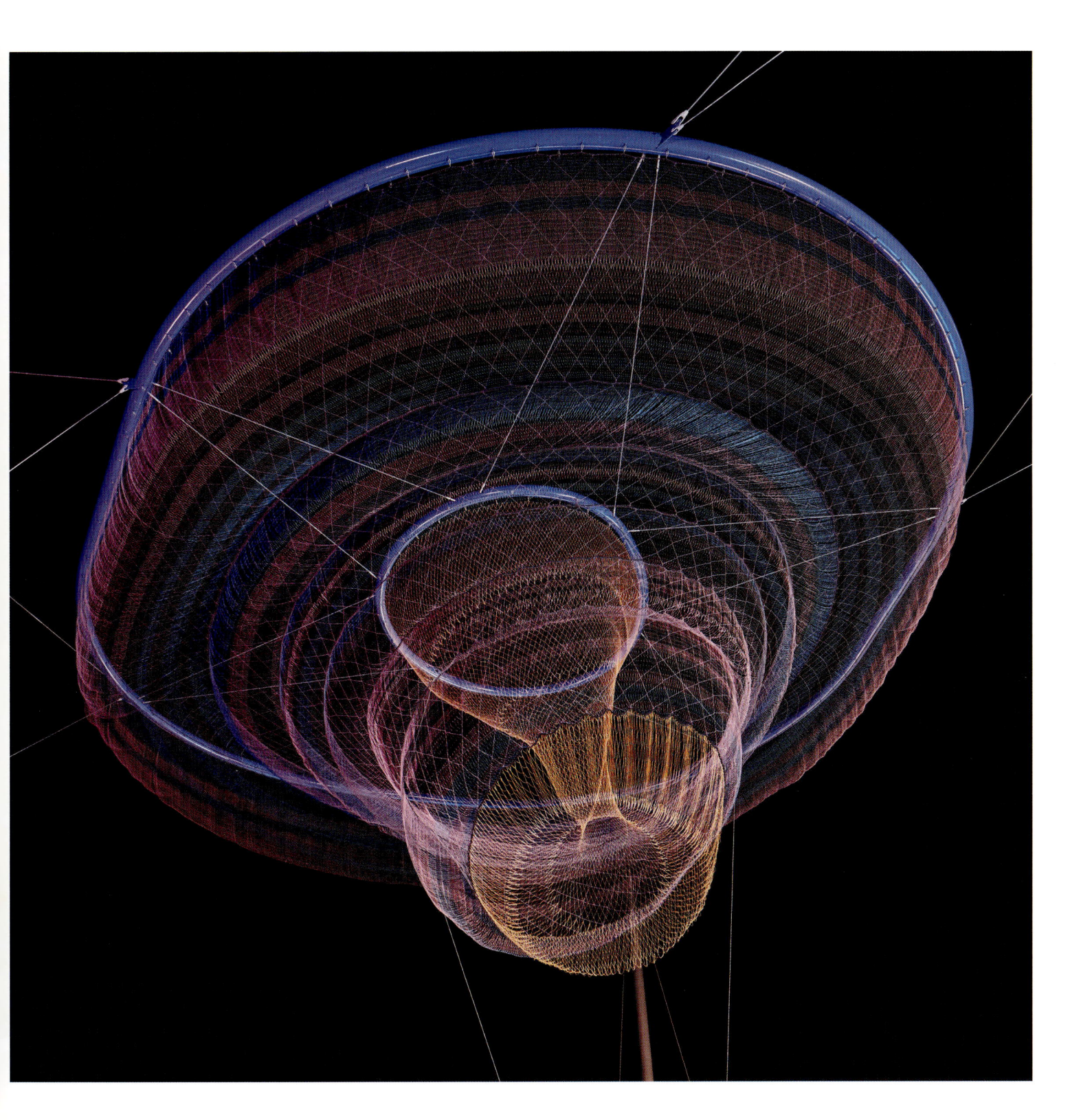

Opposite: Phoenix's Maricopa County Courthouse, or COVRT HOVSE—adopting the Romans' use of the letter v for u in their Latin alphabet—was completed in 1929 by Edward Neild and Lescher and Mahoney as the joint home of county and city administrations. But in the rippling shockwaves of the area's growth following World War II, both operations, save for the state superior court, had moved to newer buildings by 1964. Above: The title of Janet Echelman's 2009 illuminated sculpture in downtown's Civic Space Park, *Her Secret Is Patience*, is taken from Ralph Waldo Emerson's words of advice: "Adopt the pace of nature: her secret is patience."

Valley of the Sun · 31

Right: The landmark sixteen-story Westward Ho building in Phoenix, completed in 1928, was Arizona's tallest structure for more than thirty years. Its facilities included a restaurant overlook called the Top of the Ho. Below and opposite: In 1929 Frank Lloyd Wright helped Albert Chase McArthur design the city's Biltmore Hotel and Resort. Its patio features replicas of the sprite sculptures from Wright's Midway Gardens in Chicago. Overleaf: The colorful Handlebar J appeared as a saloon, dance hall, and rib joint in the 1960s in nearby Scottsdale, which the bar touted as "the West's most modern town."

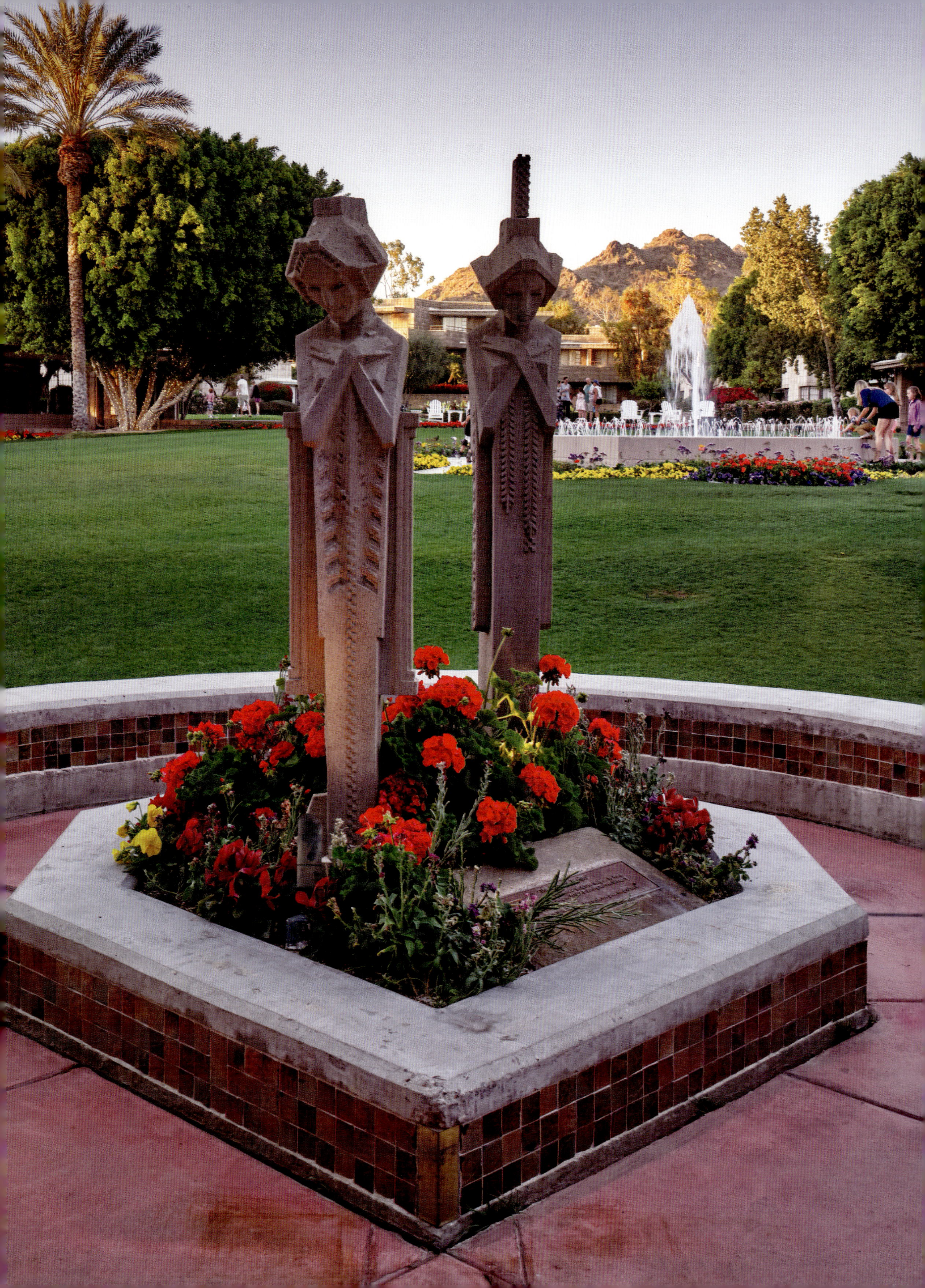

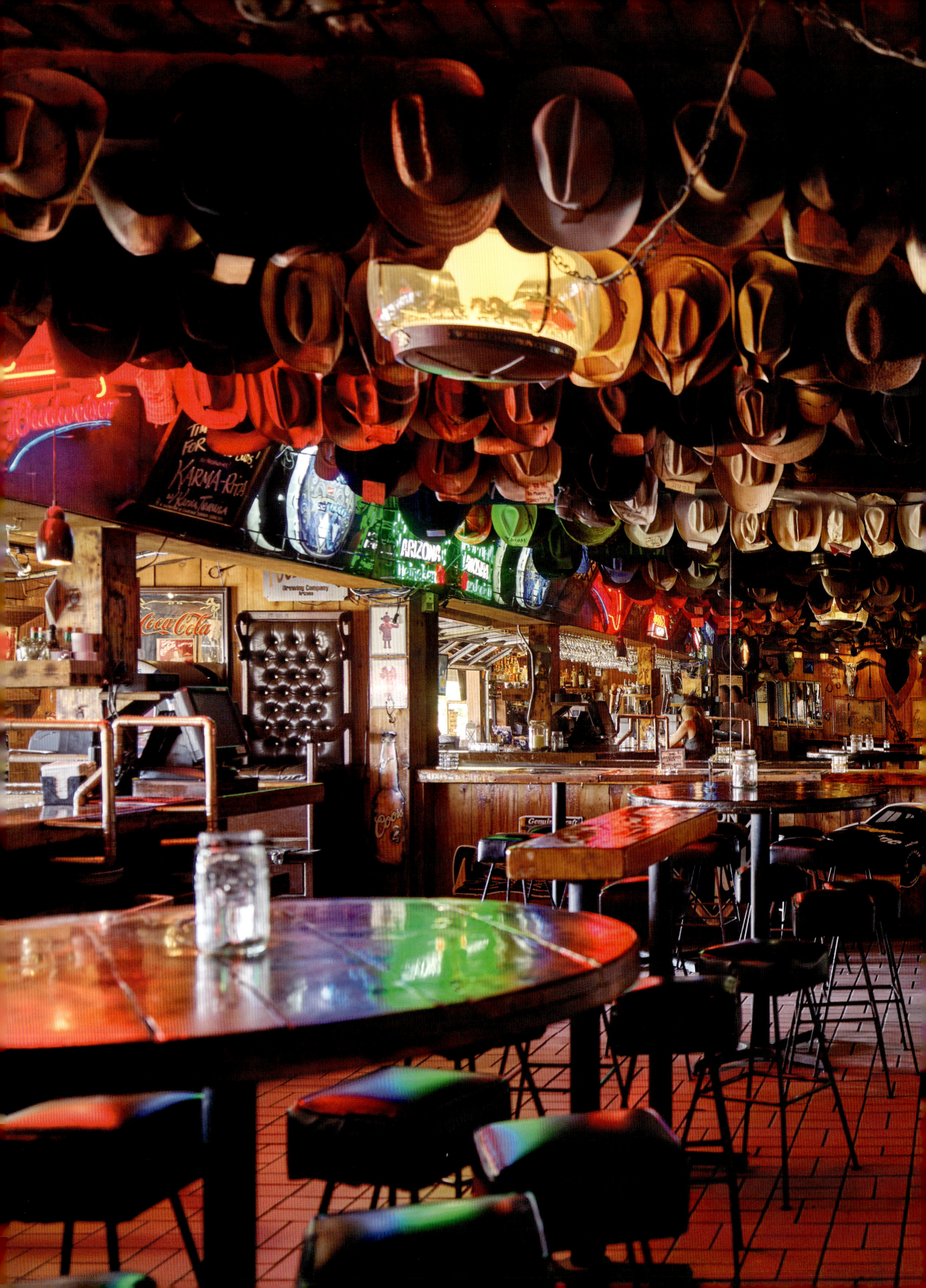
Budweiser
KARMA-RITA
ARIZONA
Coca-Cola
Coors

EMERGENCY EXIT ONLY
HERNDON
BROTHERS
BAND
Budweiser SELECT
Coors ORIGINAL
Coors BULL XING
Budweiser

Above: The Arizona artist Ed Mell's bronze work, *Jack Knife*, arrived in Old Town Scottsdale, a neighborhood packed with art galleries, in 1993. It was inspired by another cowpoke astride a bucking horse on Scottsdale's city seal.

Opposite: The cowboy artist Joe Beeler's 2004 statue of Barry Goldwater dominates the Paradise Valley park named for Arizona's five-term U.S. senator. Overleaf: Paradise Valley's Hermosa Inn includes a hotel, restaurant, and lounge.

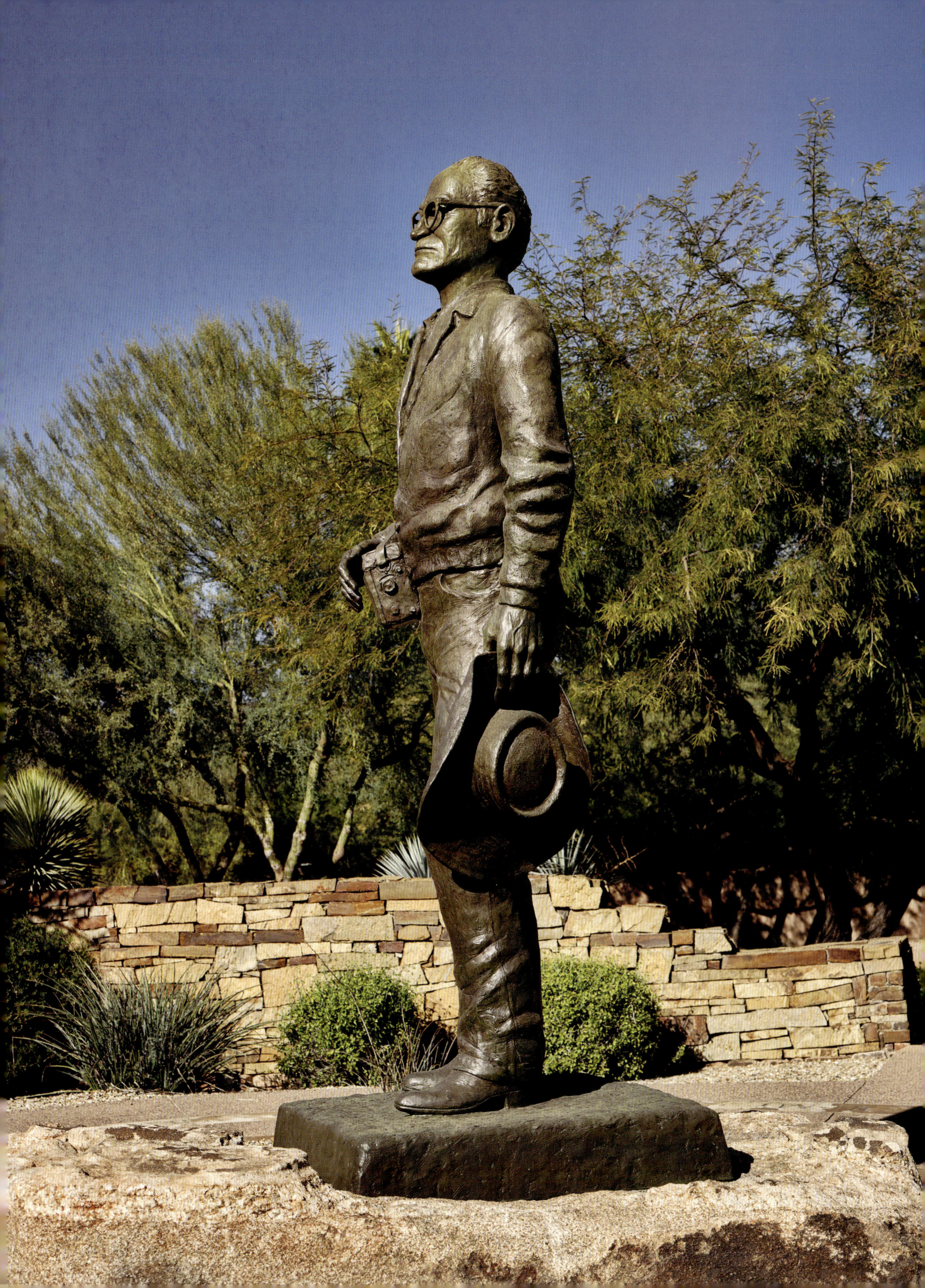

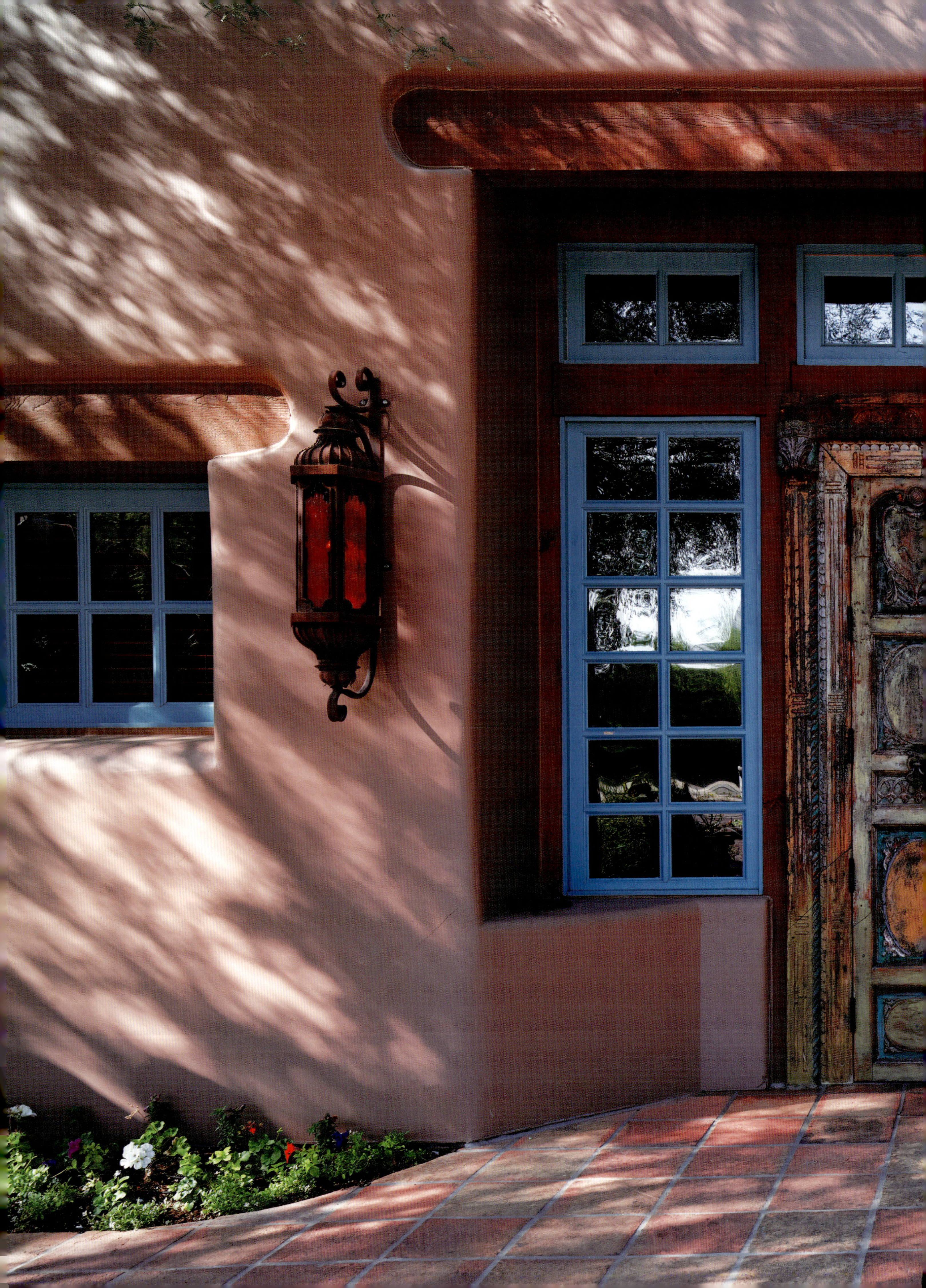

Hermosa
Inn
Registration

The 140-acre Desert Botanical Garden in Phoenix was created in 1939 by the Arizona Cactus and Native Flora Society in Papago Park, a pinecone's throw from the Phoenix Zoo. Laced with nature paths, the preserve displays twenty-one thousand plants, one-third of which are native to the area's Sonoran Desert, in more than four thousand groupings. Displays include some two hundred species that are rare, threatened, or endangered. The park relies heavily on the enthusiastic work of its seven hundred volunteers.

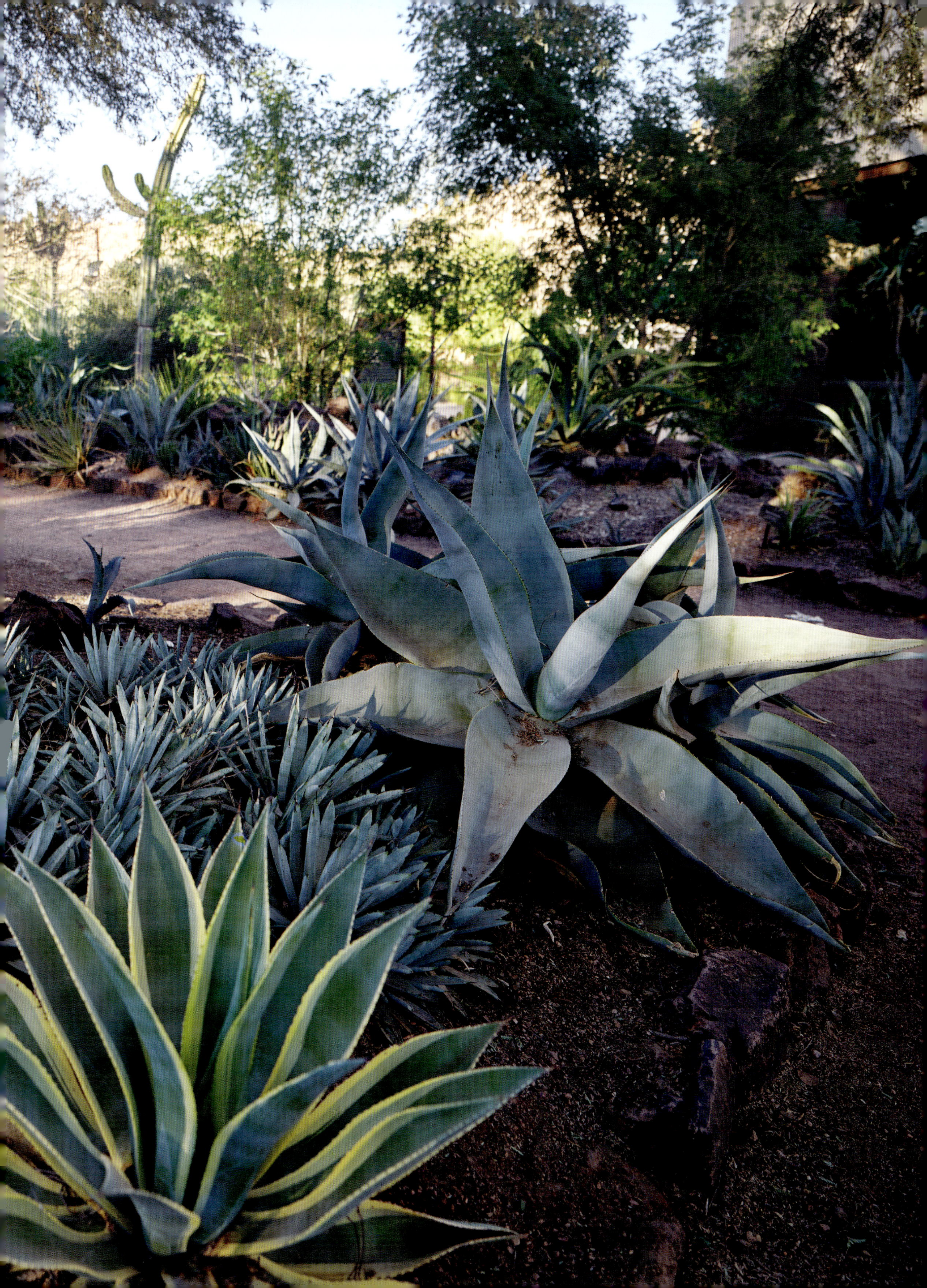

In addition to the requisite giraffes, bears, elephants, and such, a number of Southwest-specific species slither and skitter at the Phoenix Zoo. Look closely here and you will spot a superbly camouflaged roadrunner, a Hopi rattlesnake, and a burrowing owl. Overleaf: A languid community of barely one hundred thousand people in 1950, Phoenix now boasts a population of 1.7 million.

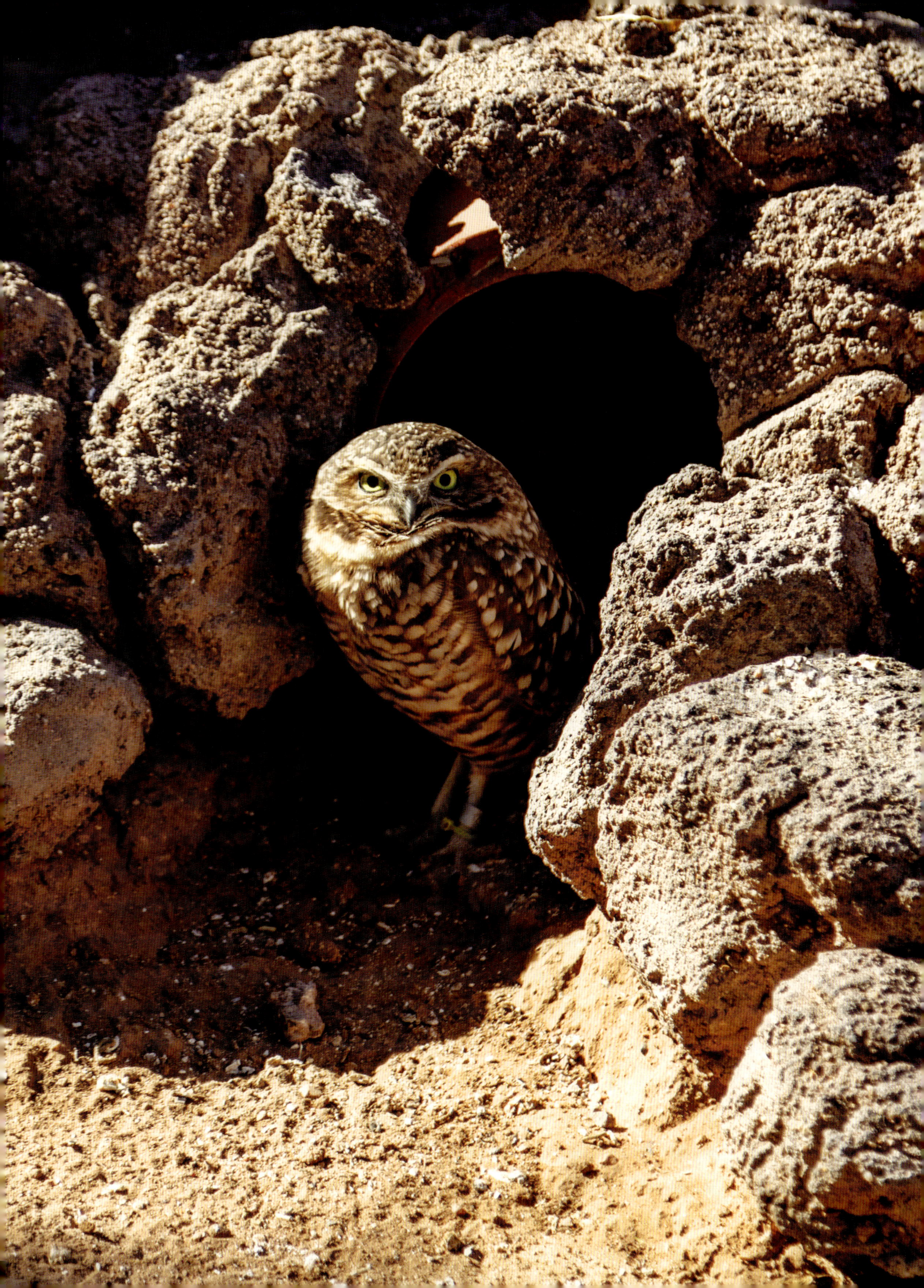

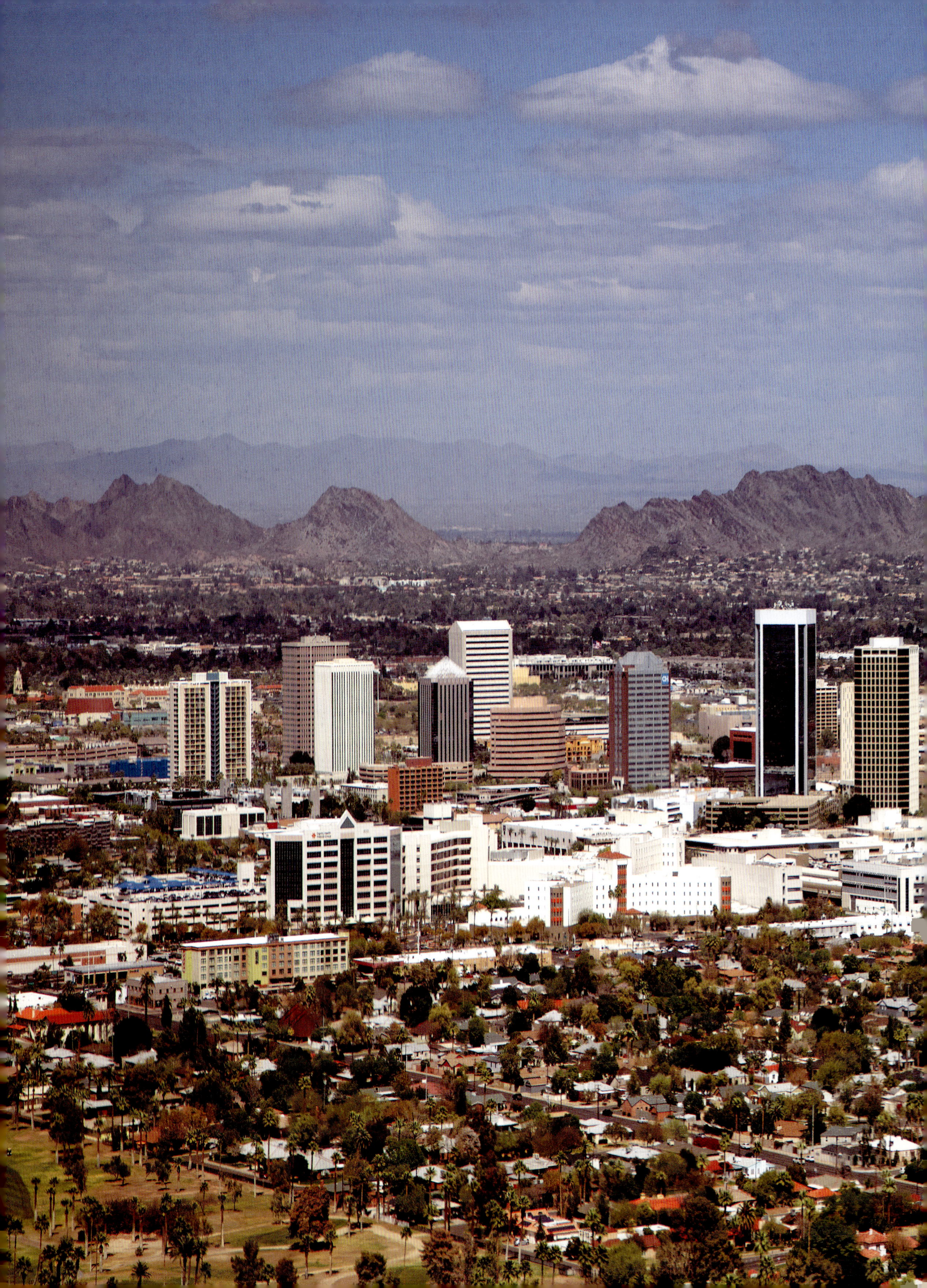

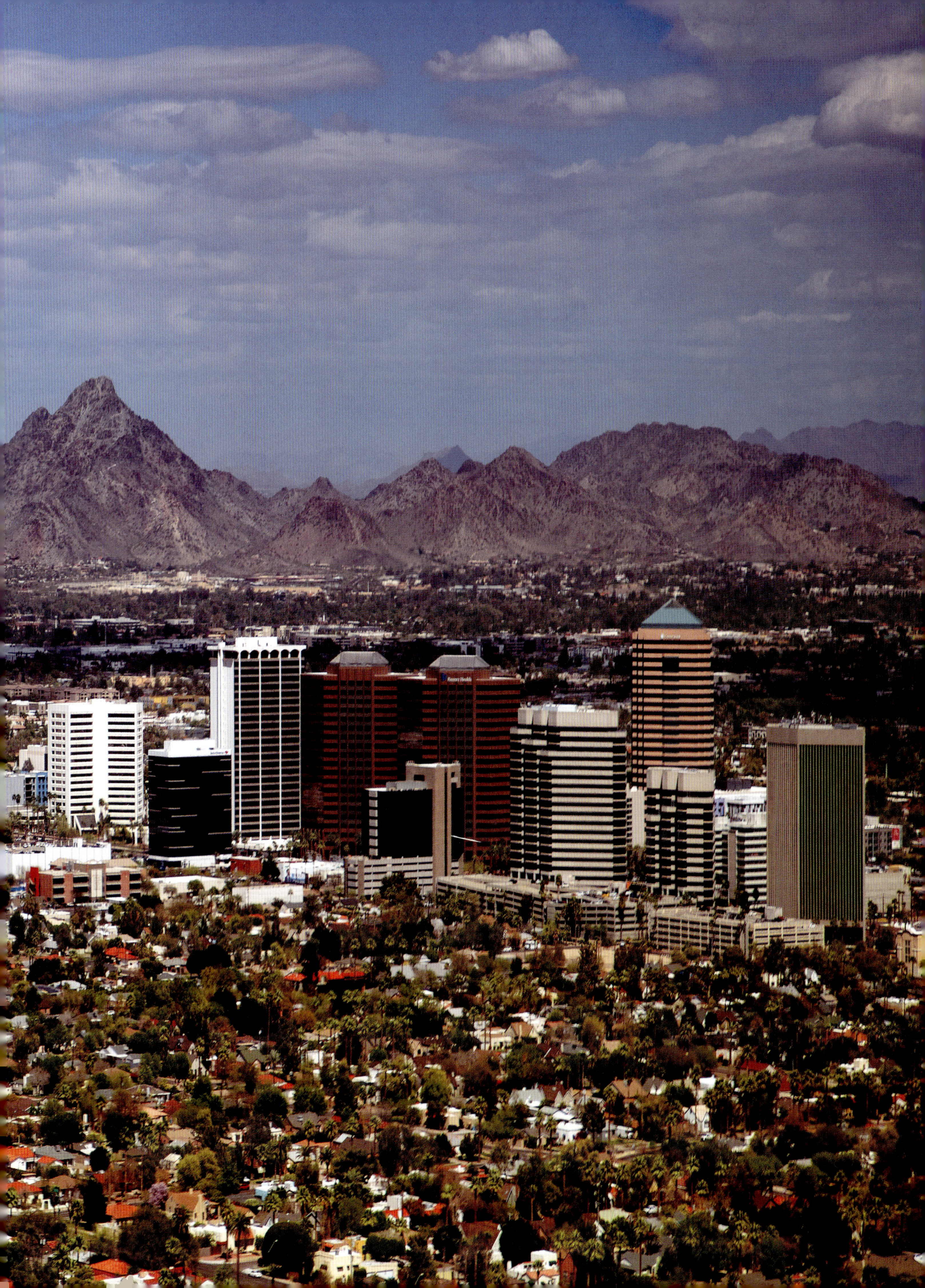

Among the prized holdings at Phoenix's Heard Museum, a private museum for the advancement of American Indian art, are Hopi katsina dolls given by Barry Goldwater during his years as a U.S. senator. Shown left to right are a Sa'lakwmana doll created in the 1890s, a Nata'aska (black ogre) doll fashioned about 1900, and an Ahöla doll from the early 1900s. Typically made of cottonwood root, kaolin clay, and paint, the figures are traditional gifts that teach about immortal beings who bring rain and other manifestations.

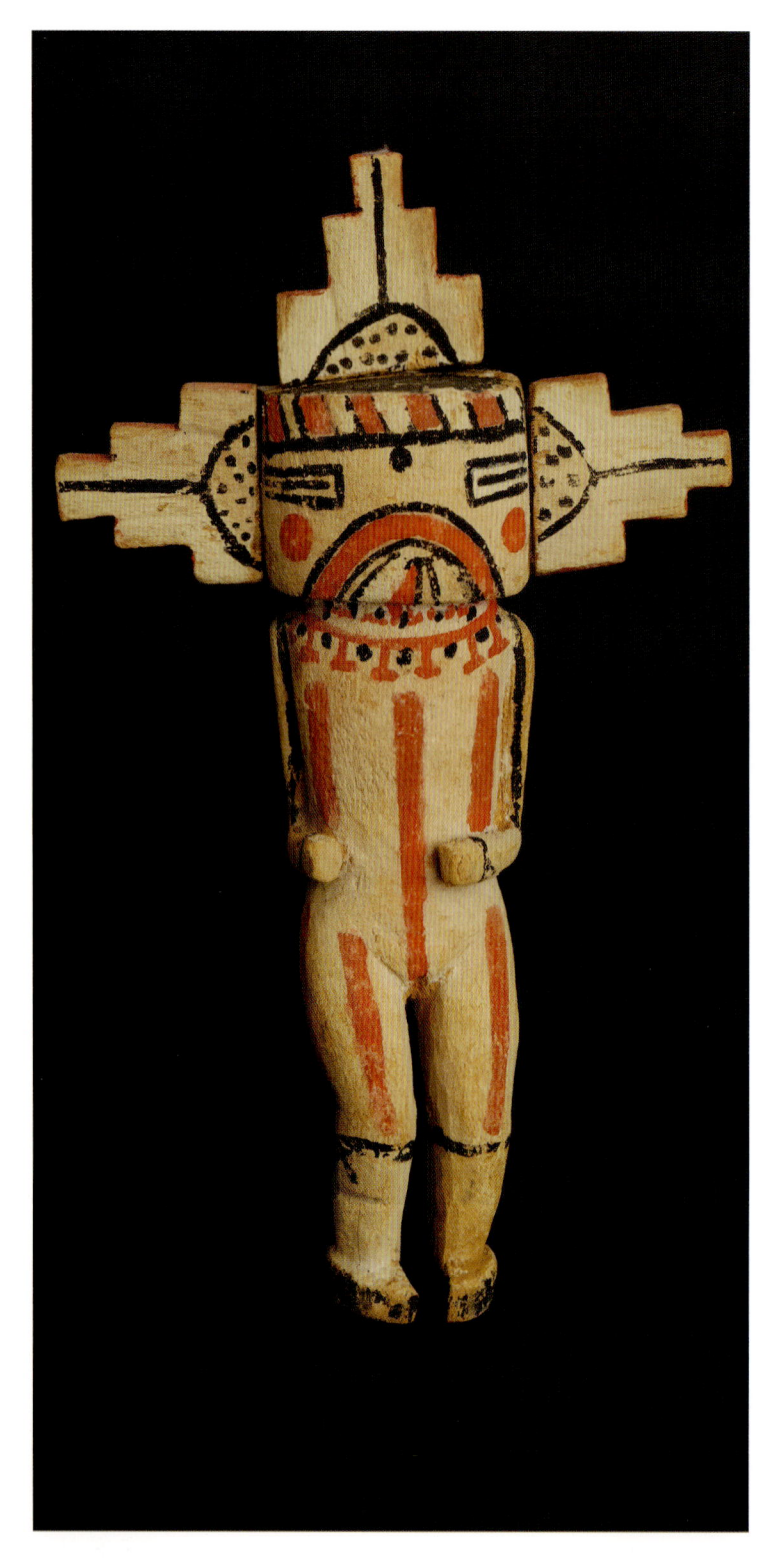

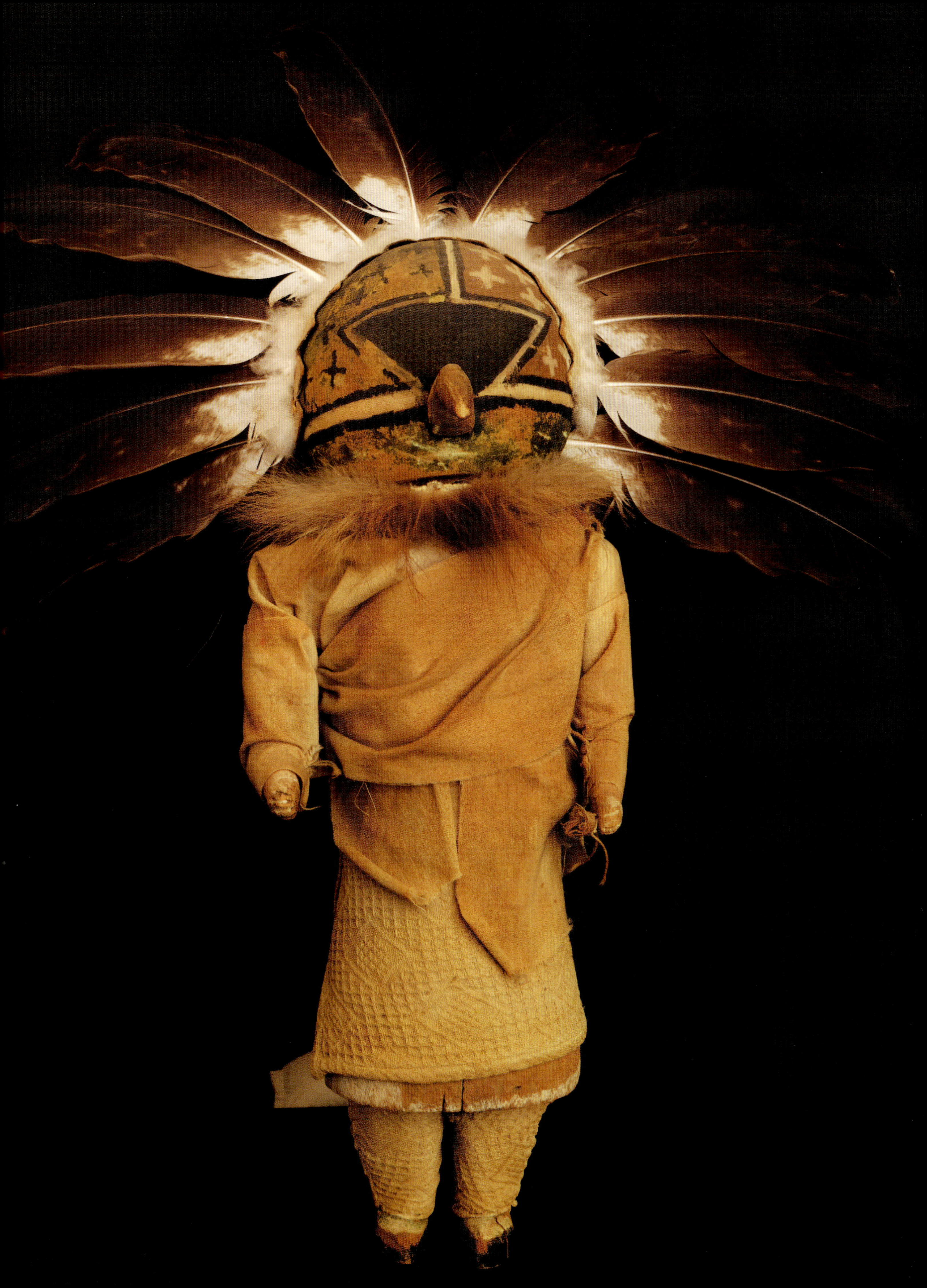

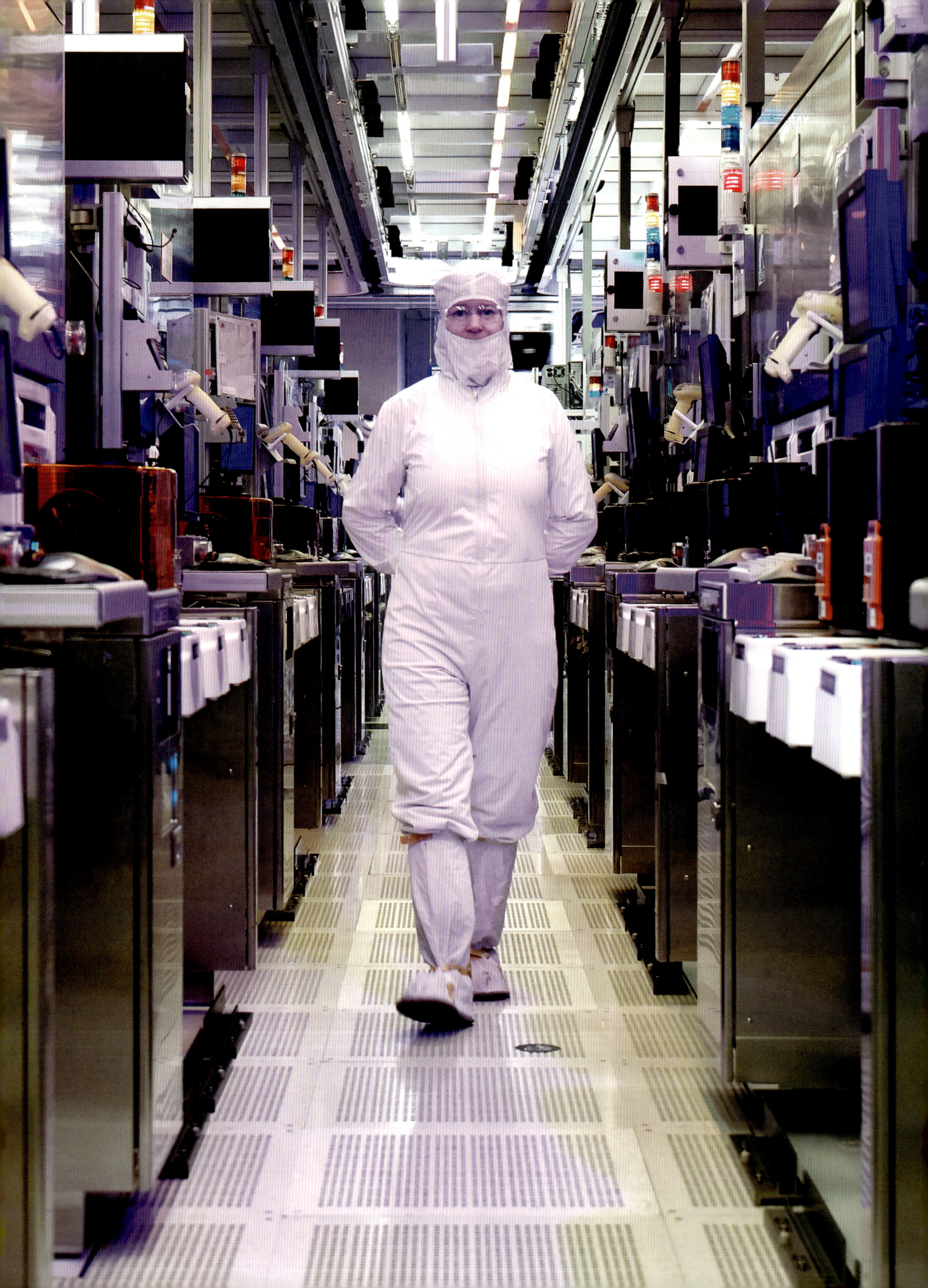

Opposite: Margaret Henschel crosses the cleanroom in her industrial "bunny suit" at the Intel Corporation's wafer fabrication facility in Chandler. Transistors and computer-chip circuits interconnect on tiny slices. Above: Dr. Michael Lawton, president and chief executive officer of the Barrow Neurological Institute in Phoenix, explains procedures inside the telepresence room, where residents observe live and recorded surgeries. Overleaf: Camelback Mountain, a landmark and a favored hiking destination, got its name from what some swear is the silhouette of the hump and the head of a kneeling camel.

Valley of the Sun · 49

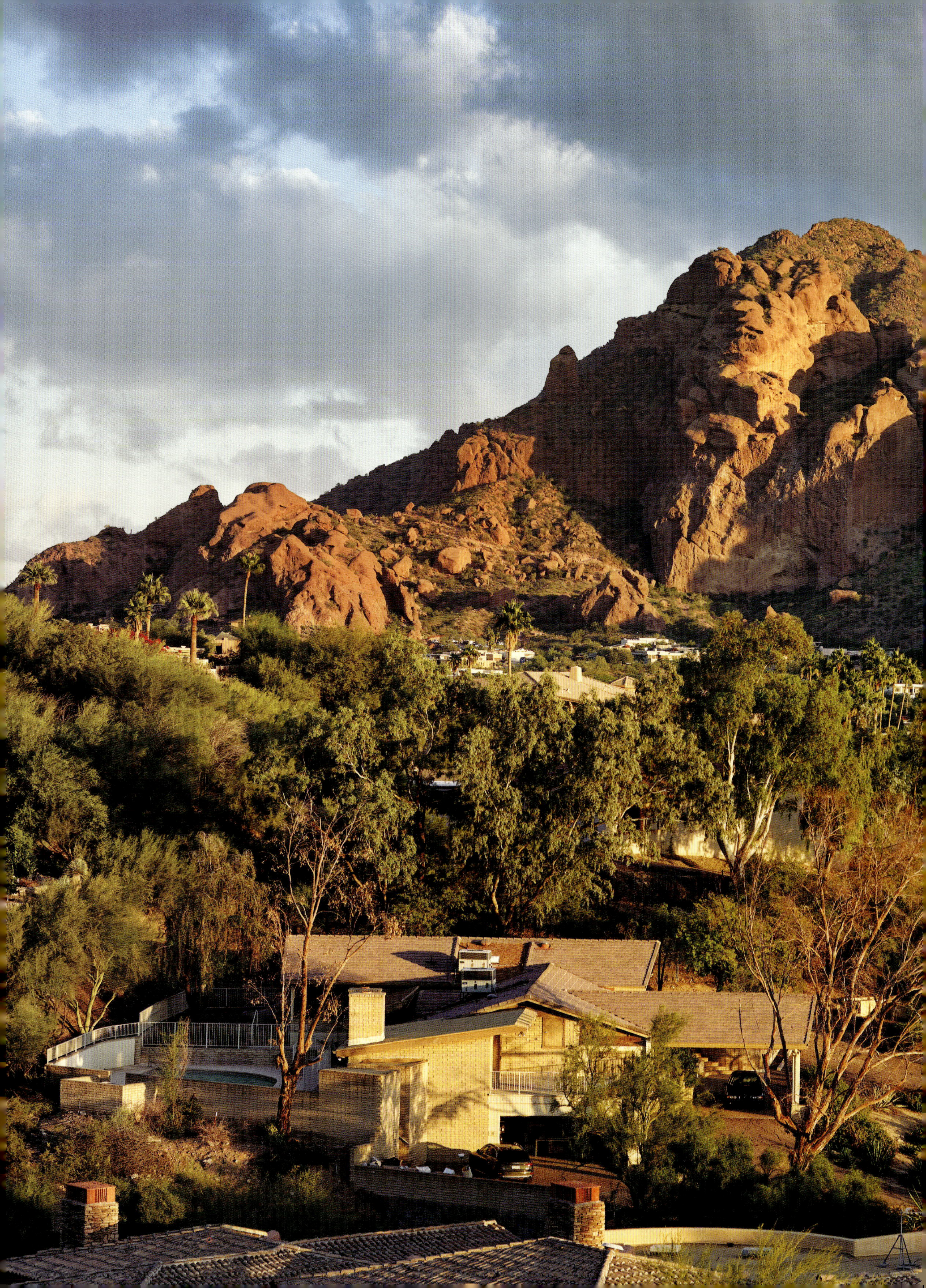

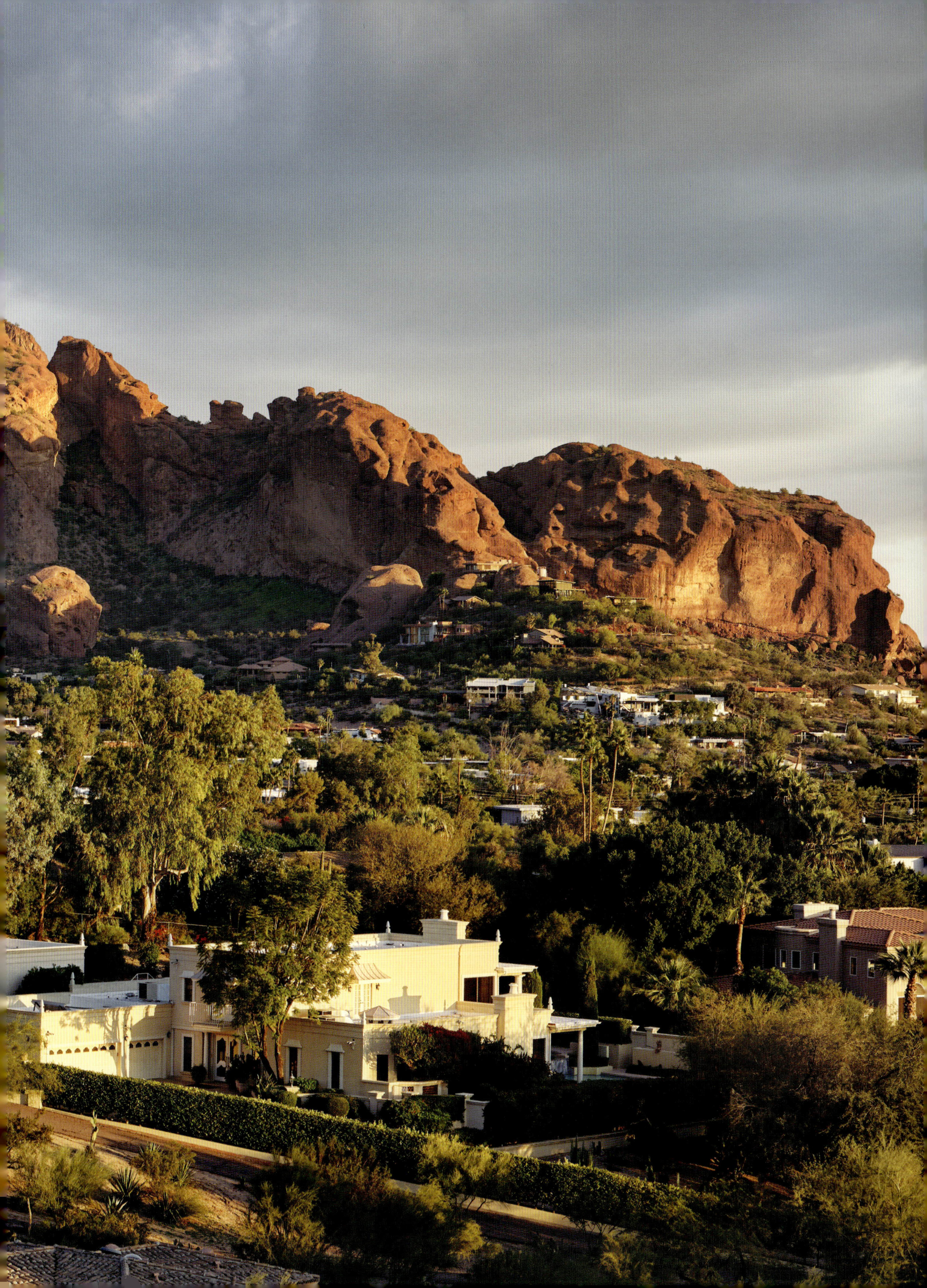

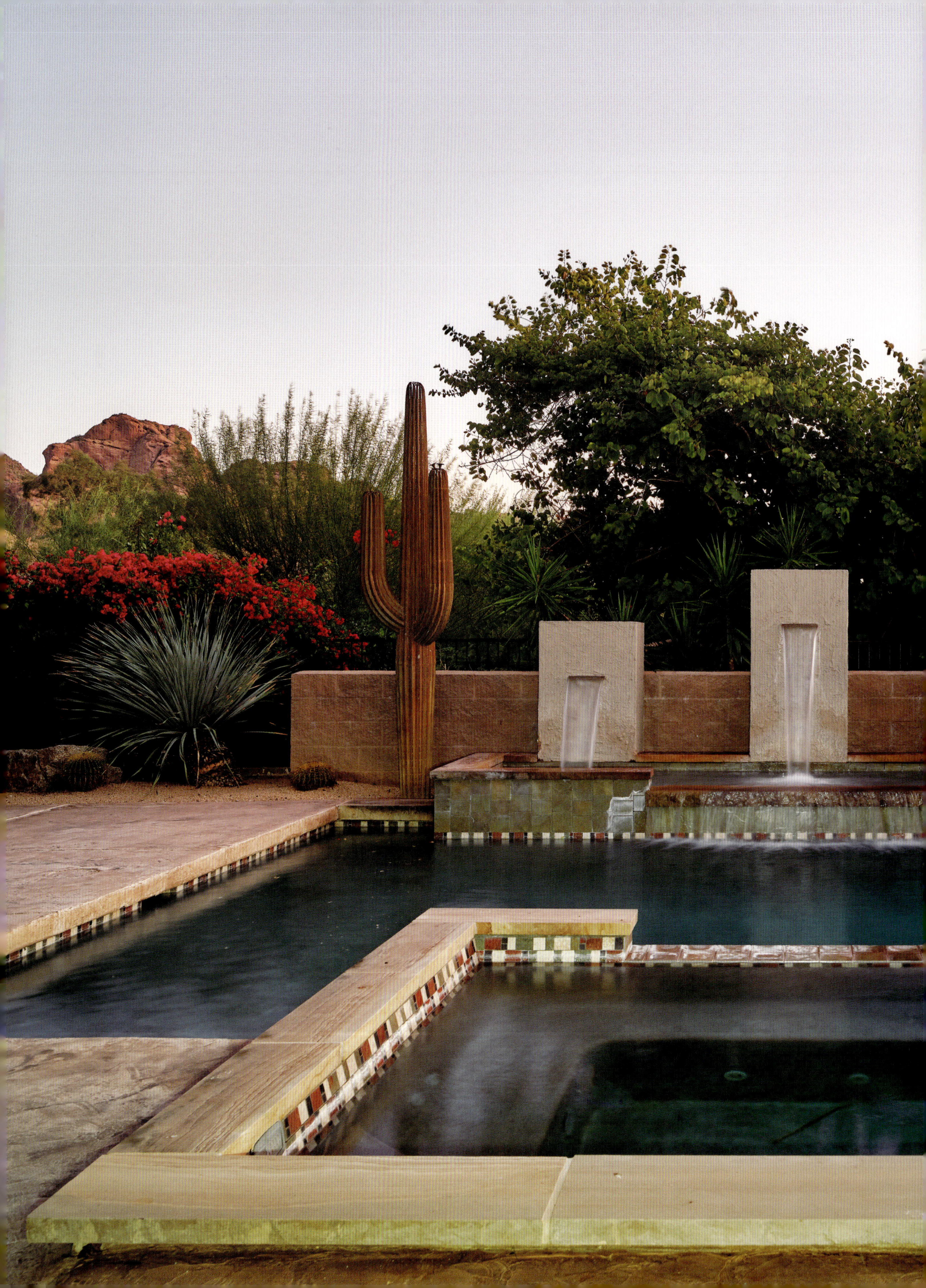

Left: Those who await a dip in this classic Paradise Valley pool behold a mélange of Arizona flora—even a metal-art saguaro. For good measure, and backdrop, distant Camelback Mountain's sunsets will soon be a soothing introduction to evening. Above: Just off poolside, a peach-faced lovebird savors a free meal. Also called rosy-faced lovebirds, the avians are native to parched southwestern Africa. Once captive amusements, they now make a comfortable free and feral life in the dry, sometimes roasting-hot, Phoenix area.

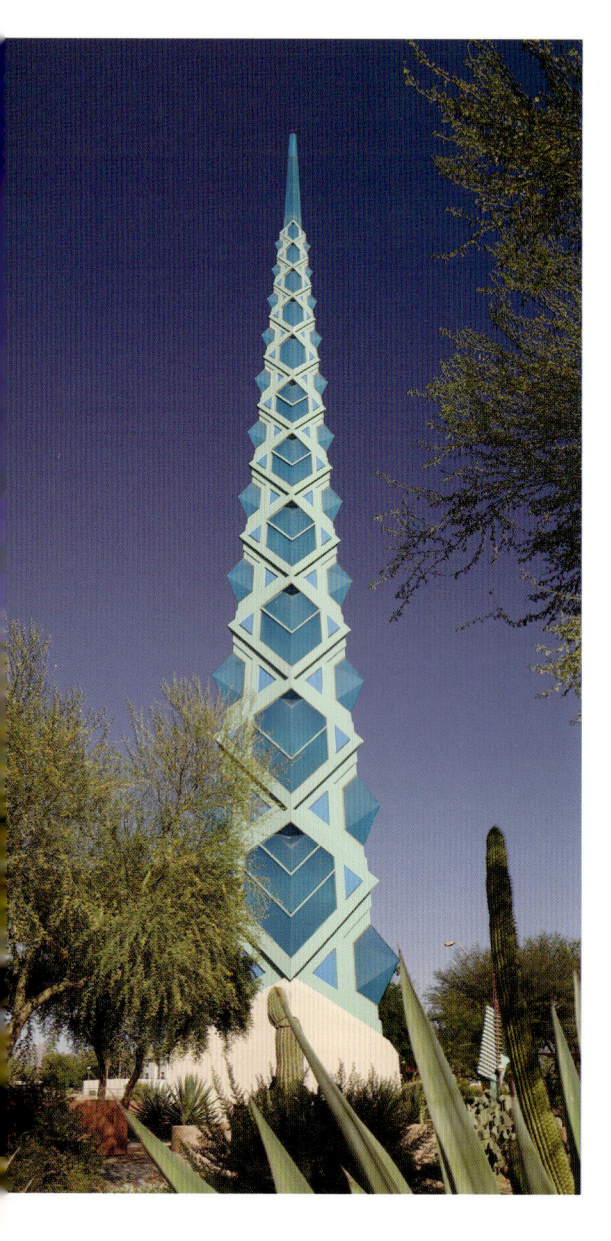

Above: Frank Lloyd Wright designed this 125-foot-tall spire for Scottsdale in 1957. The city rejected it, Wright died, and the spire was not built until 2004, for a shopping mall. At night it glows blue. Right: The Oklahoma pipeline-company magnate Harold C. Price Sr. commissioned Wright to design his family's Paradise Valley winter home in 1954. Following Price's death the Usonian-style house—the length of a football field—was sold to Sam Shoen, president of U-Haul. It is now an occasional event venue open for public tours.

54 · *Valley of the Sun*

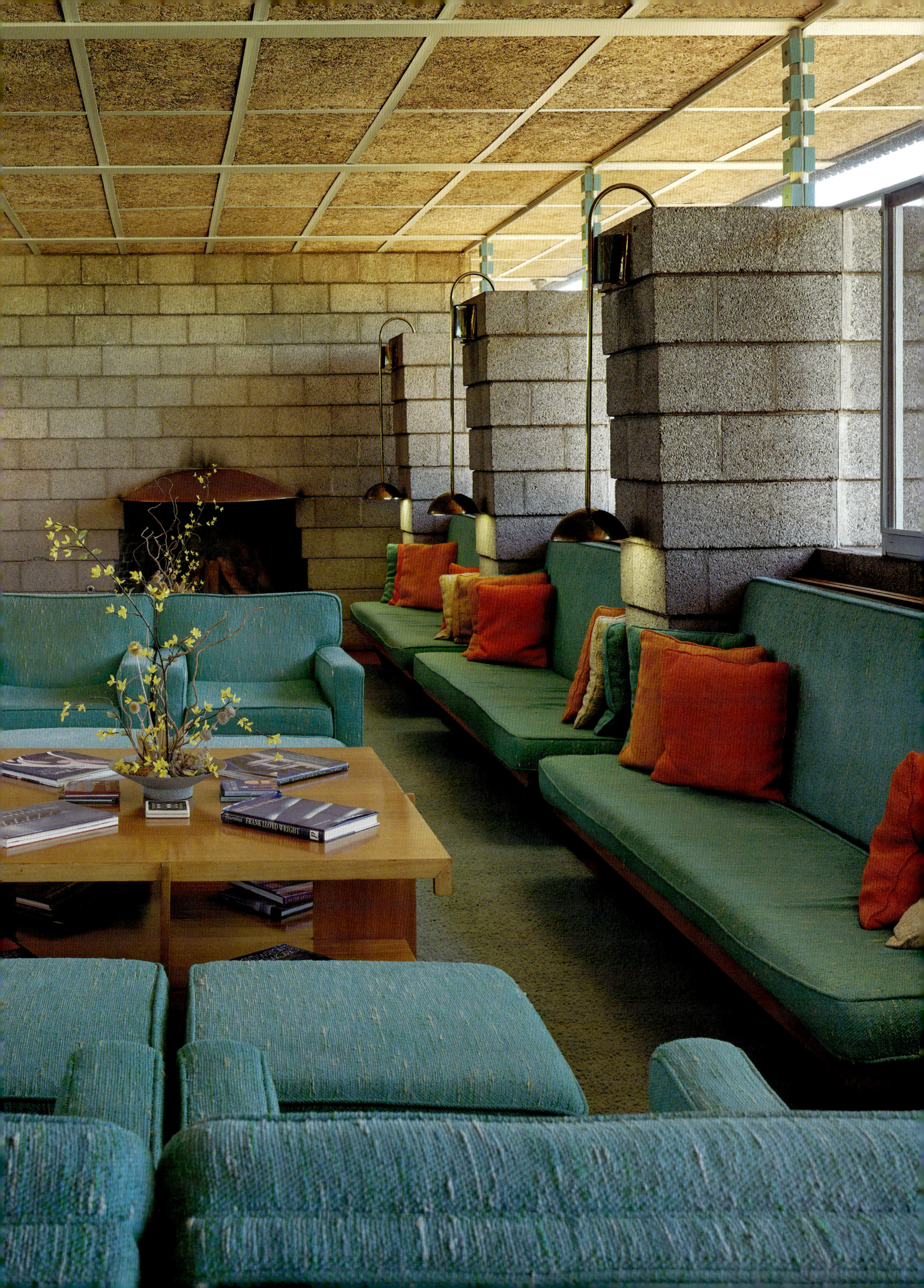
FRANK LLOYD WRIGHT

Taliesin West, begun in 1937, was Frank Lloyd Wright's winter home and studio on a desert hillside in Scottsdale. Today it is his foundation's headquarters and locus of the School of Architecture at Taliesin. Shown are what Wright called the Moon Gate, the drafting studio exterior, and the triangular "prow" pool. The name Taliesin, borrowed from the Welsh and Wright's Wisconsin summer home, means radiant brow. Overleaf: Scottsdale's Pinnacle Peak Park offers a climbable 2,889-foot crest and a glorious valley view.

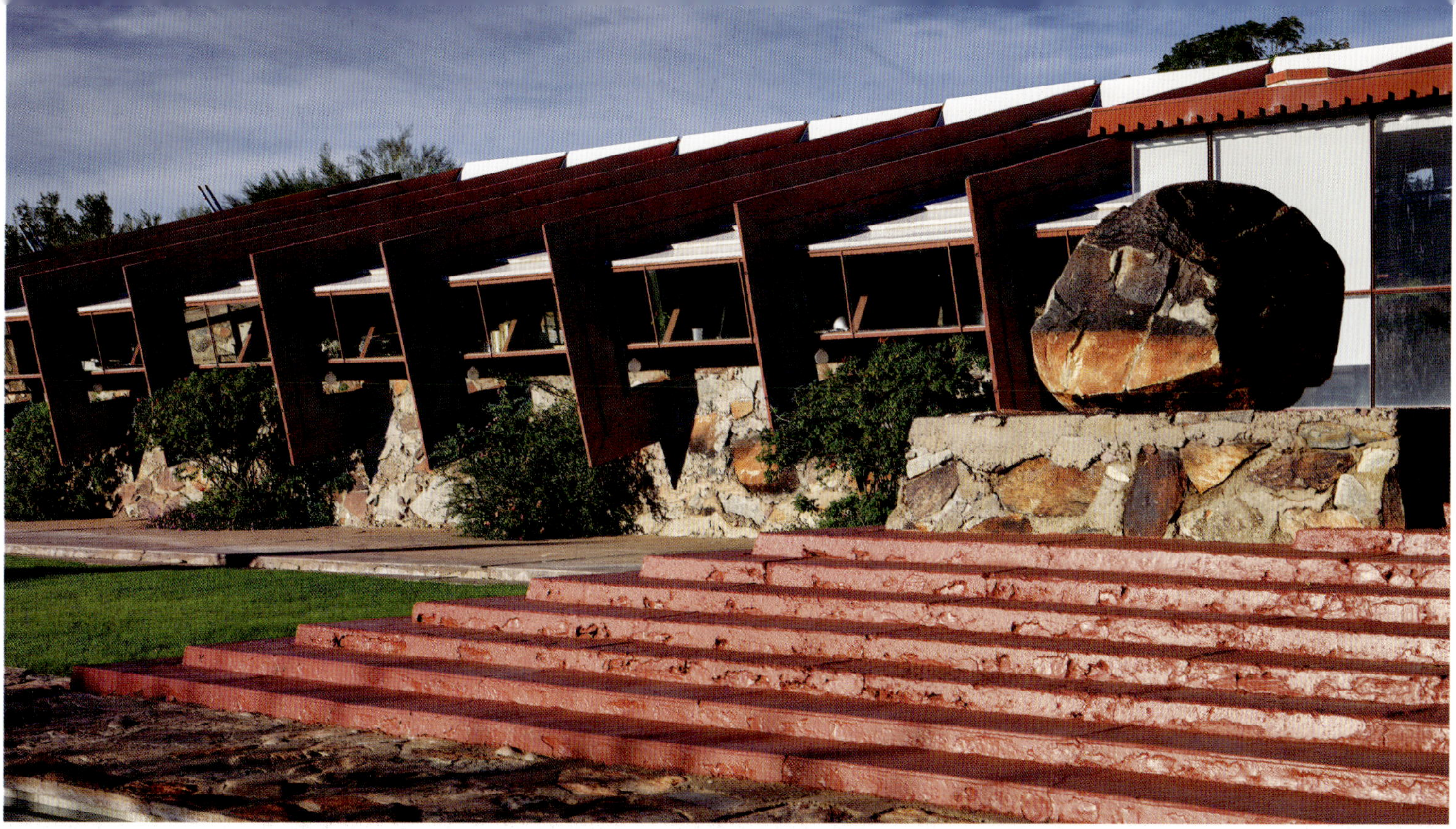

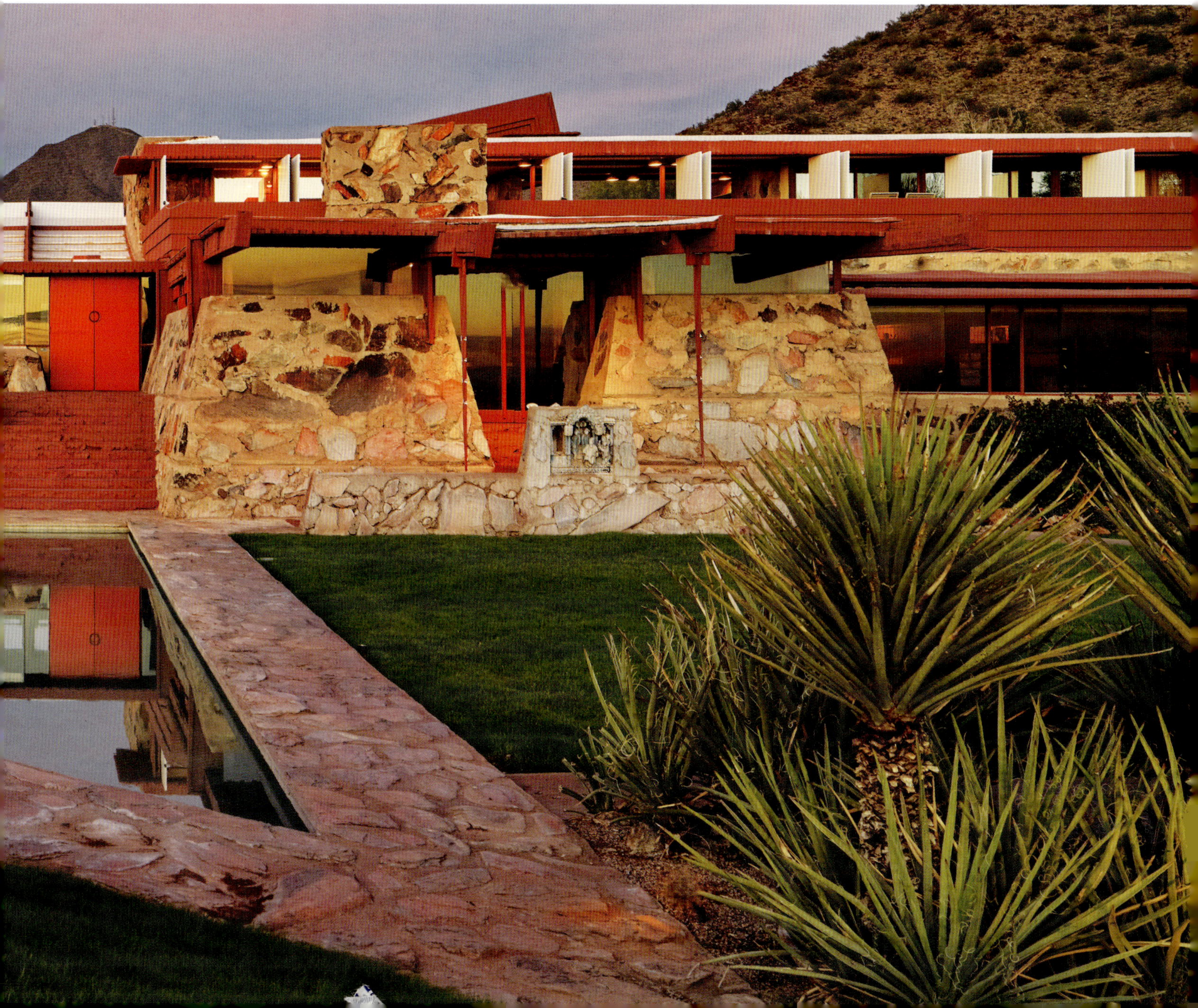

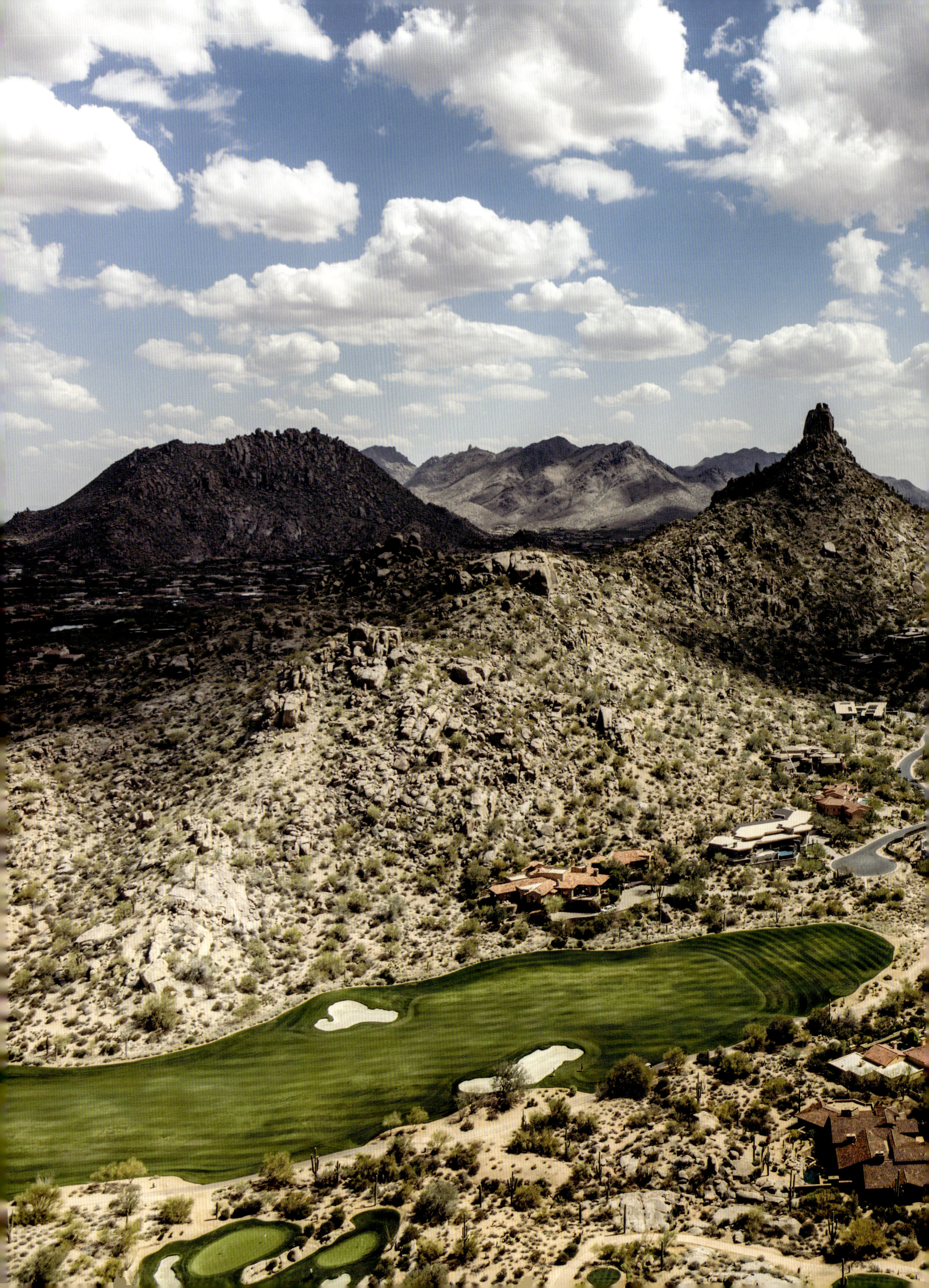

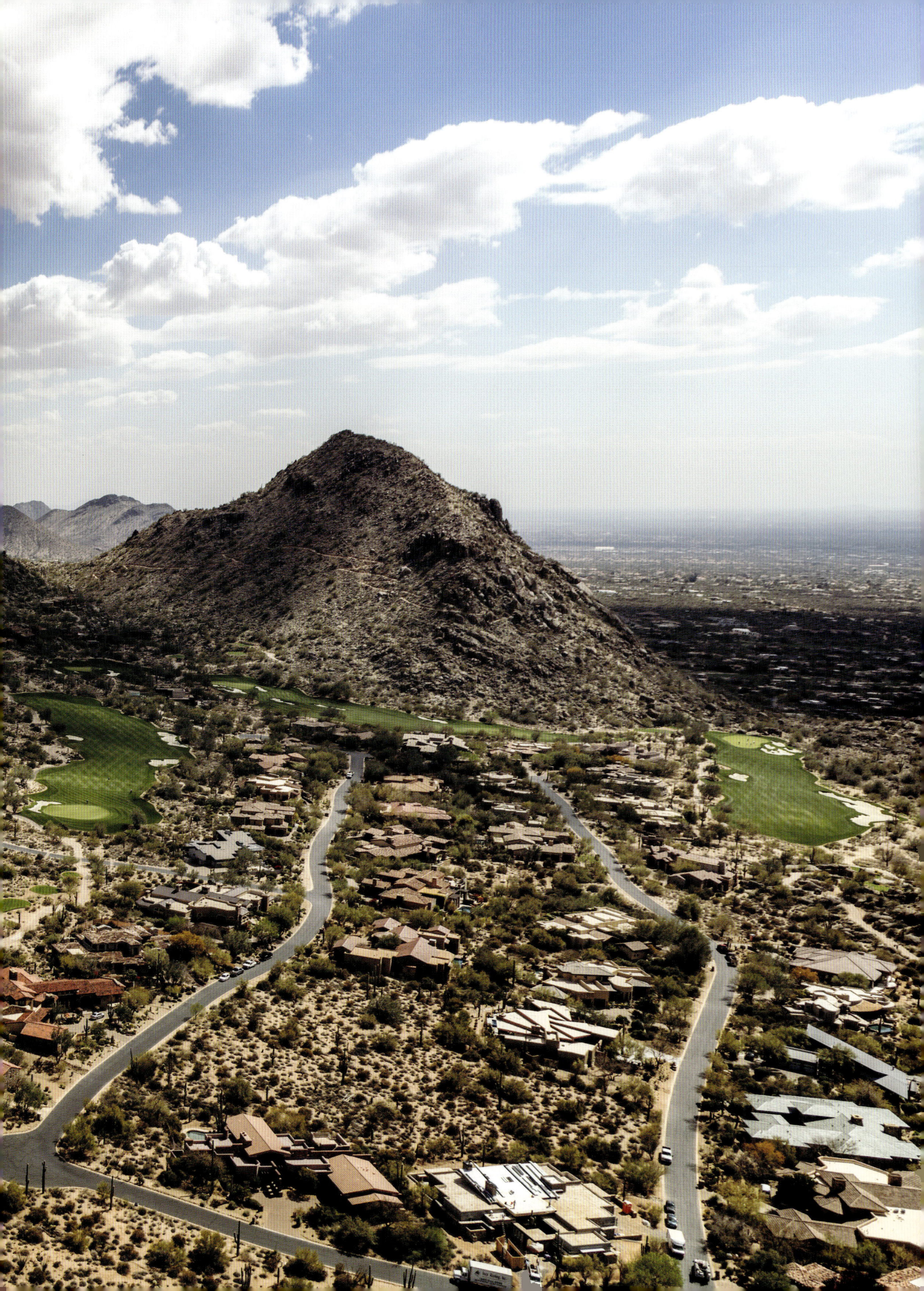

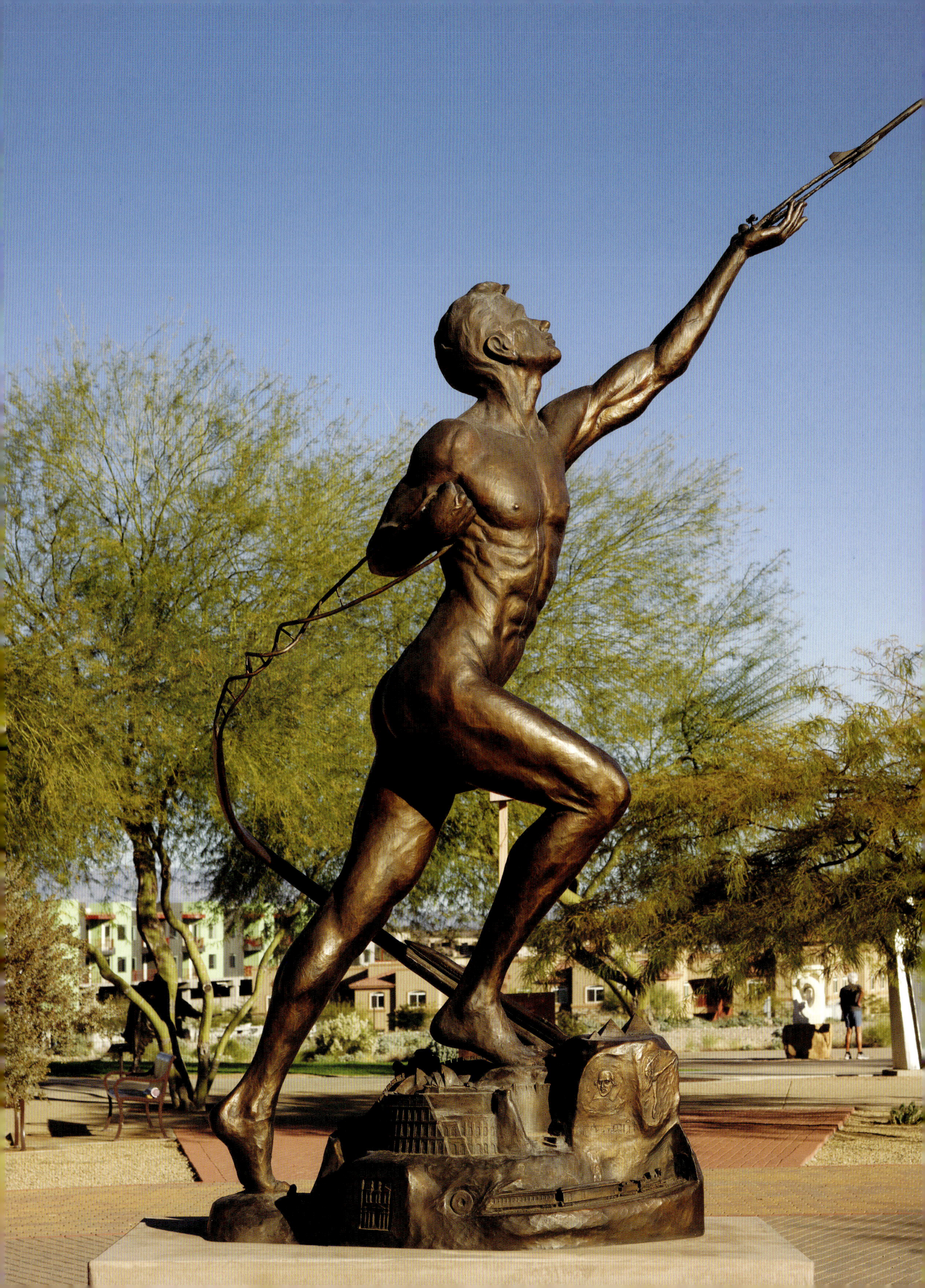

Opposite: Victor Issa's 2010 *Power of Thought* sculpture is a highlight of the community center garden in Fountain Hills. It was inspired, Issa said, "by the drive that has led men and women through the ages to expand the human experience." Below: Hoping for player autographs, the young Johnson brothers, Ethan, 6, tipping his cap, and Austin, 5, holding a ball, wait on, and by, the railing at a spring training Major League Baseball game between the Colorado Rockies and the Arizona Diamondbacks at Salt River Fields stadium in Scottsdale.

Valley of the Sun · 61

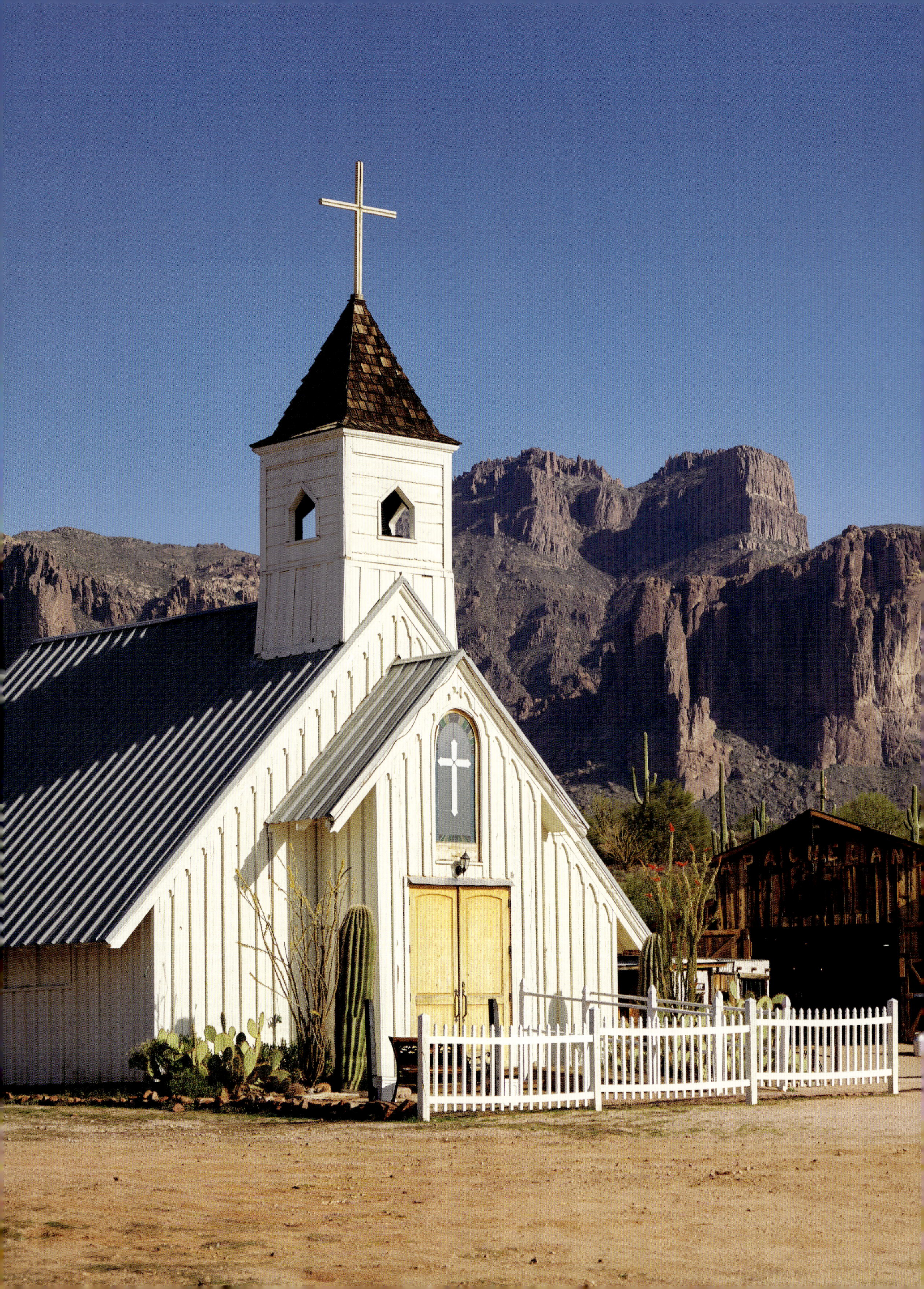

Left: The Elvis Presley Memorial Chapel at the Superstition Mountain Museum in Apache Junction is a movie prop, built for the 1969 Western *Charro!* Above: The We-Ko-Pah Golf Club on Havapai Nation land in Fort McDowell—now a community, not a fortification—makes effective use of native saguaros. Overleaf: Superstition Mountain Golf and Country Club in Apache Junction's Gold Canyon offers a stunning view.

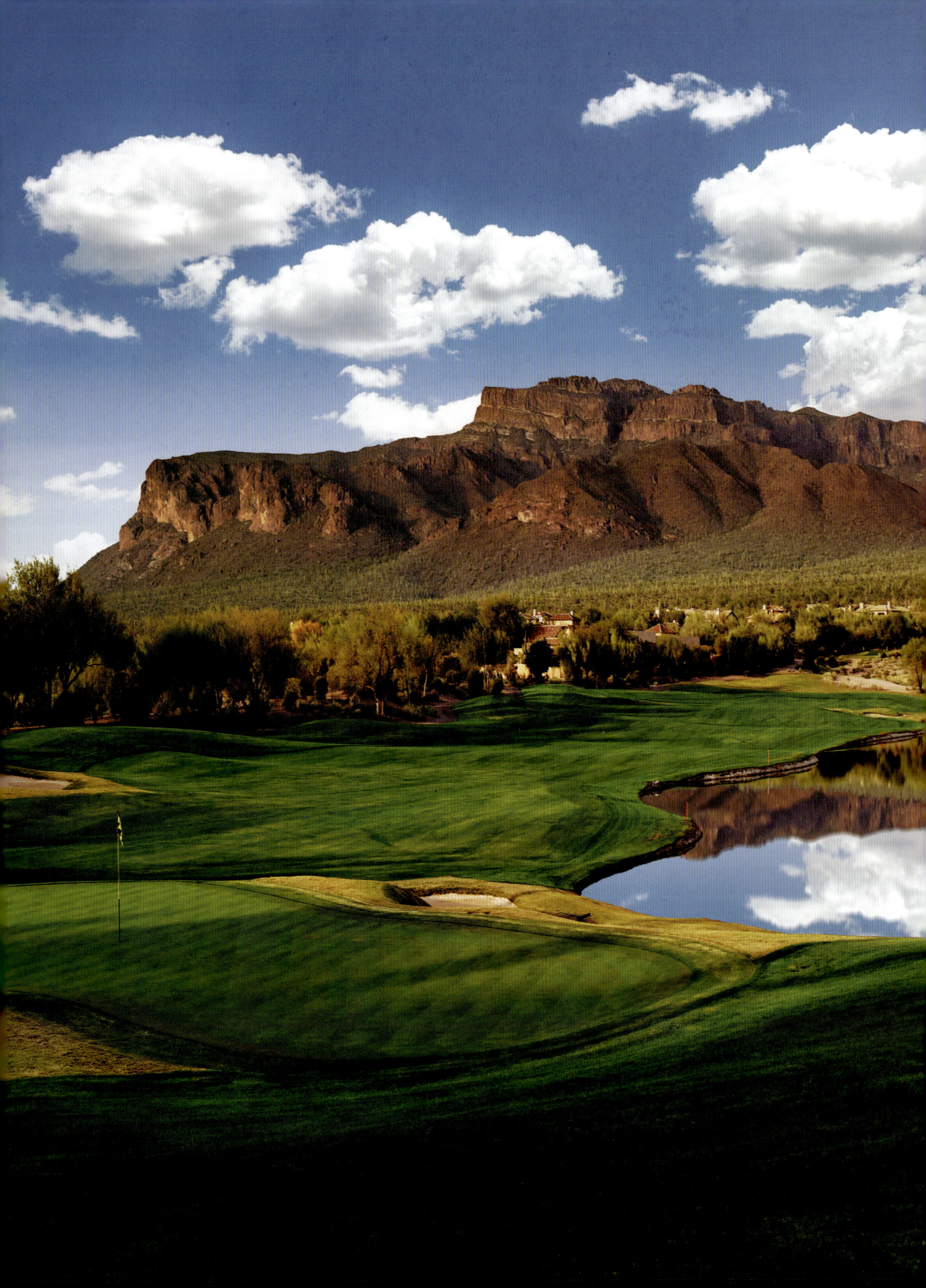

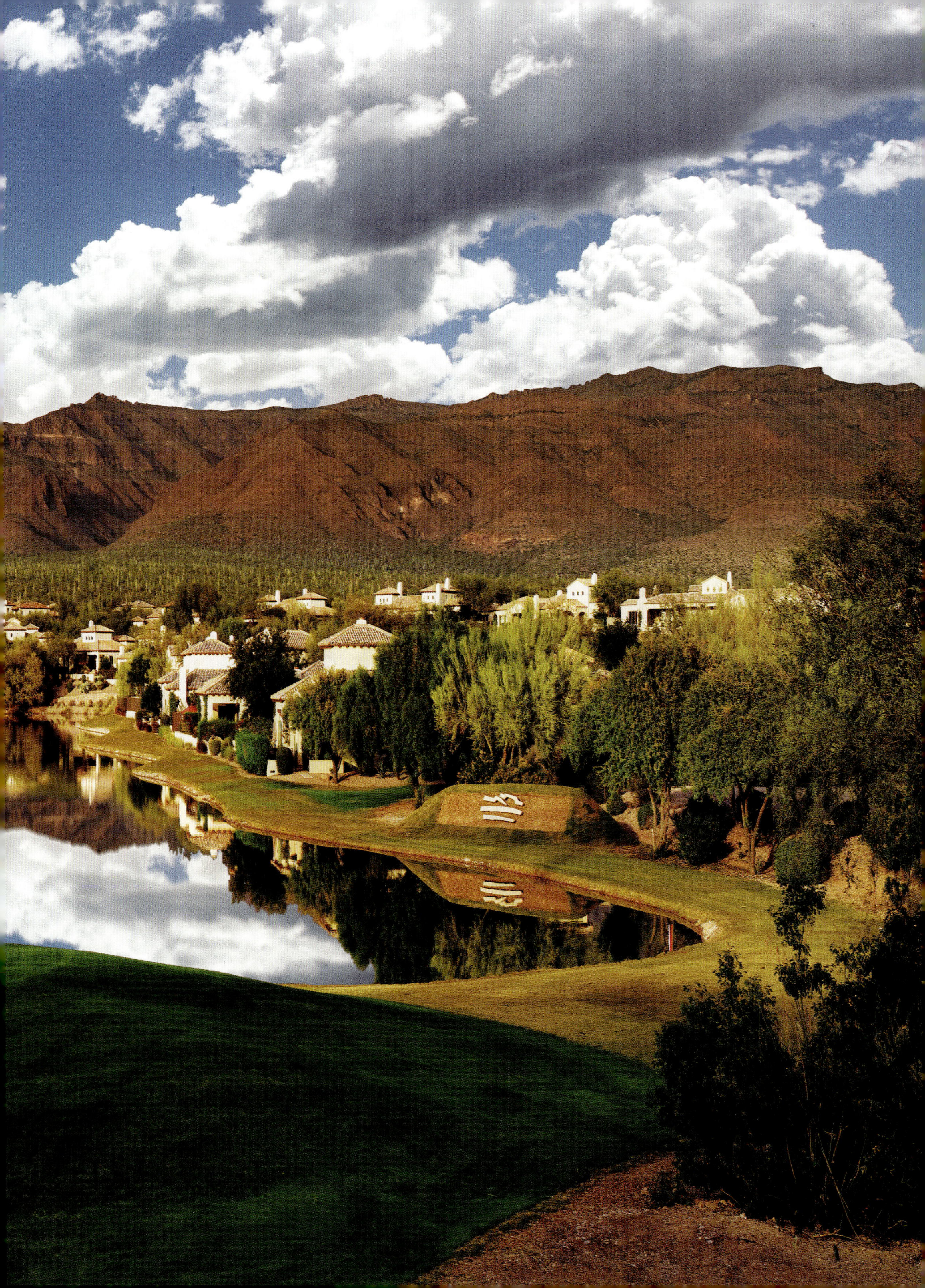

Below: A palm-lined pathway leads to the main campus of Arizona State University in Tempe. Opposite: Grady Gammage Auditorium is an exotic Frank Lloyd Wright creation on campus. After Wright's death in 1959, the auditorium's design was completed by his protégé William Wesley Peters. Overleaf: Bougainvilleas dazzle outside this house in Tempe's Cyprus Southwest neighborhood.

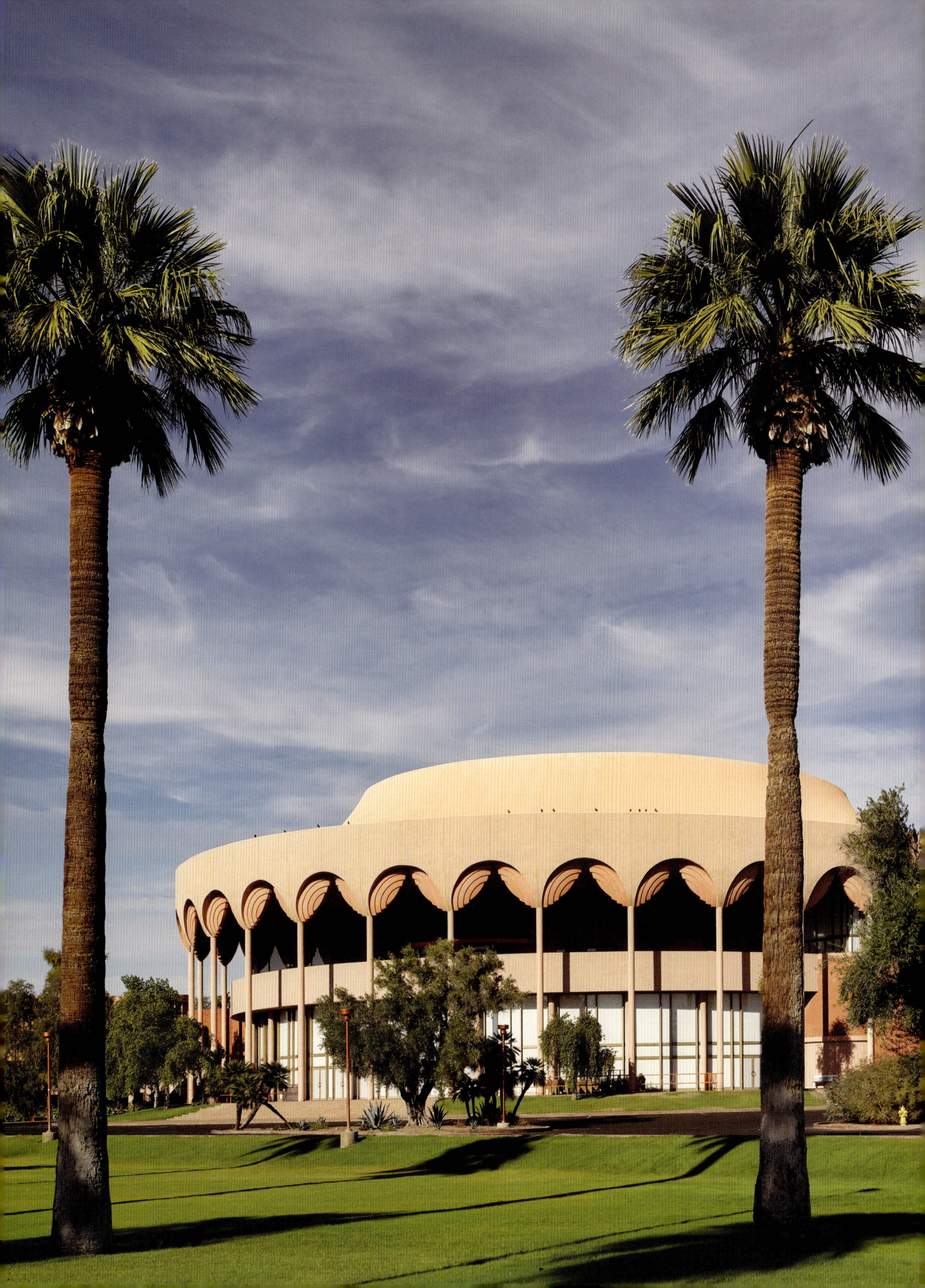

1036

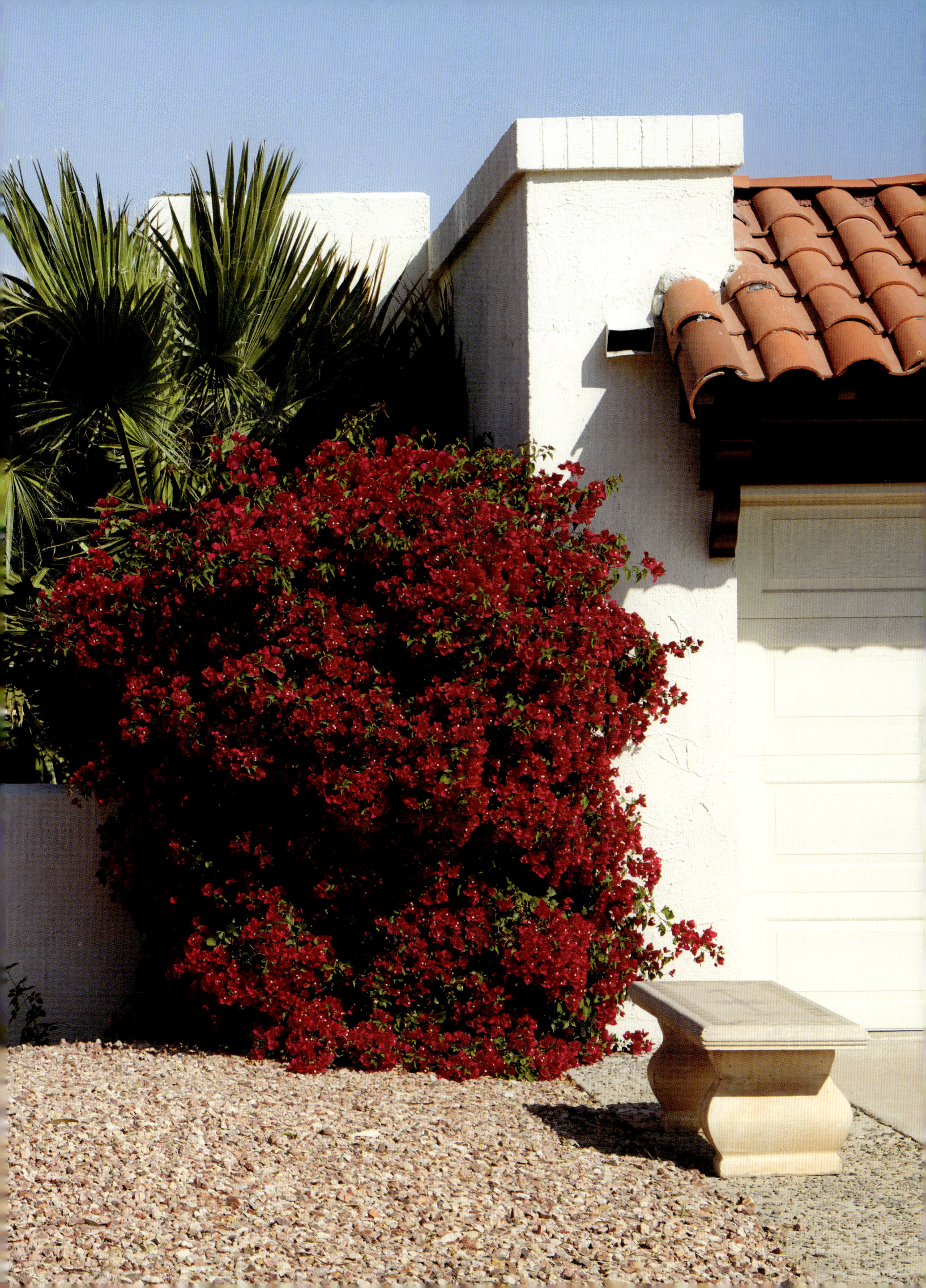

Above: An F-35 Lightning II fighter jet takes off at Luke Air Force Base in Glendale. For years this arm of the Air Education and Training Command emphasized instruction on the F-16 Fighting Falcon, a successful all-weather multirole aircraft. In 2011 the emphasis switched to training on Lockheed Martin's F-35 Lightning II, a single-seat, single-engine, all-weather stealth fighter designed for both ground-attack and air-to-air missions. Opposite: The Phoenix Temple in Glendale, which opened in 2014, became the 144th temple of the Church of Jesus Christ of Latter-day Saints worldwide.

70 · *Valley of the Sun*

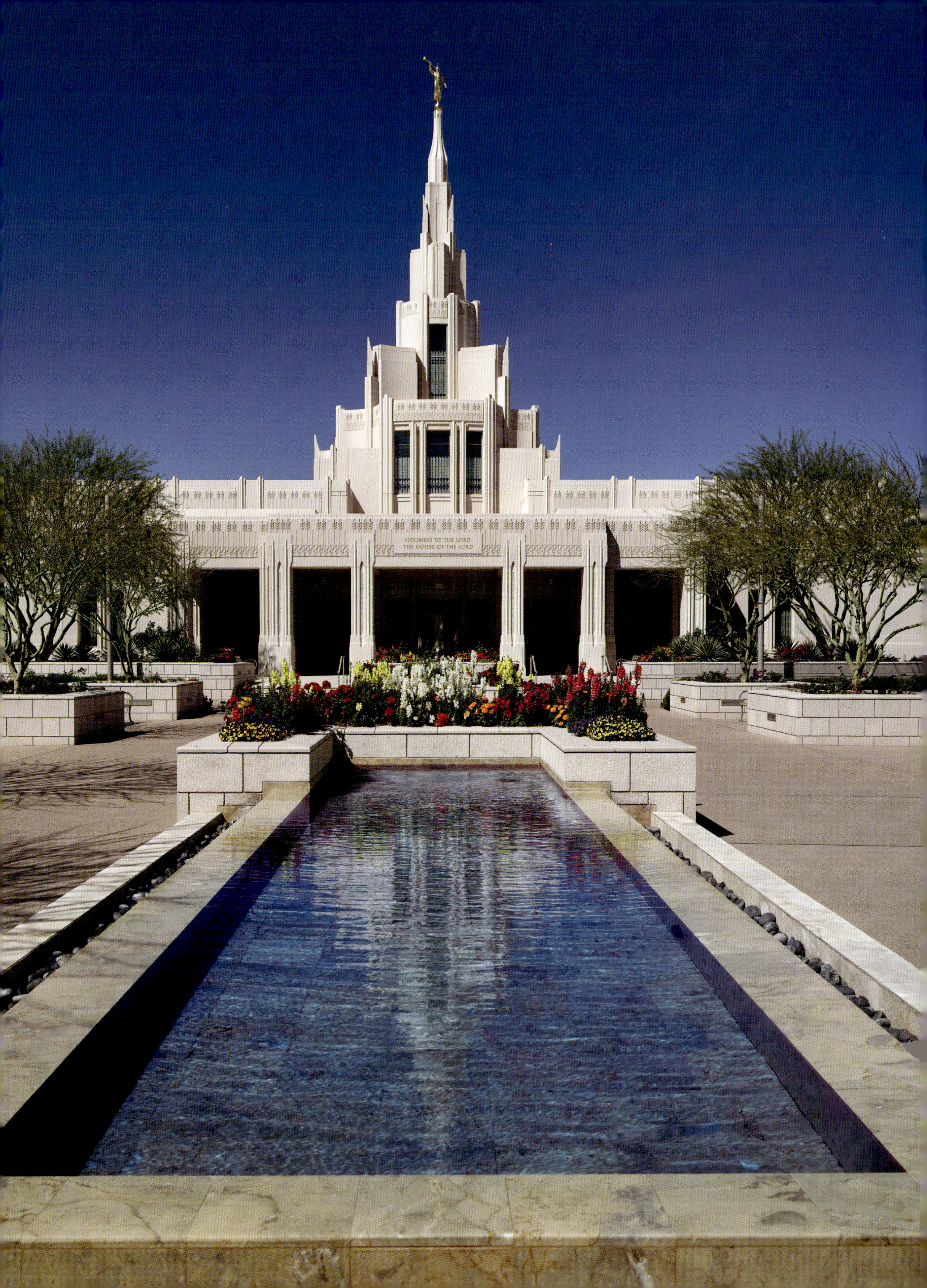
HOLINESS TO THE LORD
THE HOUSE OF THE LORD

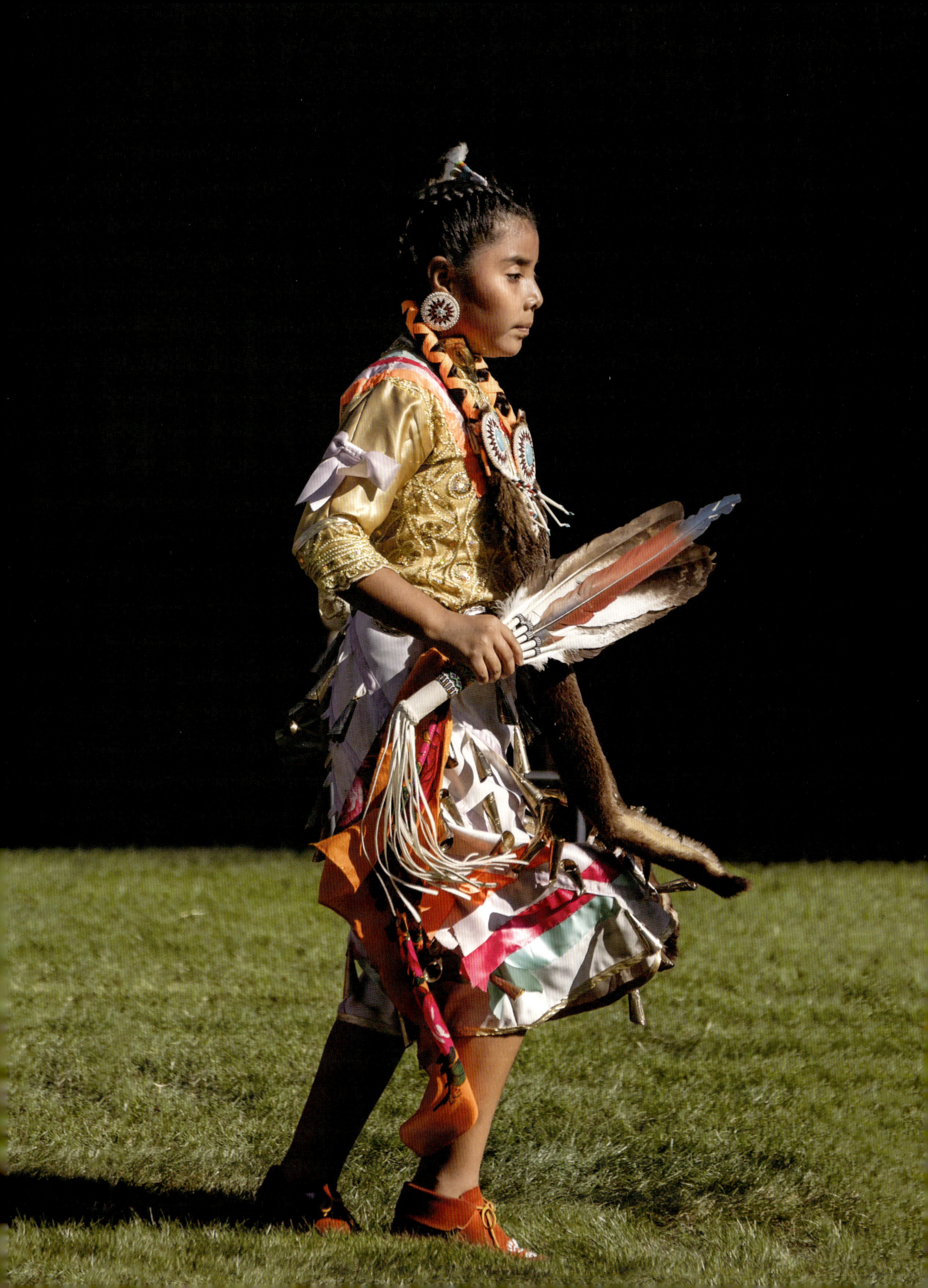

Dancers perform at the Native American Heritage Festival and Pow Wow on Arizona State University's west campus in Glendale. Many Indian communities enliven such social gatherings with dancing, drumming, and singing in full regalia. The ASU event, held each Veterans Day, also salutes tribal elders and honors veterans of U.S. military conflicts. Overleaf: The restored Castle Hot Springs resort, deep in the Bradshaw Mountains north of Phoenix, dates to 1896. Closed for several years, the historic retreat and spa reopened for business in 2019.

Valley of the Sun · 73

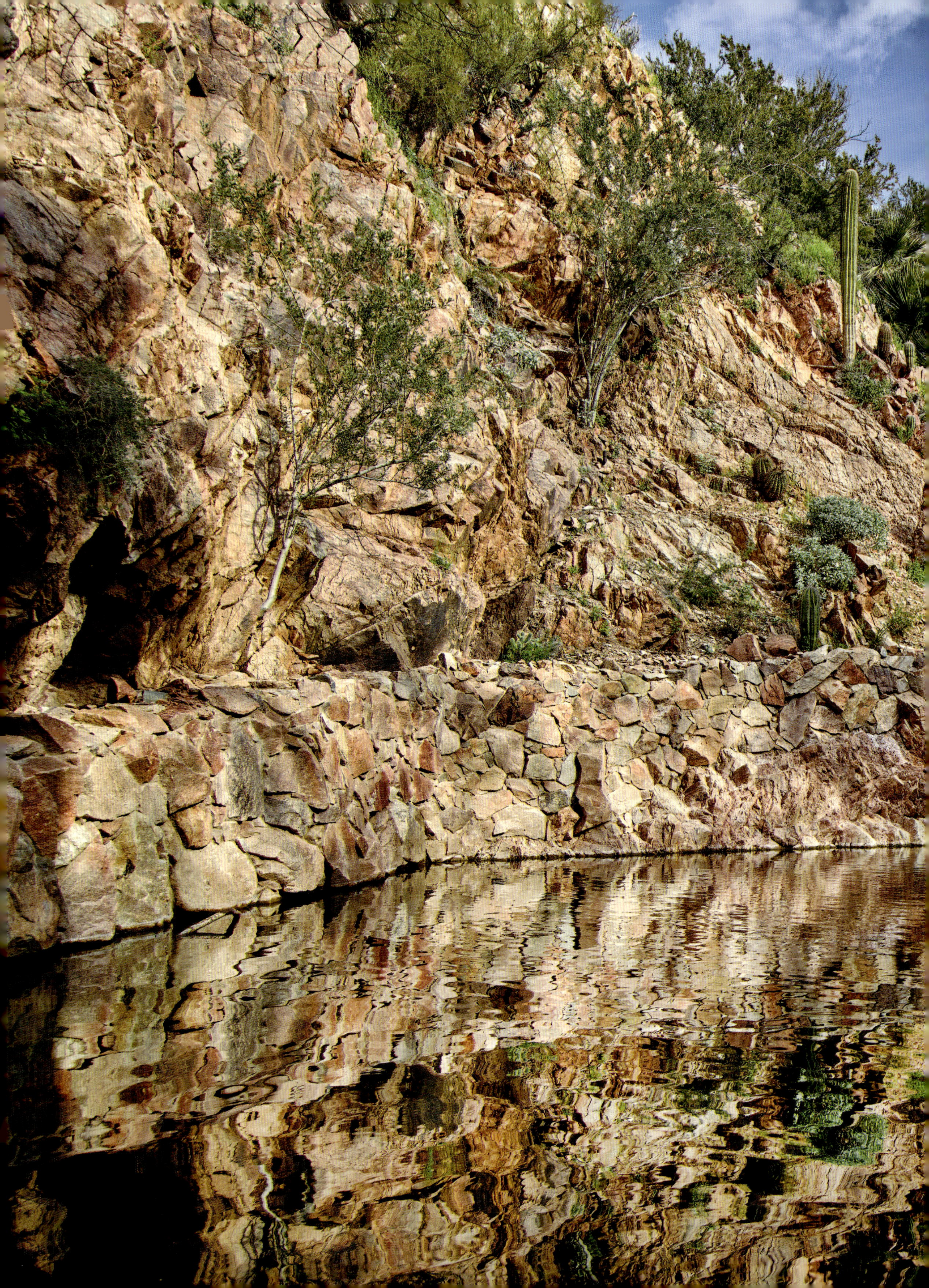

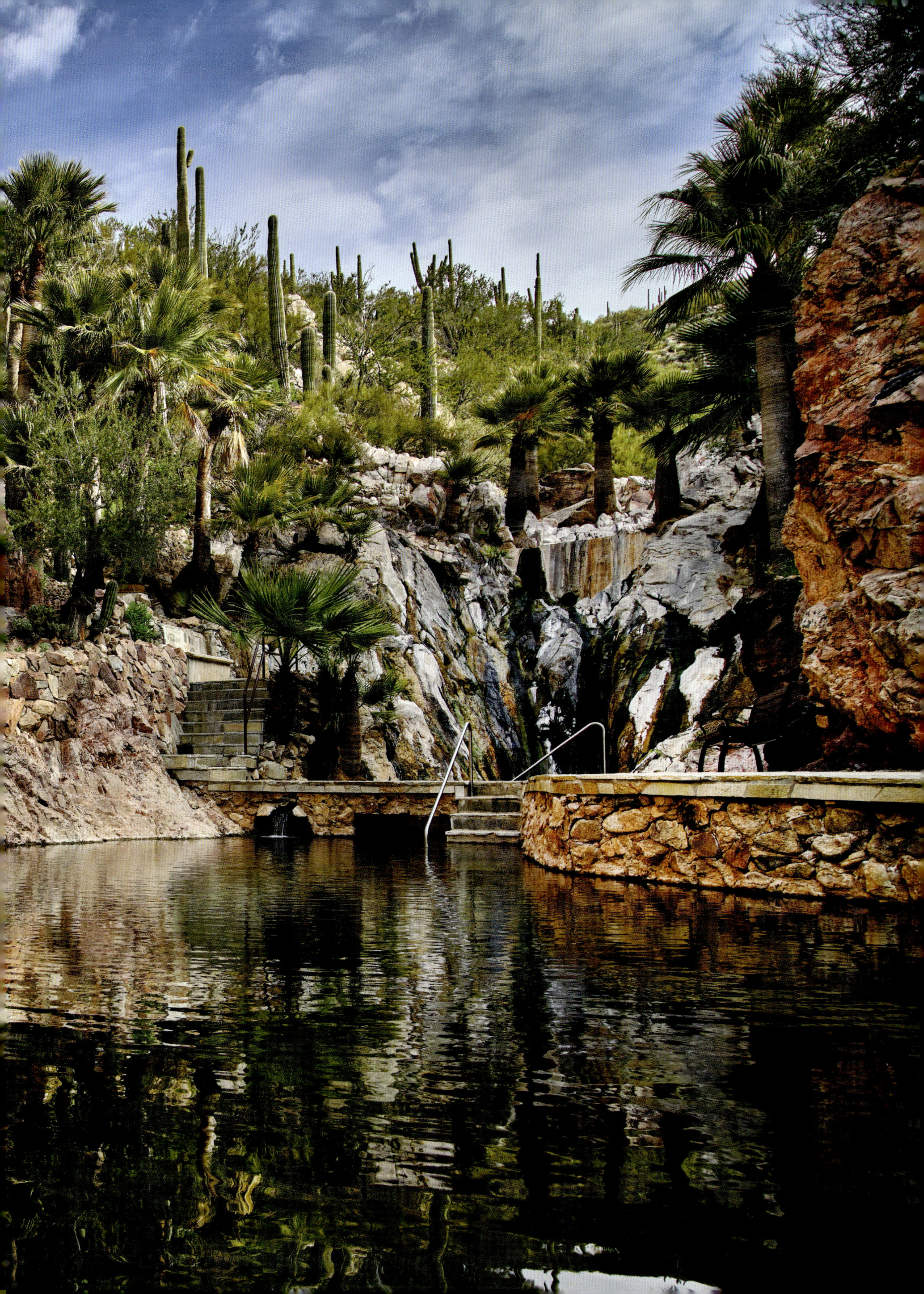

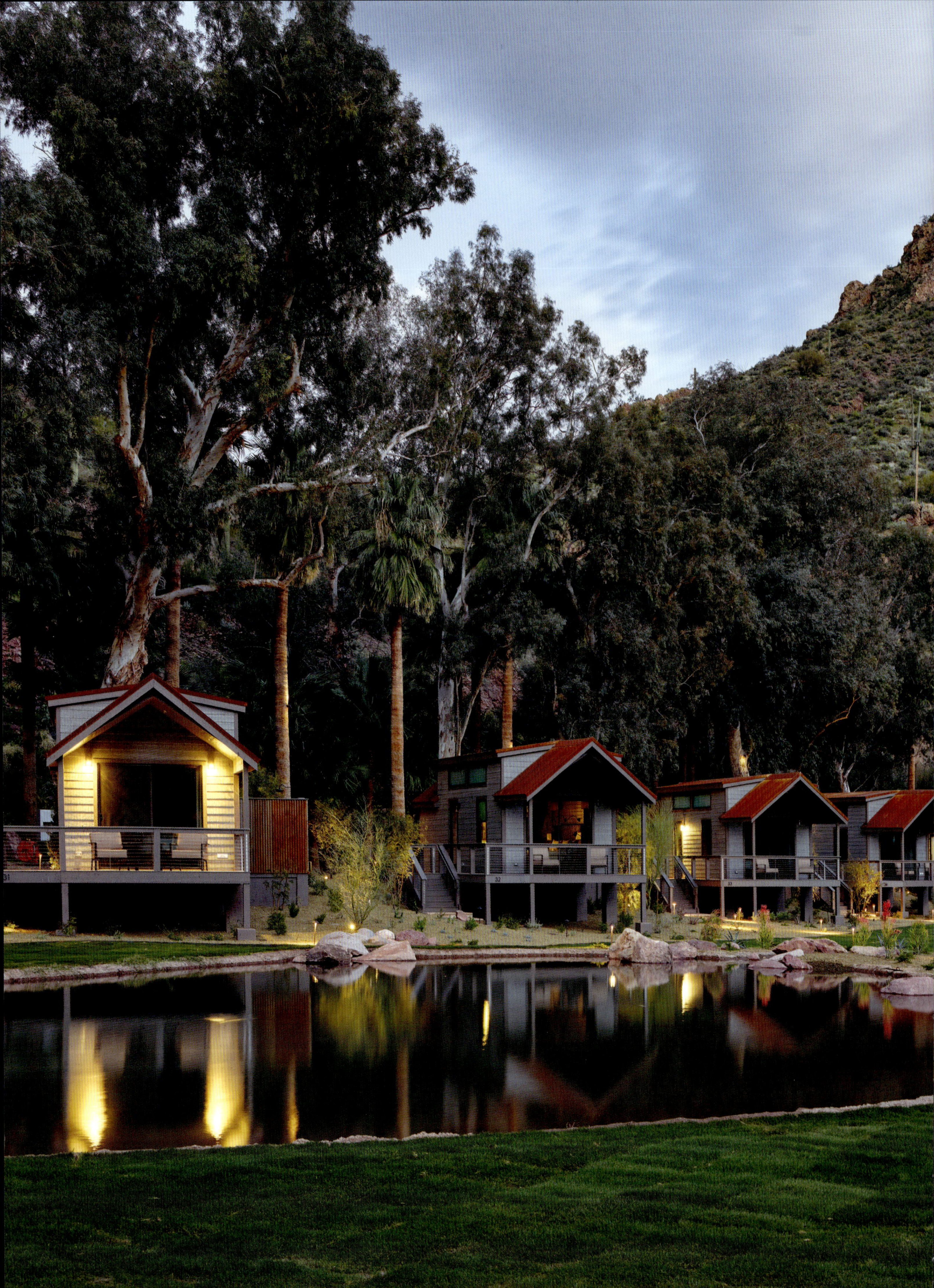

Castle Hot Springs is one of many therapeutic health resorts that popped up around the turn of the twentieth century. The 180,000 gallons of water produced by its thermal springs also served as a balm for injured American service members during World War II.

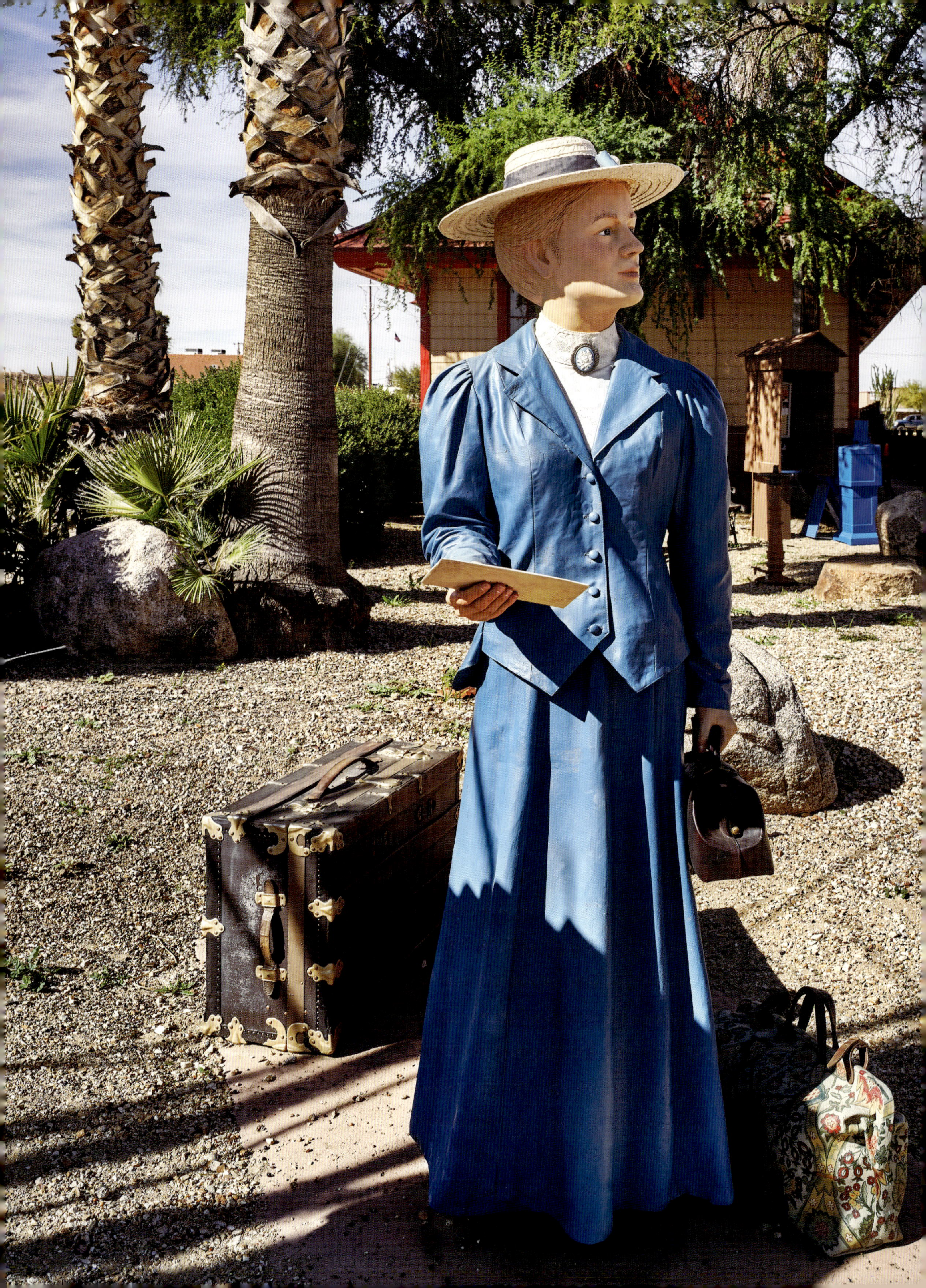

Opposite: J. Seward Johnson's statue depicts a schoolteacher arriving "out Wickenburg way," as the local motto goes—perhaps in part, according to its placard, "to corral a local cowboy." Below: When residents up the road in Flores thought that a new traffic circle could use a frontier adornment, Kelly and Jennifer Hill designed this sculpture, each spur of which weighs forty-three hundred pounds.

Overleaf: Arcosanti is an experimental arcology (architecture and ecology) commune in Yavapai County's high desert. It was begun in 1970 by Paolo Soleri, an Italian architect and former Frank Lloyd Wright apprentice who came to Arizona in 1947. This semidome apse in his futurist desert city now shelters casting equipment for bronze bells whose sales support the community.

Wickenburg · Flores · 79

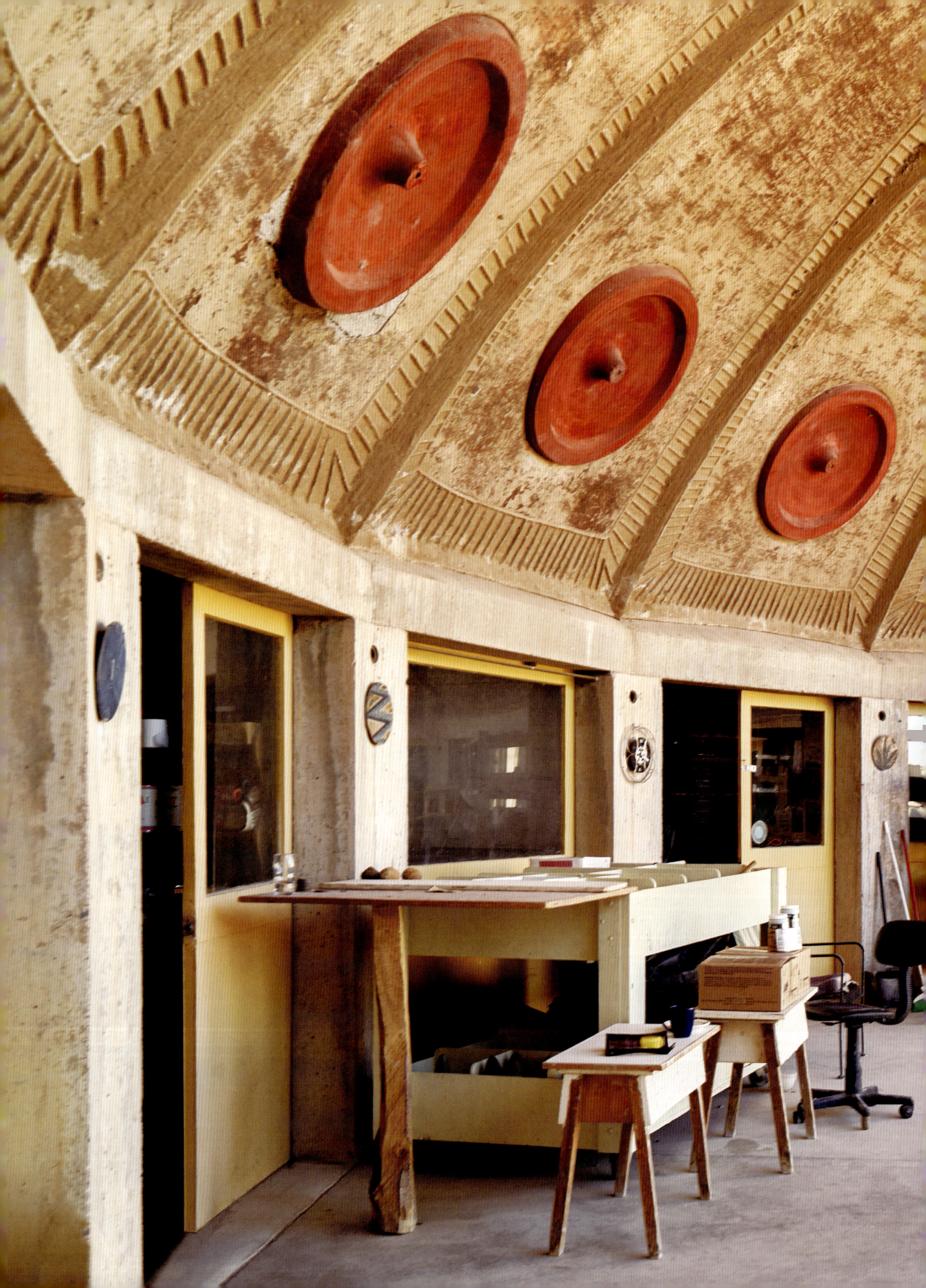

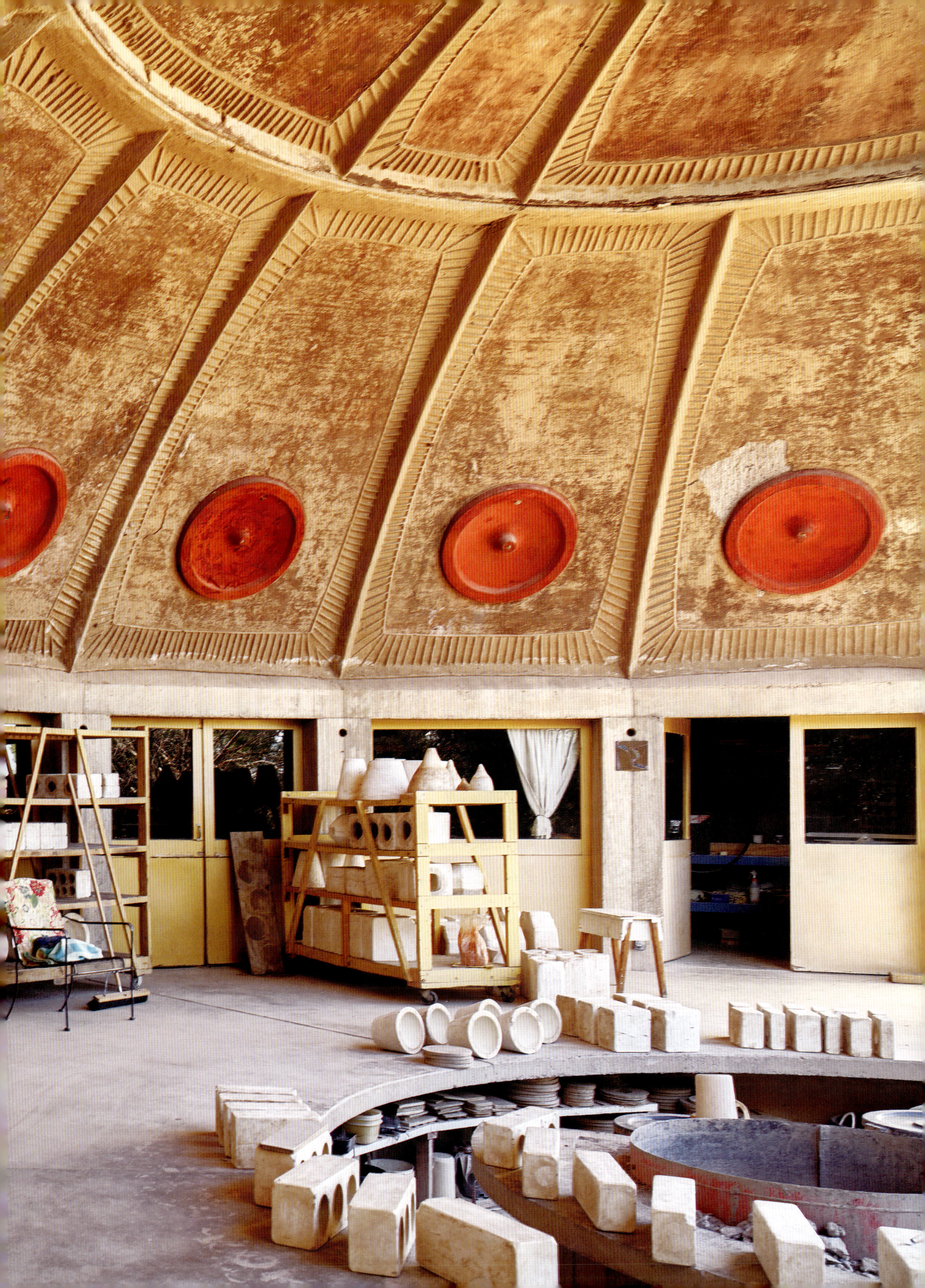

Above: Bill Nebeker sculpted the 1985 *Early Settlers* brass monument in Prescott, which was founded in 1864 as the capital of Arizona Territory. That briefly included a swath of present-day New Mexico and reached as far west as what is now Las Vegas, Nevada. Right: Slate-black skies and fetching rainbows such as this beauty outside Humboldt-Dewey usually presage a drenching downpour. Overleaf: Almost hidden in a pocket of the area's boundless prairie is a surprise: Granite Dells—exposed formations of 1.4-billion-year-old igneous rock.

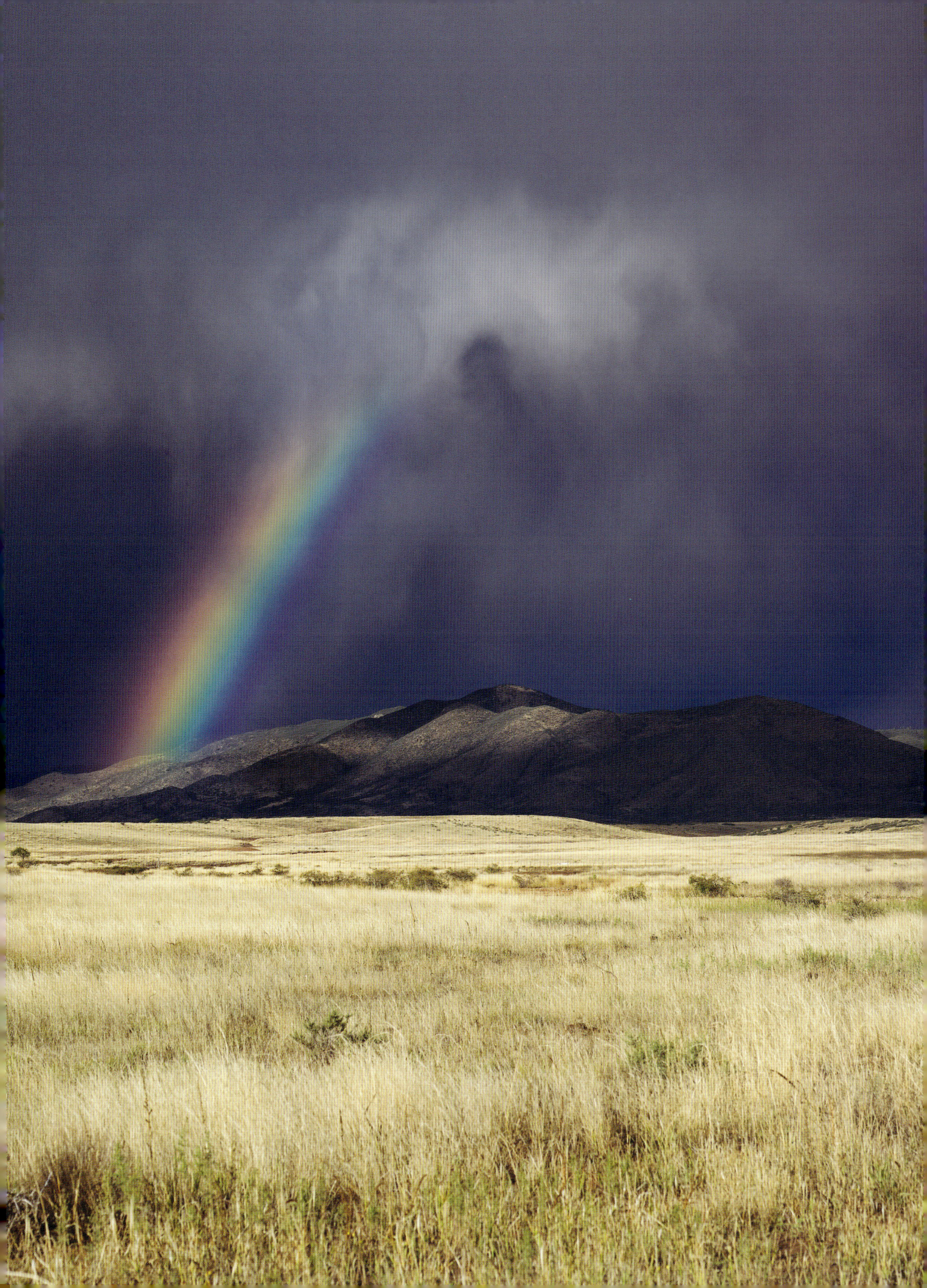

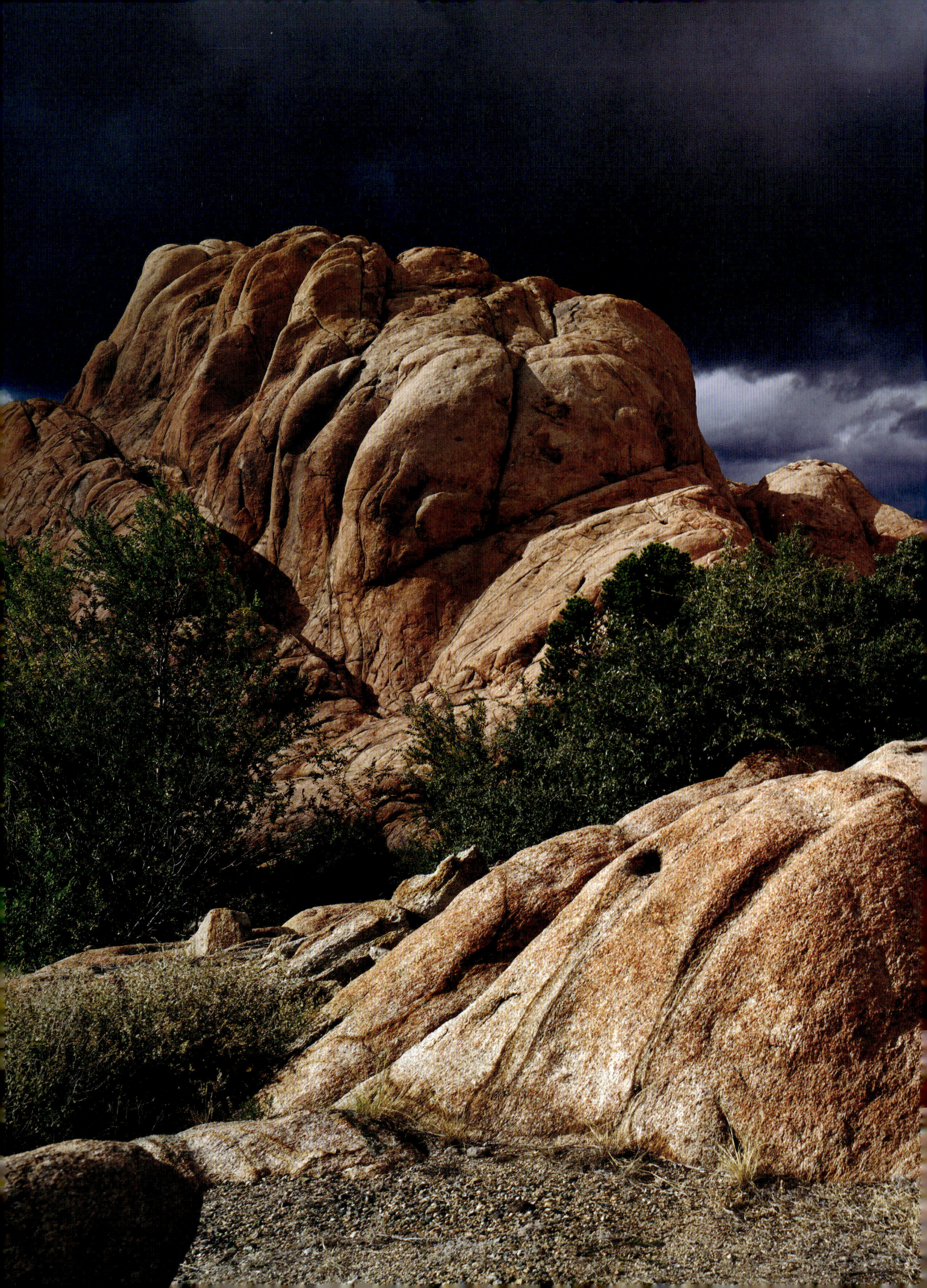

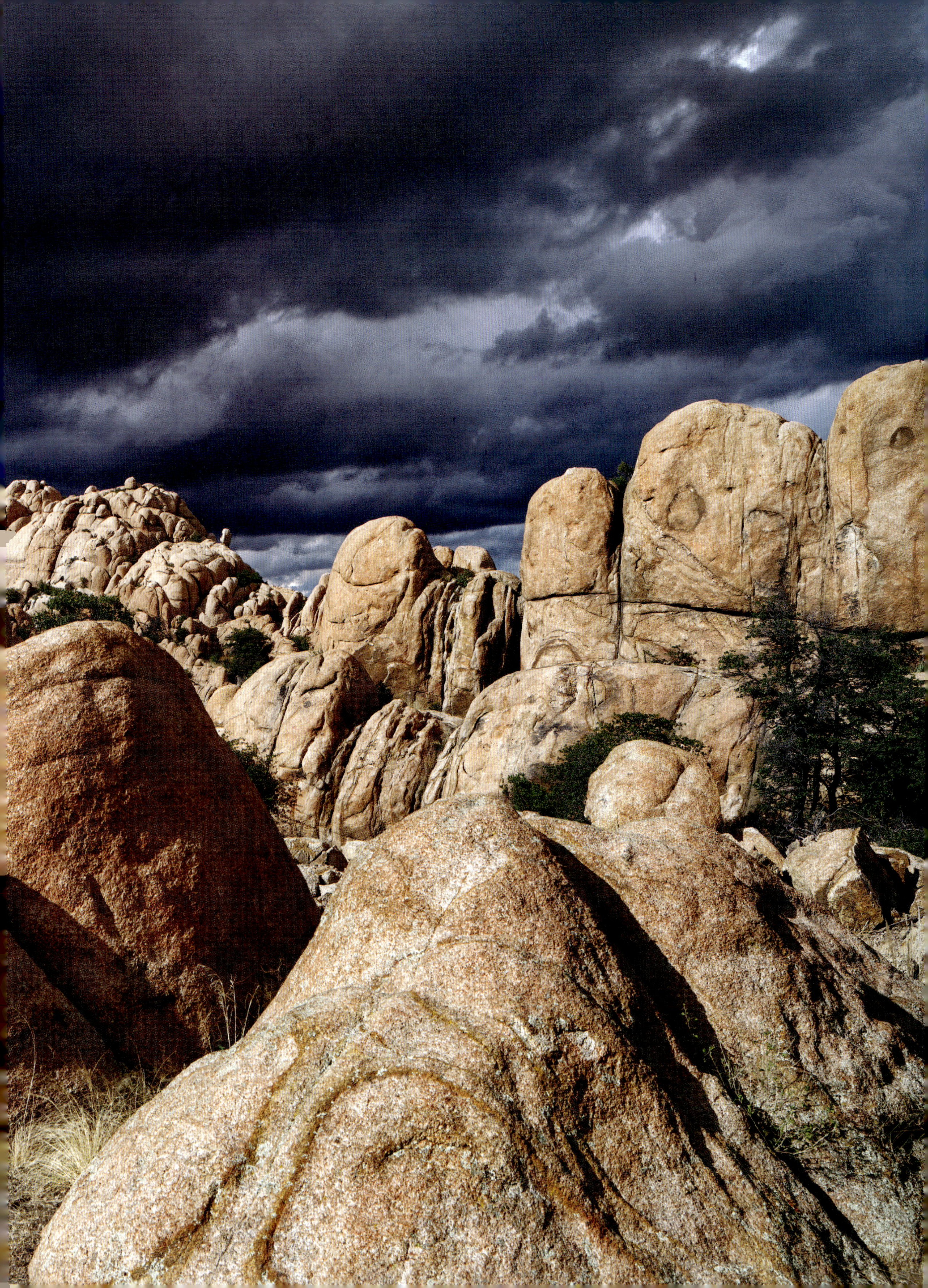

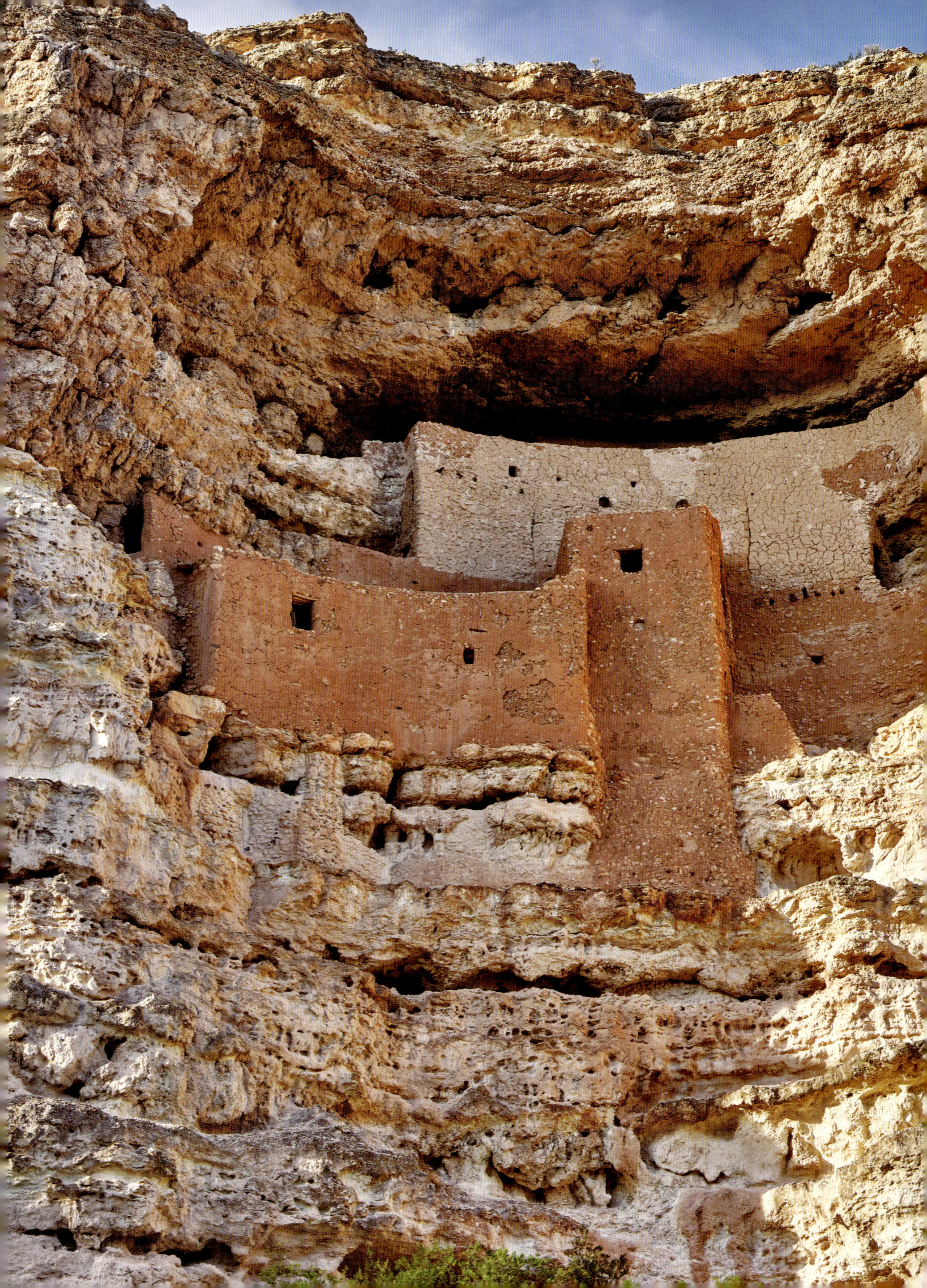

Left: Near Camp Verde are vestiges of stone dwellings, now called Montezuma Castle National Monument, built about seven hundred fifty years ago by the Southern Sinagua people, a pre-Columbian culture. Below: Tuzigoot, a 110-room stone pueblo of similar vintage and Sinagua heritage, was rubble in 1933 when the archaeologists Louis Caywood and Edward Spicer rebuilt it while employing local families in the throes of the Great Depression. *Tuzigoot* (crooked water) is an Apache word for a nearby meandering of the Verde River.

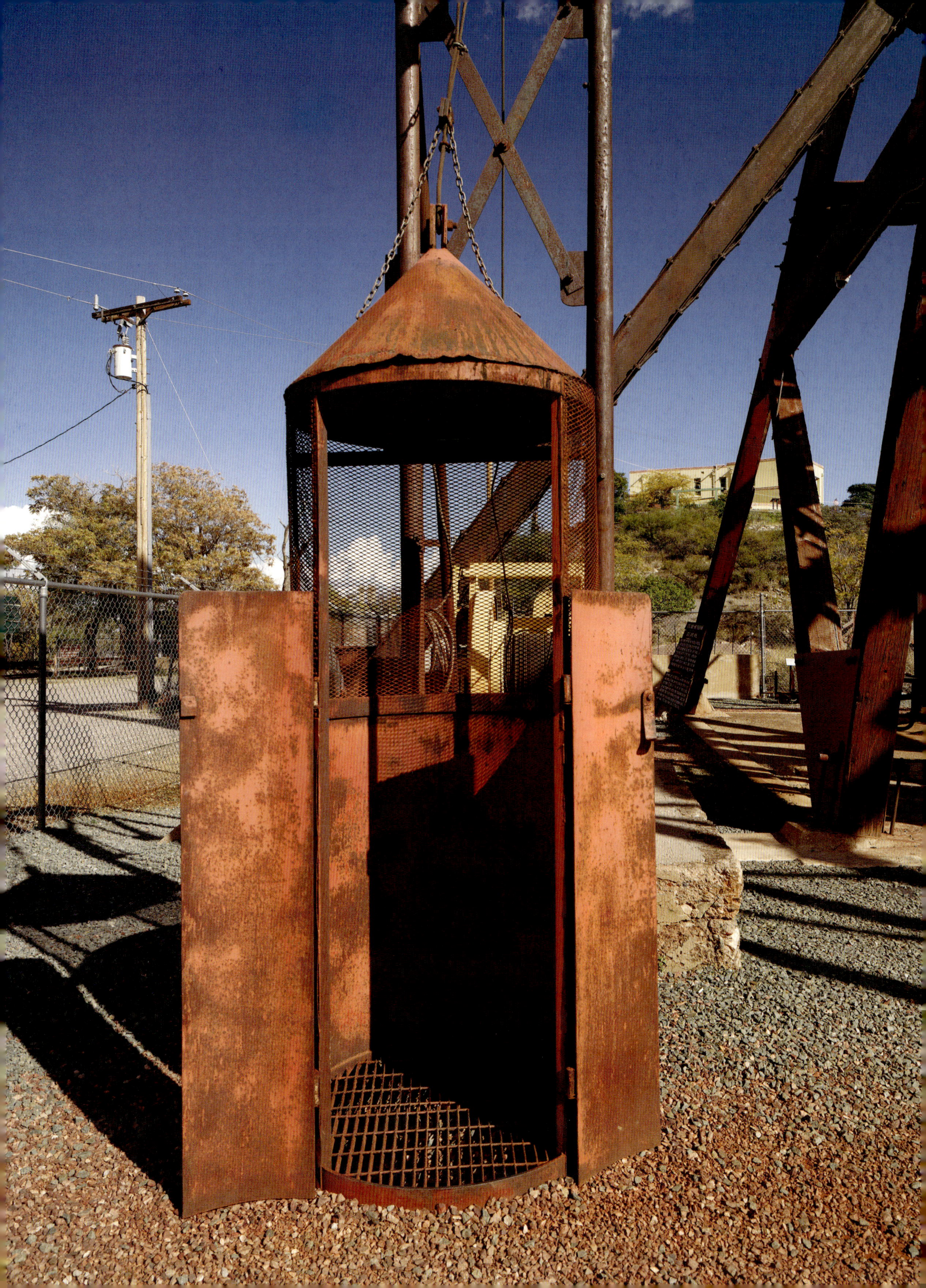

Opposite: The old Audrey Mine headframe, a winding tower atop a deep mine shaft, is a vestige of the historic mining boomtown of Jerome on Cleopatra Hill, overlooking the Verde Valley. Left: In little McGuireville, proprietors of the Pistols & Petticoats studio present customers with a wide selection of old-timey Western outfits in which to pose for souvenir photographs. Below: A Verde Canyon Railroad excursion train, moments out of Clarkdale, heads into the canyon en route to the veritable ghost town of Perkinsville.

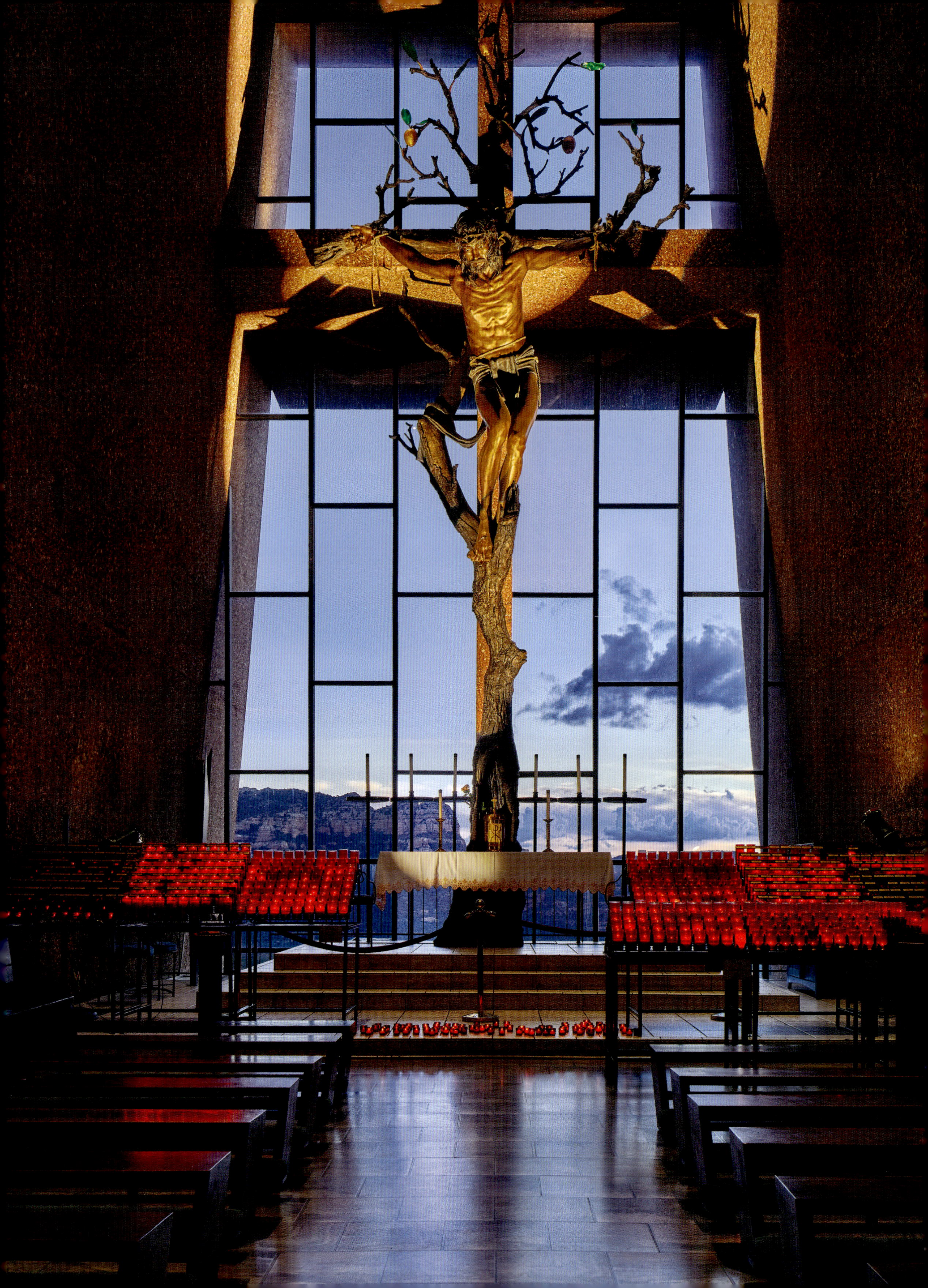

Along with Sedona's bevy of art galleries and eclectic shops, the Roman Catholic Chapel of the Holy Cross is a popular tourist draw, thanks in great measure to its setting among brilliant red-sandstone formations. The sculptor Marguerite Brunswig Staude commissioned the chapel, which was completed in 1956. Overleaf: The red rocks that surround Sedona—named after the postmistress Sedona Miller Schnebly, whose mother said that "it sounded pretty"—turn exceptionally vivid when the setting sun envelops them.

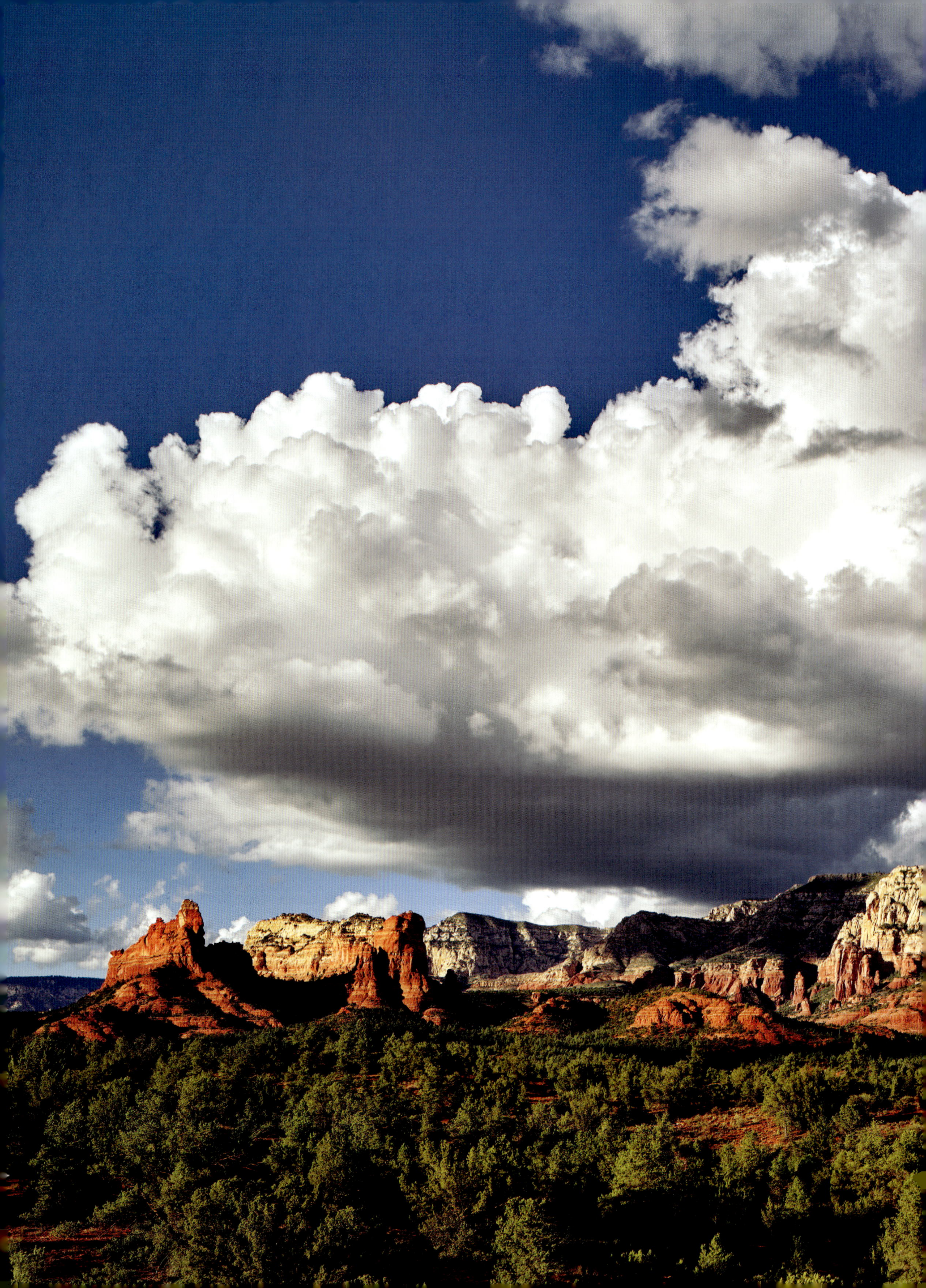

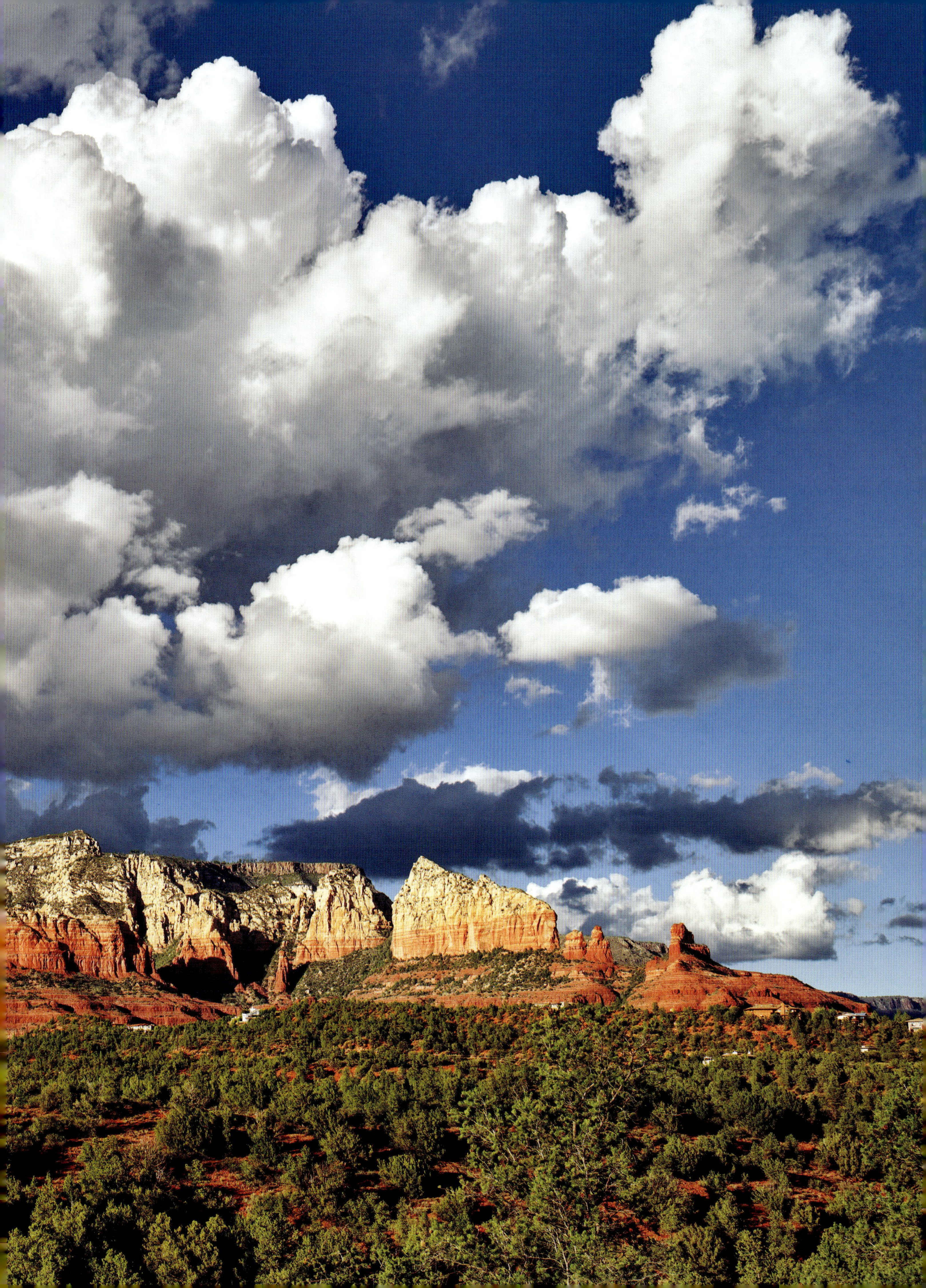

1966 Happy Jack
Donated
In Memory of
EARL E. HARRIS
307 6/8
DONATED BY
RUSS KRUEGER
1999
The Zane Grey Century

Left: Mementos and trophy heads accent the Mormon Lake Lodge in a settlement named for pioneers in the valley. After a fire incinerated this saloon and steakhouse in 1974, ranchers from throughout Arizona volunteered their time and strength to rebuild it. Below: Even the cacti are part of a metal-art installation near Sedona. Overleaf: This patch of ponderosa pine forest is part of the remote Coconino National Forest near Mormon Lake.

Mormon Lake · Sedona · 95

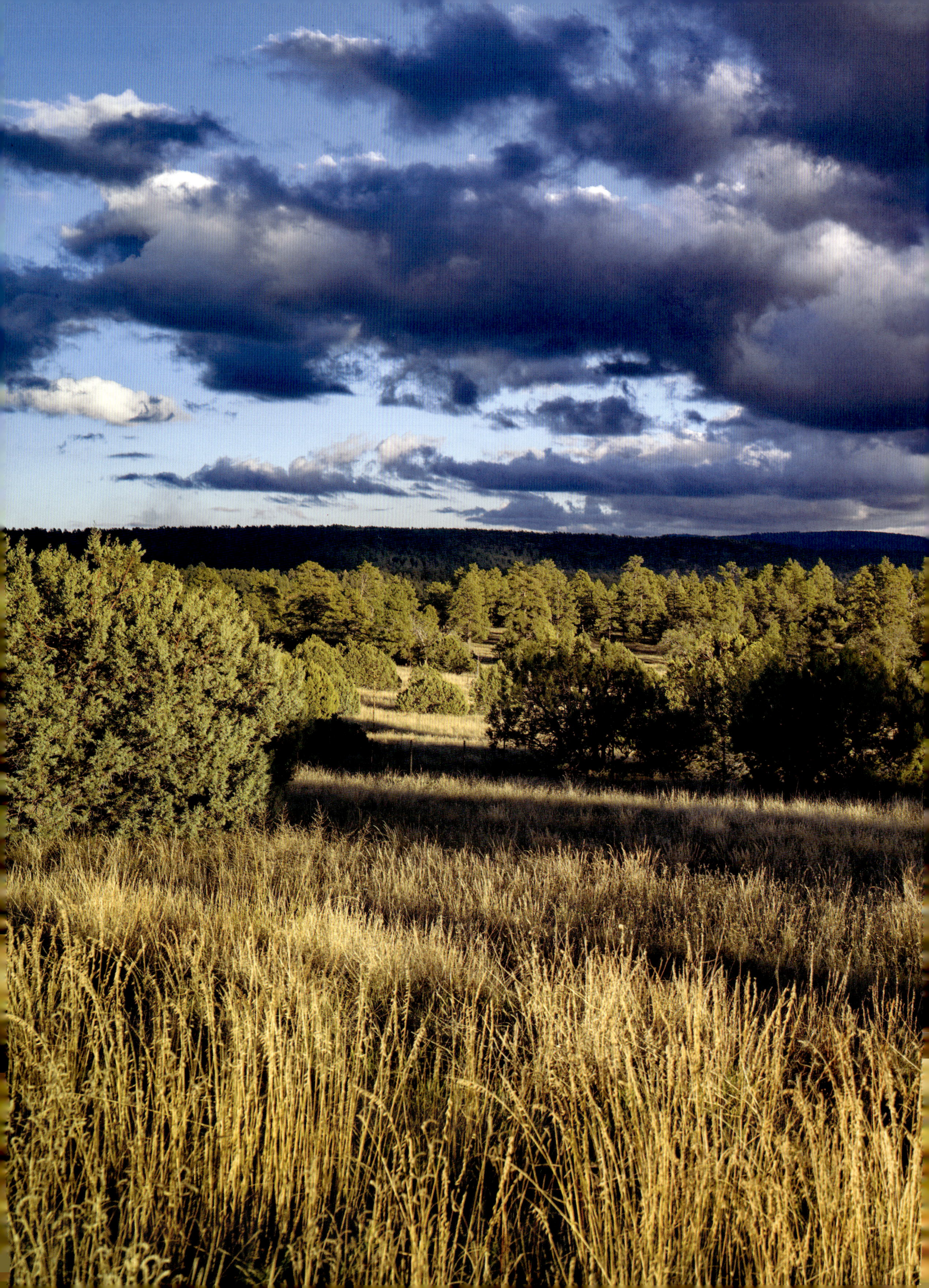

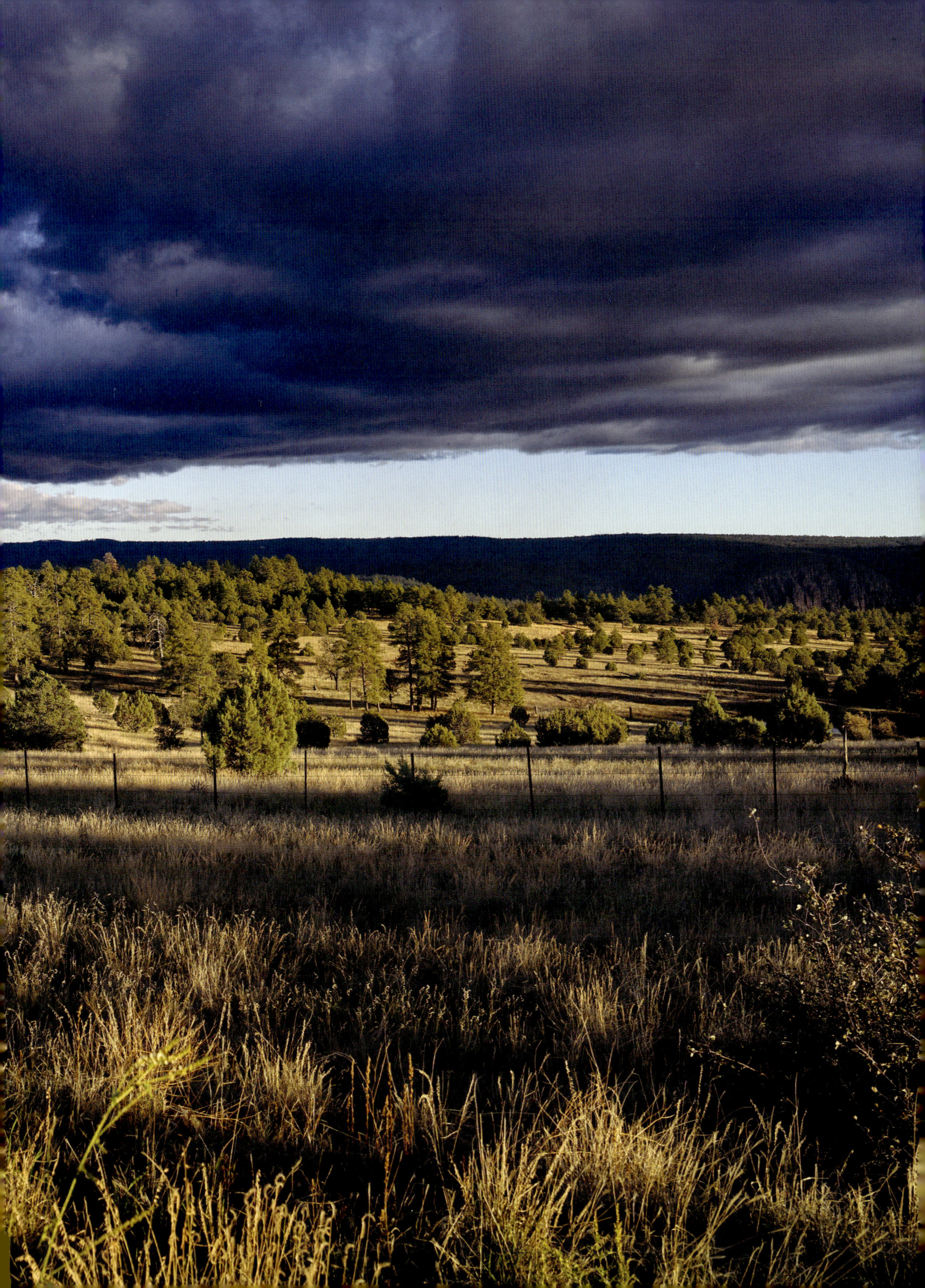

In the Painted Desert, the crater of a long-extinct volcano provides an otherworldly setting for the artist James Turrell's network of tunnels, chambers, and viewing areas that form what he calls a "naked-eye observatory." Two of the intriguing Roden Crater features are the Alpha Tunnel, at right, which leads to the East Portal, opposite. Overleaf: At 12,633 feet, Humphreys Peak (*Aaloosaktukwi* in Hopi and *Dook'o'oosłííd* in Navajo) is Arizona's tallest peak, looming over a woodsy Flagstaff neighborhood.

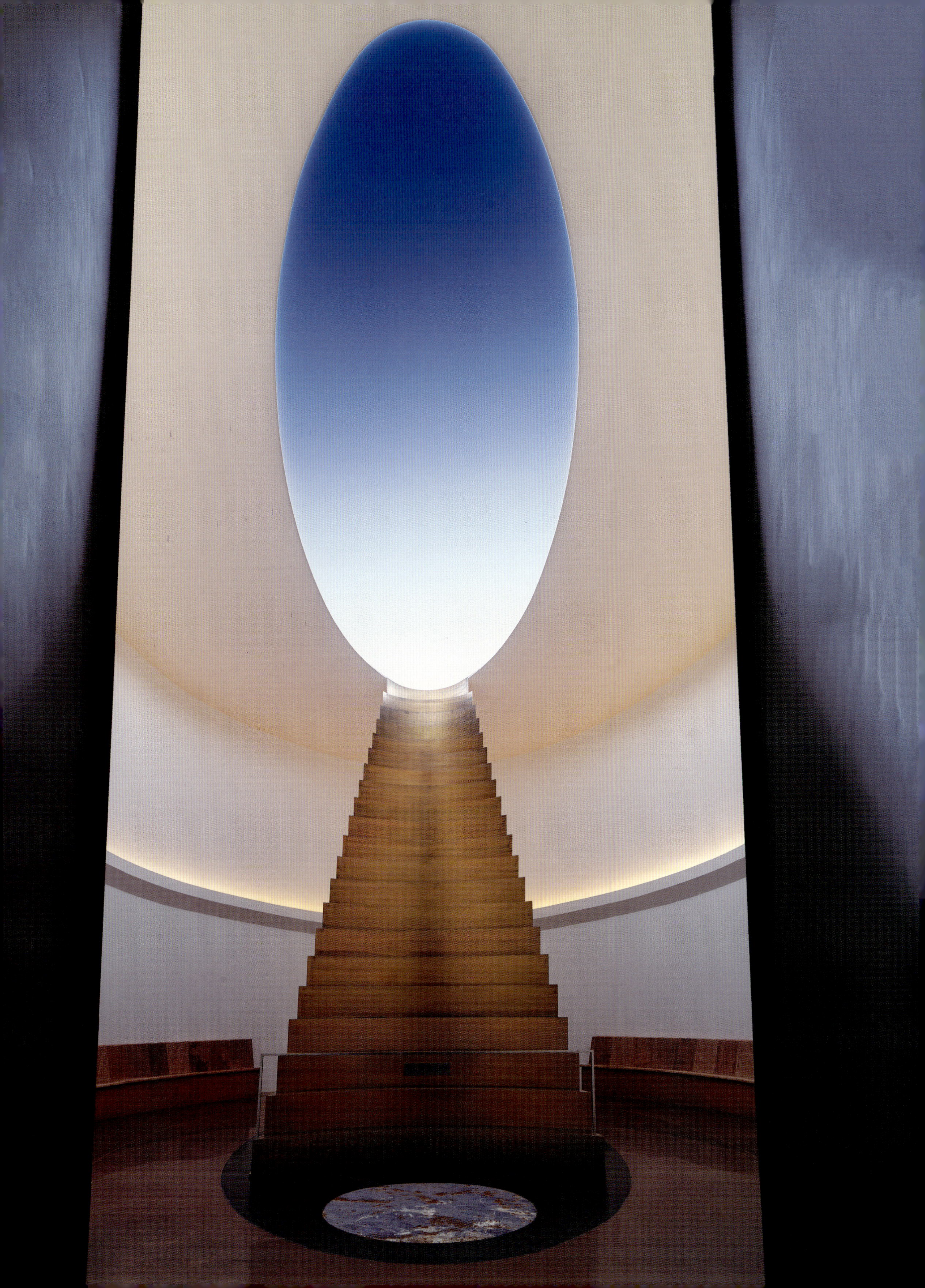

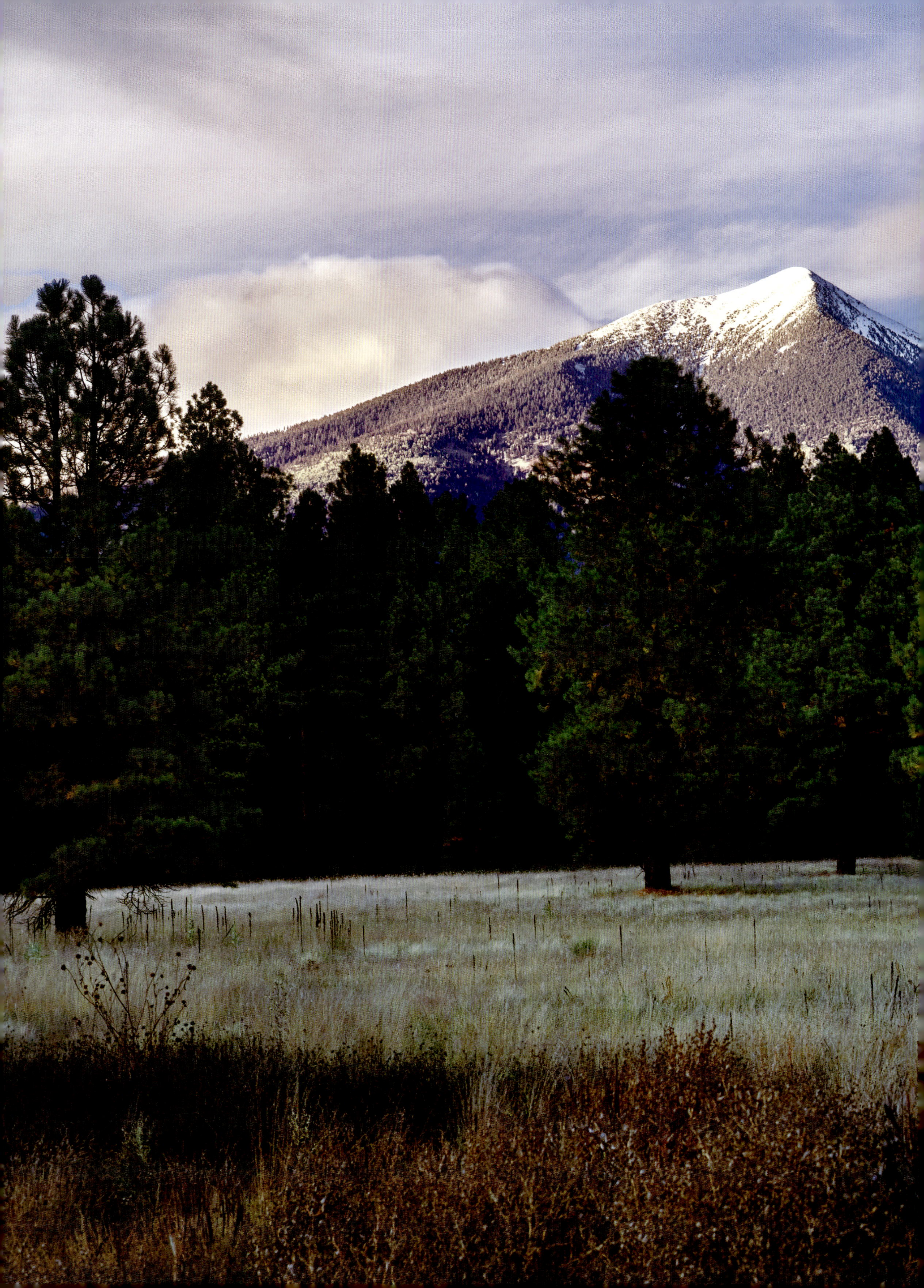

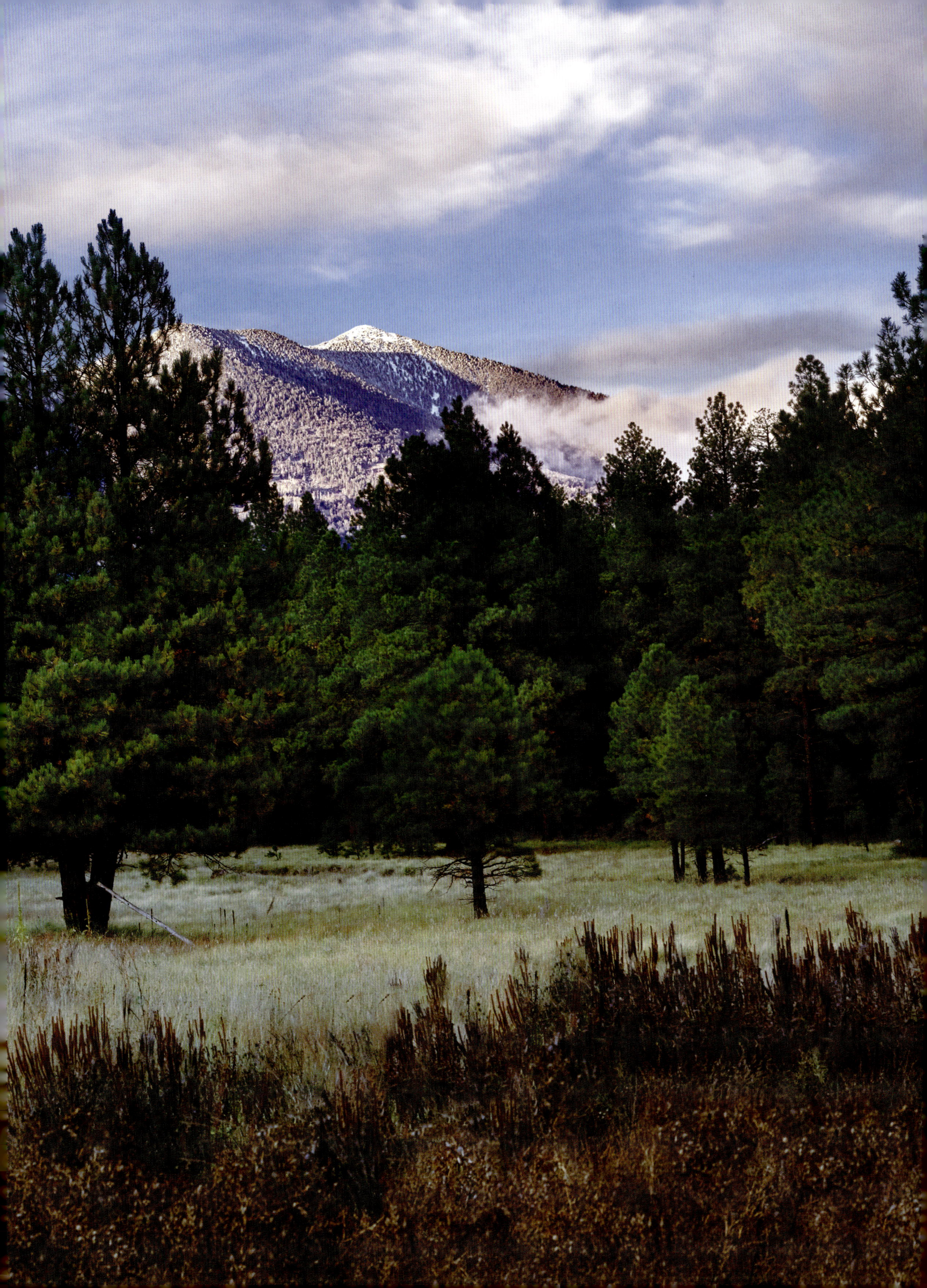

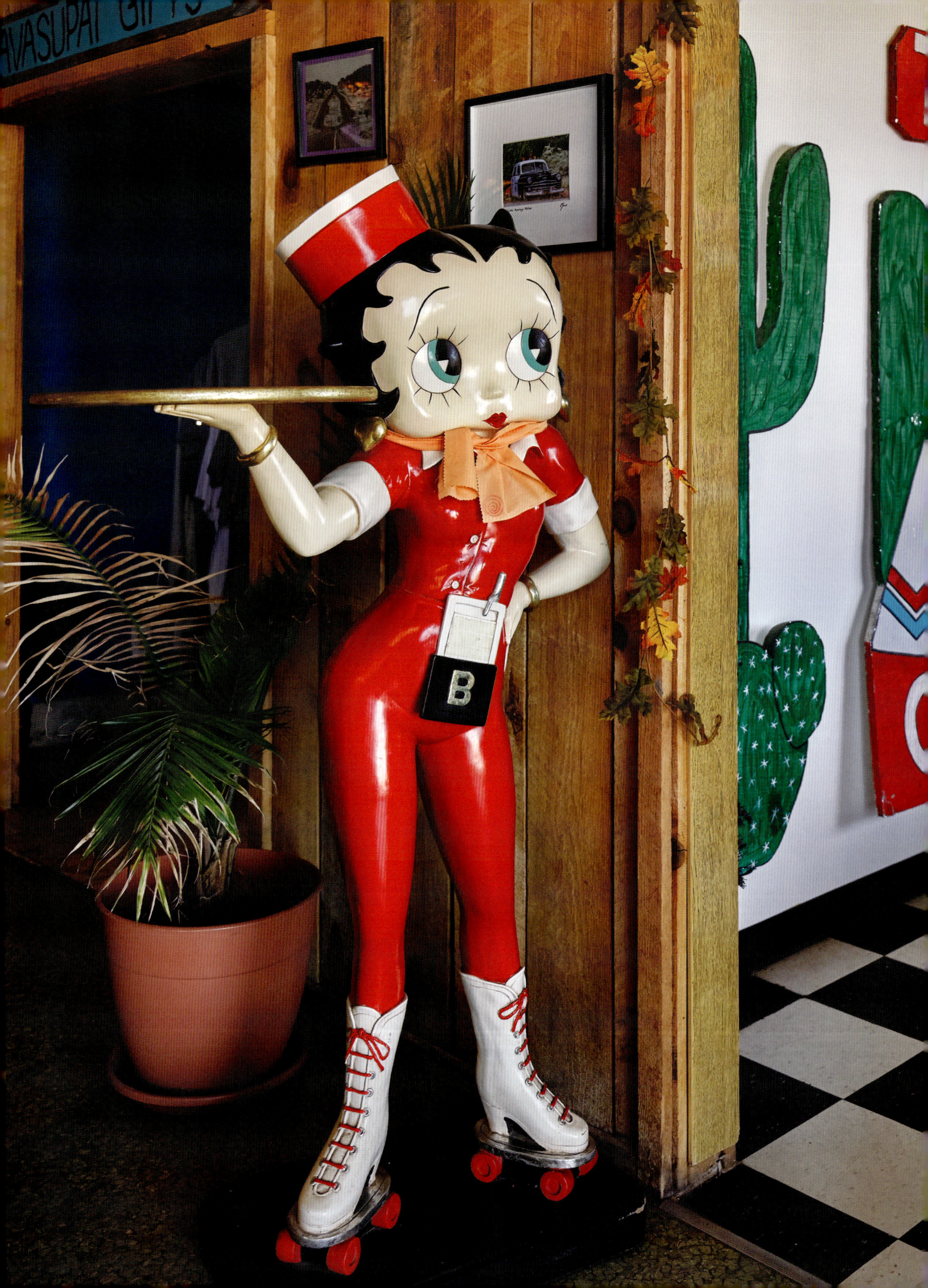

AVASUPAI
B

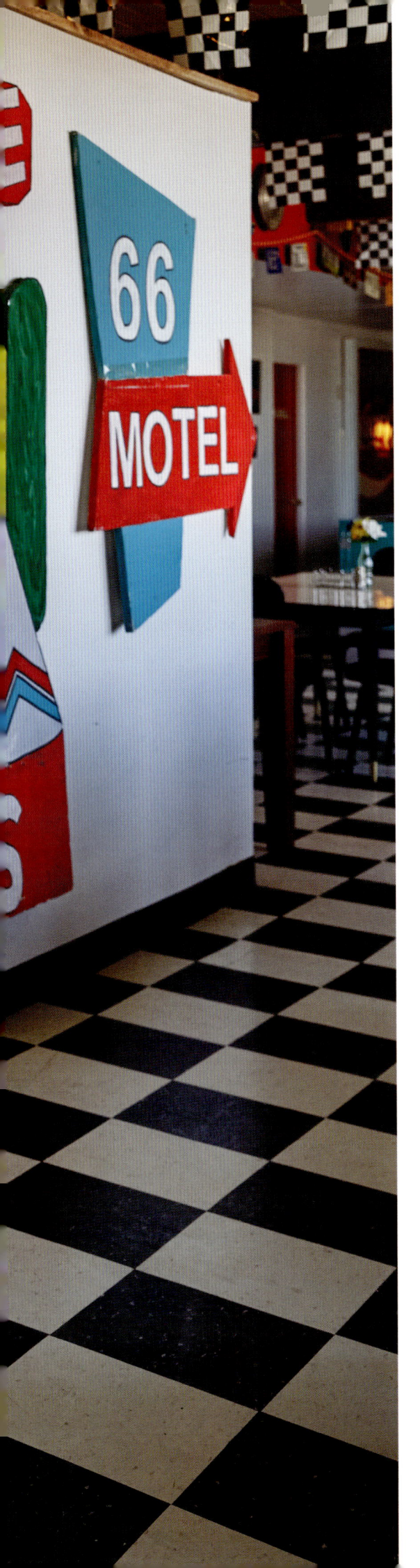

Left: Betty Boop, the flirtatious caricature of a Jazz Age flapper, serves up memories at the Grand Canyon Caverns' old-fashioned diner near Peach Springs. Below: In Williams, a steam engine of the Grand Canyon Railway prepares for departure to the South Rim of the natural landmark, far up the track. Built by the Atchison, Topeka and Santa Fe Railway in 1901, the line helped swell tourism to the area and prompted the development of Grand Canyon Village.

Peach Springs · Williams · 103

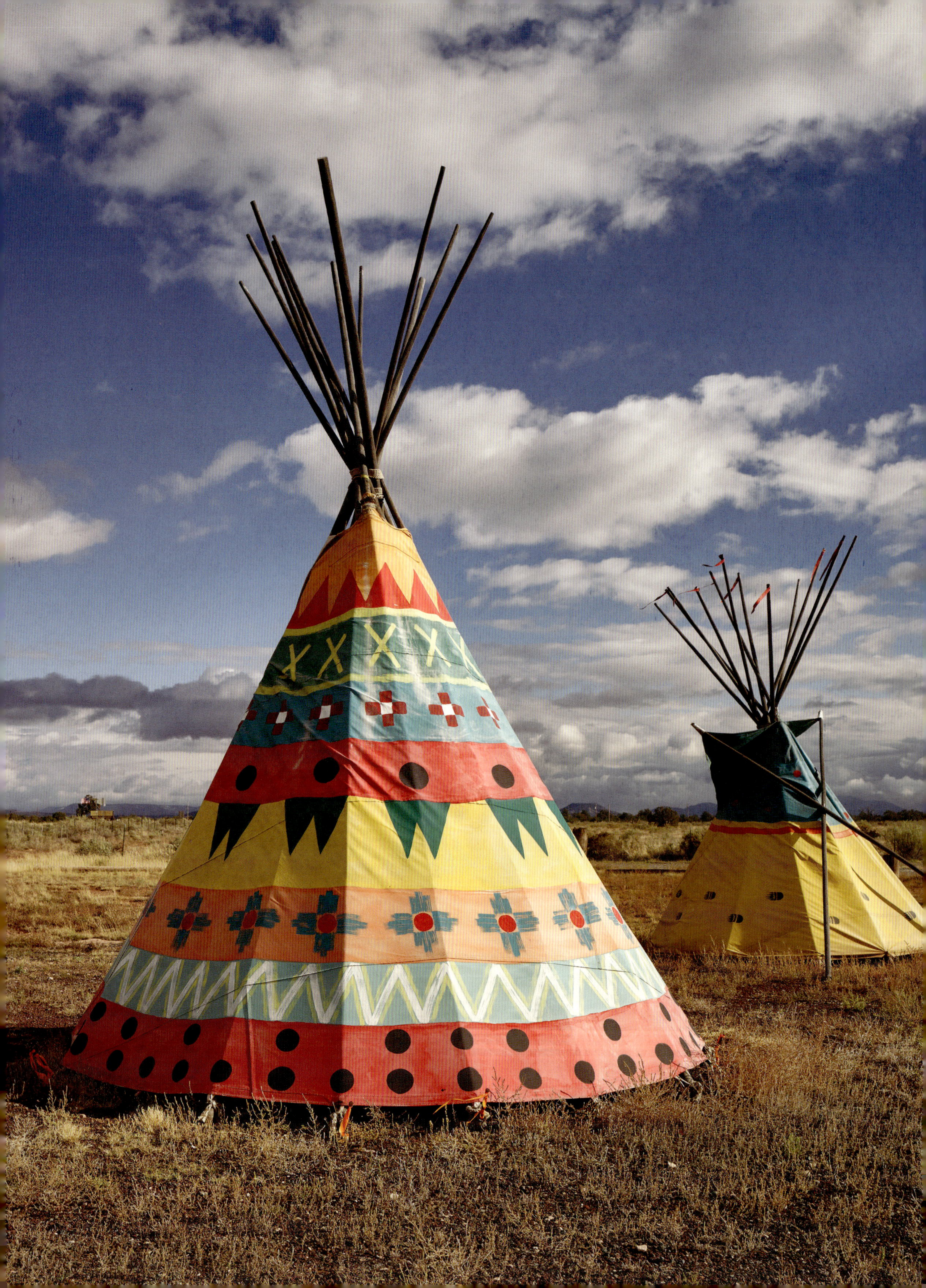

Although it is a modest, fairly remote town of just three thousand folks, Williams gets a host of visitors, owing to its location along America's "Mother Road"—the historic Route 66 from Chicago to Santa Monica. Williams is also the Gateway to the Grand Canyon, sixty miles through the ponderosa pines to the north. One of the places in this small city that captures the tourist trade—with souvenirs, jewelry, and animal trophies inside and eye-catching representations of Indian tipis outside—is the Double Eagle Trading Company.

Below: What better place to observe this black bear on the move than at Bearizona, a drive-through wildlife park featuring an assortment of North American species outside Williams? Right: The Clark Telescope at Lowell Observatory in Flagstaff was built in 1896. Commissioned by the observatory's founder, Percival Lowell, the twenty-four-inch-aperture refractor telescope has pointed toward the heavens ever since. Established two years before this scope arrived, Lowell is among America's oldest astronomical observatories.

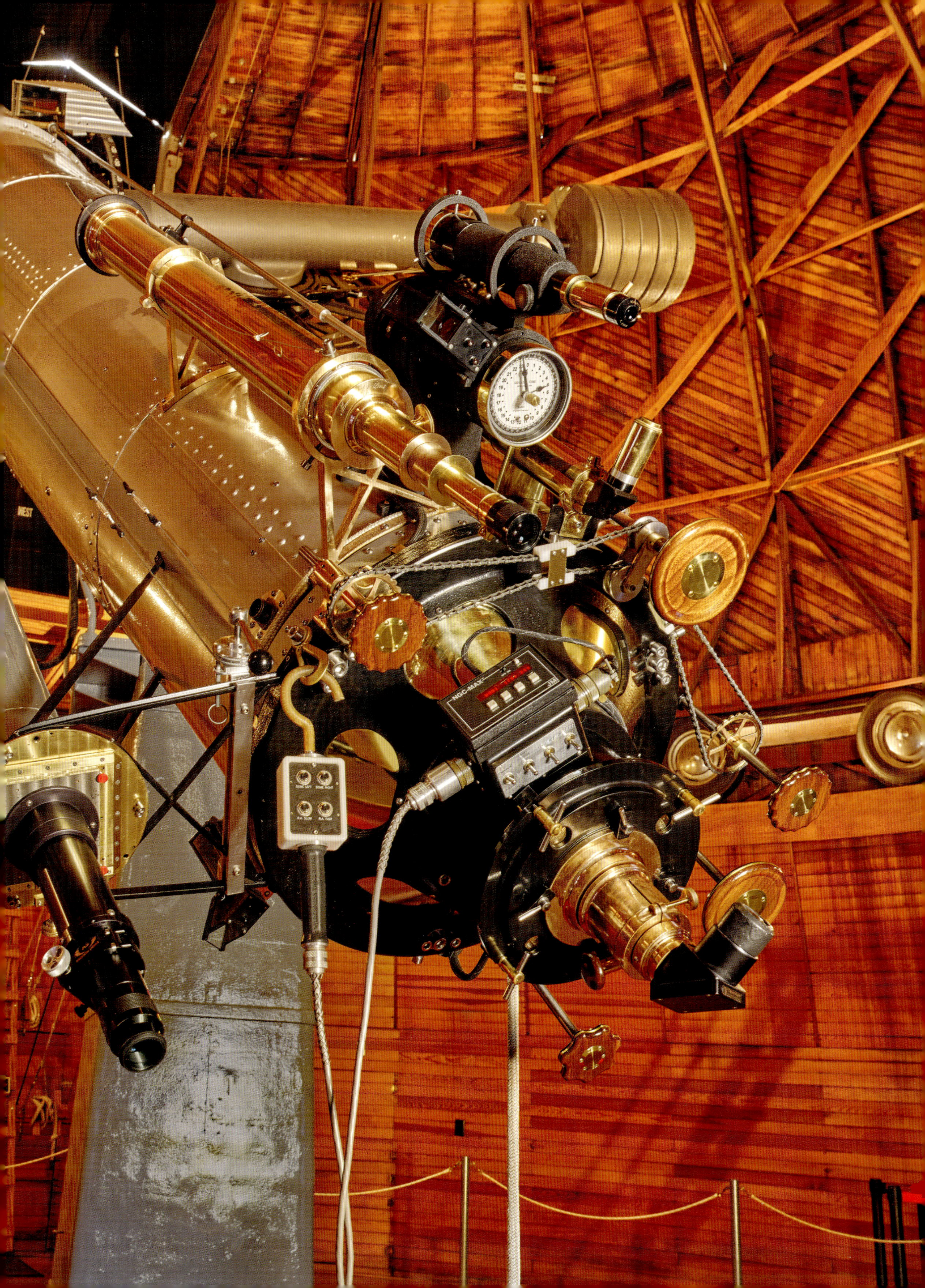
NGC-MAX

Walnut Canyon National Monument, just ten miles from downtown Flagstaff, preserves twenty-five of what were once eighty twelfth-century cliff dwellings of a northern branch of the same pre-Columbian Sinagua people who fashioned what are now Montezuma Castle and Tuzigoot National Monuments. A looping trail guides visitors three hundred fifty feet beneath the canyon rim into the gorge. Like the cliff dwellers who abandoned Colorado's Mesa Verde, the Sinagua mysteriously up and left Walnut Canyon, perhaps because of a drought.

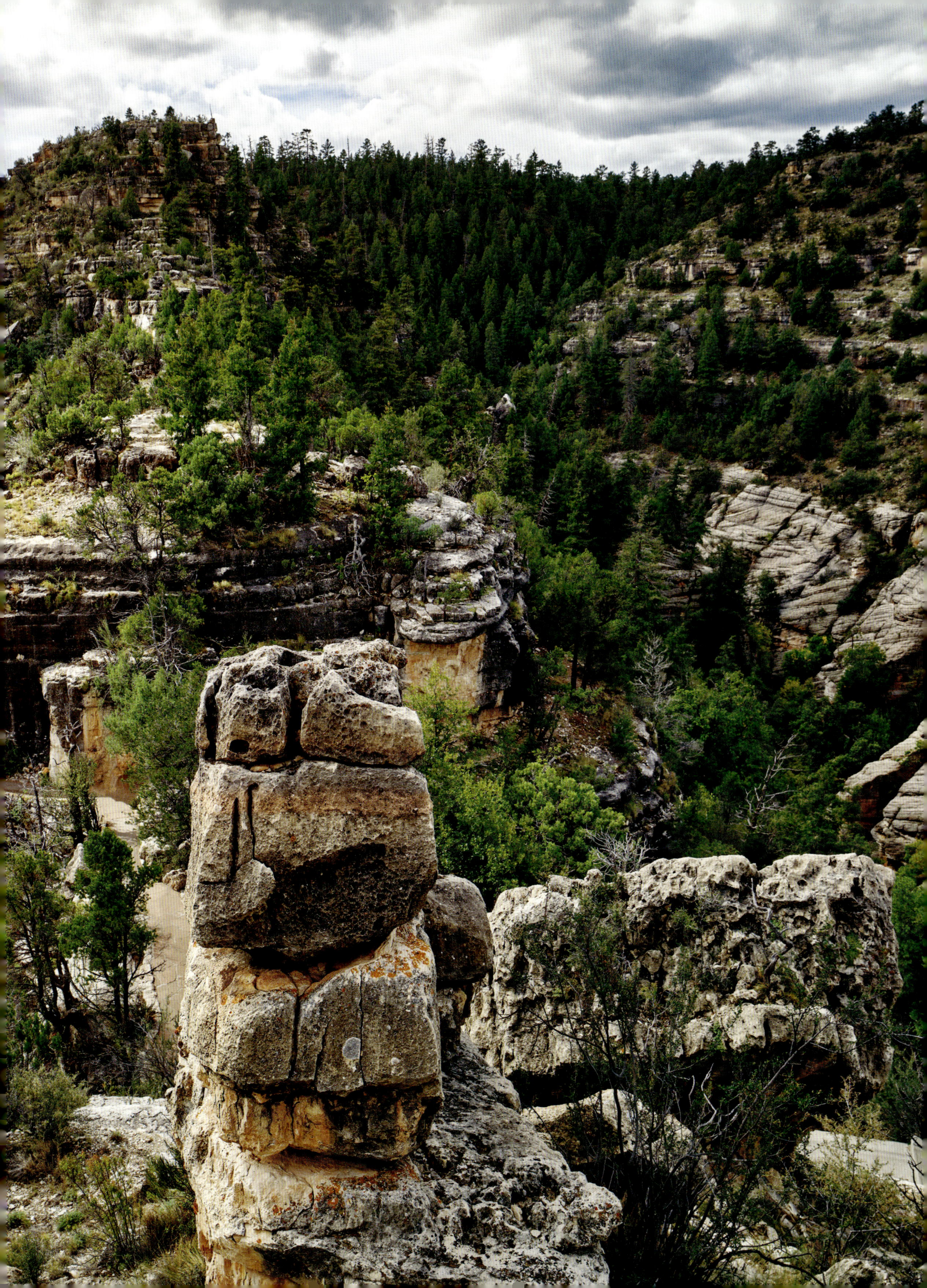

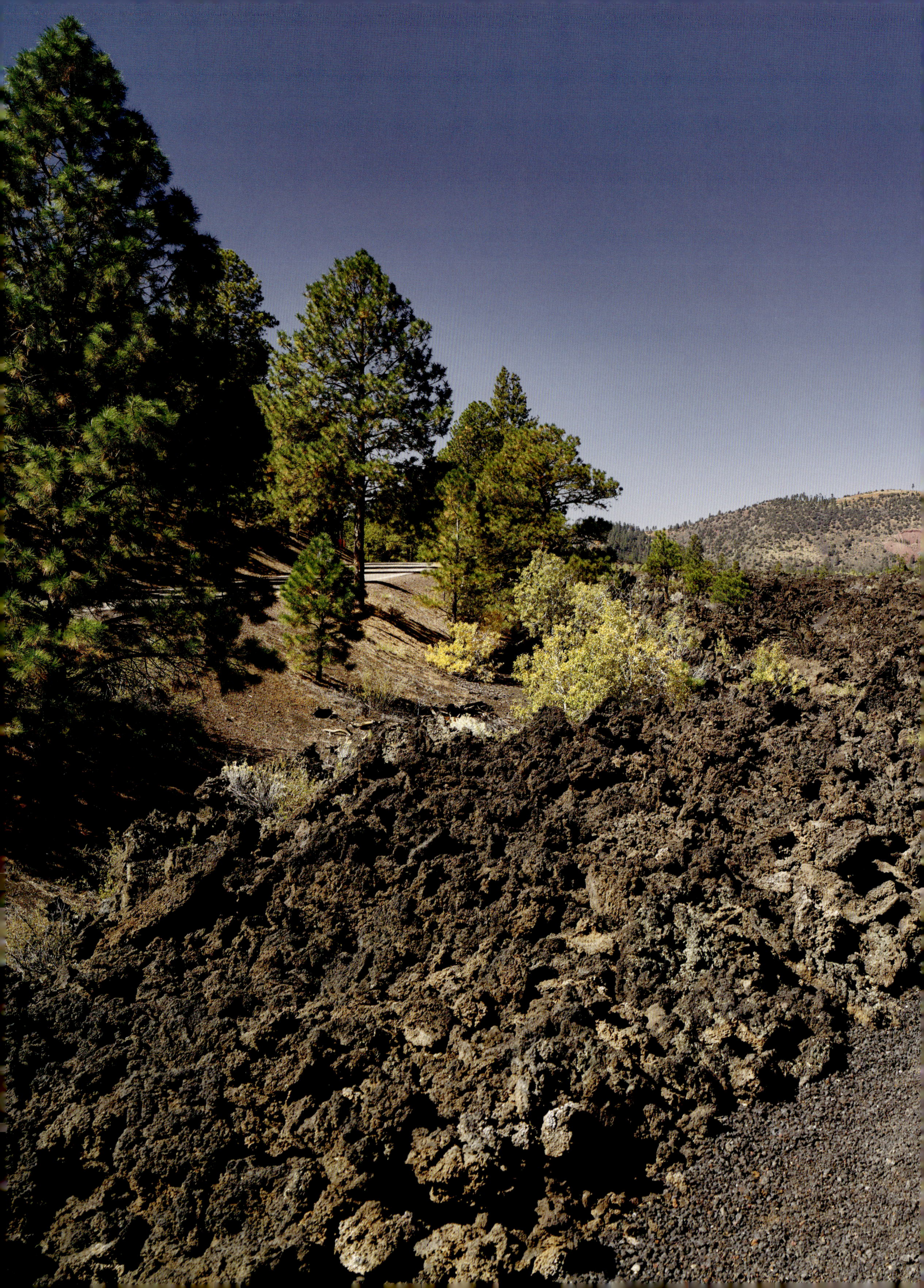

Left: Lava beds beside the road north of Flagstaff are the residue of a fearsome explosion that occurred about AD 1085. Now this 1,115-foot-high hill of volcanic rubble is part of Sunset Crater National Monument. Above: Nearby, at Wupatki National Monument, is the largest of several red-rock pueblos scattered across miles of desolate prairie. Eight centuries ago, this multi-story, hundred-room "tall house" (*Wupatki* in Hopi) may also have been the richest and most influential structure made by humans for fifty miles.

Flagstaff · 111

Below: In tiny Cameron, a speck along the road from Flagstaff to Page, one of several works by the remarkable Chip Thomas brings a run-of-the-mill building to life. A doctor on the Navajo reservation, Thomas employs the *nom d'art* Jetsonorama for his poignant murals. They are blown-up versions of his photographs, wheat-pasted onto otherwise unremarkable structures. Opposite: Near The Gap, another blur on Navajo Nation land, horses trot beneath barren, striated hills. Overleaf: Clouds race, seemingly within touching distance, above the northeastern Arizona desert.

112 · *Cameron · The Gap*

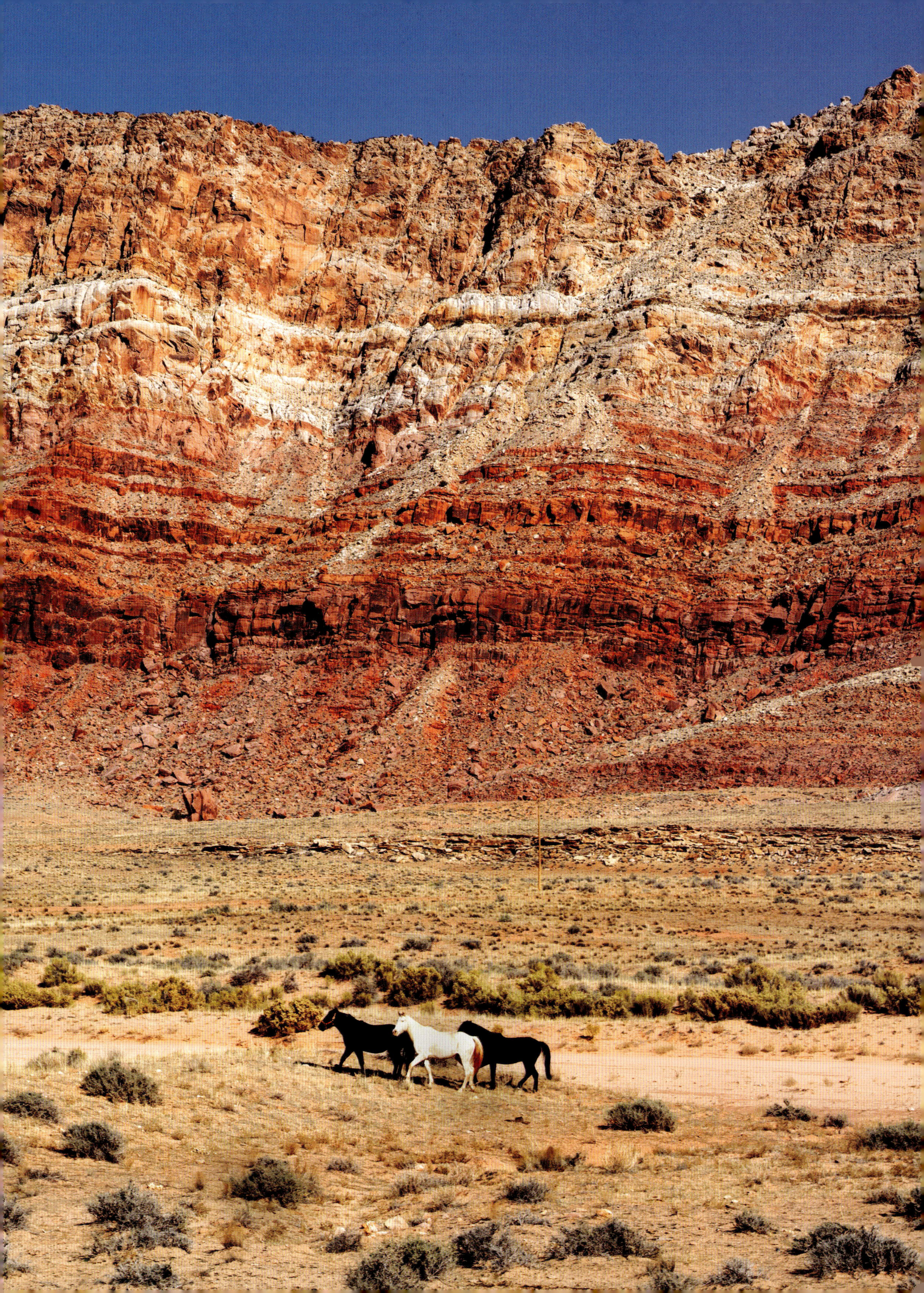

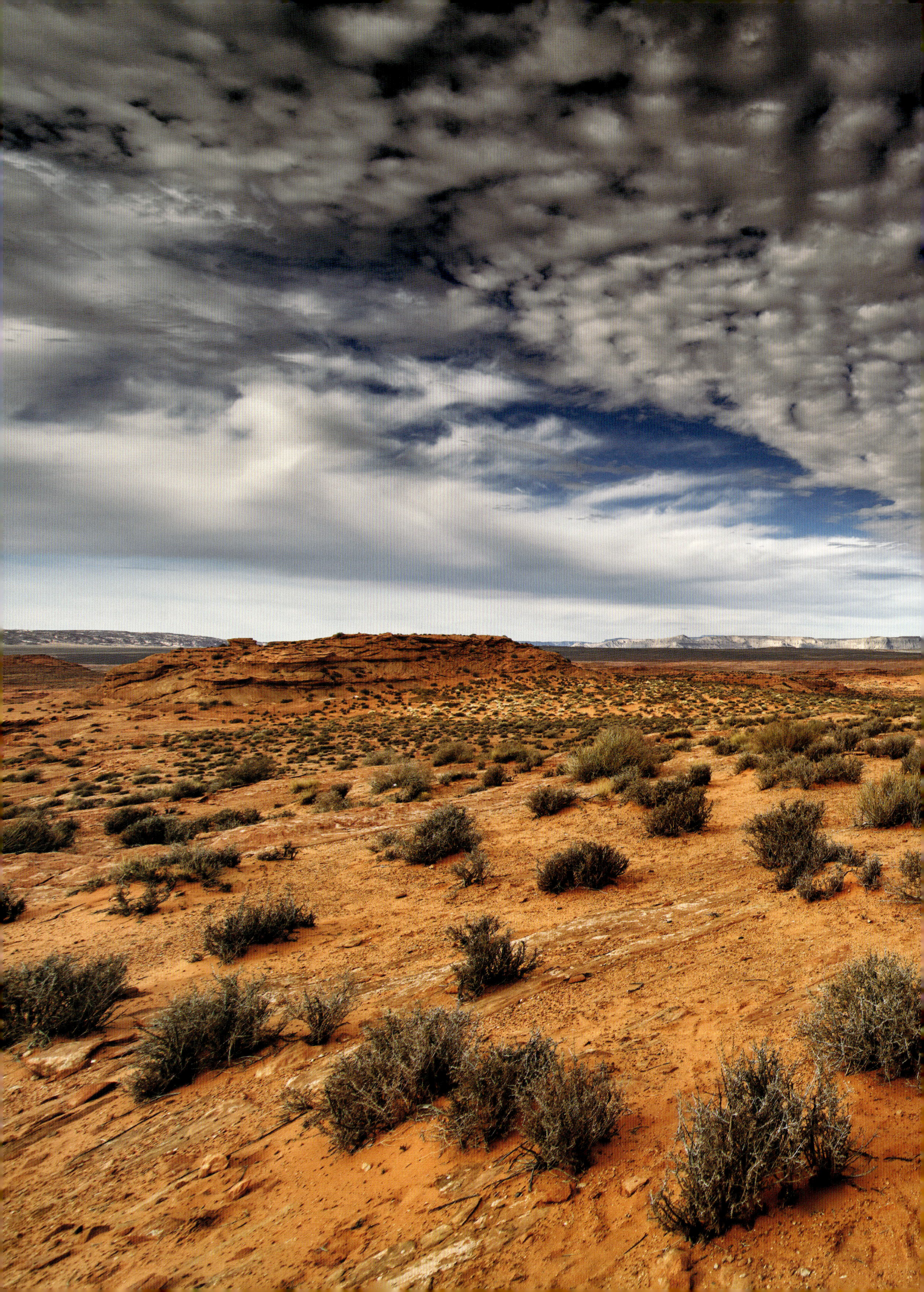

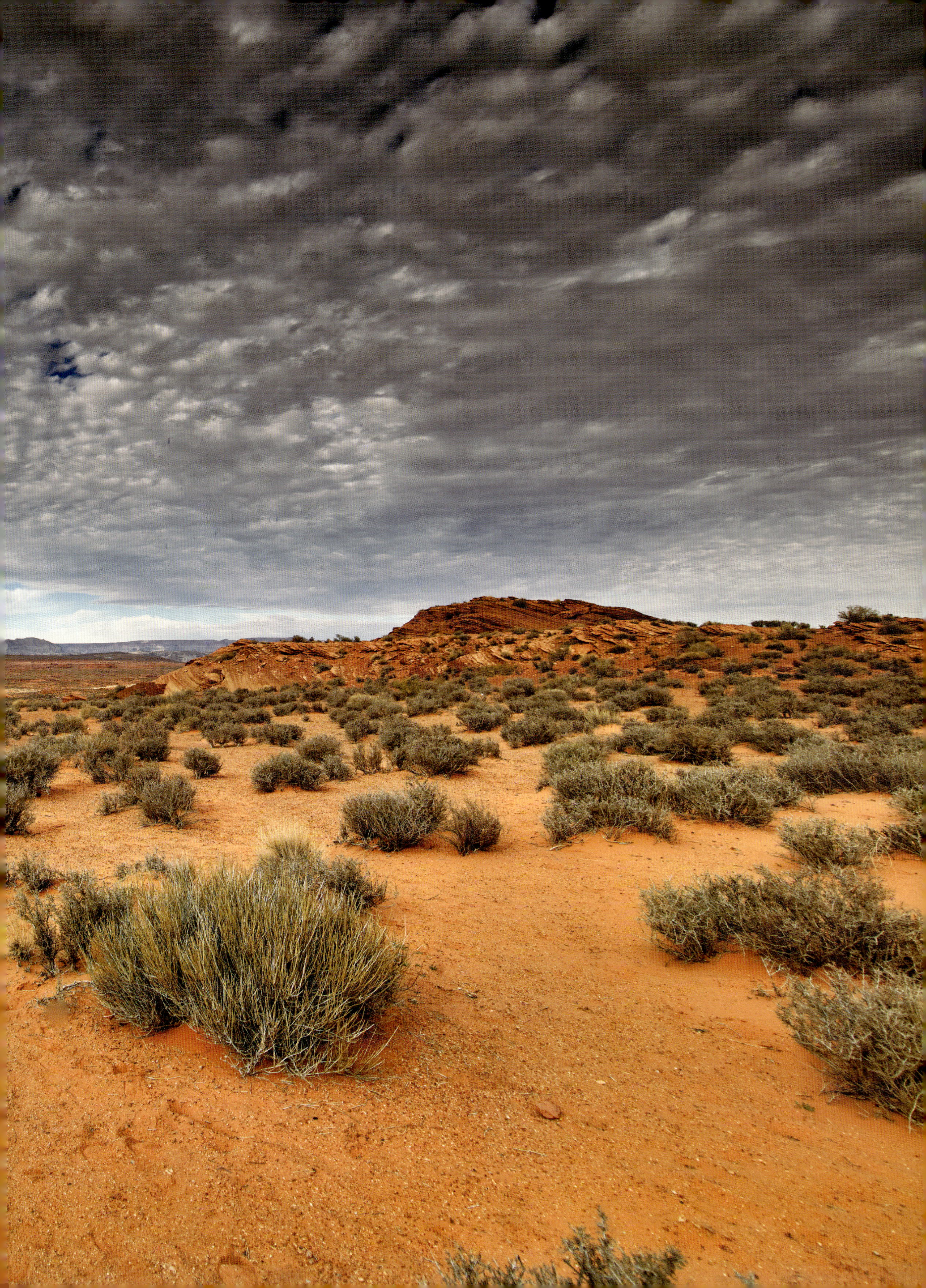

Below: Fish got to swim. Birds got to fly. And rivers will twist and turn, although rarely as dramatically as the Colorado, which nearly completes a circle at Horseshoe Bend, outside Page. It is a thousand-foot drop from this aerie to the riverbed. Right: The dam of the Colorado in Glen Canyon, one of several gorges scoured by the river, took ten years to build, ending in 1966. The project formed Lake Powell, named for John Wesley Powell, the region's legendary one-armed explorer.

116 · *Page*

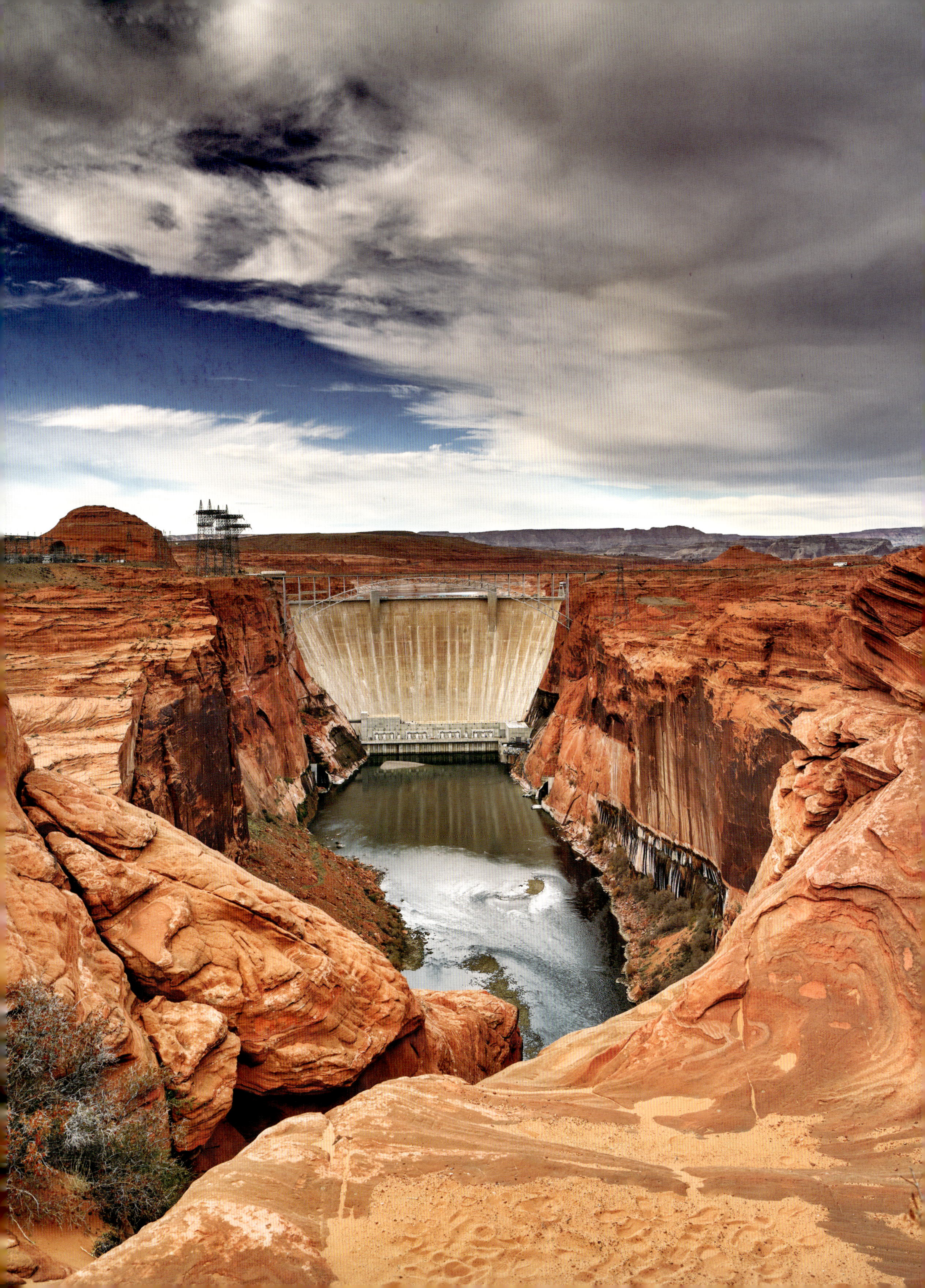

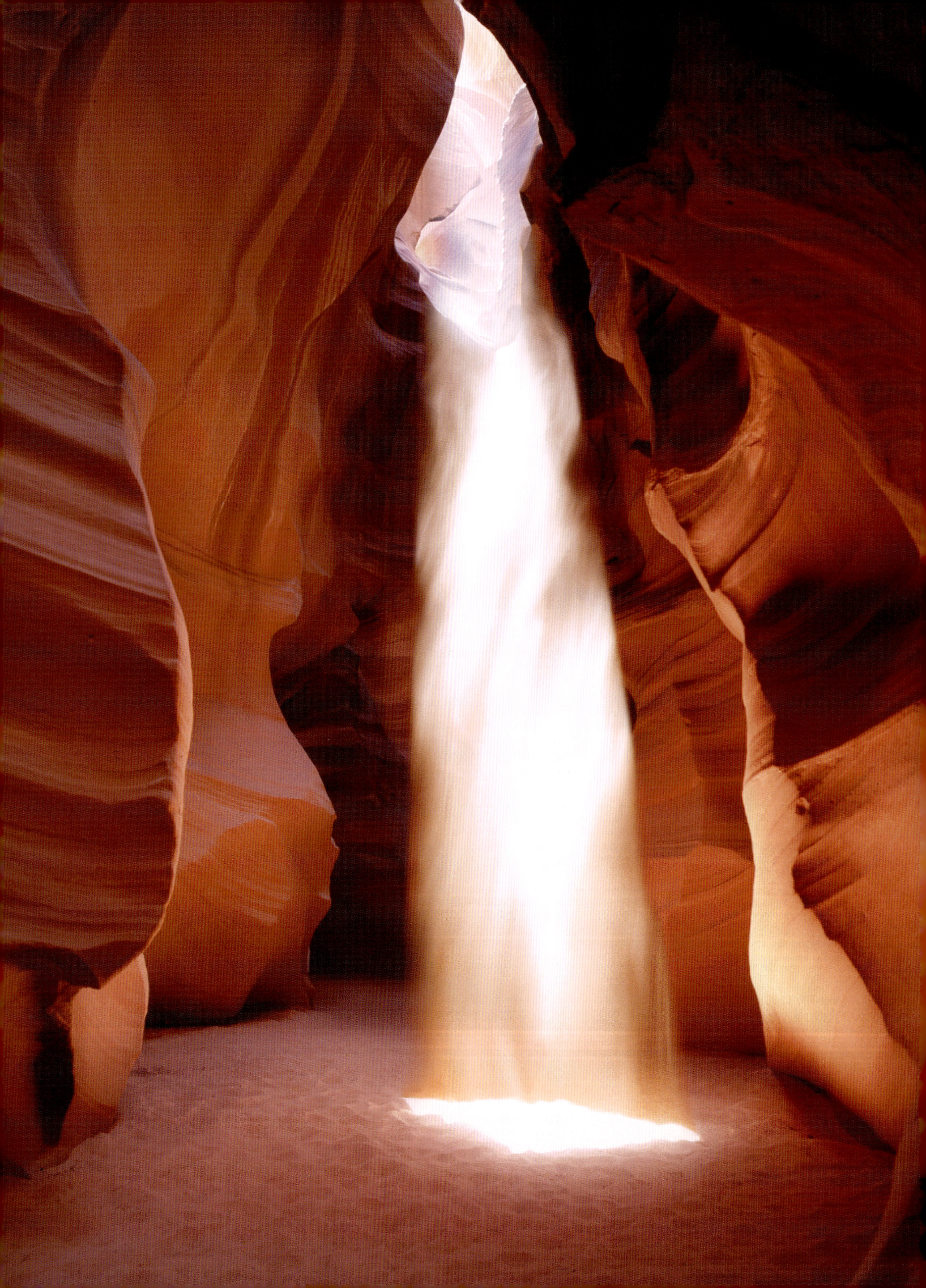

Opposite: Light pours through a slit in one of Arizona's slot canyons, named Upper Antelope, near Page. This view, with a vivid and steady light beam, is possible only certain times of the day and few times of the year because of the sun's capricious angles. Above and overleaf: Not many people have heard of Coyote Buttes North, next to nowhere near the Utah line. Fewer still have seen the wonder, better known as the Wave for its swirling, brush-stroked appearance. Federal officials keep it nearly inaccessible by design.

Page · Coyote Buttes North · 119

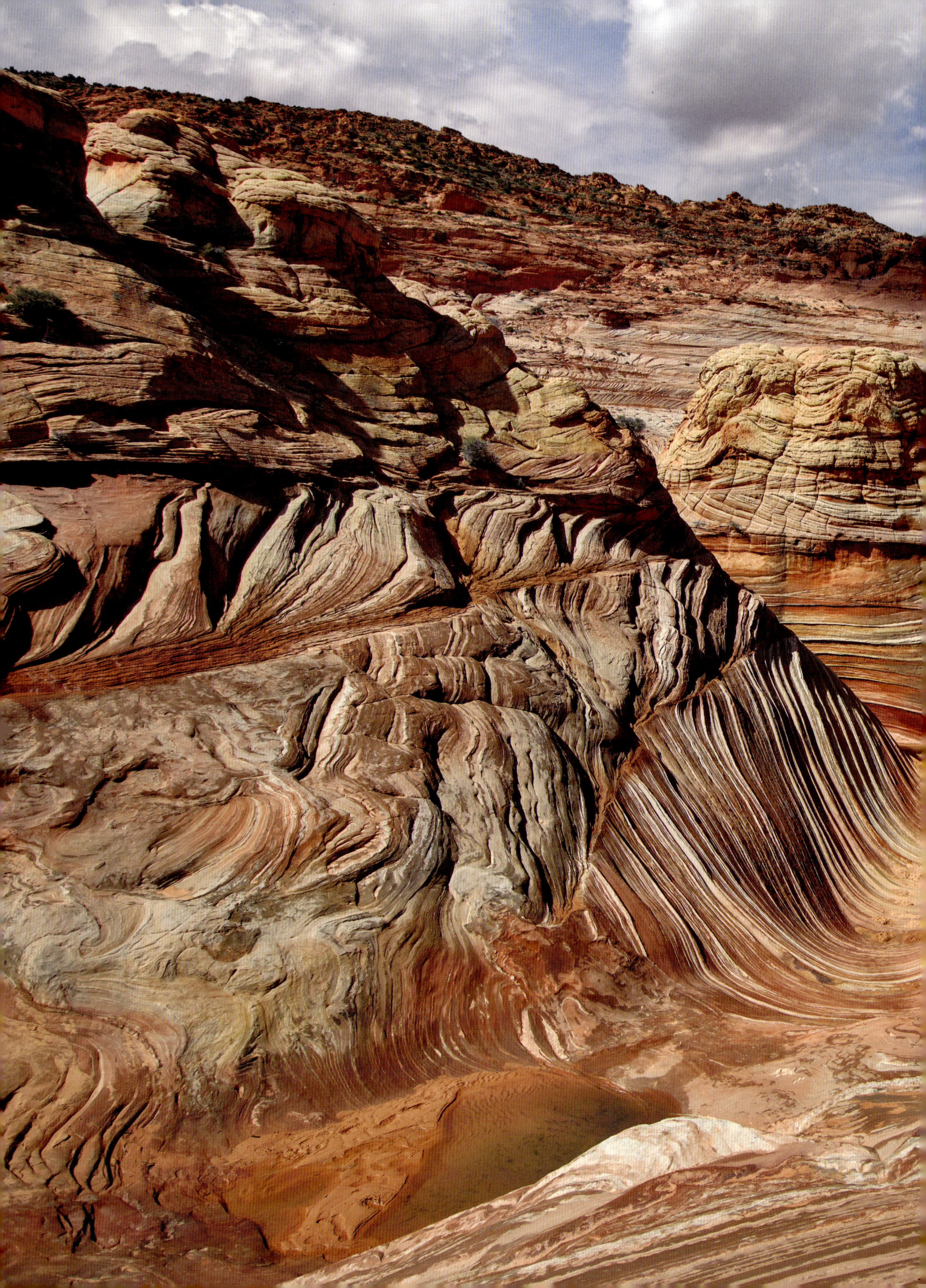

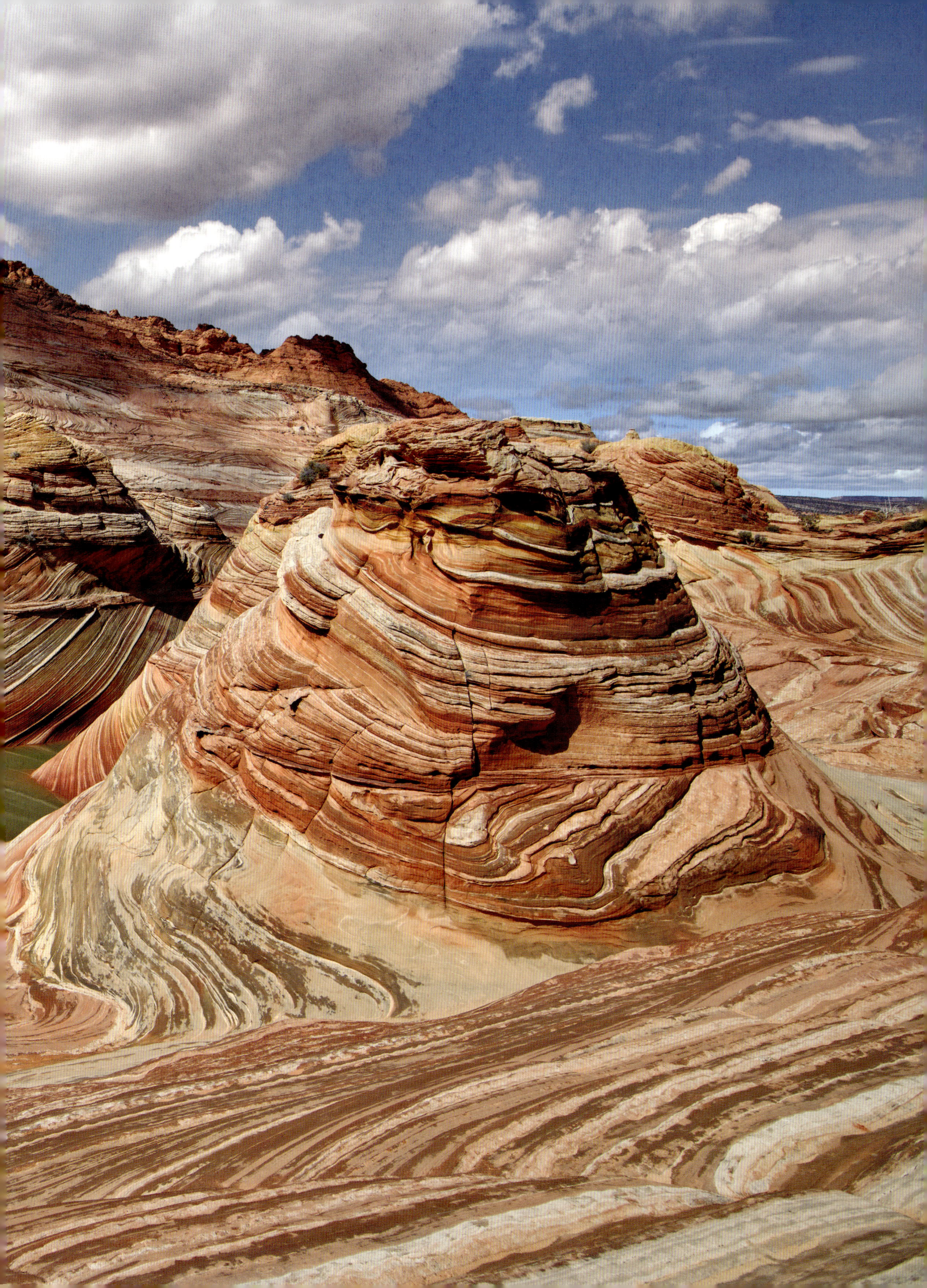

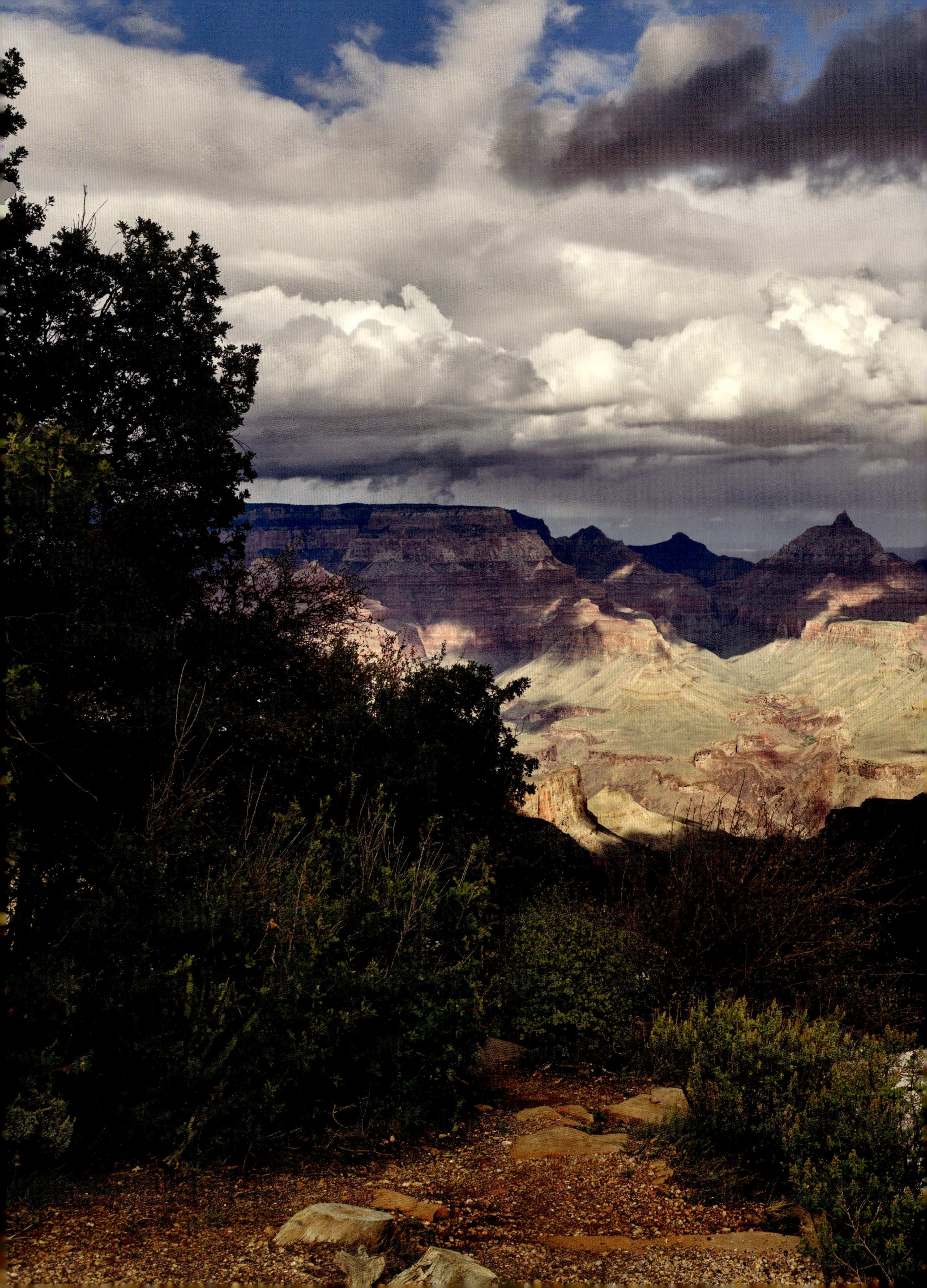

The Grand Canyon inspires poetry, rapture, even ecstasy in those who first behold it. Its world-renowned gorge is a deep, jagged, 277-mile-long slice into a nearly featureless topographical tabletop. Visitors to the breathtaking American Southwest are used to looking up at natural wonders. Here the astonishment comes from looking down. Overleaf: The Grand Canyon's centerpiece, and reason for being, is the Colorado River, which carved its route through the vast plateau more than five million years ago.

Grand Canyon · 123

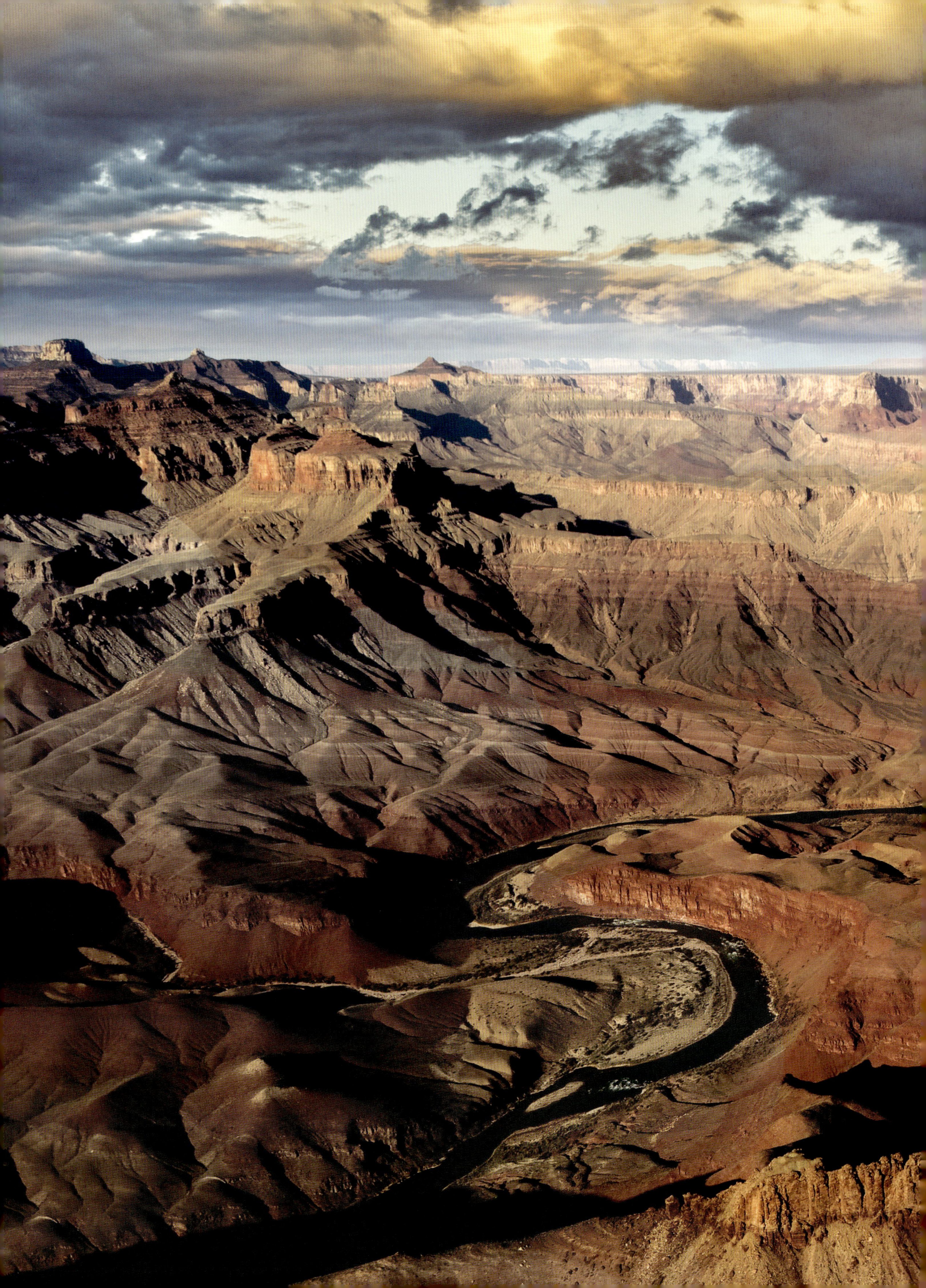

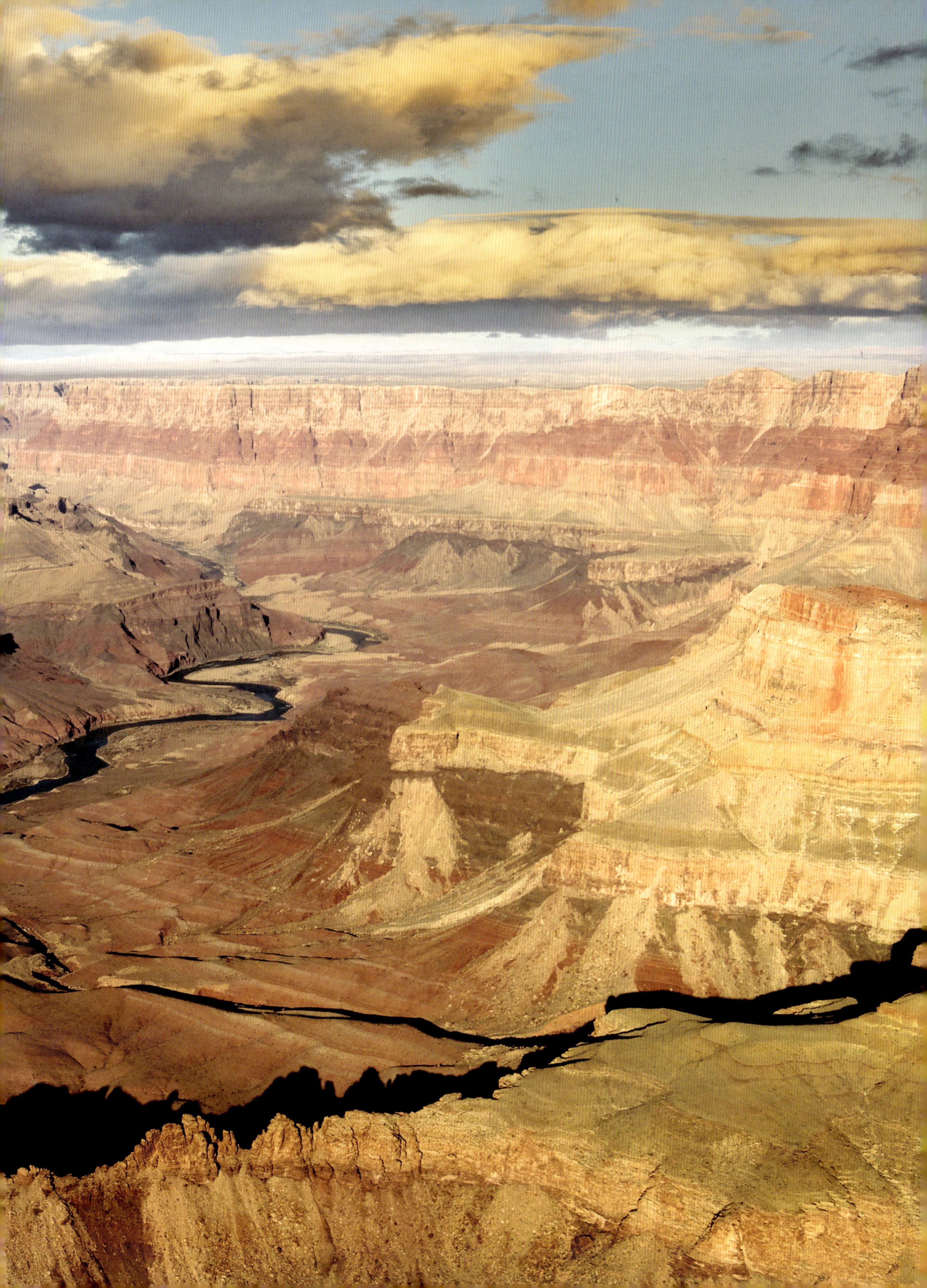

Above: Grand Canyon Depot, completed in 1910, is one of three remaining American railroad stations made primarily of logs. Right: The 1905 Hopi House, built to the architect Mary Colter's design to resemble a Hopi pueblo, originally served as the Fred Harvey souvenir shop. The company's crisply attired Harvey Girl waitresses worked in restaurants elsewhere in the park. Opposite: Indian motifs are employed extensively at Bright Angel Lodge, a 1935 Colter design, and elsewhere throughout Grand Canyon Village.

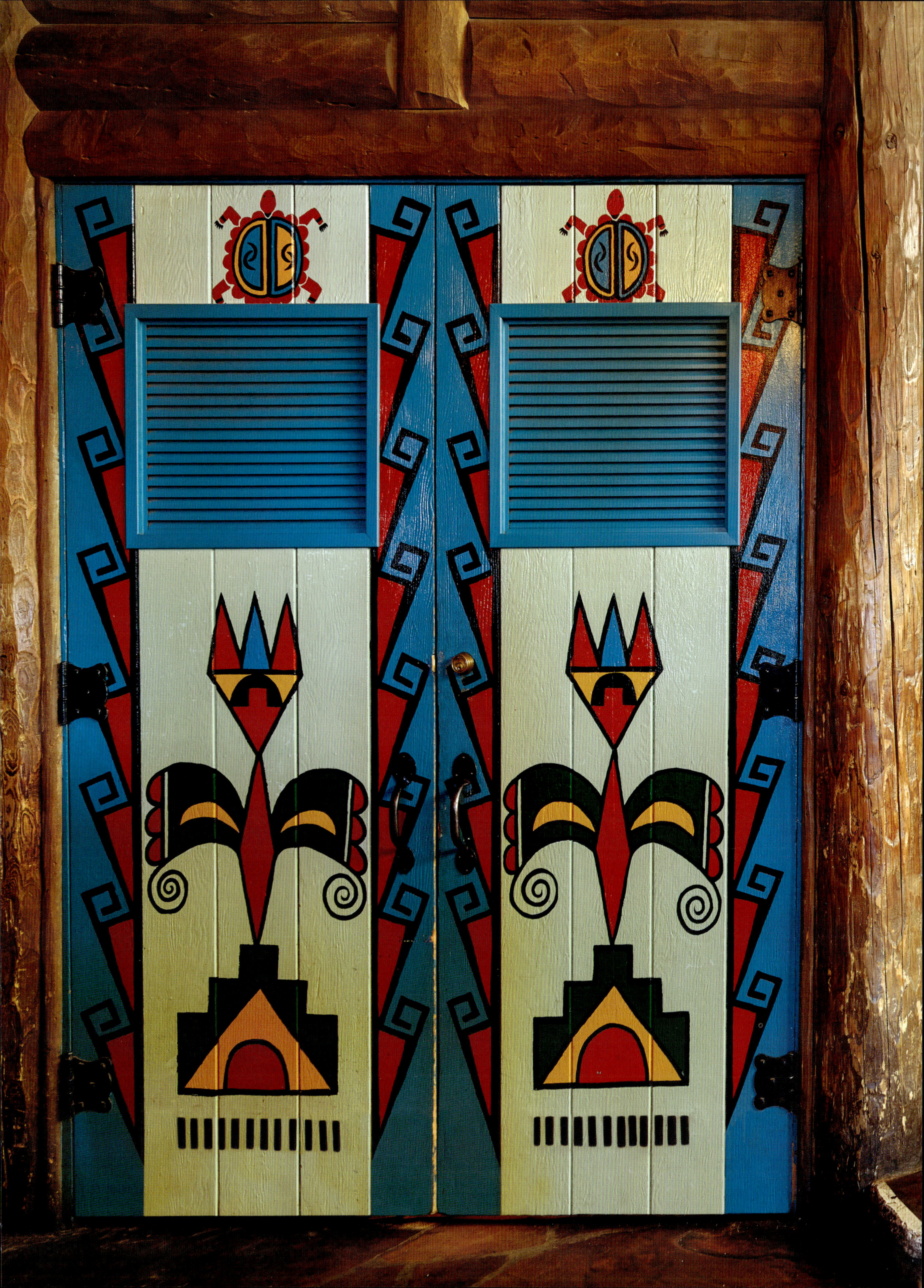

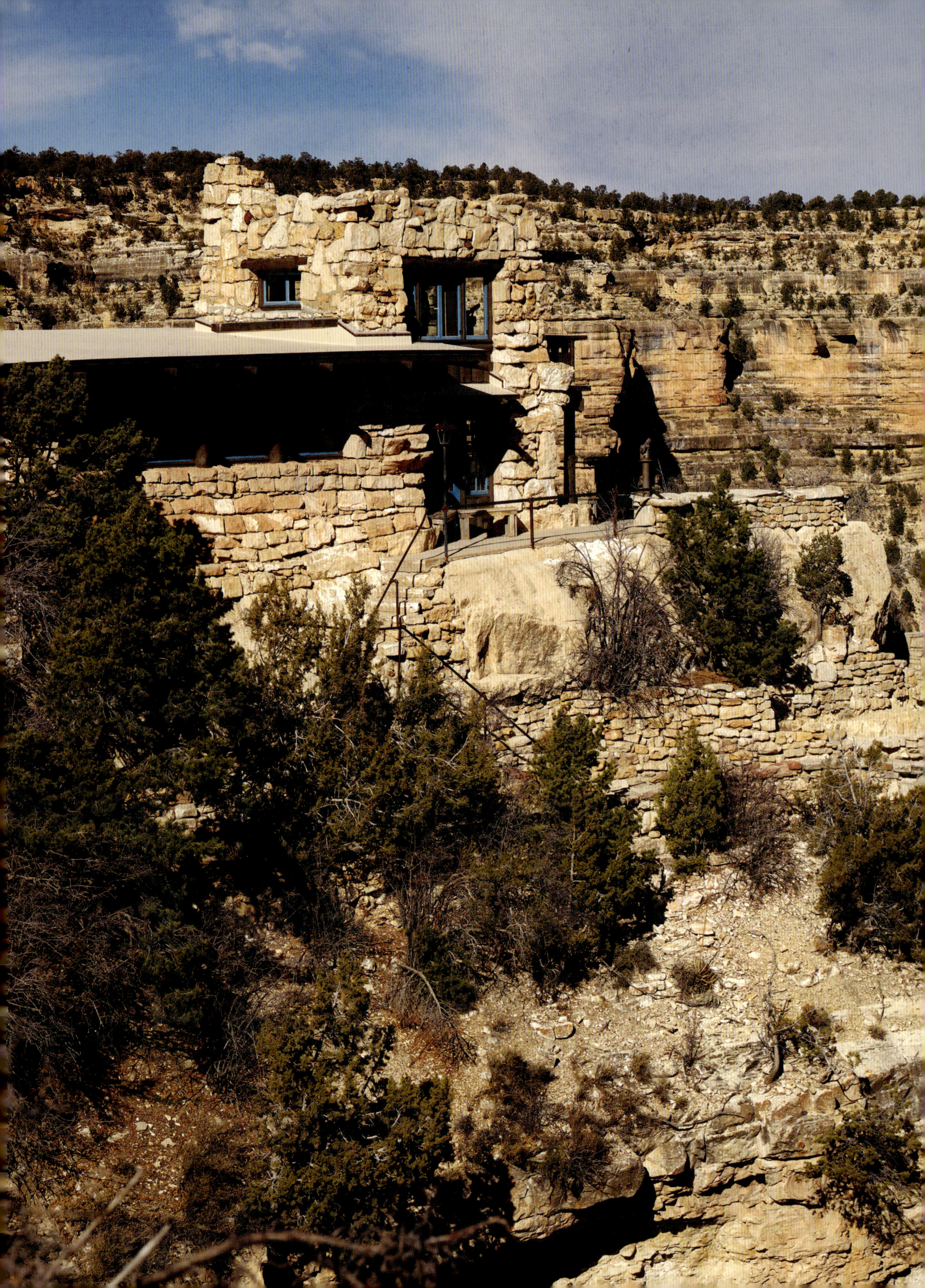

Left: Realizing that grandeur sold train tickets, the Santa Fe Railway built Lookout Studio, another Colter design, in 1914 at a prime spot for photographing the Grand Canyon. Below: Mule rides down Bright Angel Trail are almost always uneventful, if daunting with the abyss looming below. But this fellow flew butt-over-teakettle when his mount reared—only to calmly arise, remount, and continue his trek.

The Desert View Watchtower, a seventy-foot-high stone structure on the Grand Canyon's South Rim, was designed by Mary Colter and completed in 1932. Colter, who traveled throughout the Southwest seeking inspiration at ancient sites, loosely patterned the tower after prehistoric villages built of and among stones and boulders at Hovenweep and Mesa Verde. The Hopi painter Fred Kabotie did the bold wall paintings in the Hopi Room, while Fred Geary of the Fred Harvey Company added petroglyph-like ornamentation, seen above, on the tower's upper ceilings.

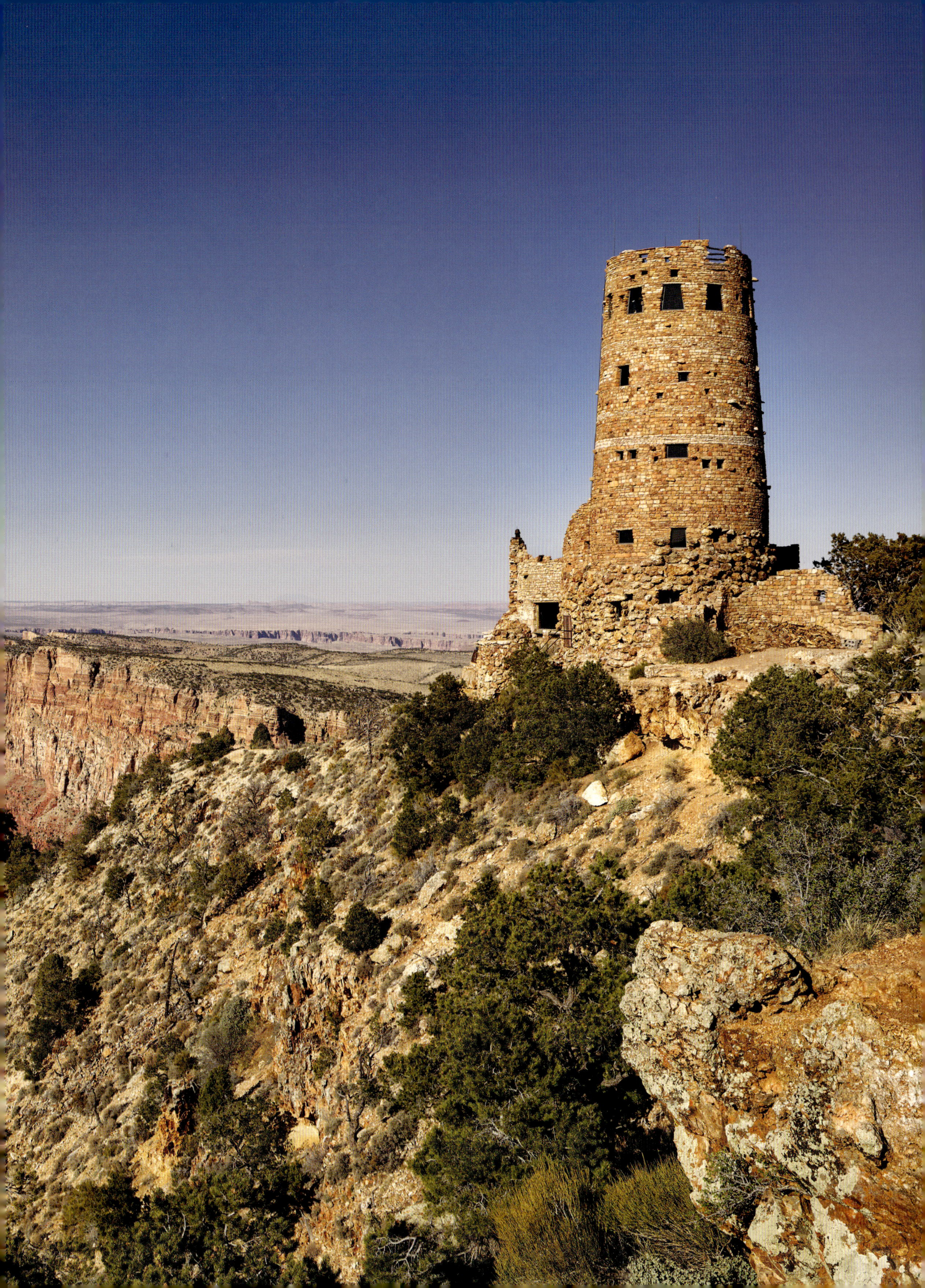

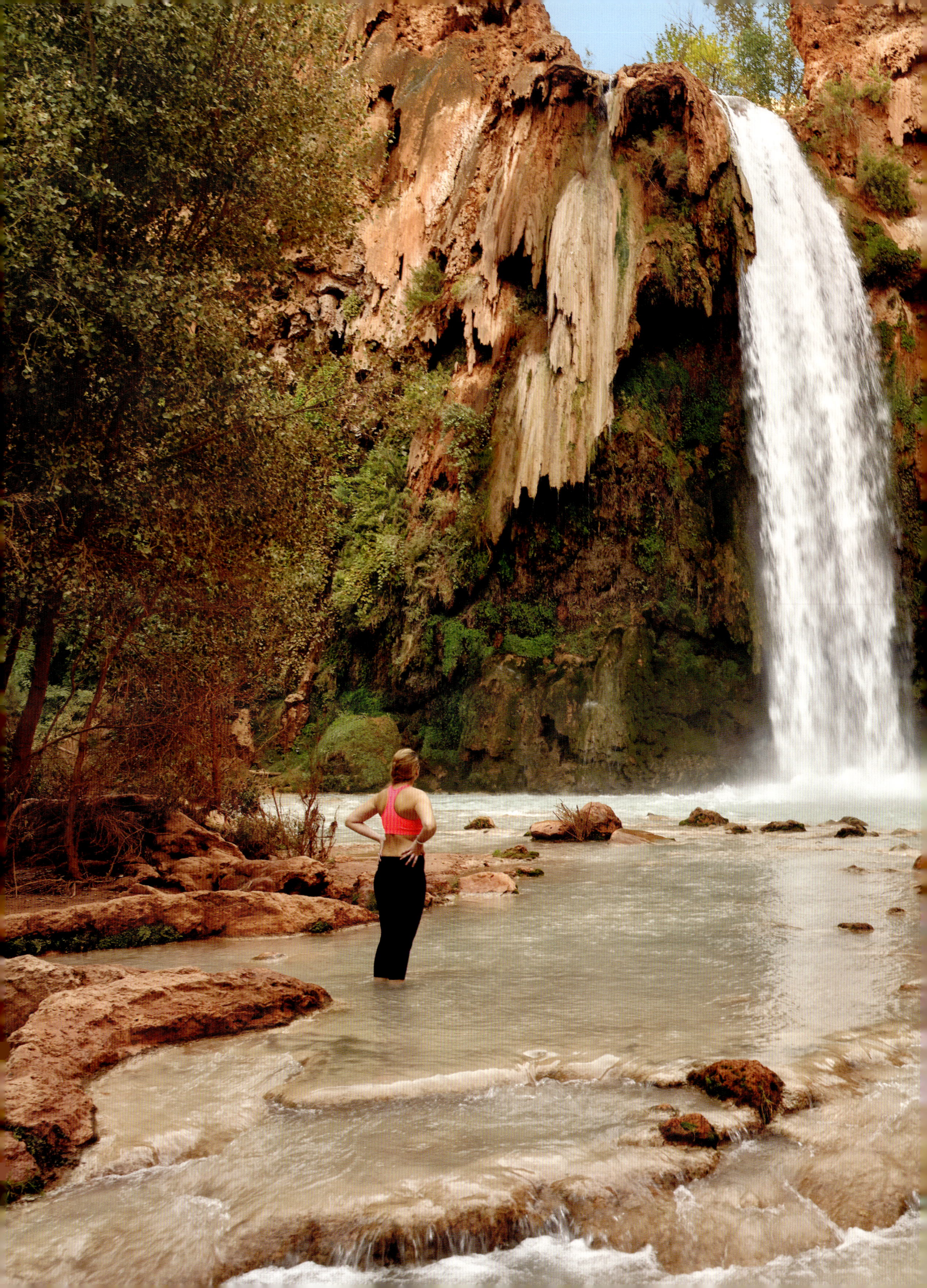

Left: Havasu Falls is one of five waterfalls deep in Arizona's Havasu Canyon, an offshoot of the Grand Canyon on lands administered by the Havasupai tribe. No roads or drivable overlooks lead to the falls or the tiny Supai village nearby. But hikers who obtain a tribal permit may make the steep, zigzagging—and arduous—thirty-mile slog by foot to reach them. Above: Mooney Falls splashes into an aquamarine pool elsewhere in the remote canyon.

Supai · 133

Above: The trail to Mooney Falls is comfortable but narrow, and hikers must be vigilant for mules that sometimes gallop past. Frequently one must gingerly tiptoe along narrow canyon ledges. Right: Once a hiker has made it safely to the canyon floor, tranquility awaits at a campground on Havasu Creek, which babbles between Mooney and Havasu Falls. Overleaf: Lake Mead straddles the Arizona-Nevada border, like Hoover Dam, which created it in the early 1930s. It quickly became the locus of a widespread national recreation area, adored by boaters and fishers.

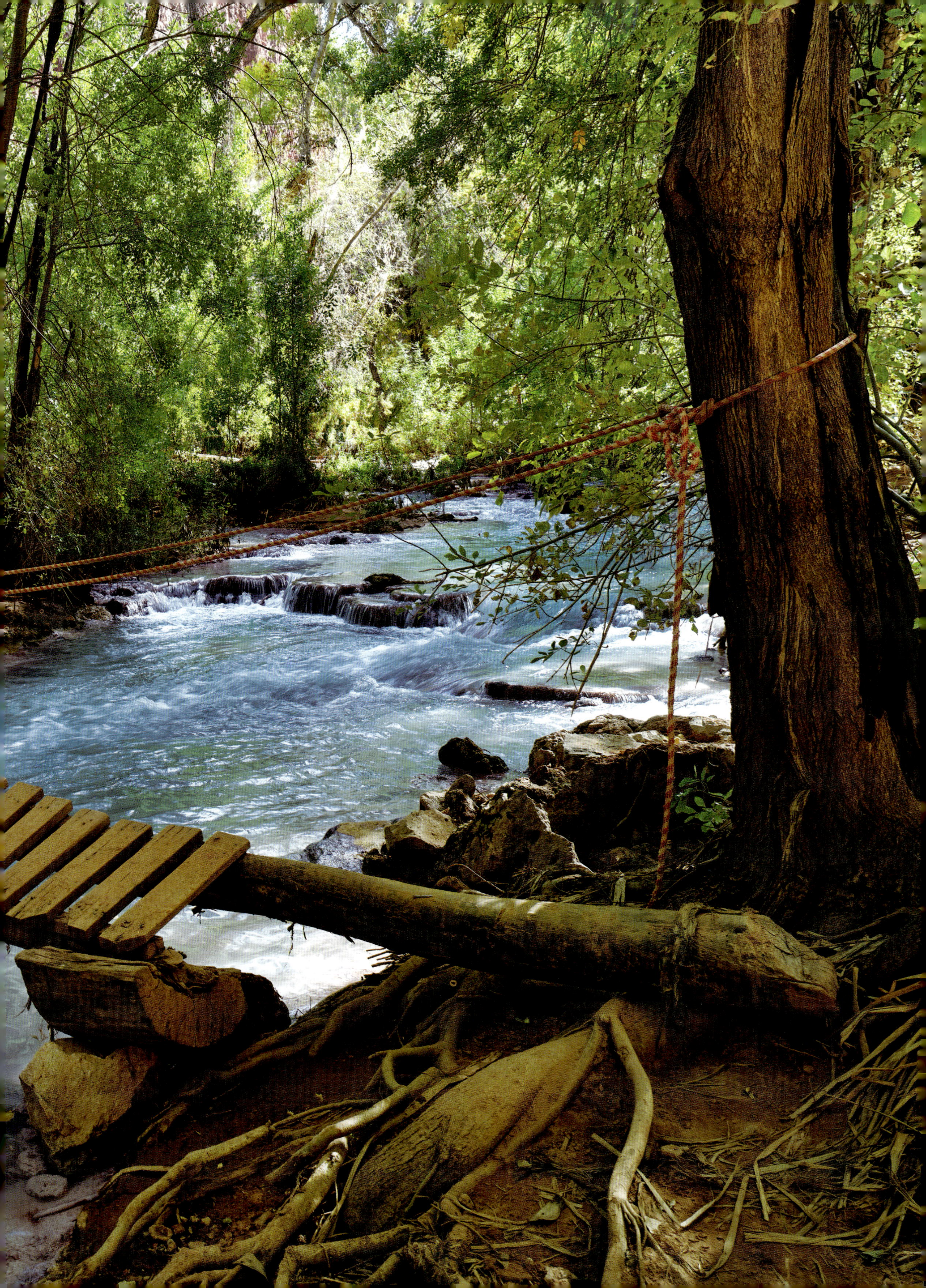

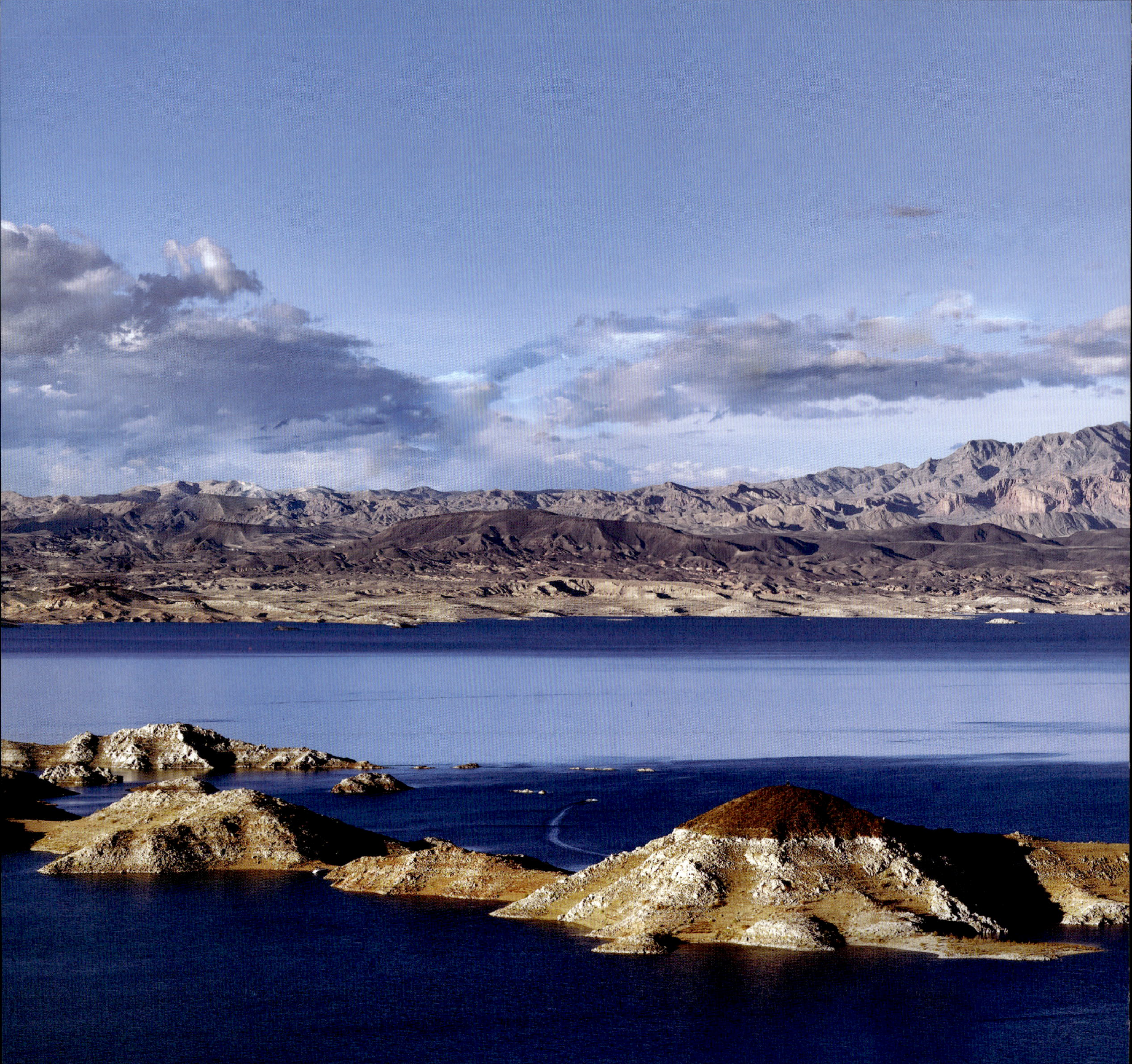

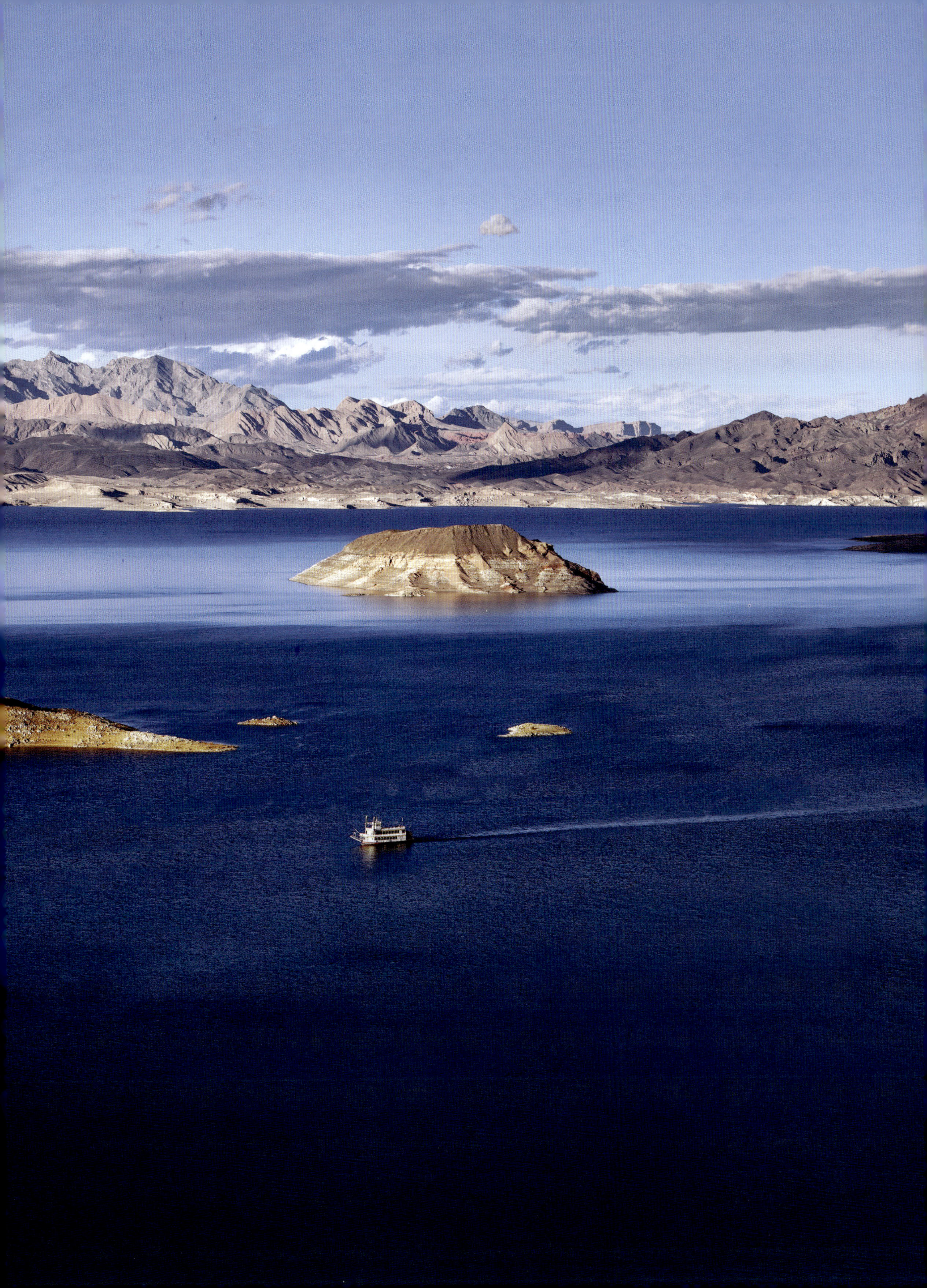

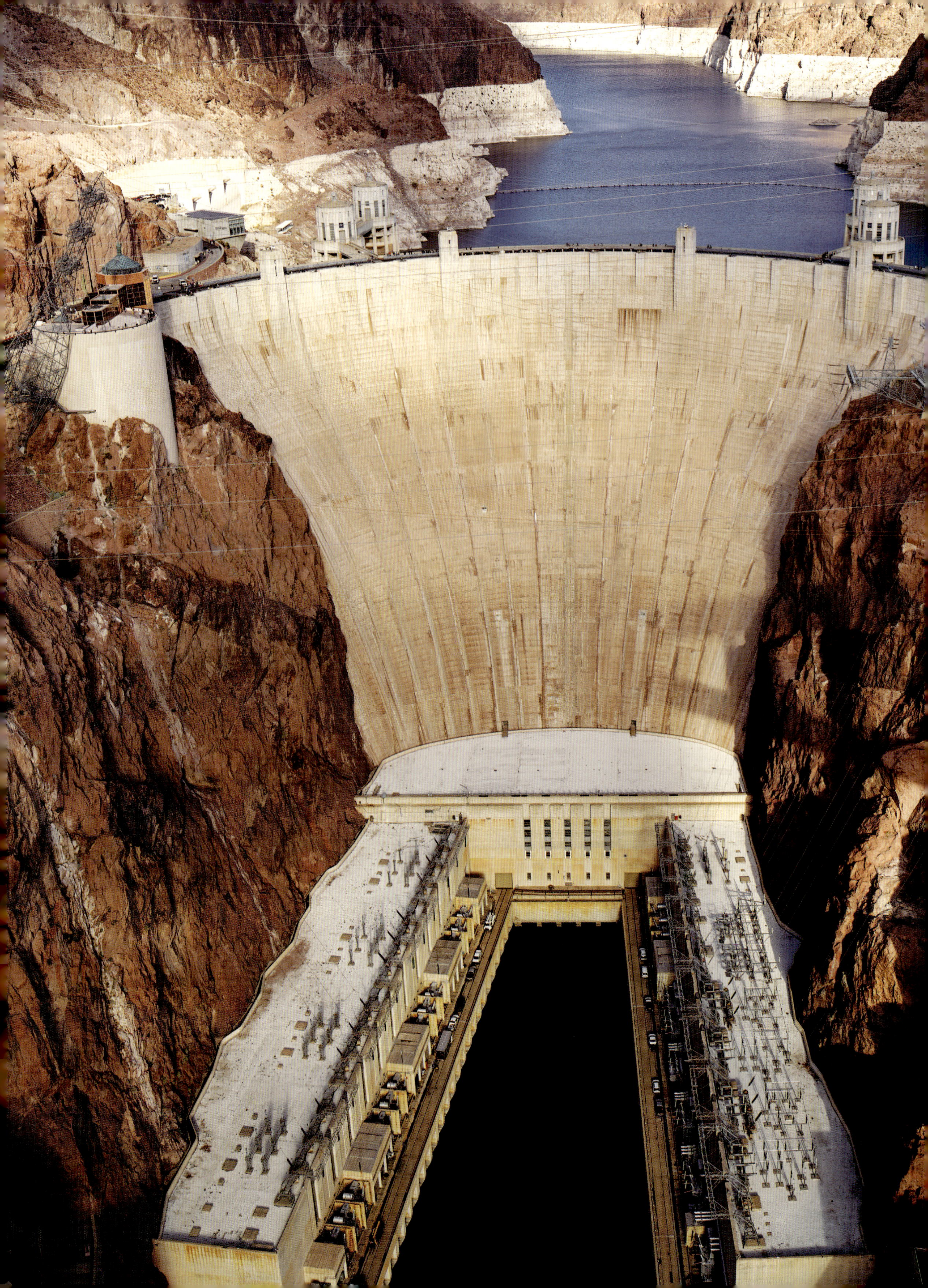

Left: The massive Hoover Dam, which surmounts the border between Arizona and Nevada in the Black Canyon of the Colorado River, was called Boulder Dam at its completion in 1935. It was renamed after former President Herbert Hoover in 1947. The dam's generators provide power for electric utilities as far away as California. Below: For the dam's visitors entrance, the Norwegian immigrant Oskar J.W. Hansen designed two *Winged Figures of the Republic* statues—part angel, part symbol of the strength of man, he said.

Willow Beach · 139

Above: This Arizona plaque is embedded in a walkway at Hoover Dam. (Nevada got one, too.) *Ditat Deus* (God Enriches) is Arizona's state motto. Right: These and two other 338-foot-high intake towers stand in Lake Mead behind the massive dam. Overleaf: The lake, named for Elwood Mead, the Bureau of Reclamation commissioner who oversaw the Hoover Dam project, holds some ten trillion gallons of water.

140 · Willow Beach

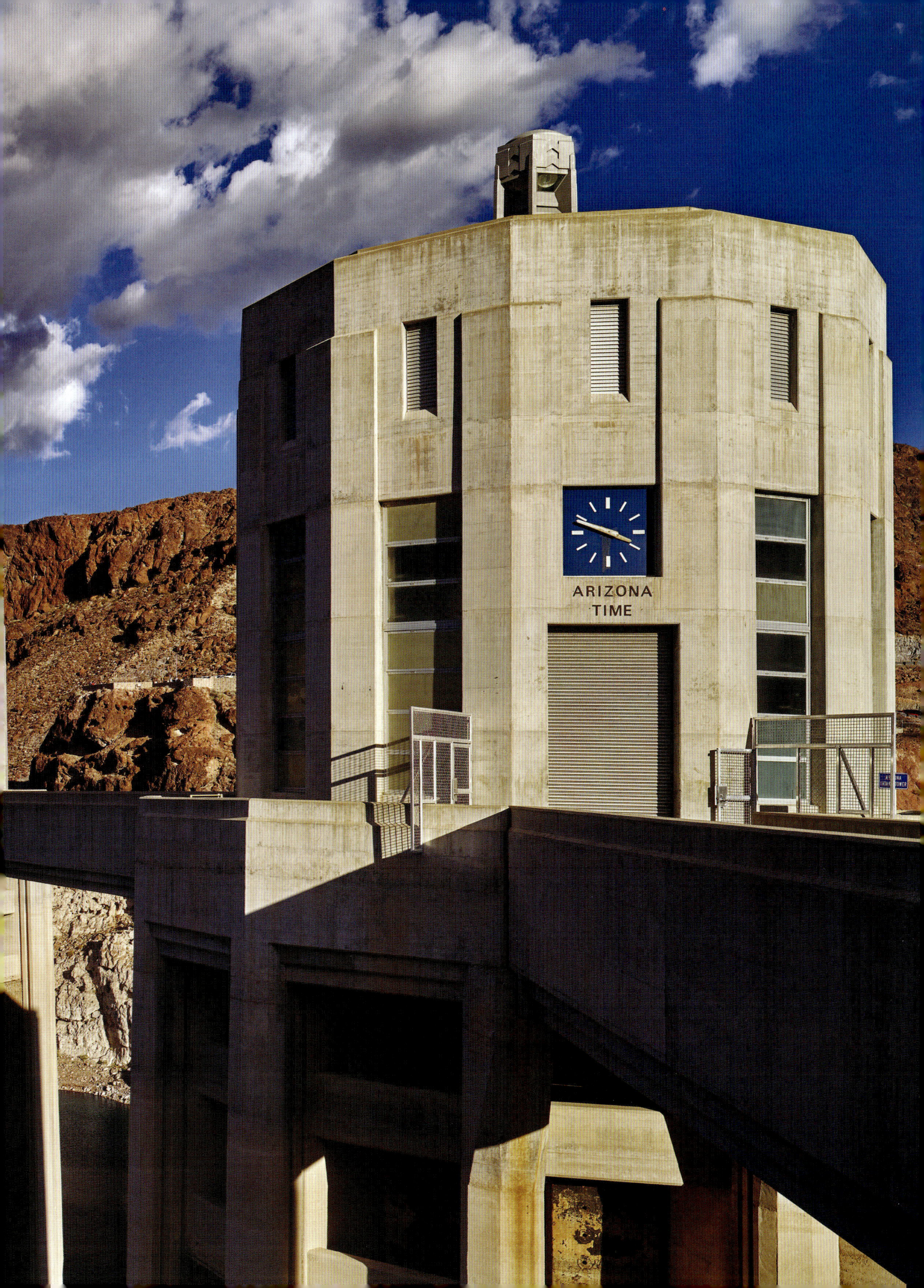
ARIZONA
TIME

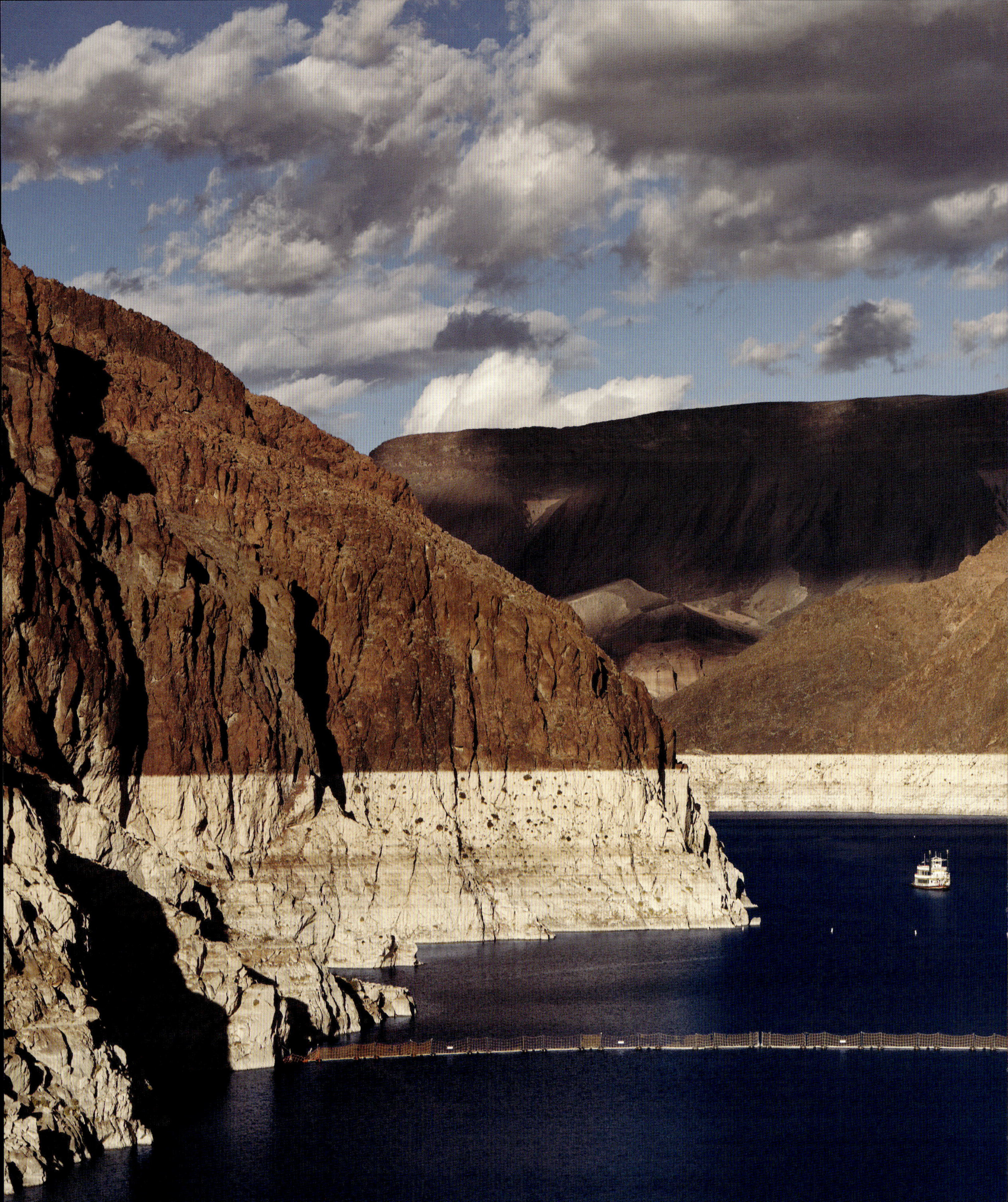

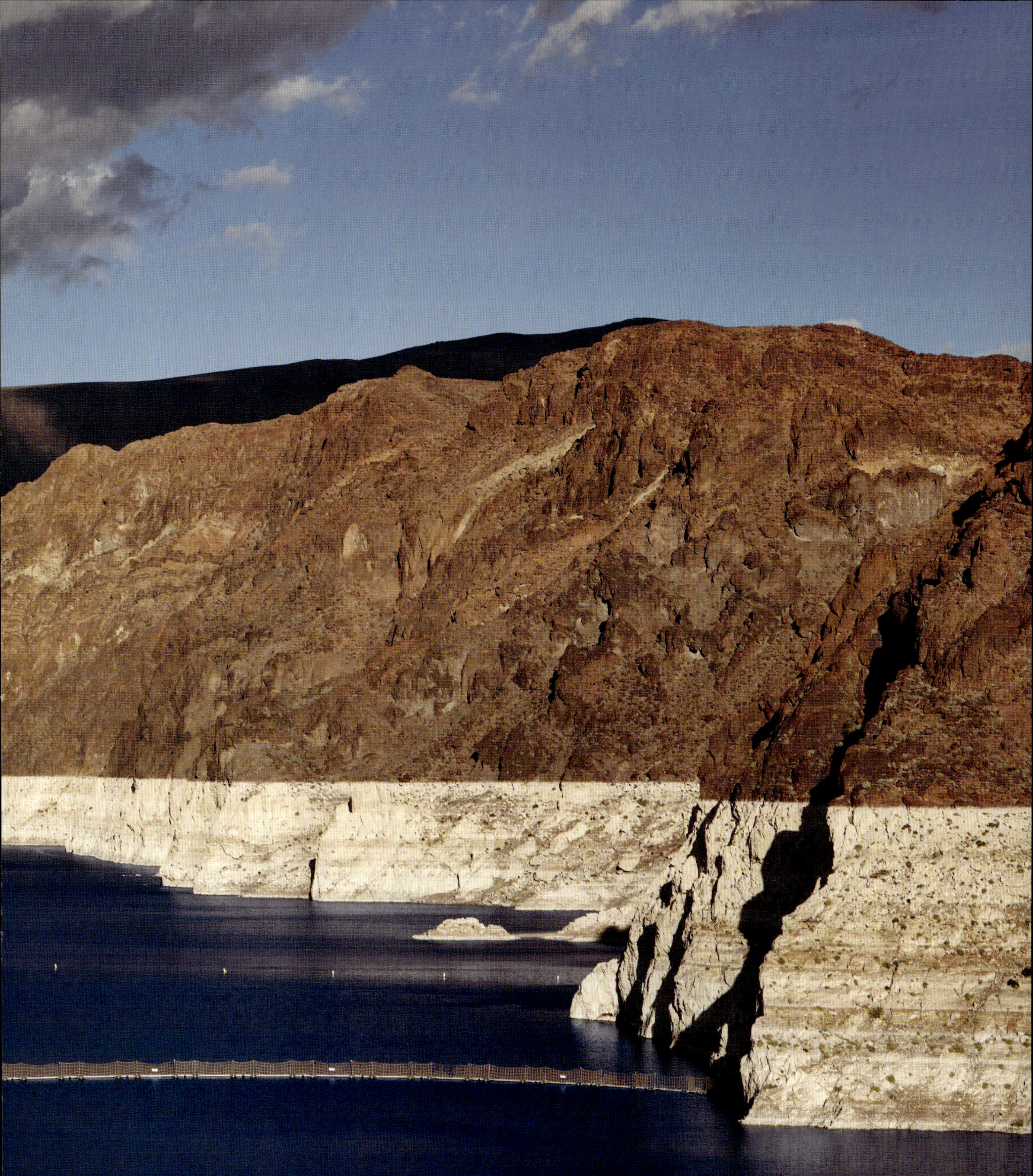

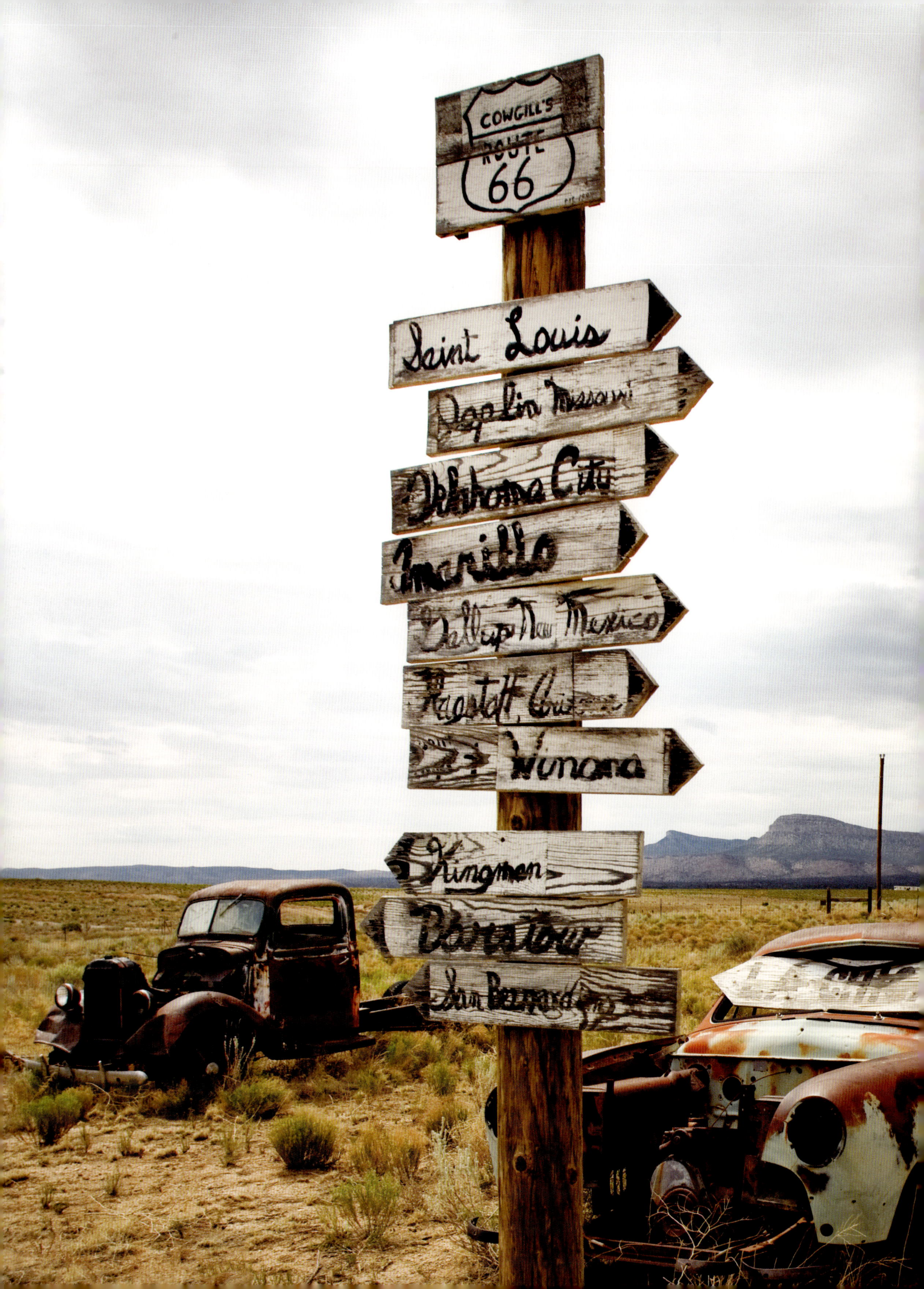

Left: Directions to towns selected for this weather-beaten sign along the old Route 66 near Truxton have not changed over the years. However, the vehicles beneath it assuredly have. Above: A spiny dragon?—the type of roadside attraction that was the rage in the days of cross-country, two-lane-road travel—hangs on outside the old-fashioned Arizona Trading Post in Dolan Springs. Overleaf: A stunning reflection of the setting sun limns the clouds above a passing freight train near Valle Vista.

Truxton · Dolan Springs · 145

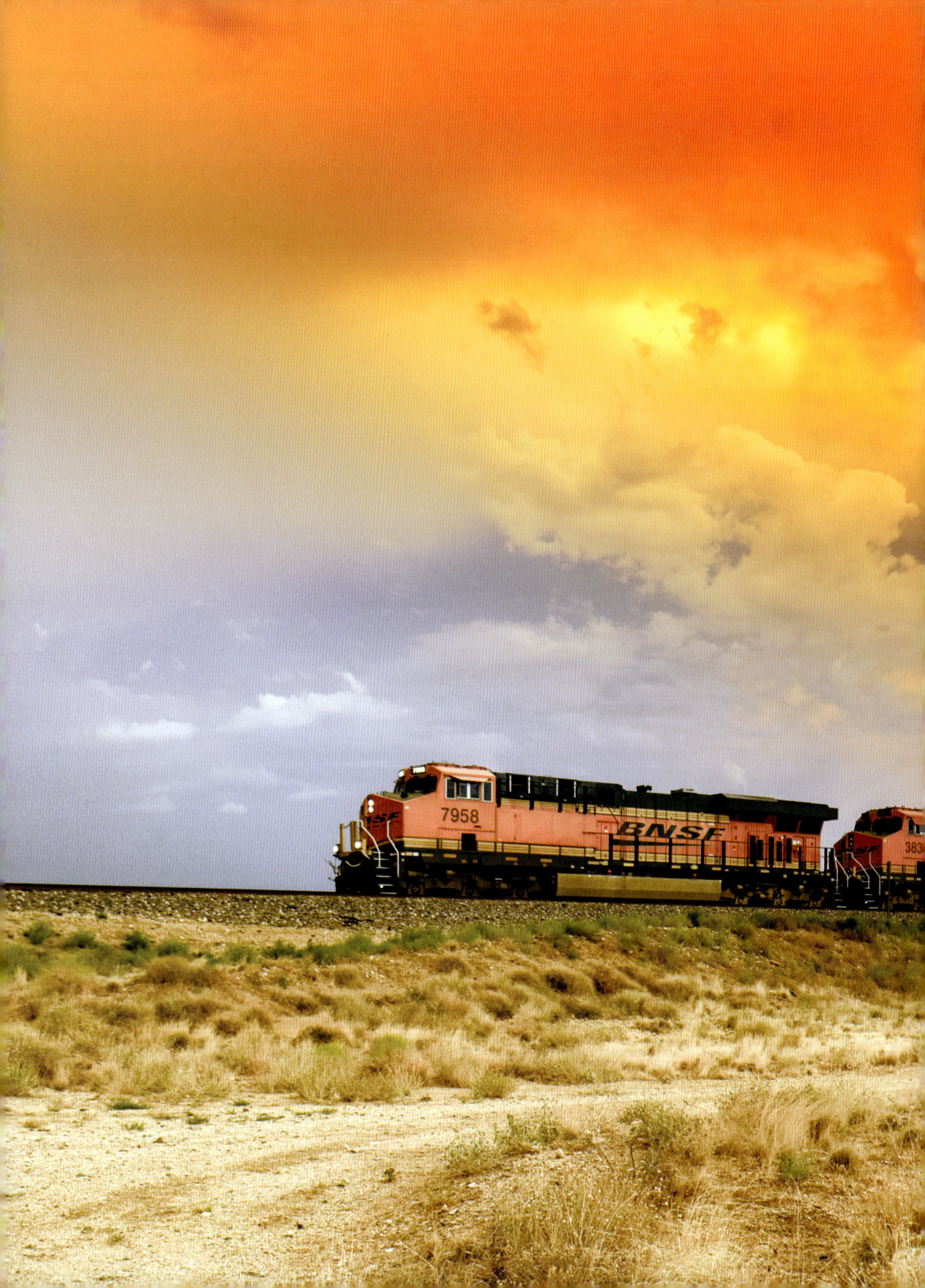
7958
BNSF

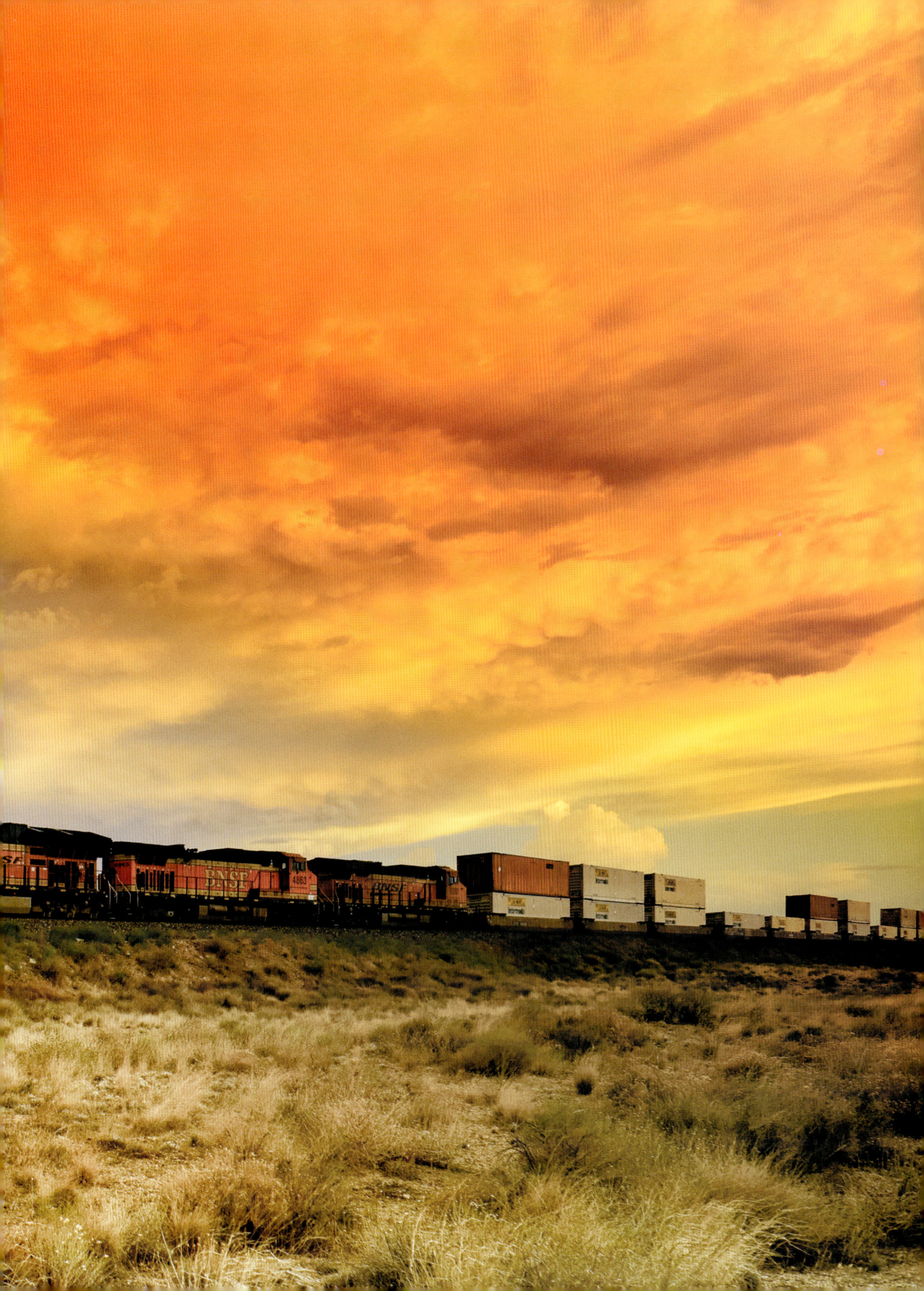
BNSF

Above: In Kingman, Solomon Bassoff created this sculpture of a chuckwalla, a stocky, human-fearing lizard that lumbers around the area. Opposite: Not far away is this endearing *Running Hare* metal sculpture crafted by Donald Gialanella. Overleaf: The Hackberry General Store, a fixture on the old Route 66—once the two-lane road of choice west from Chicago—offers snacks, drinks, a chubby cat, a couple of mules to pet, and what might be called Sixtysixiana souvenirs. Once, small silver and gold mines were found nearby. Now, not much of anything.

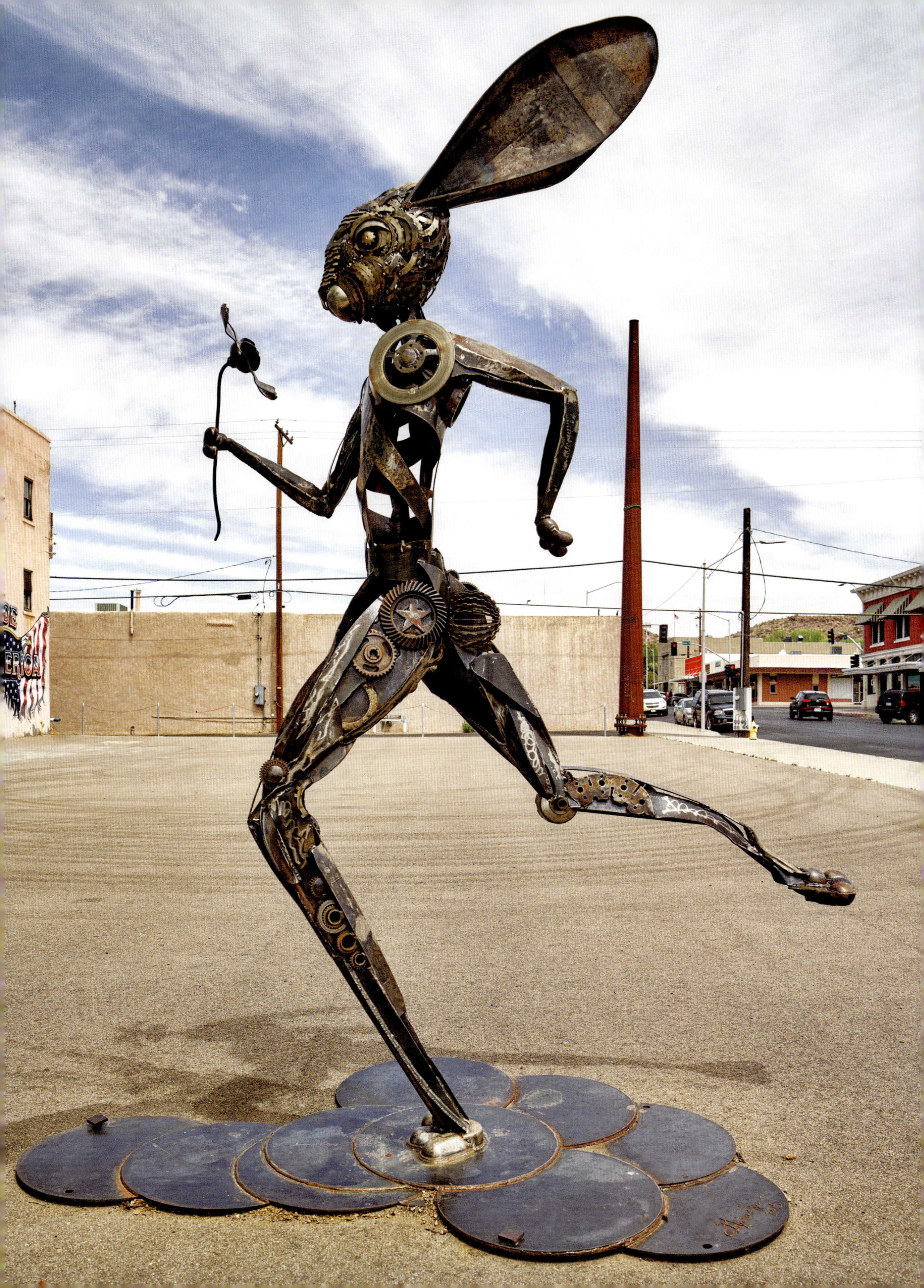

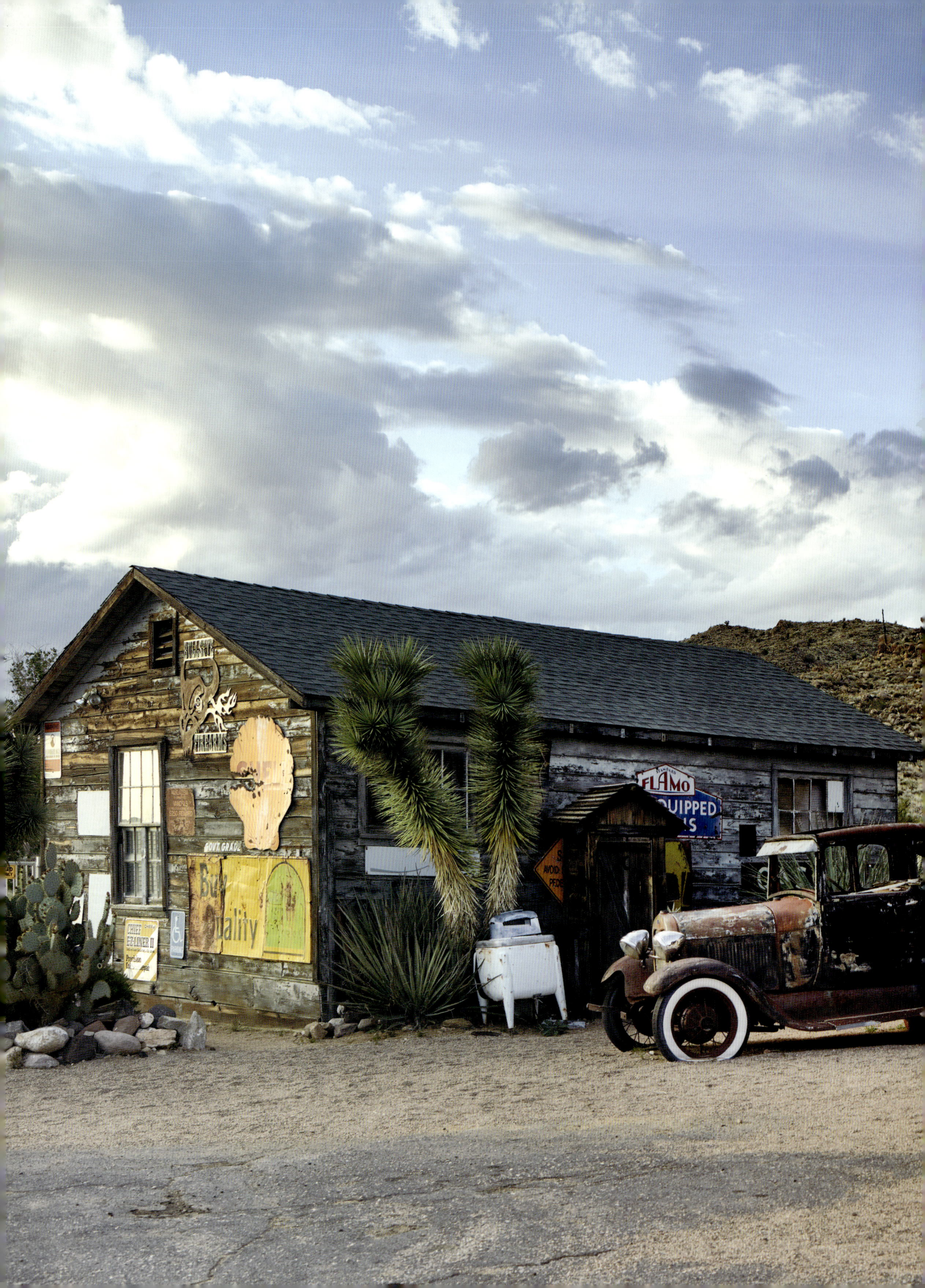
FLAMO
GOVT. GRADE

SANTA FE RAILROAD
66
REGULAR
ROUTE
66
7up
PREMIUM
Phillips
66

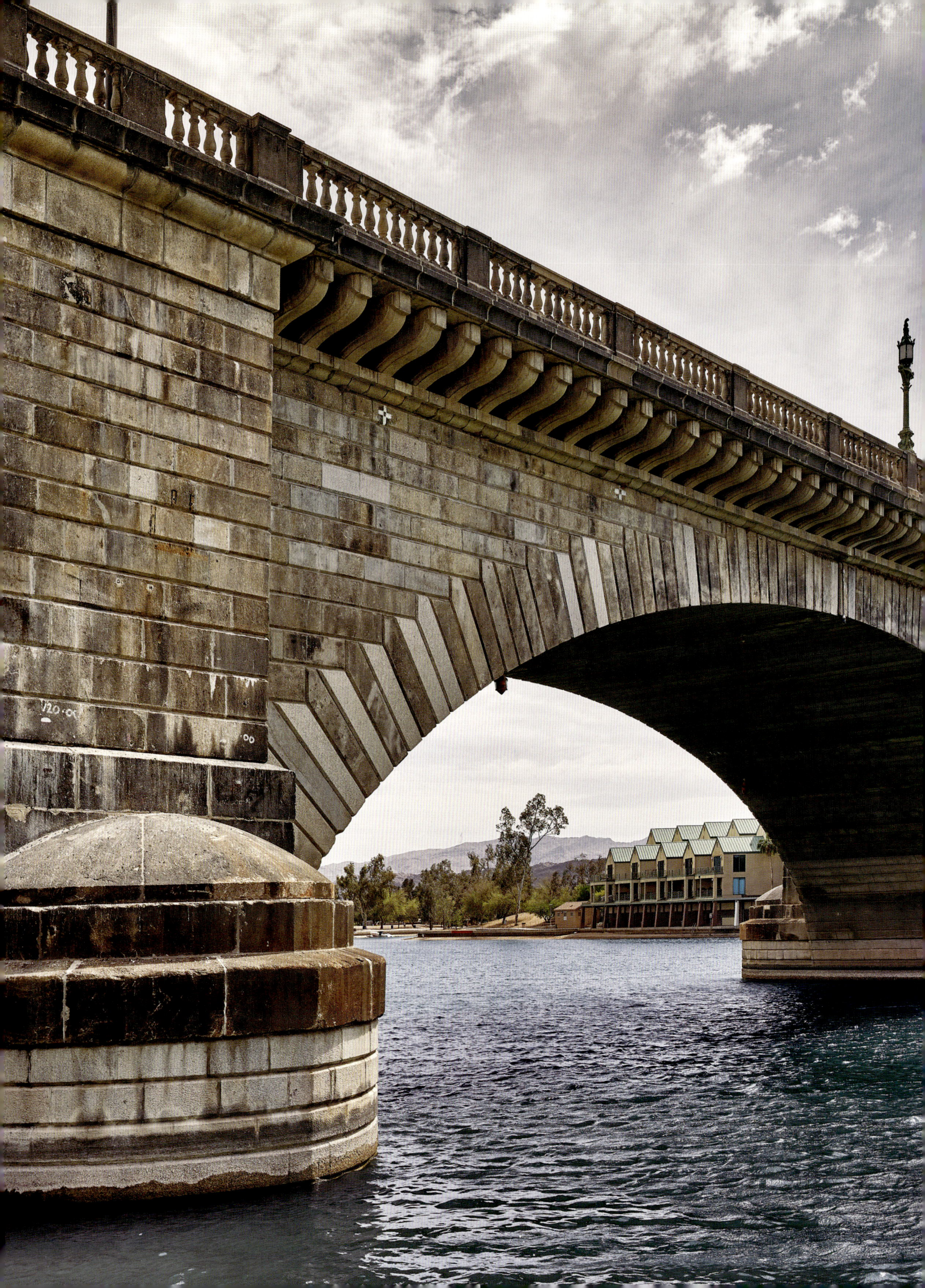

Left: London Bridge was very British until 1971, when Robert P. McCulloch bought its dismantled granite blocks, shipped them fifty-three hundred miles to Lake Havasu City, and turned the rebuilt bridge into an Arizona tourist attraction. Above: In Topock, the 1914 Old Trails Bridge now carries pipelines, not vehicles, across the Colorado River to California. Overleaf: Spray ponds serve as cooling agents at the Palo Verde Nuclear Generating Station near Tonopah. Its electric power serves communities all the way to Los Angeles.

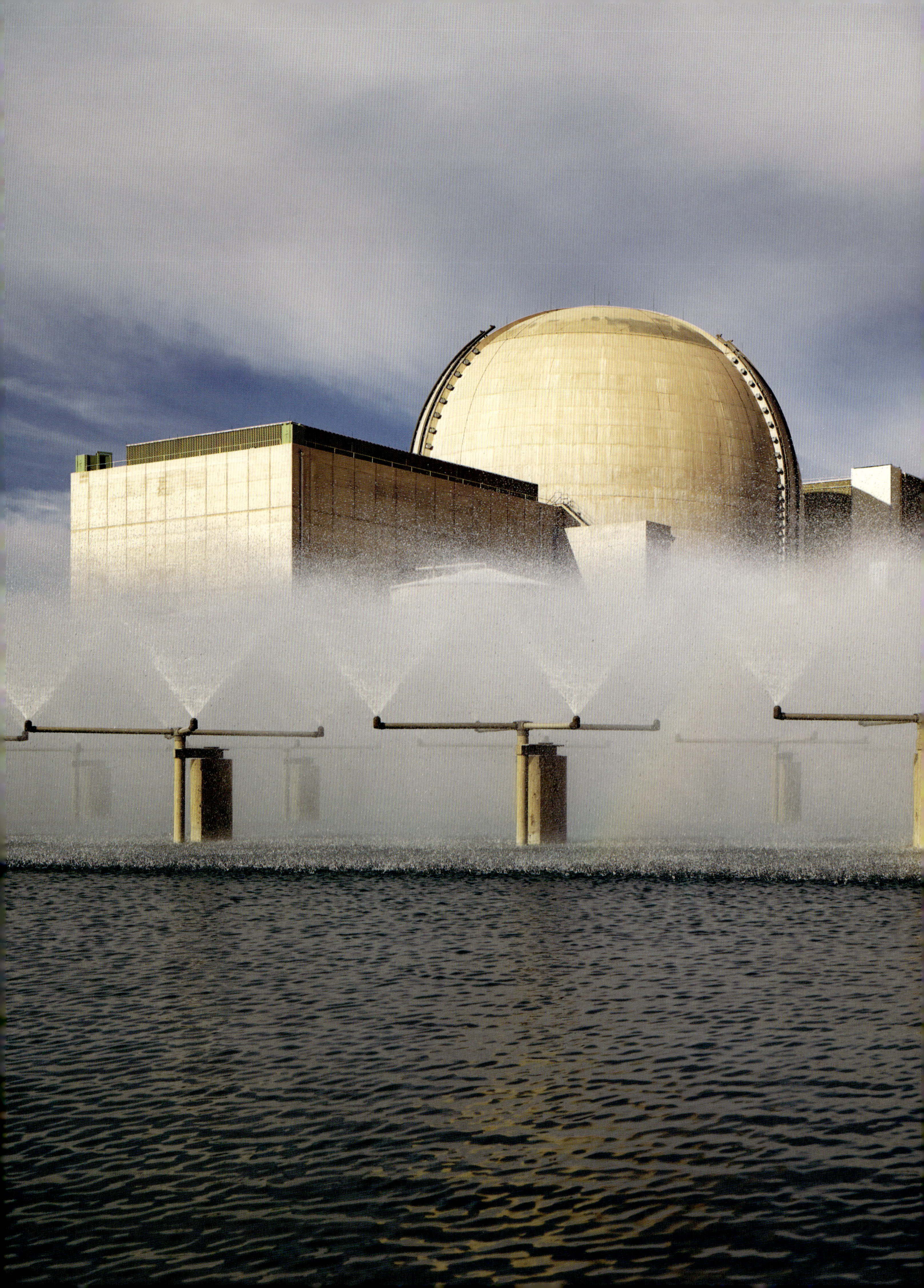

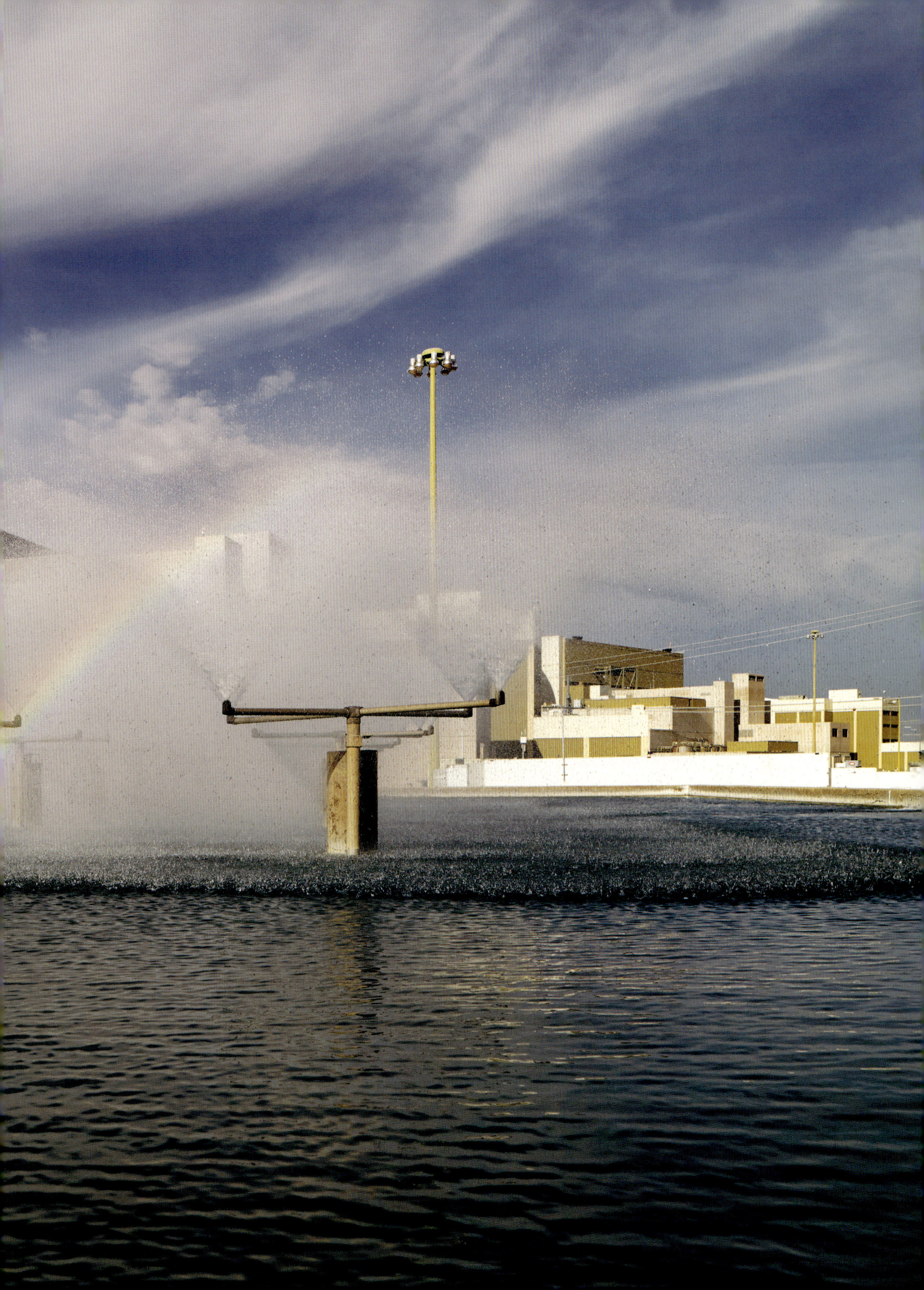

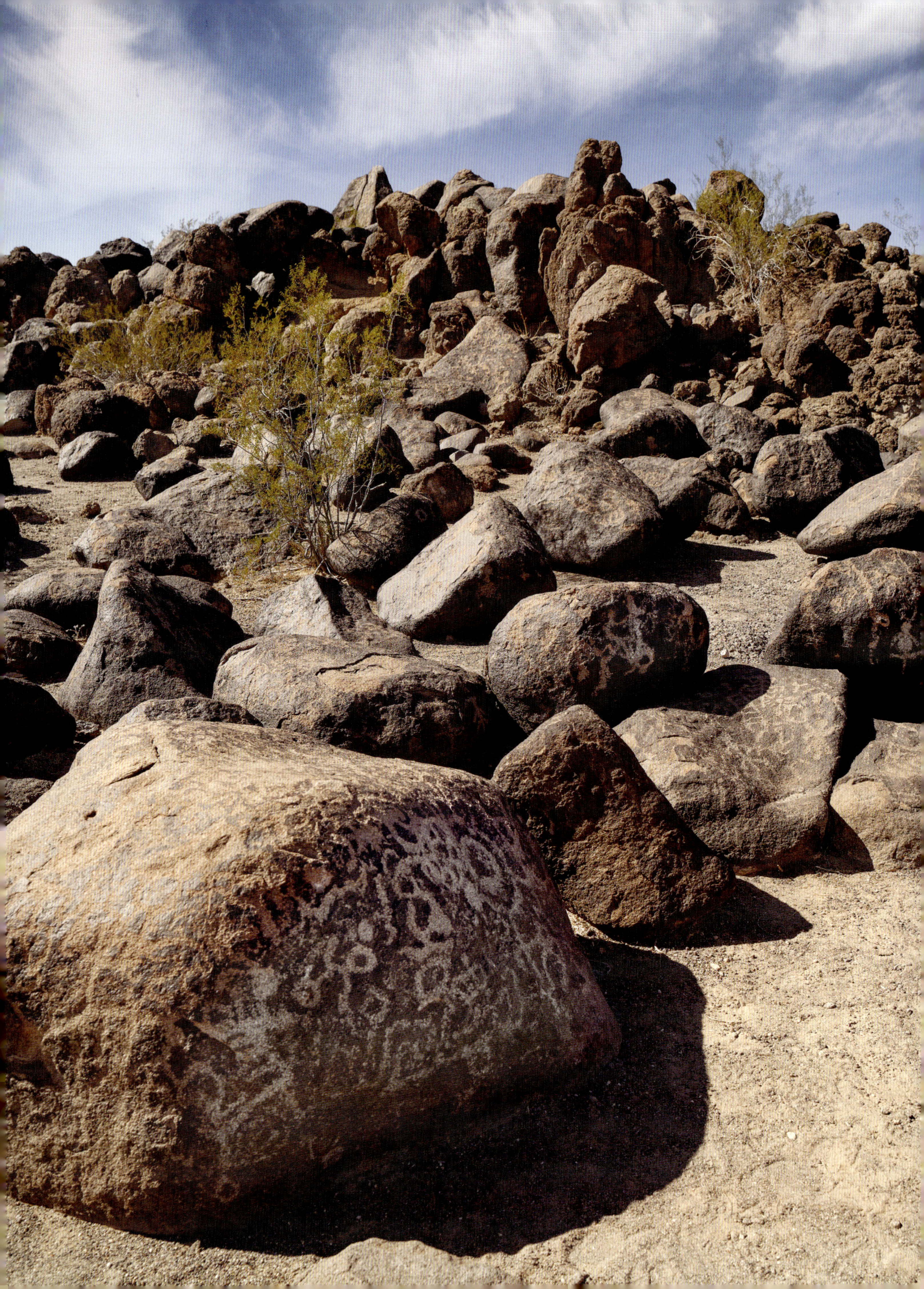

Opposite: Visitors to a campground near Dateland get an extra-added attraction: Painted Rock Petroglyph Site, where both prehistoric designs and "I was here" inscriptions left by modern travelers are etched into the rocks. Above and left: At Holt's Gas Station and Gift Shop in Gila Bend, spatting metal dinos and a sculpted gila monster entertain customers. The town is named for a river, not the venomous lizards.

Dateland · Gila Bend · 157

Above: The NexGen Yuma organization of young professionals commissioned the artists Josh Tripoli and Rebekah Lewis to create this postcard-style welcome sign on a wall of the Yuma Art Center. Opposite: Two of the city's most uninhibited characters, Bob Lutes, left, and his brother, Bill, ham it up inside one of the town's most eclectic locations: their Lutes Casino, which no longer is a gambling joint but an offbeat restaurant and bar. Its own newspaper, the *Gazette*, writes that "the décor is early eclectic, what might be called interesting junk."

158 · *Yuma*

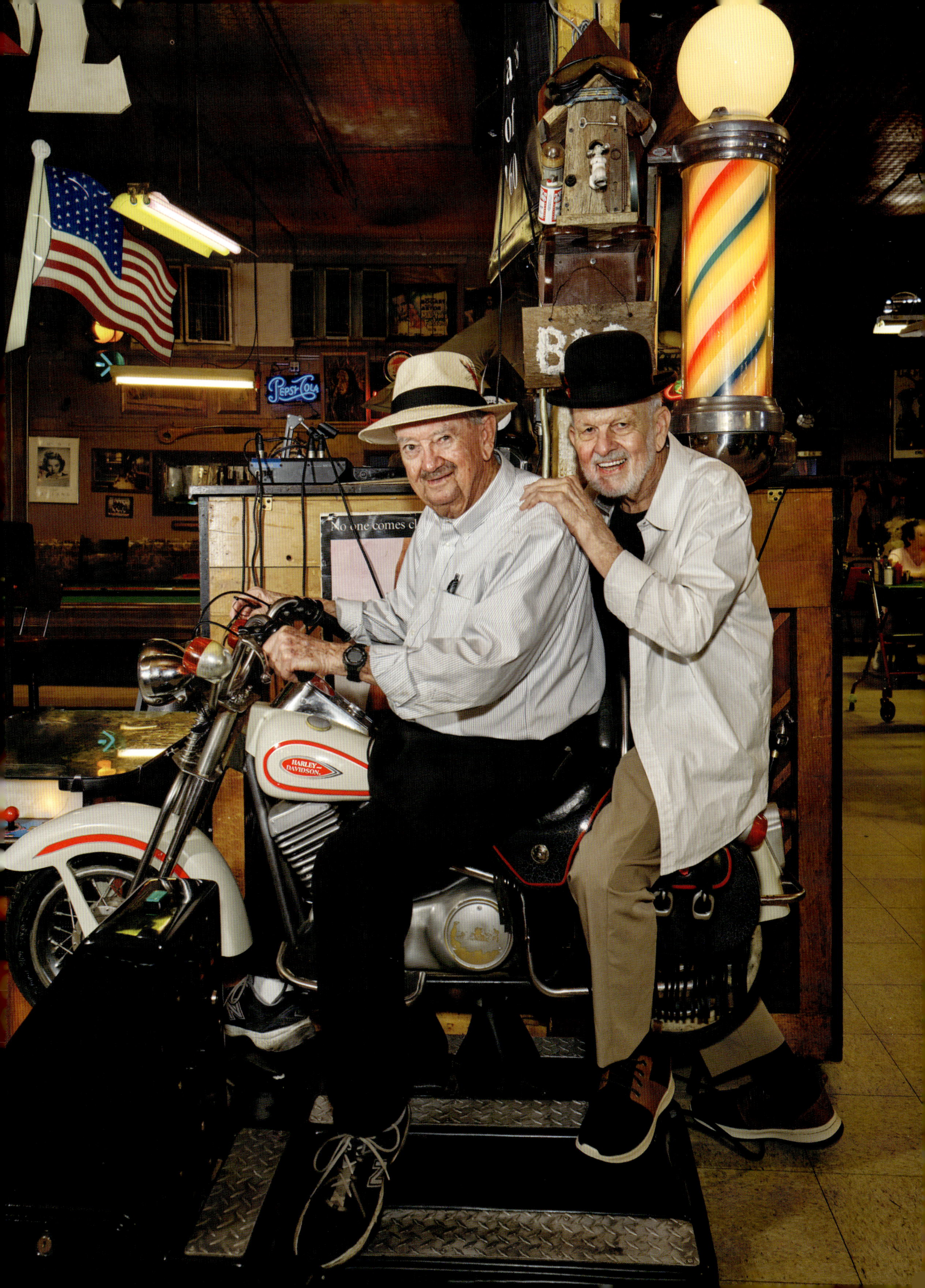
Pepsi-Cola
HARLEY DAVIDSON

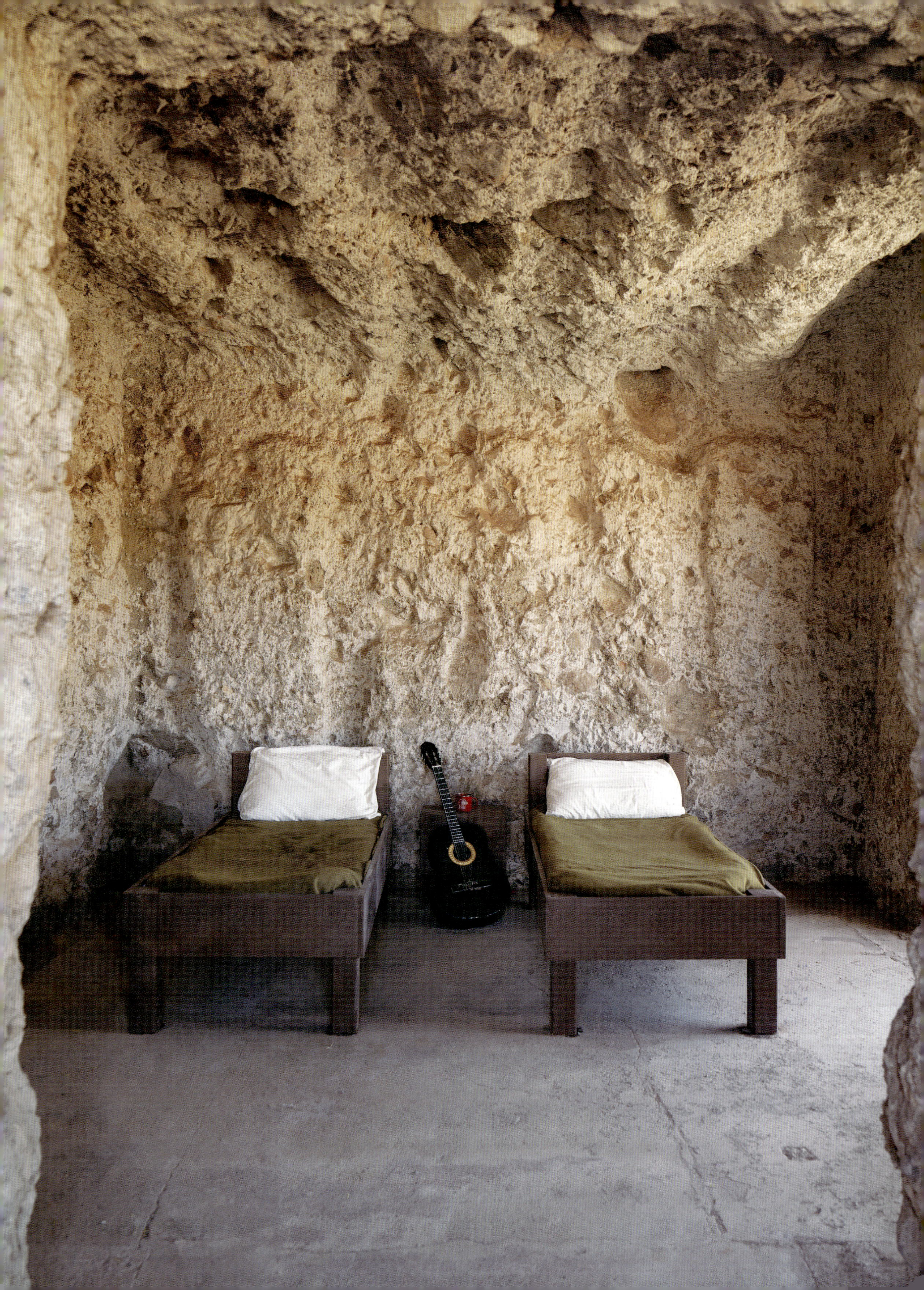

The display of an ordinary inmate's quarters at the Yuma Territorial Prison State Historic Park contrasts sharply with that of a solitary-confinement cell. One can imagine the many connotations of the term "Dark Cell" here. The prison operated from 1876 until 1909, during which time more than three thousand inmates passed through its iron gates, sleeping in overcrowded rock and adobe cells. After the prison closed, its buildings were used for a time as a high school.

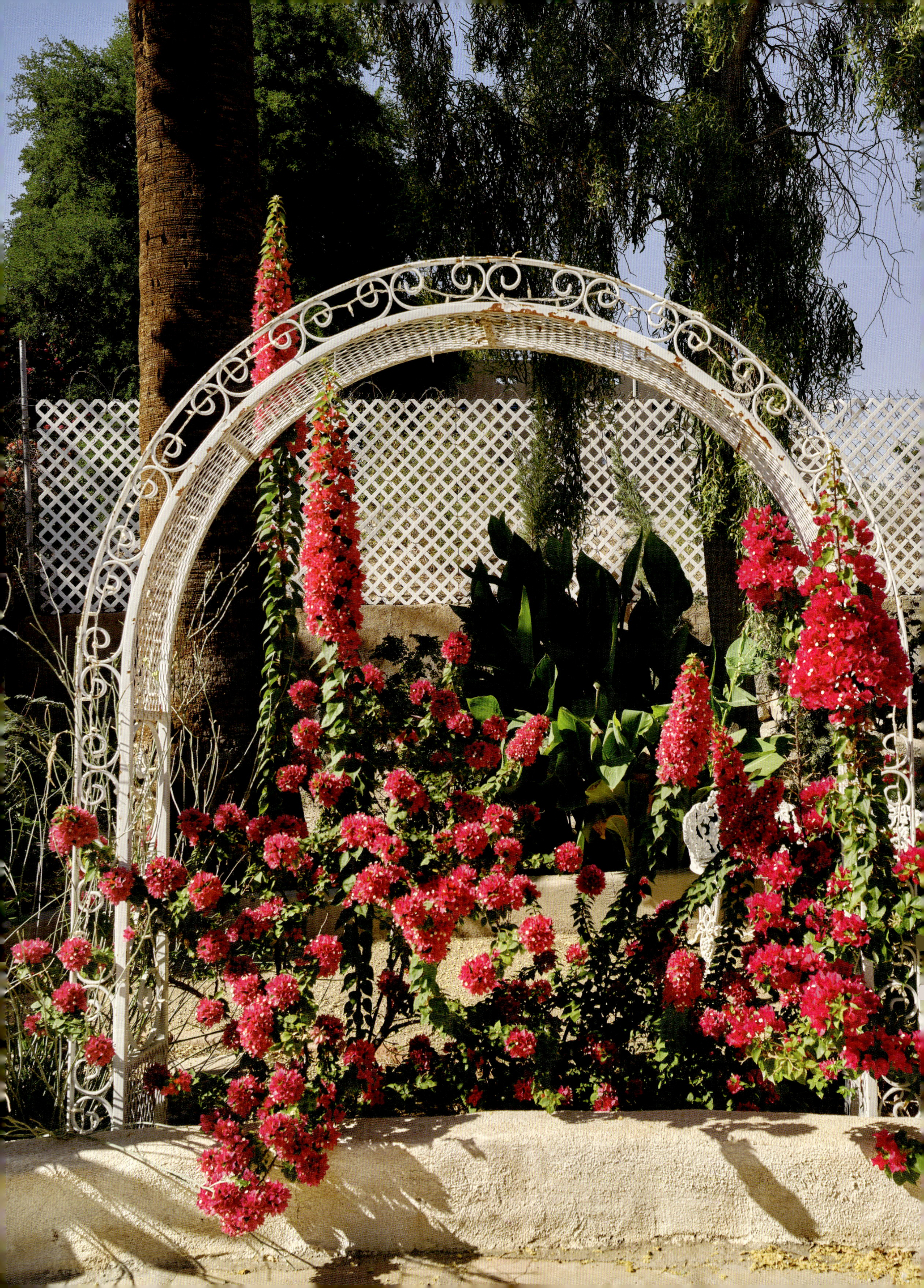

Opposite: Flowers in this Yuma city park do not lack for sunshine, but water is a different matter. On average, the city receives 3.36 inches of rain a year; in all of 2007, it got just one-seventh of an inch! Below: In 1994 Allen Armstrong, shown here, and his wife, Stephanie, bought and began restoring the Castle Dome City ghost town, once a boomtown above silver and lead mines that thrived near Yuma. They centralized vintage buildings, tidied up a scrawny old cemetery, and opened part of one mine for gemological tours.

Yuma · 163

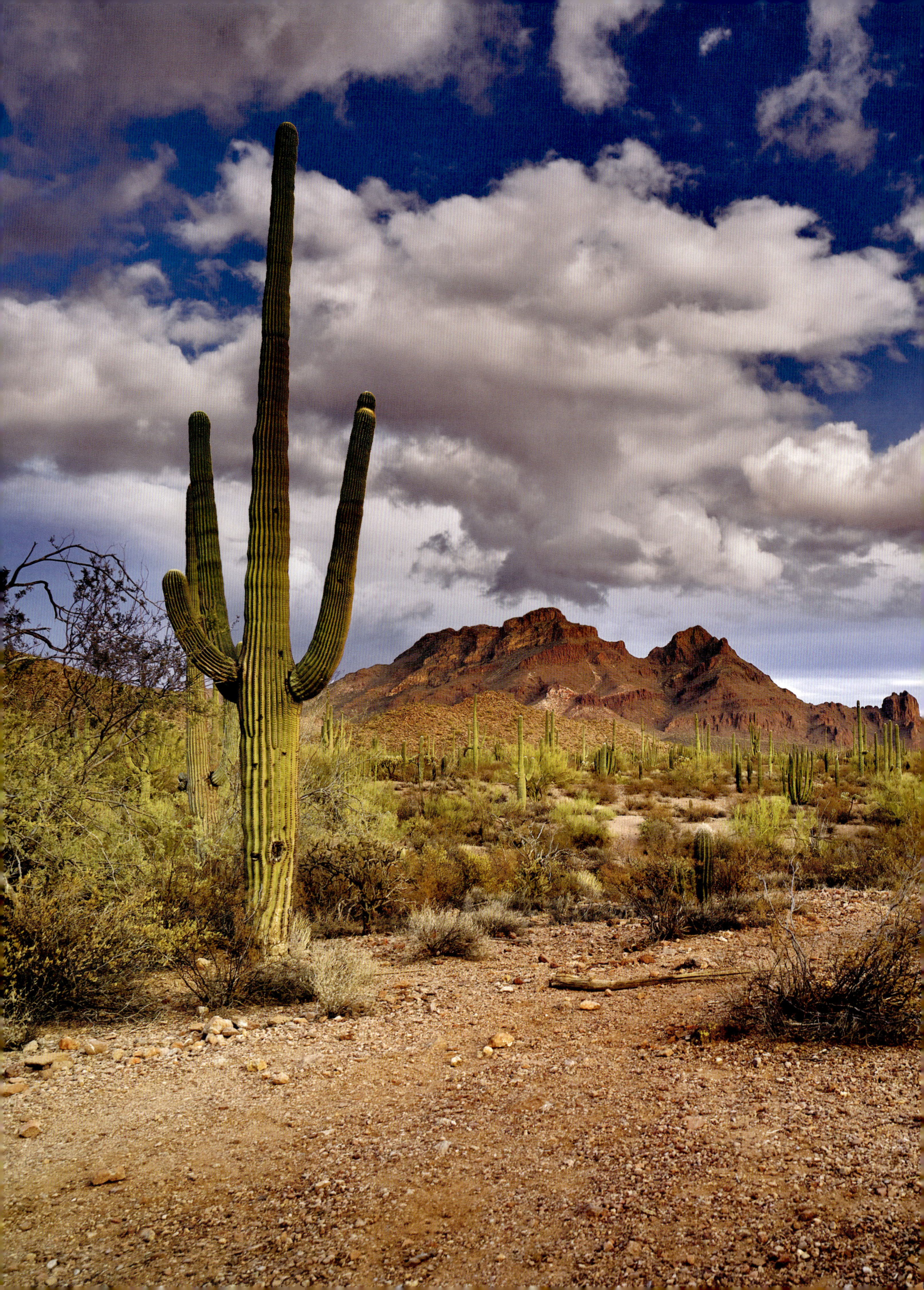

Organ Pipe Cactus National Monument, adjacent to the Mexican border, is a 517-square-mile reserve featuring its unusual namesake flora, notable for their upward-spreading, asparagus-looking stems. Various other cacti, including the ever-present saguaro, also thrive in the remote park. Overleaf: Surrounding an ocotillo *(Fouquieria splendens)* at Organ Pipe are fluffy cactus specimens known as teddy bear cholla *(Cylindropuntia bigelovii)*. Their blossoms, open mostly at night, are pollinated primarily by bats.

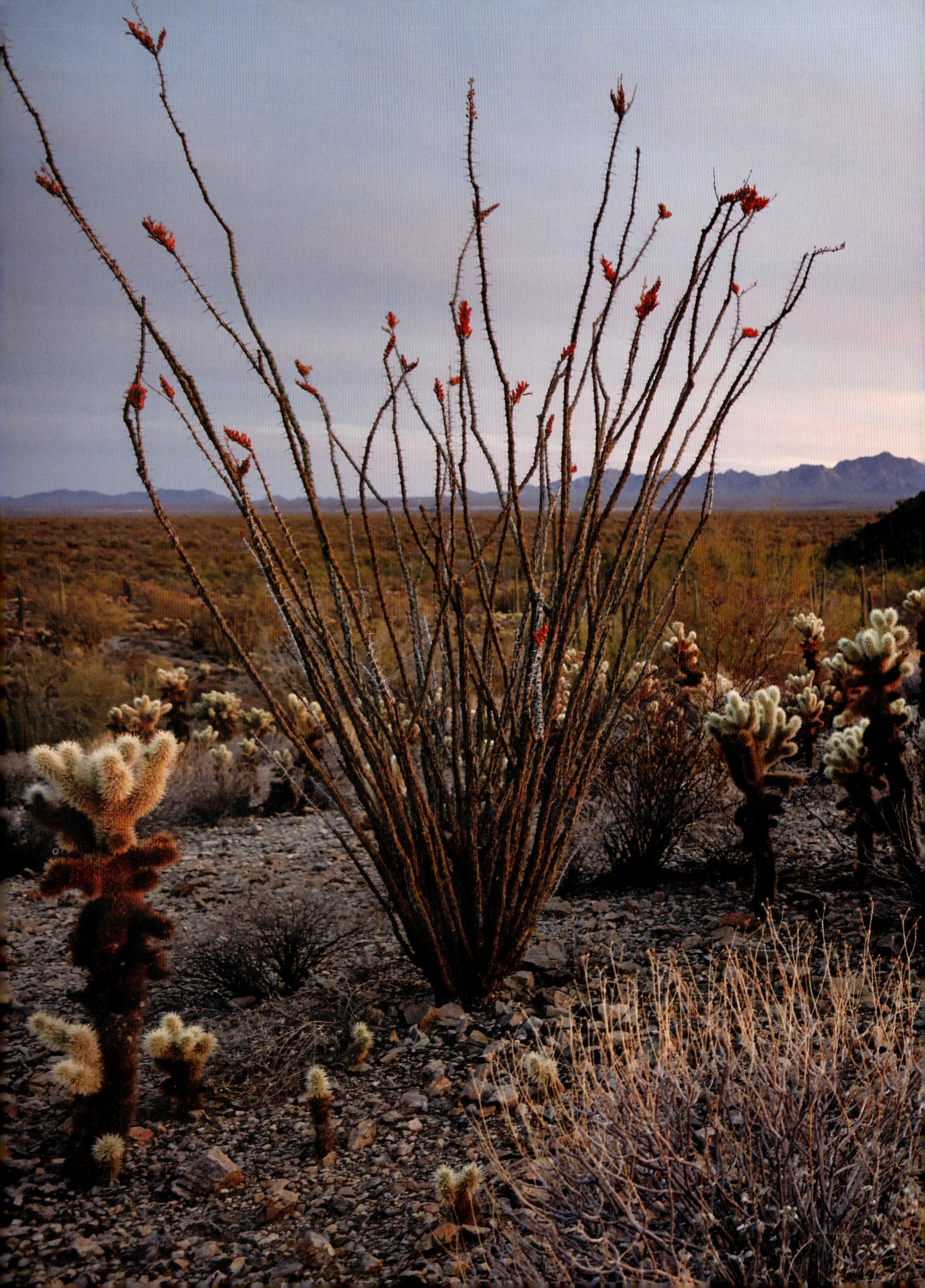

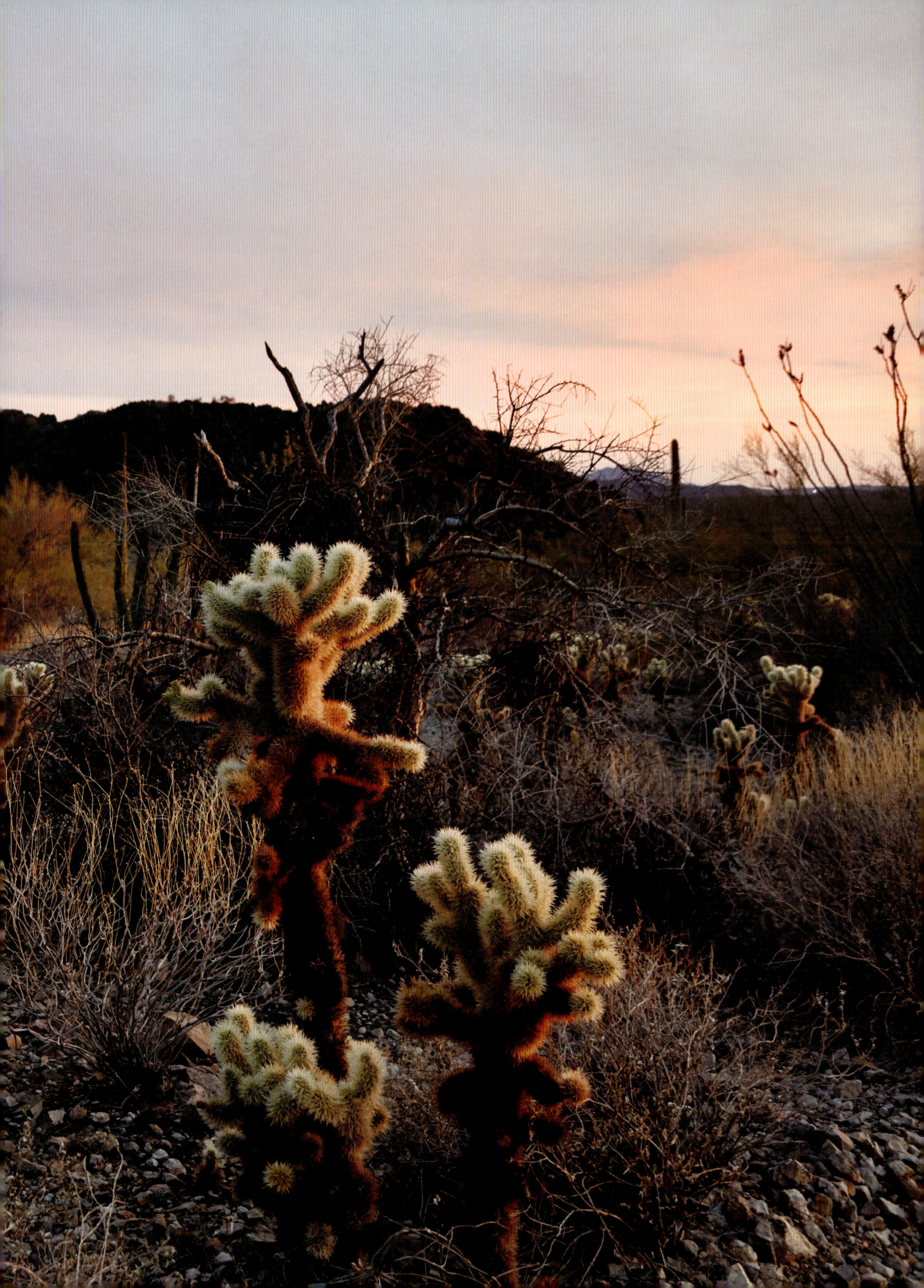

Above: When the Second Pinal County Courthouse was completed in 1891, funds were lacking for its tower's clockworks. So someone painted clock hands set at 11:44. The building fell into disrepair and was closed in 2005, only to later reopen as a county office building. Right: Florence uses the Spanish word *parada* to describe the downtown parade associated with its junior rodeo—the oldest in the nation. Opposite: Florence is a cotton town where the old "lift that bale" task is by no means simple.

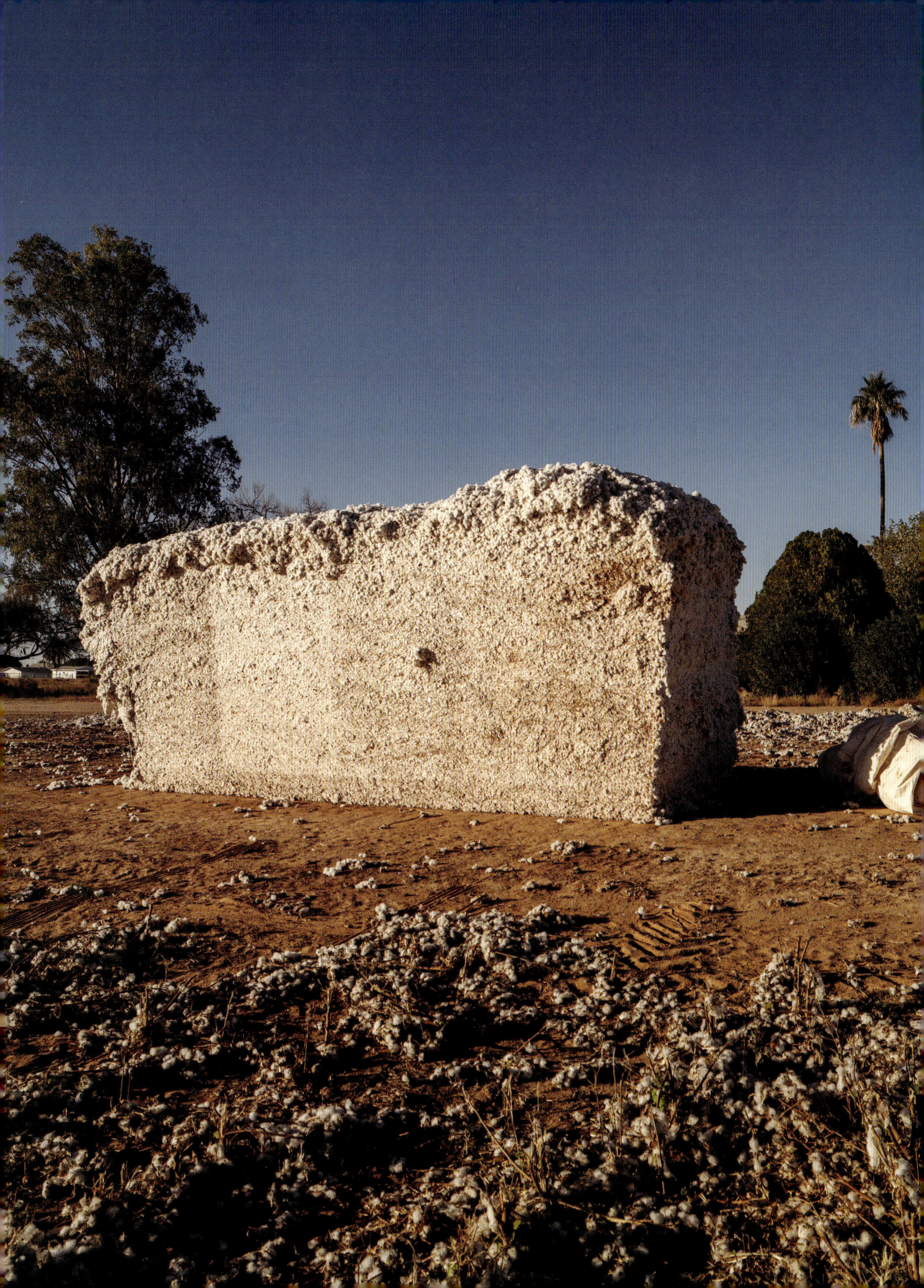

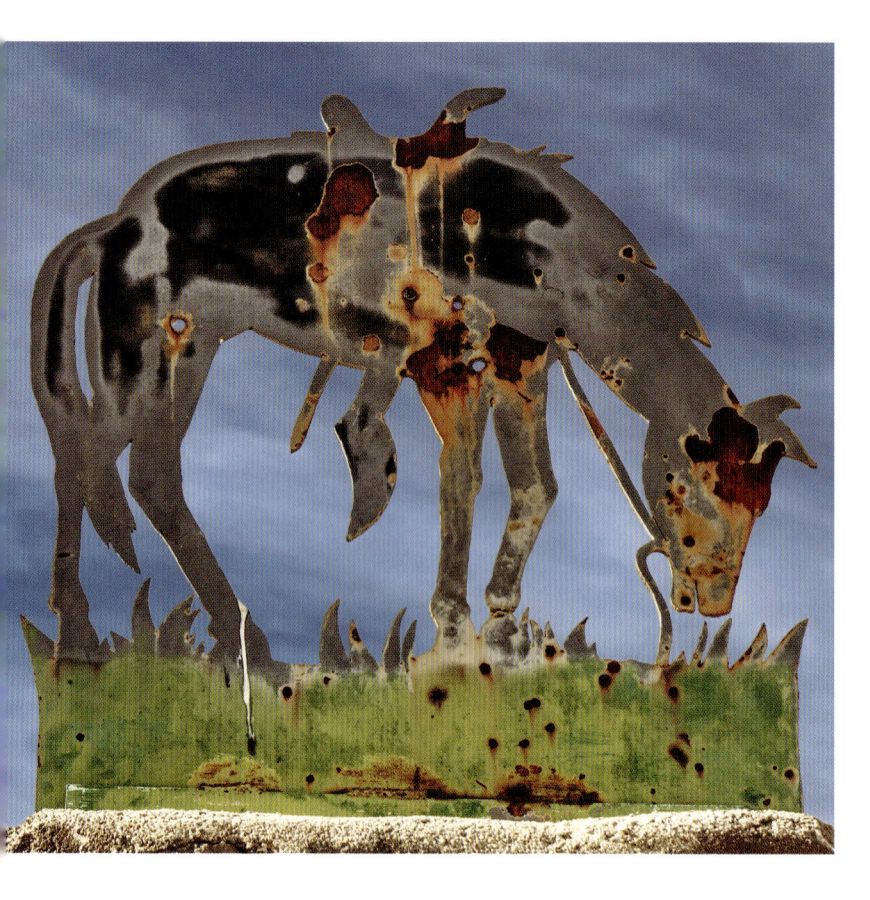

Above: South of Florence on Route 79, a highway pull-off memorializes Tom Mix, the silver screen's King of the Cowboys, at the spot where he died in a 1940 car accident. It features not Mix but his beloved and talented mount, Tony the Wonder Horse. Right: The Quijotoa cemetery on Tohono O'odham Indian Nation lands is reverently maintained. Overleaf: Biosphere 2 in Oracle, completed in 1991 and now owned by the University of Arizona, is used for ecological and agricultural experiments in a sealed environment.

170 · *Florence · Quijotoa*

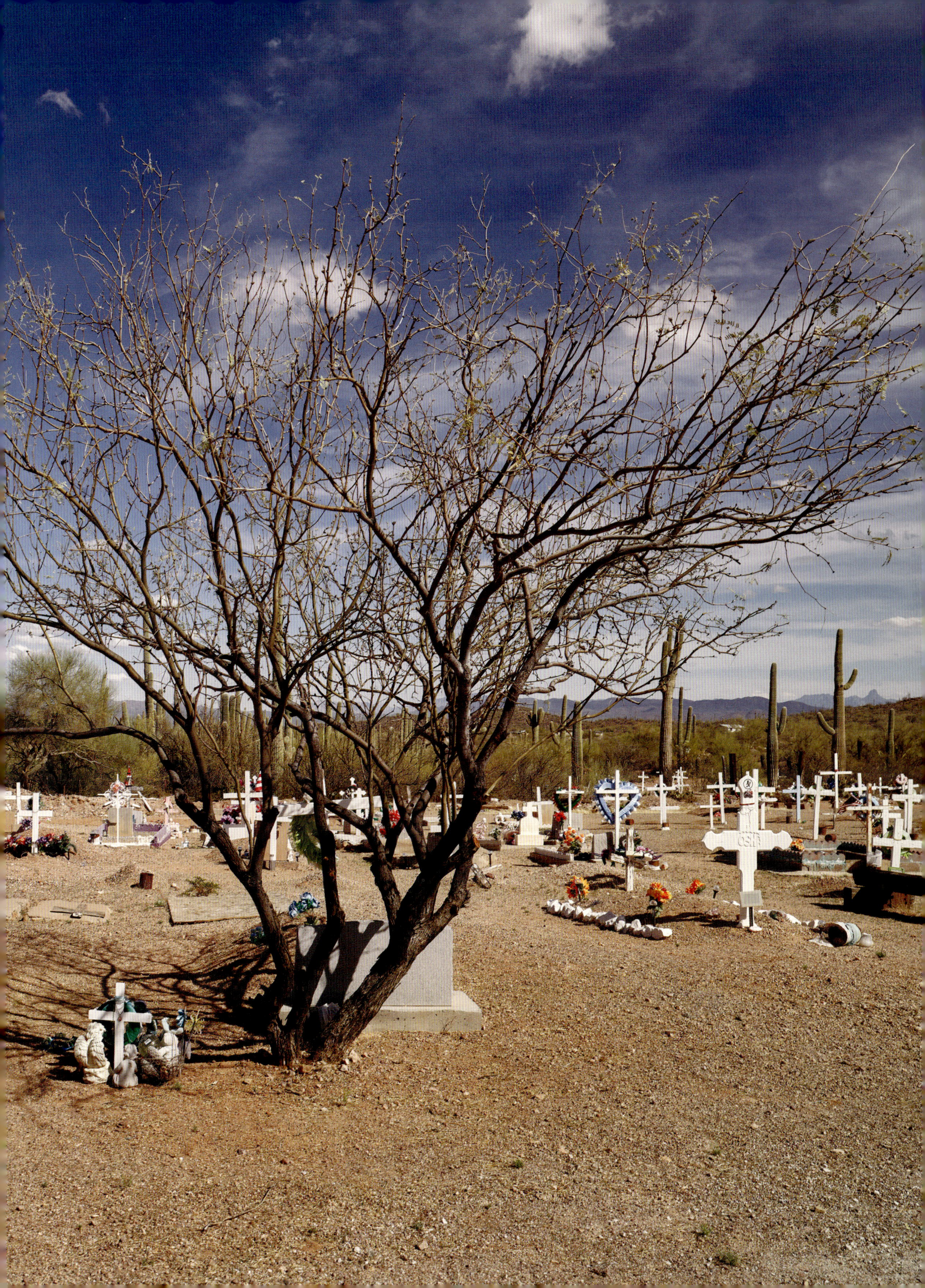

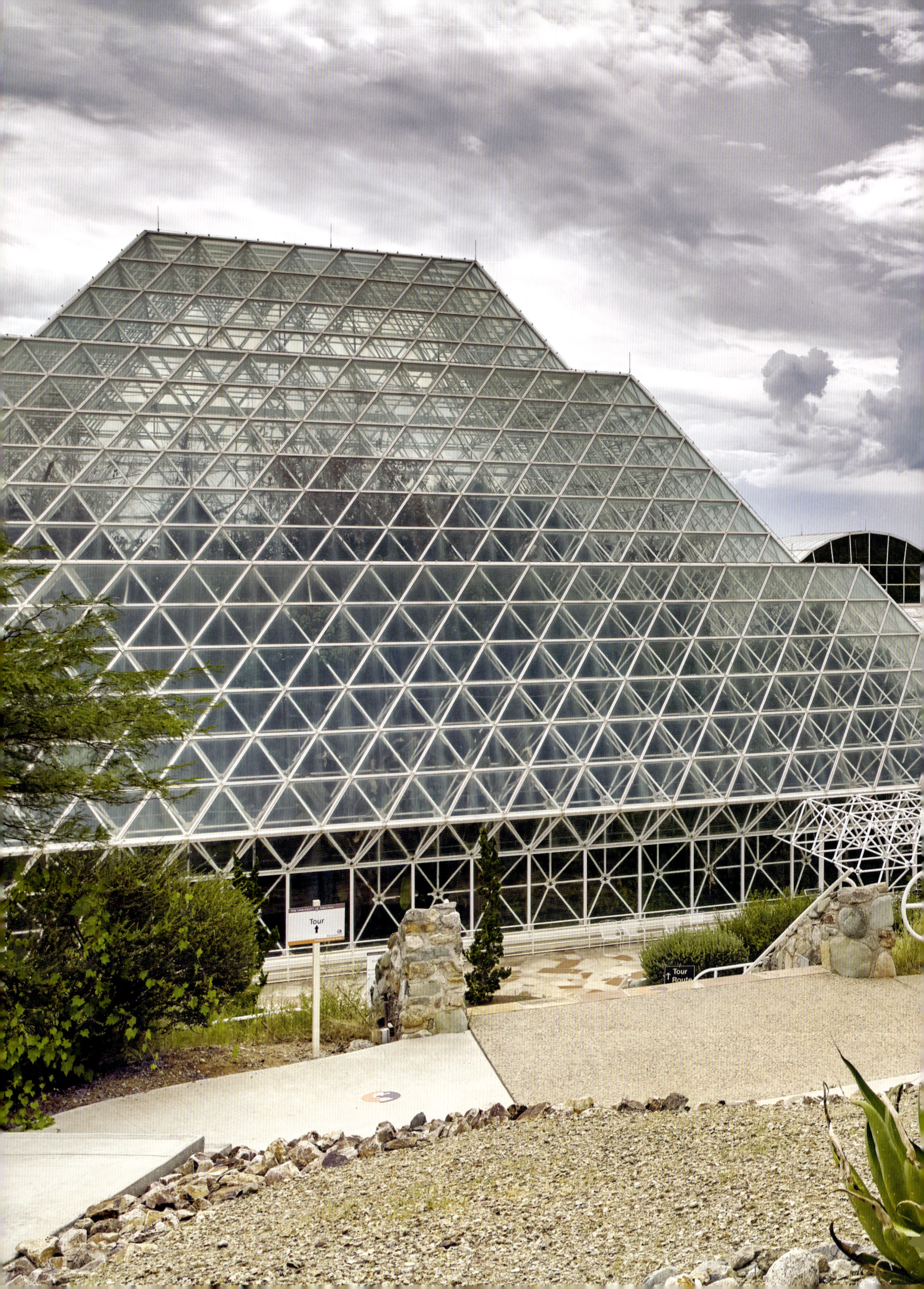
Tour

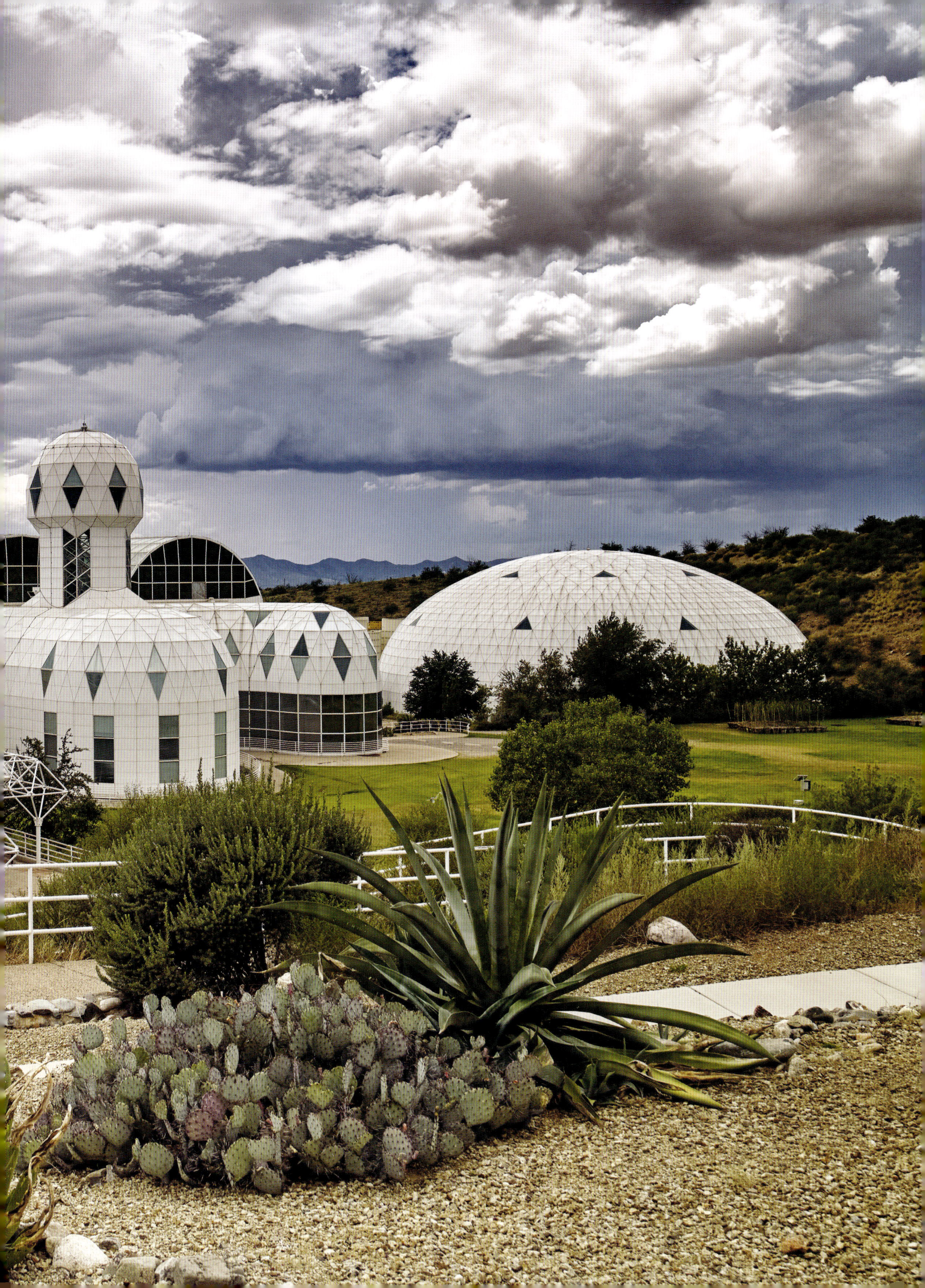

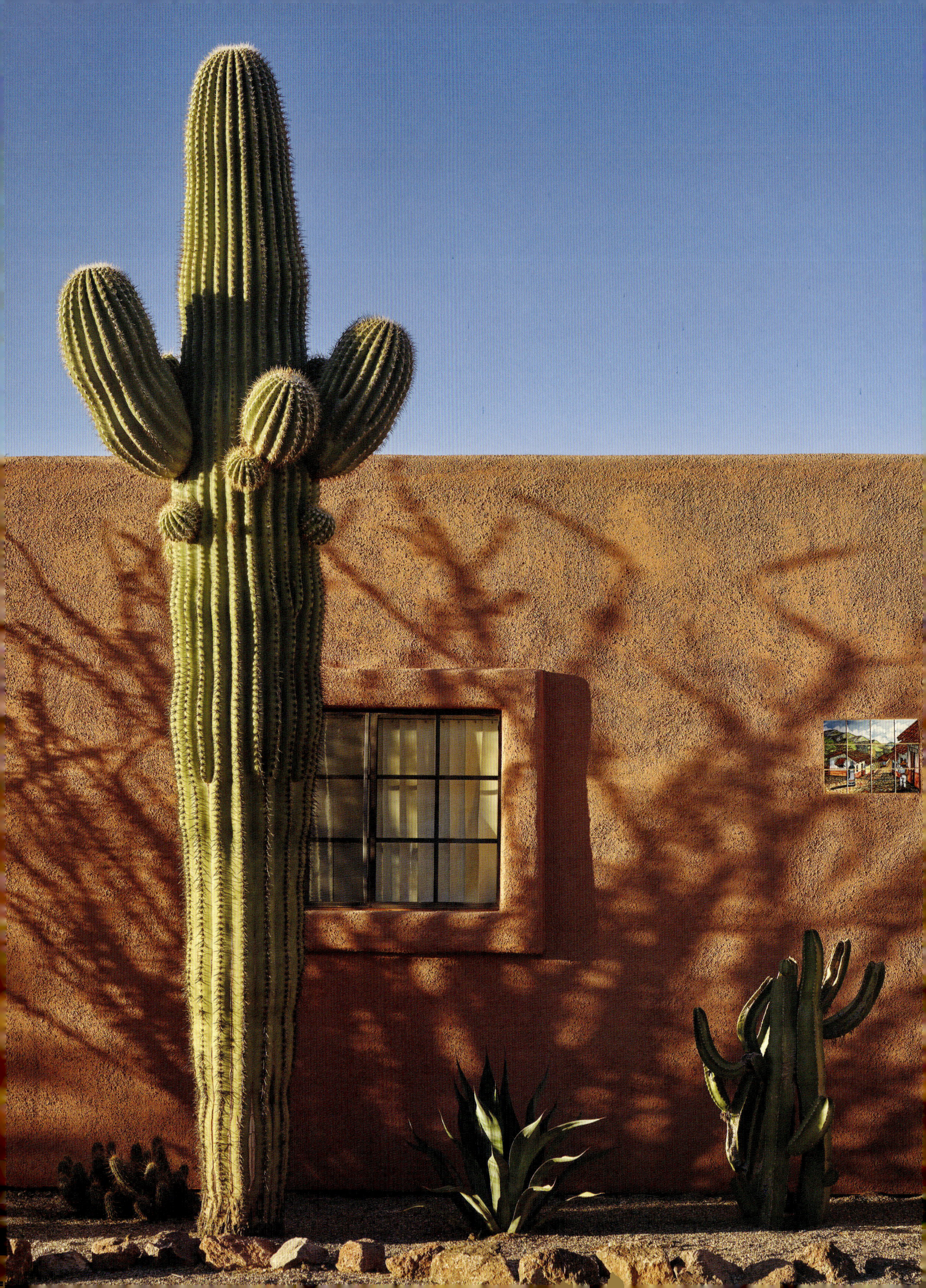

Tucson's White Stallion guest ranch proclaims that it is located "where the pavement ends and the West begins." (The name Black Stallion was discarded because BS would not work as a brand.) Since 1965 the ranch's True family owners have built one of Arizona's largest riding-horse herds. Overleaf: Perched on the highest point of the Quinlan Mountains, the Kitt Peak National Observatory boasts more than twenty telescopes, including the dominant Mayall four-meter telescope.

Tucson · 175

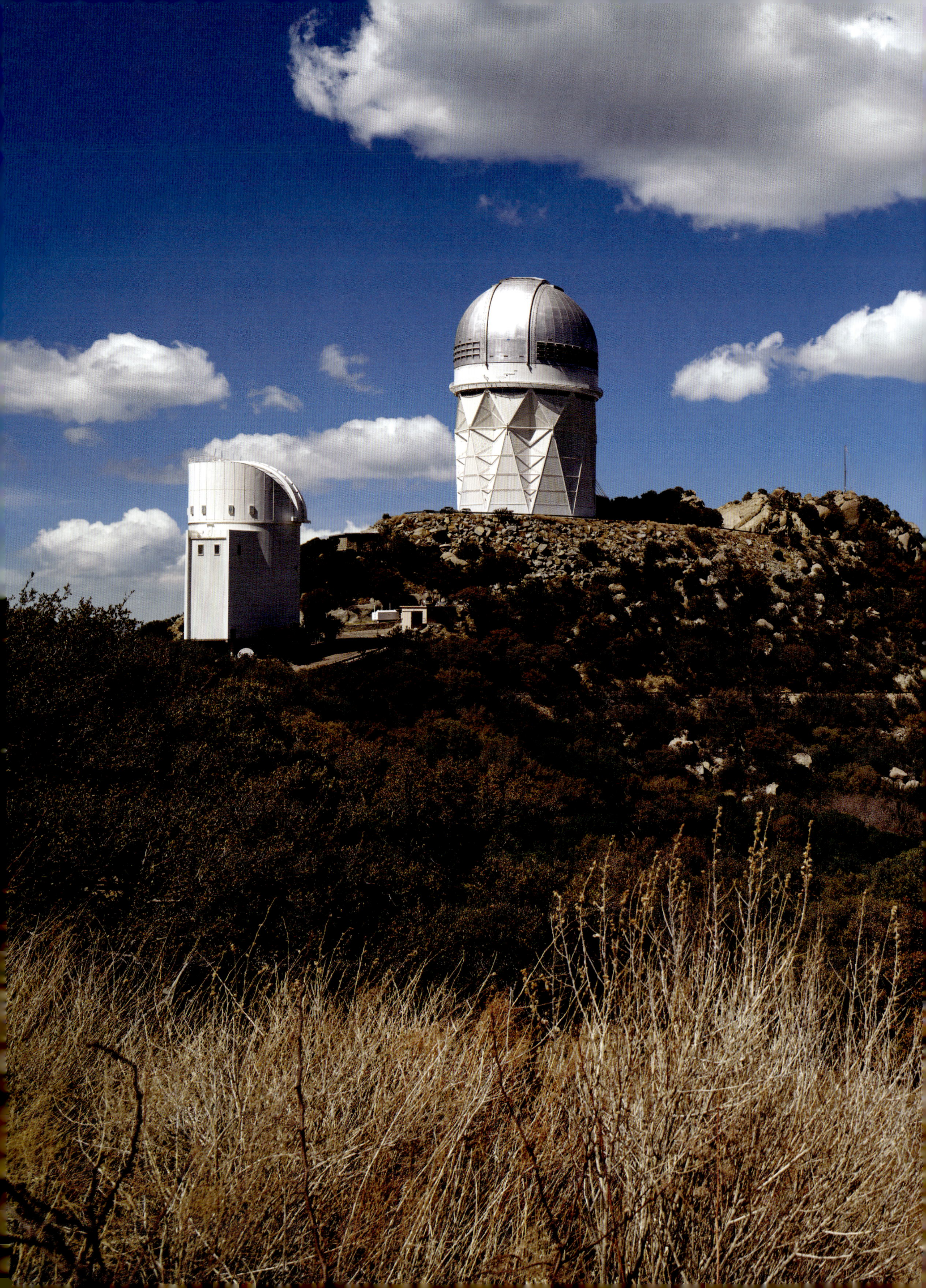

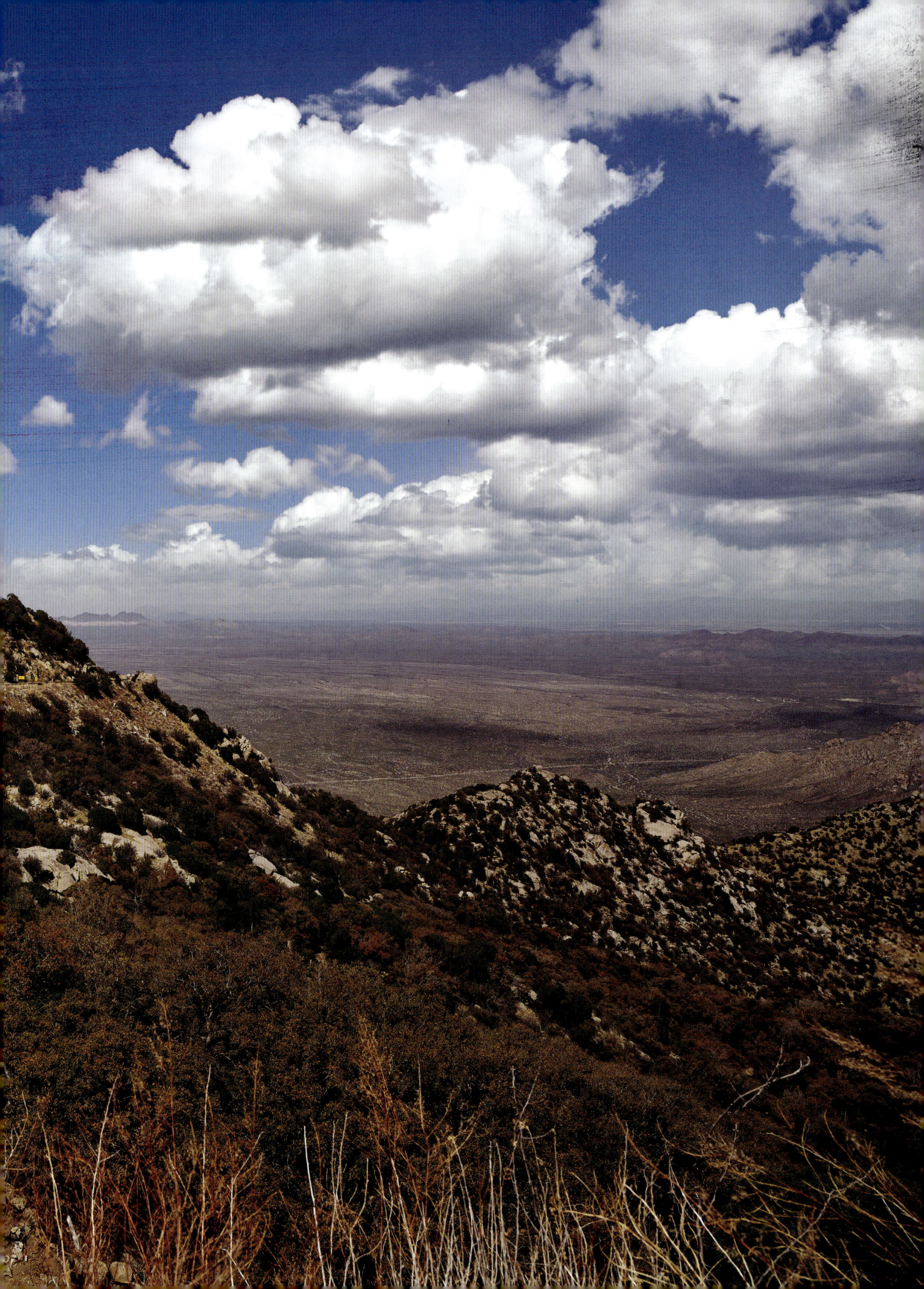

Saguaro National Park showcases thousands of the ubiquitous cacti in separate areas to the east and west of Tucson. The saguaro is native to, and grows in any abundance only in, Arizona's Sonoran Desert, the adjacent Mexican state of Sonora, and a bit of neighboring California. The cactus is best known for its upraised arms, but many have just a central trunk because extensions do not usually appear until the cactus is at least seventy-five years old.

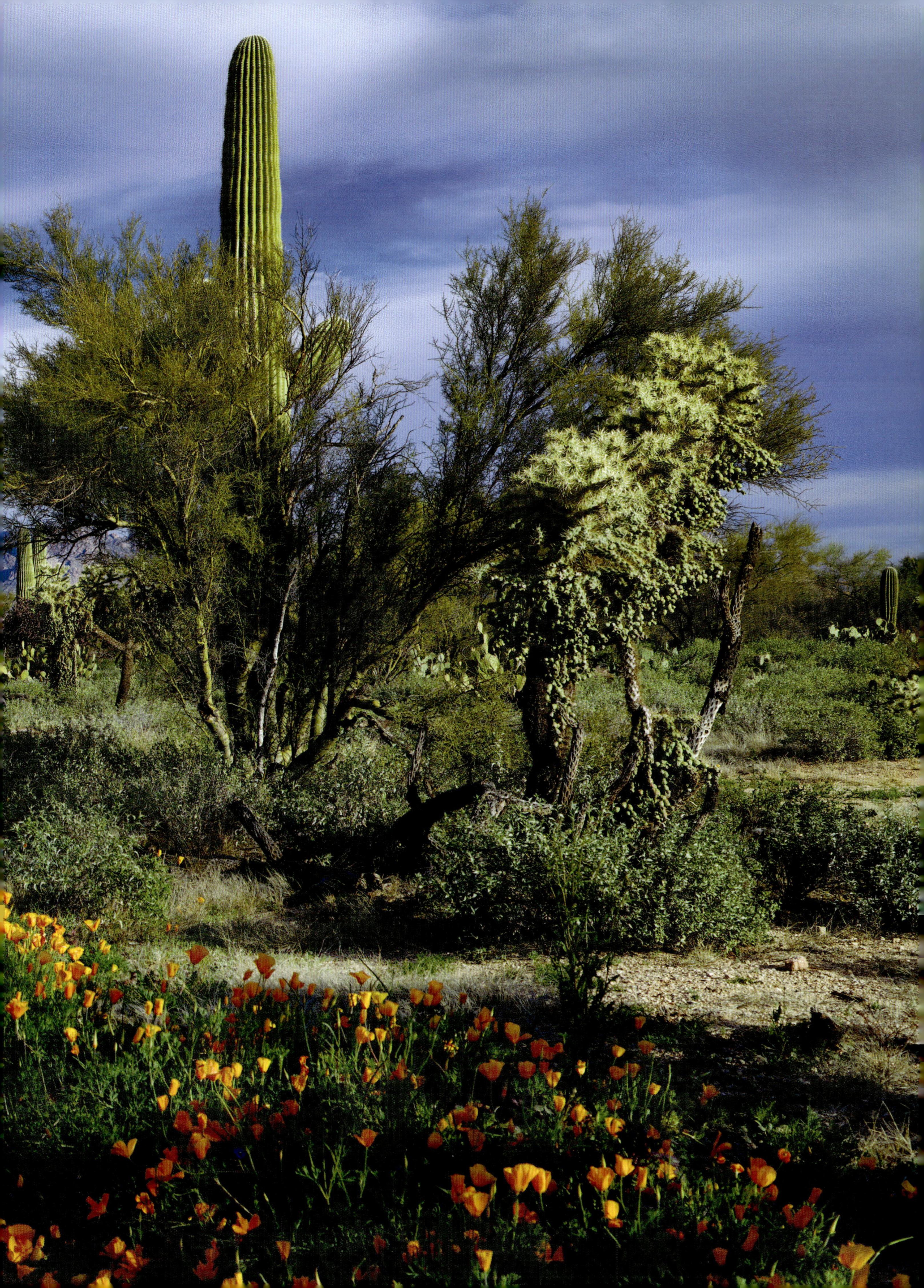

Situated on ninety-eight acres bursting with hundreds of animal species and plant varieties, the outdoor Arizona-Sonora Desert Museum maintains a series of trails through woodlands, grasslands, and desert gardens. A crested (or cristate) saguaro, seen opposite, is a rare mutation. One saguaro expert has referred to its fanlike crown as "an icon on top of an icon."

180 · *Tucson*

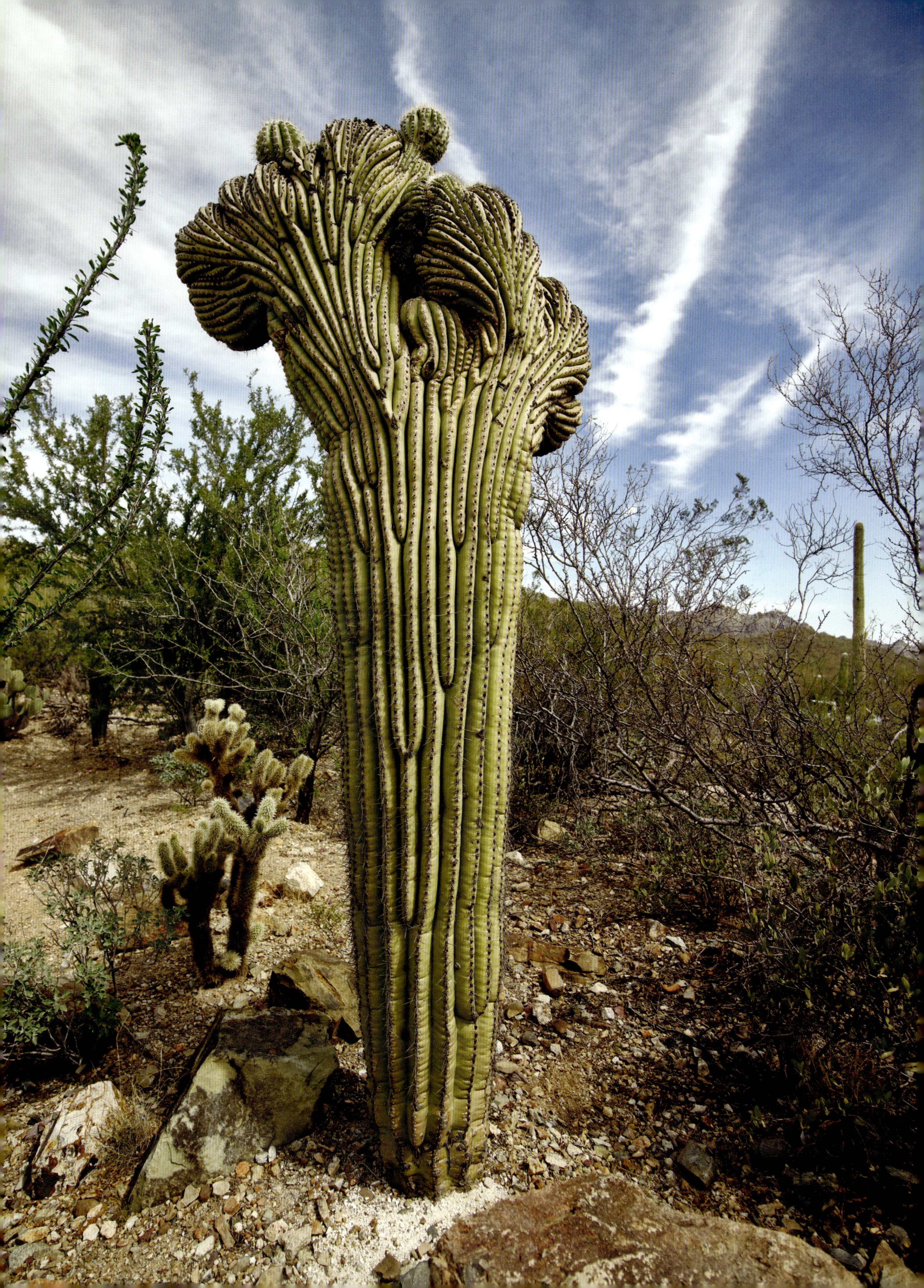

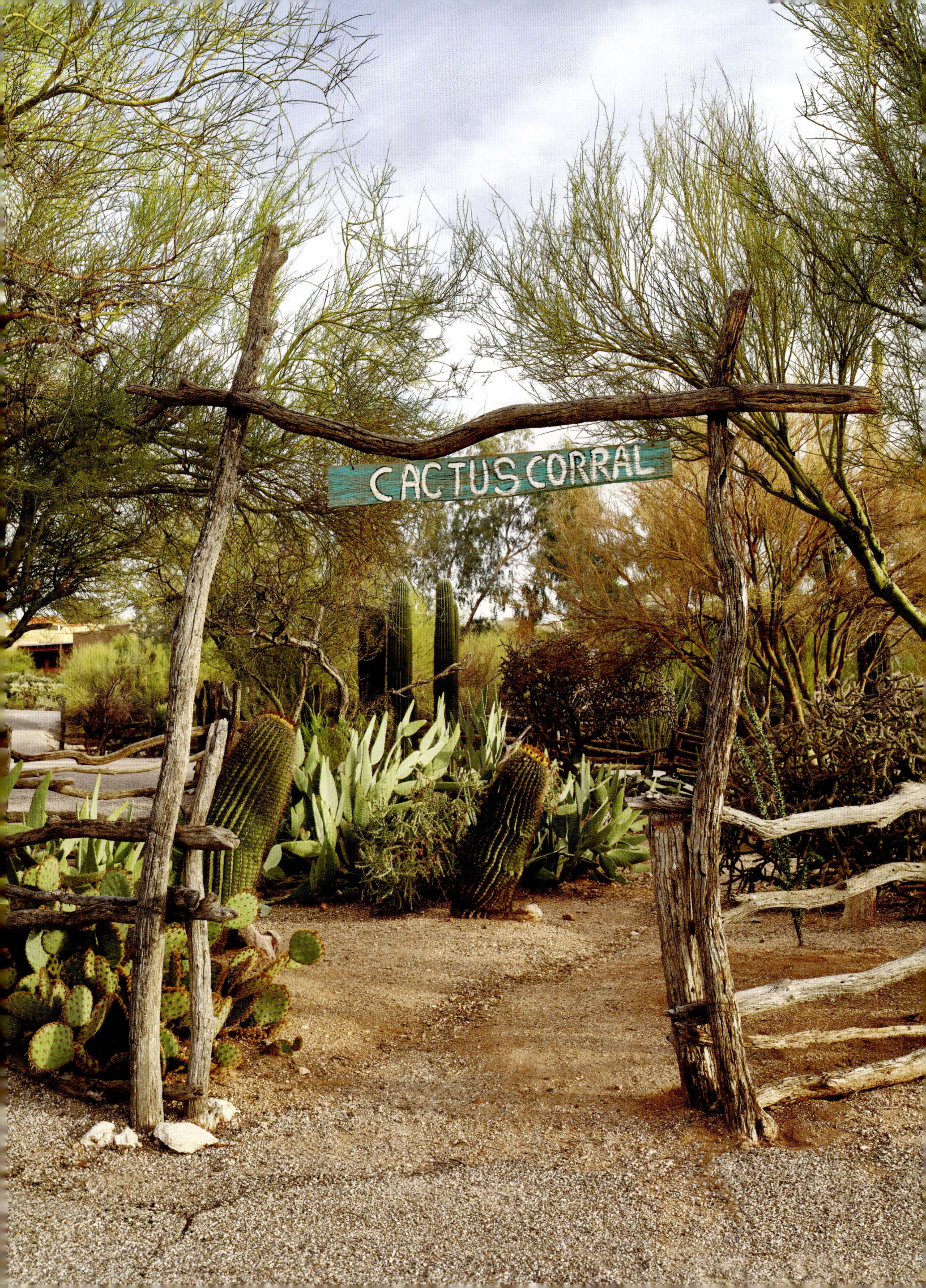
CACTUS CORRAL

Opposite: The DeGrazia Gallery in Tucson's foothills, now a ten-acre national historic district, salutes the work of Ettore DeGrazia, a multifaceted Italian immigrant artist and sculptor. In its heyday in the 1960s and '70s, it drew hundreds of thousands of visitors annually. Below: Josias Joesler's architectural touches helped turn an elite Tucson preparatory school for girls into the fashionable Hacienda Del Sol guest ranch in the 1940s. It became a favored destination for Hollywood nobility, including Clark Gable and John Wayne, who filmed several Westerns in the region. Overleaf: Nearby at the Old Tucson Studios theme park, built in 1939 for the movie *Arizona*, things get a good bit more animated—even explosive.

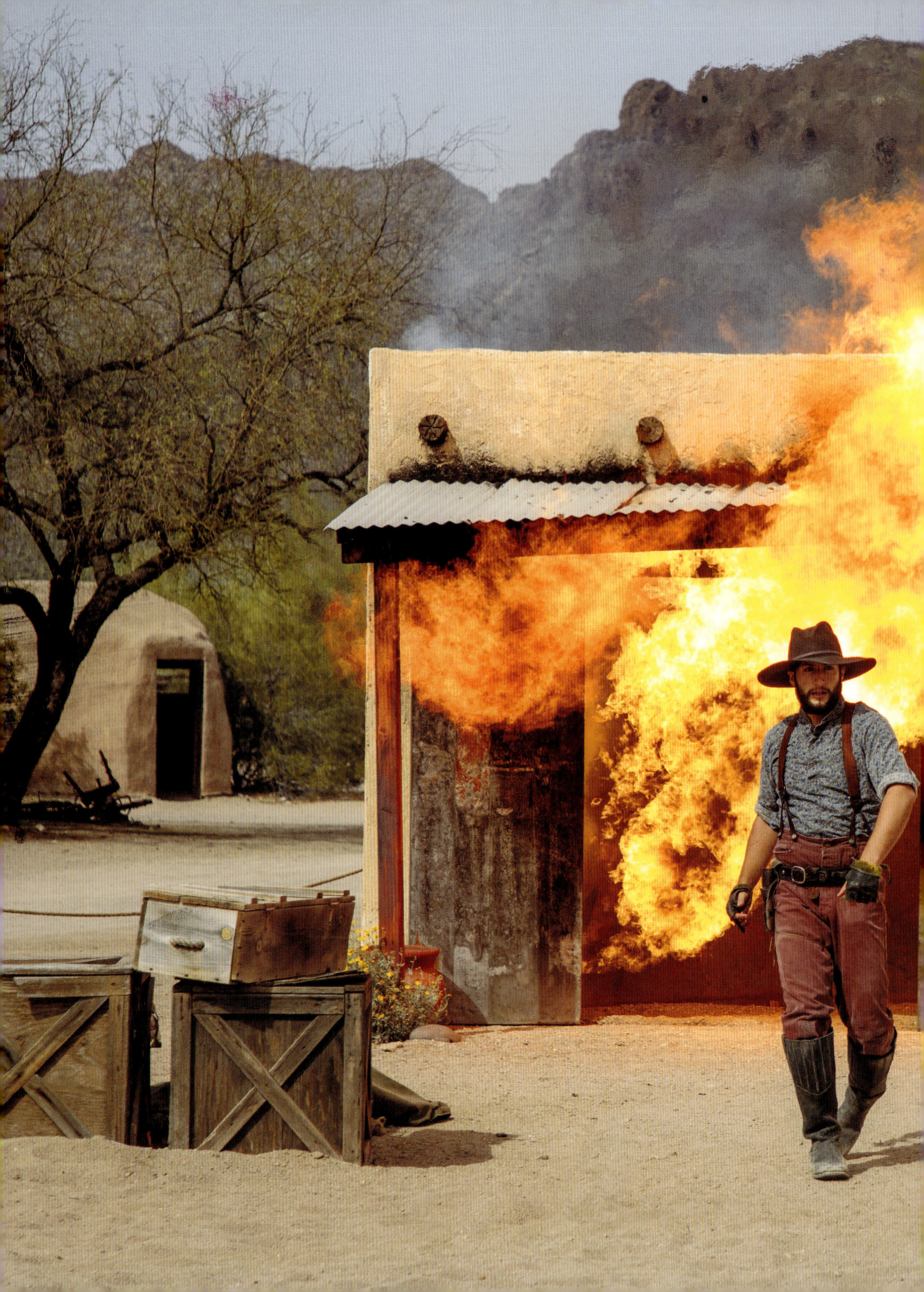

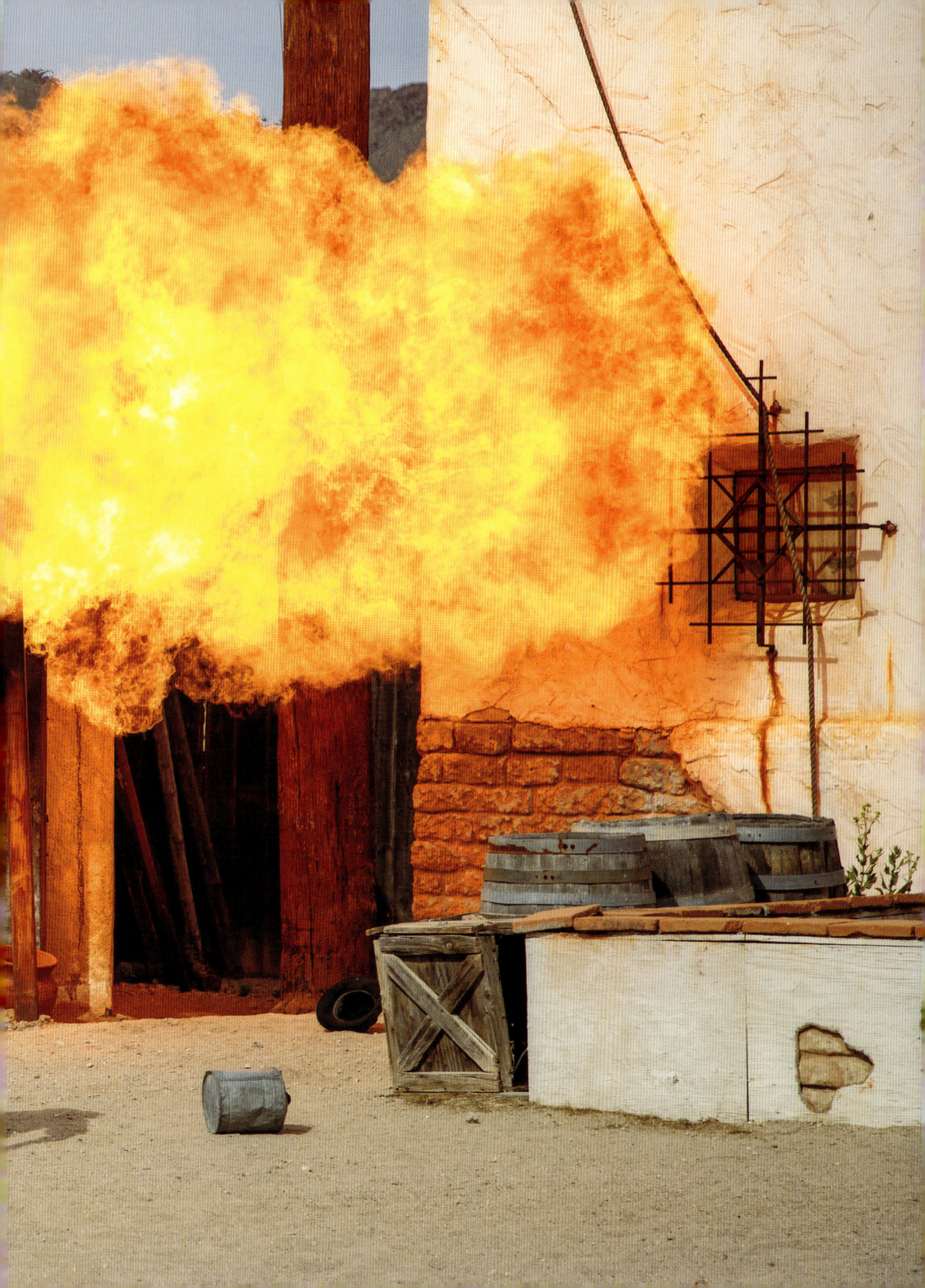

Above: This mosaic is part of the Ben's Bells Project, which Jeannette Maré founded in Tucson to spread kindness through bells and art after her two-year-old son, Ben, died. Right: Part of the city's pedestrian Rattlesnake Bridge, designed in 2002 by Simon Donovan, mimics the serpents that sidewind throughout the sun-drenched region. Opposite: After Tucson boomed as a tourist destination, its boulevards came alive with dazzling neon signs. Dirk Arnold's eye-catching welcome sign is relatively new. It was installed in 2010.

186 · *Tucson*

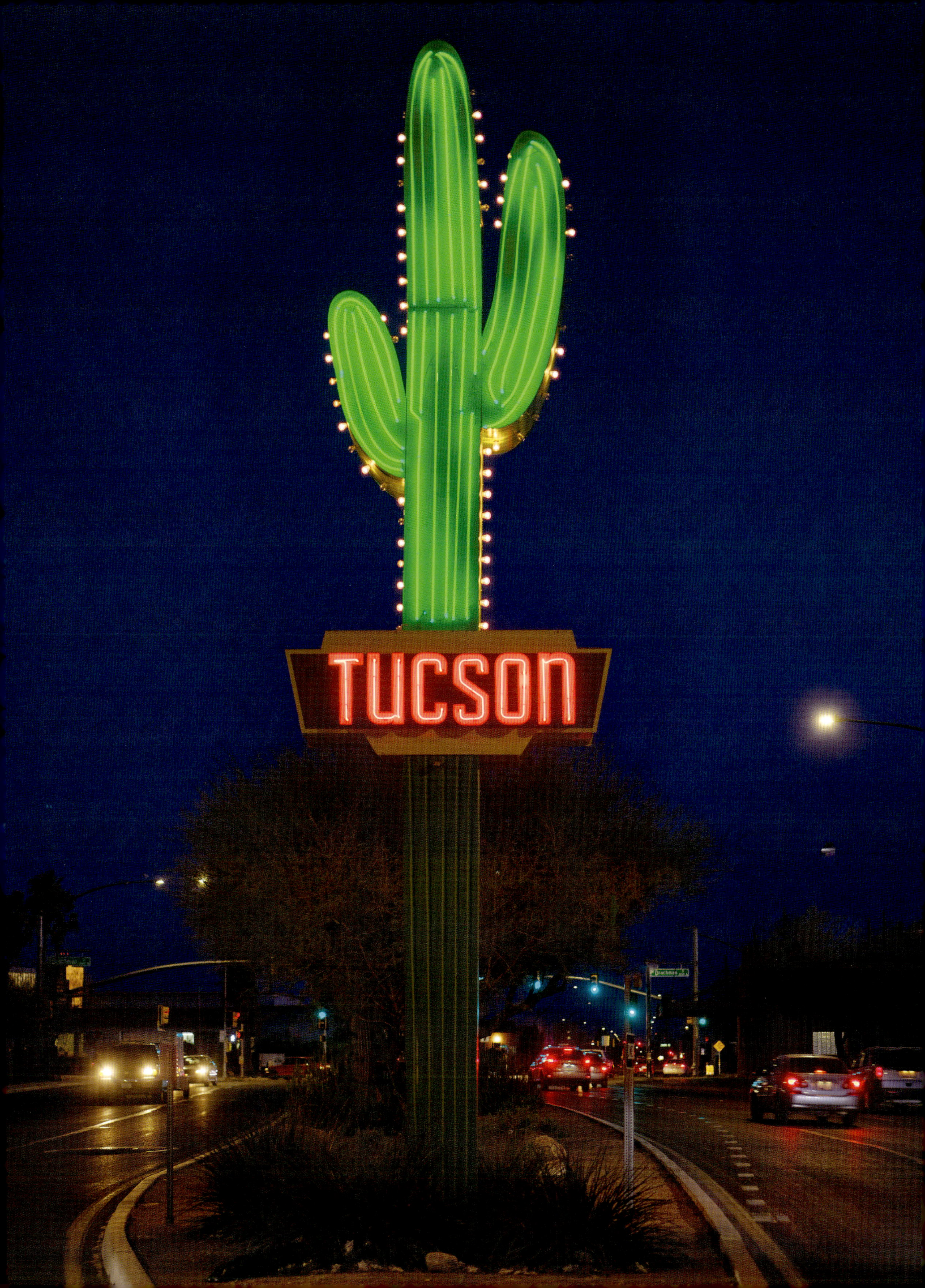
TUCSON

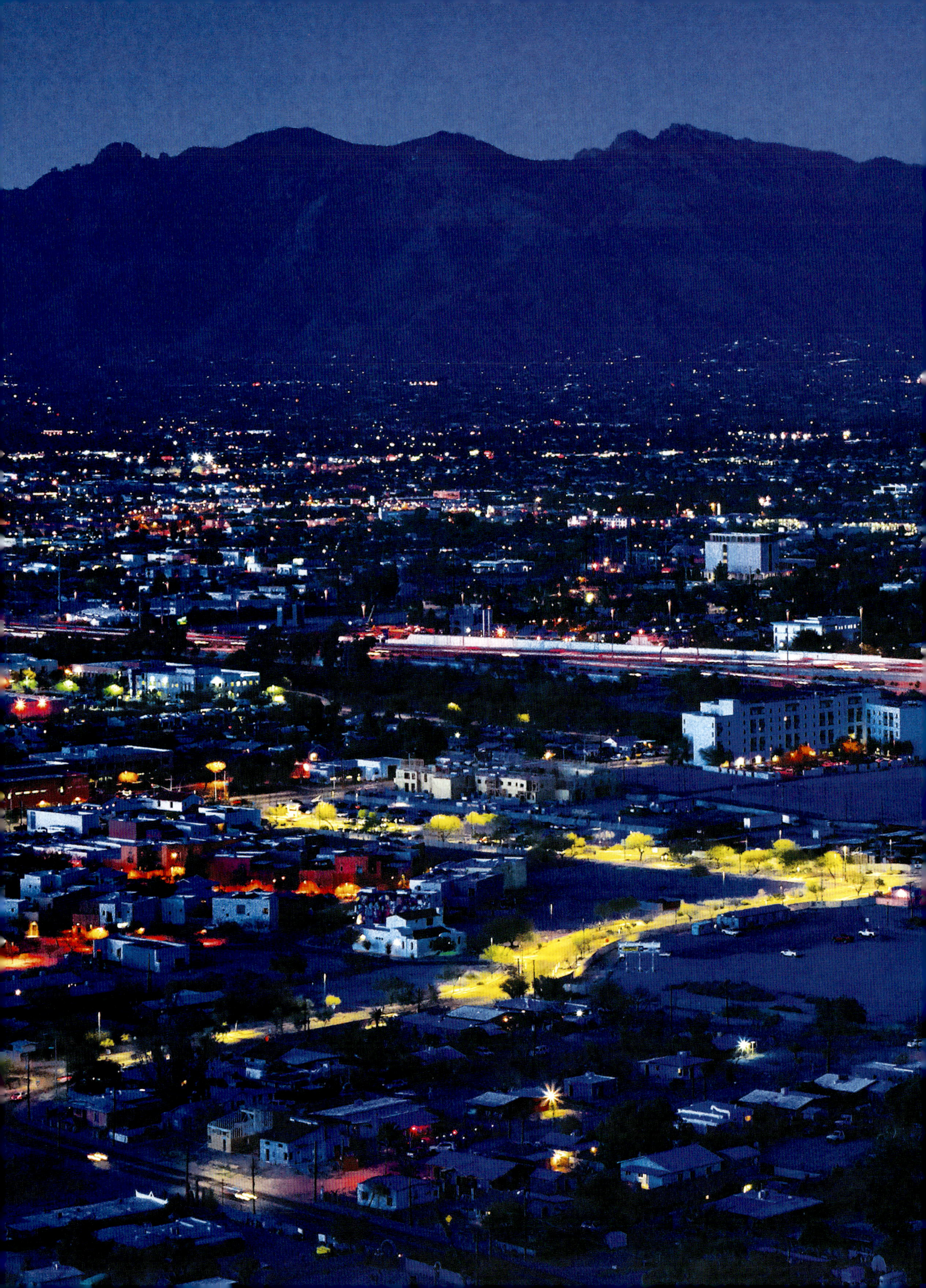

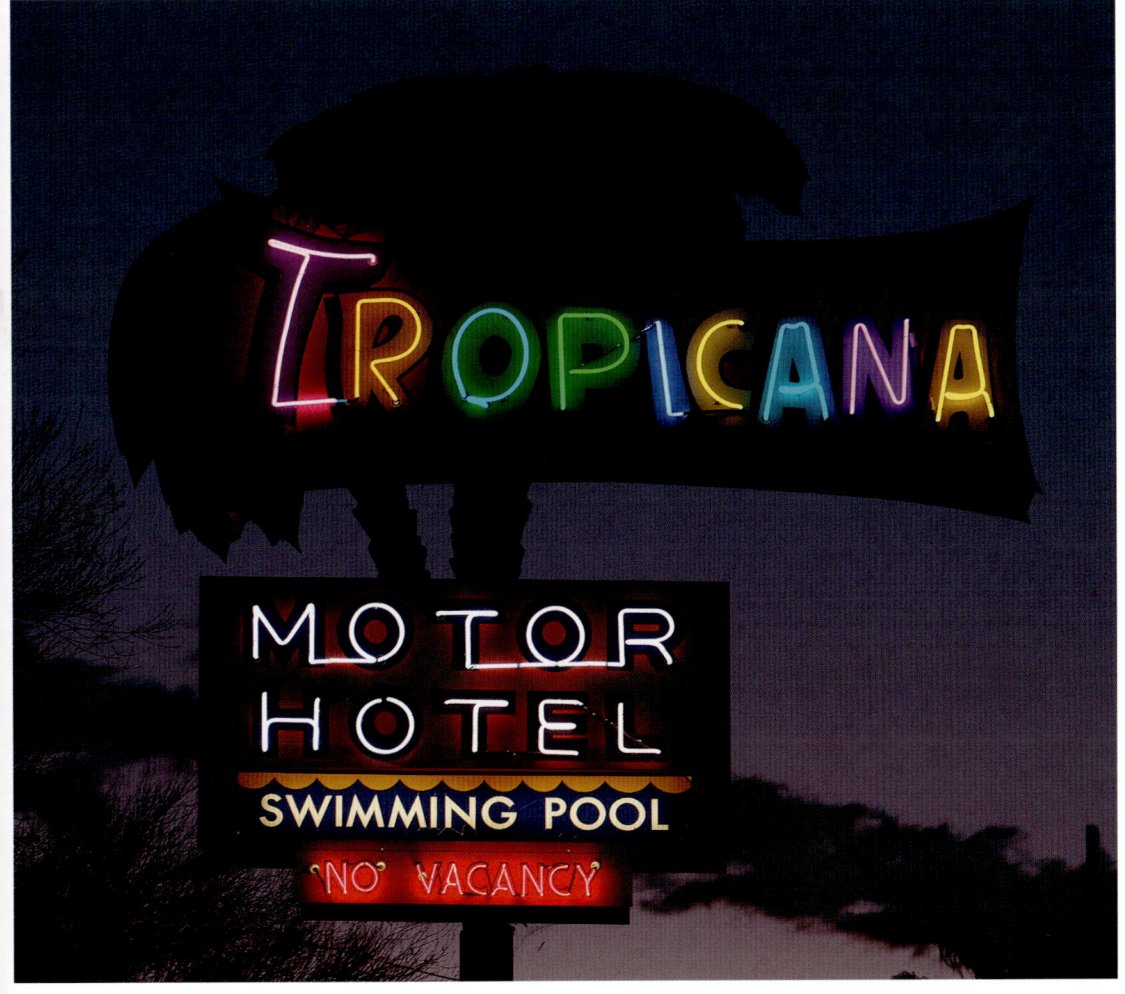

Opposite: The lights of Tucson enliven what was once the dark and sleepy Santa Cruz River floodplain. Left: Although many of the city's early tourist courts and visitor attractions have tattered or disappeared, more and more glittering signs that touted them have been saved and relighted. Some locals have even taken to calling Tucson the Neon Pueblo.

Tucson · 189

Right: The domed Pima County Courthouse in Tucson was designed by Roy Place in 1928 in the Mission Revival style. Below: The "ground" floor of Old Main, the 1891 signature building on the University of Arizona's main campus, was deliberately sunk six feet below the surface so the cool earth would minimize the effects of Tucson's hot summers. Opposite: Initial work on Tucson's 1897 St. Augustine Cathedral accentuated Gothic details. Eventually the church exterior was completed in a restrained baroque style drawing on Mexican influences and motifs featuring local vegetation.

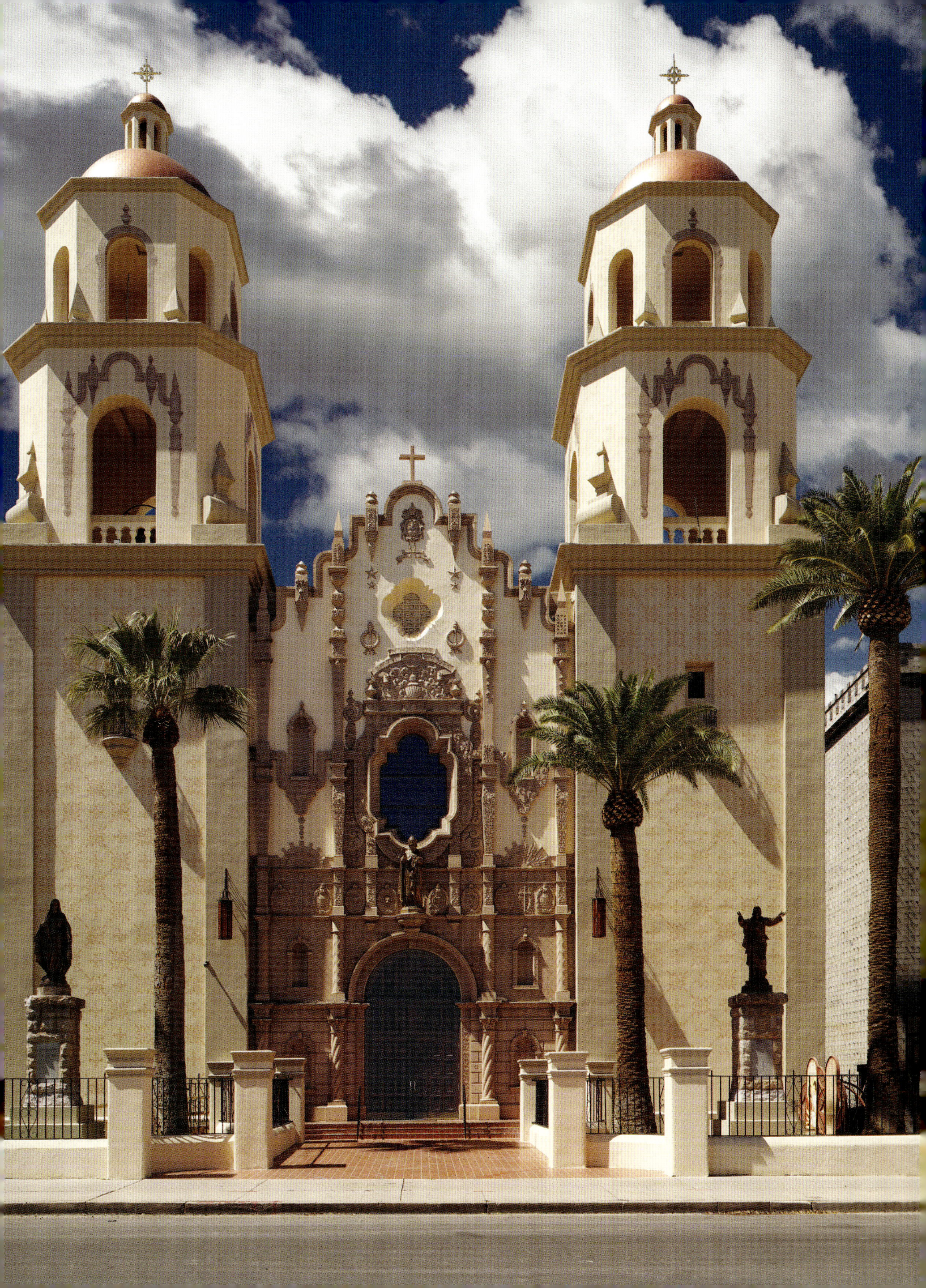

Isabella Greenway, a friend and bridesmaid of Eleanor Roosevelt, built Tucson's Arizona Inn in 1930 and went on to become Arizona's first female representative in the U.S. Congress. The Spanish Colonial Revival–style hotel, which remains in the Greenway family, was designed by Merritt Starkweather. Pink-stucco buildings in the fourteen-acre complex incorporate blue accents. The gardens, within still more walls of pink, were the work of James Oliphant. Overleaf: Antique furnishings, such as those found in the hotel's library, help fulfill Greenway's promise of privacy and serenity in the sun.

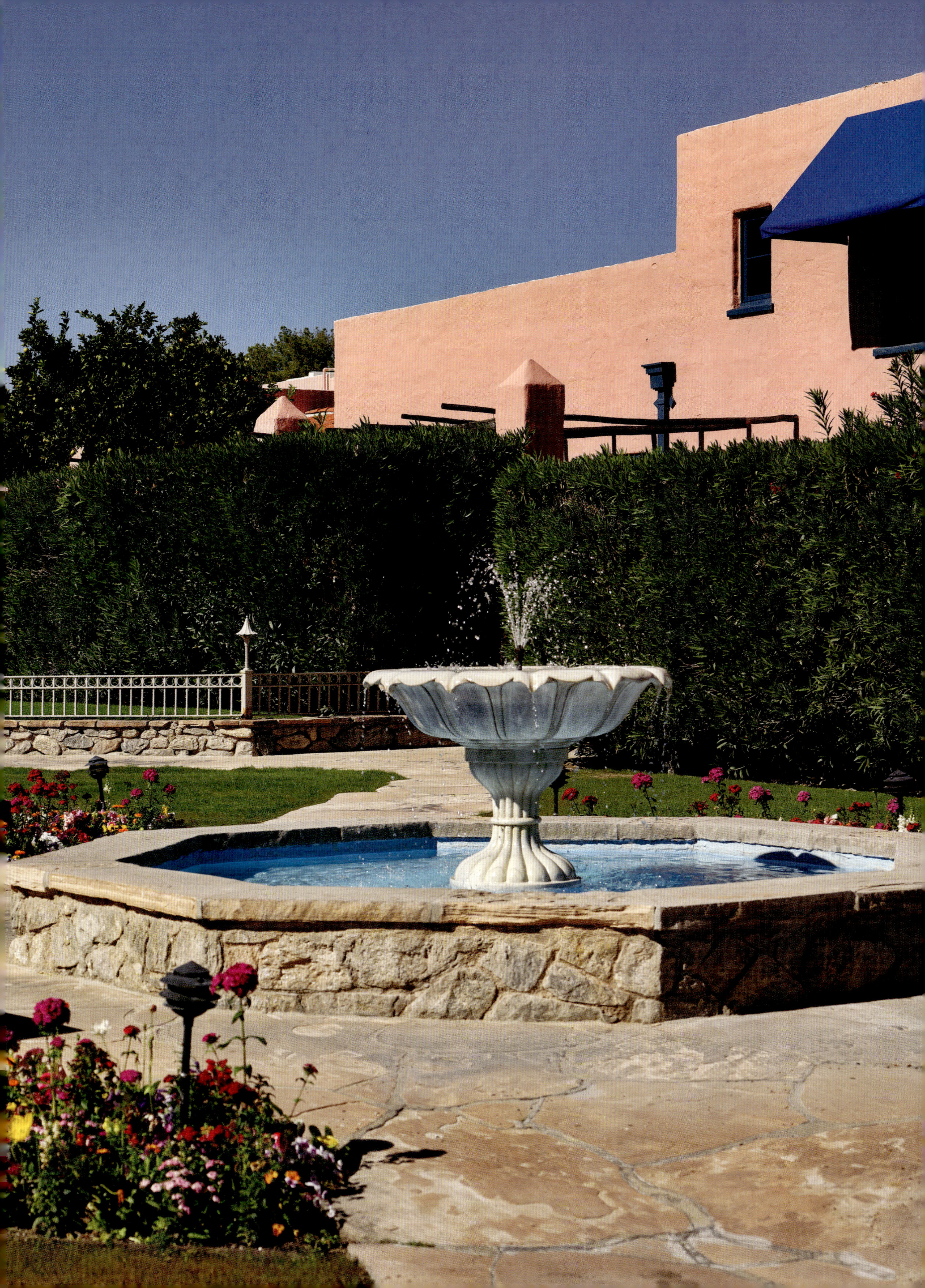

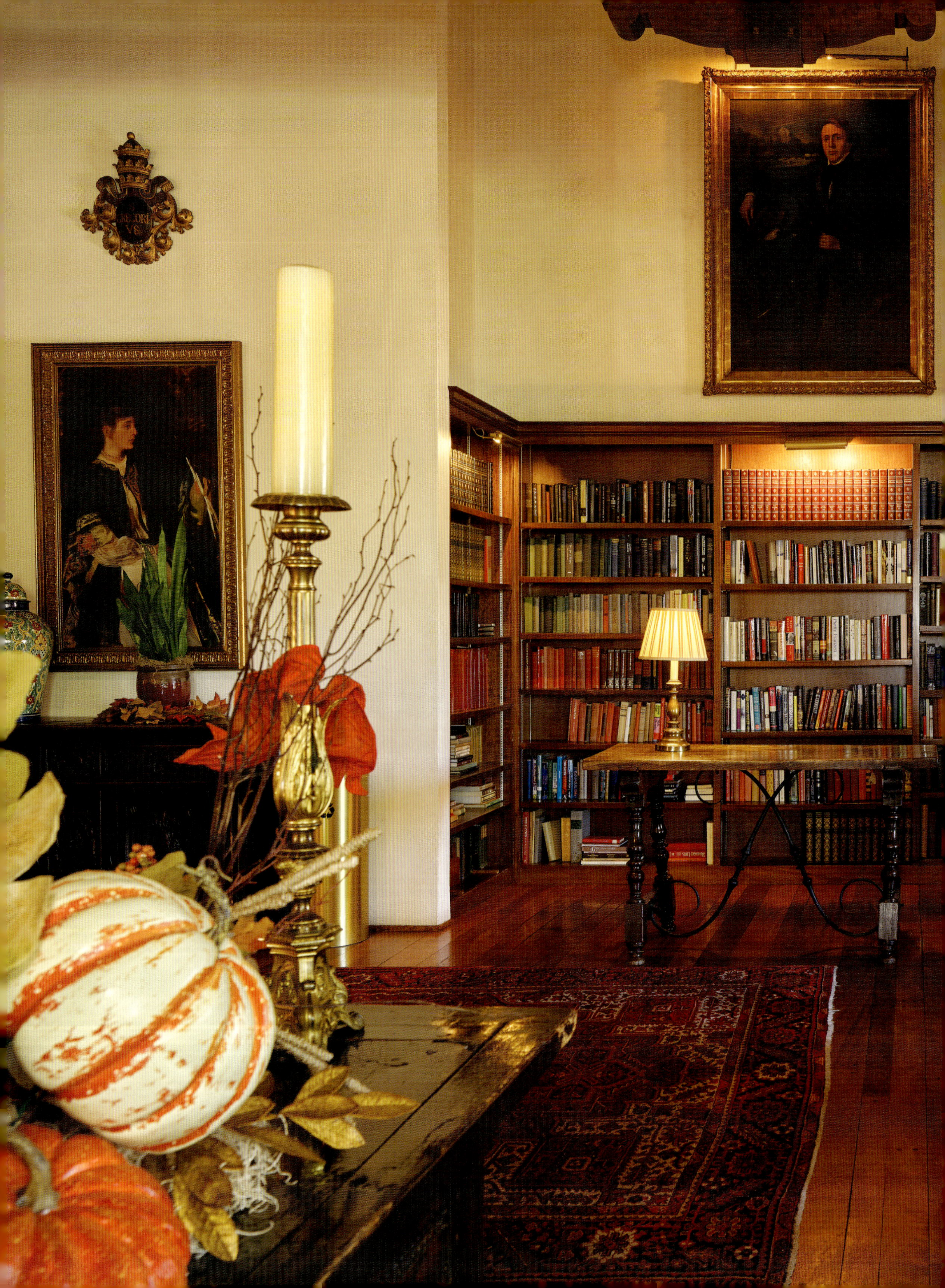

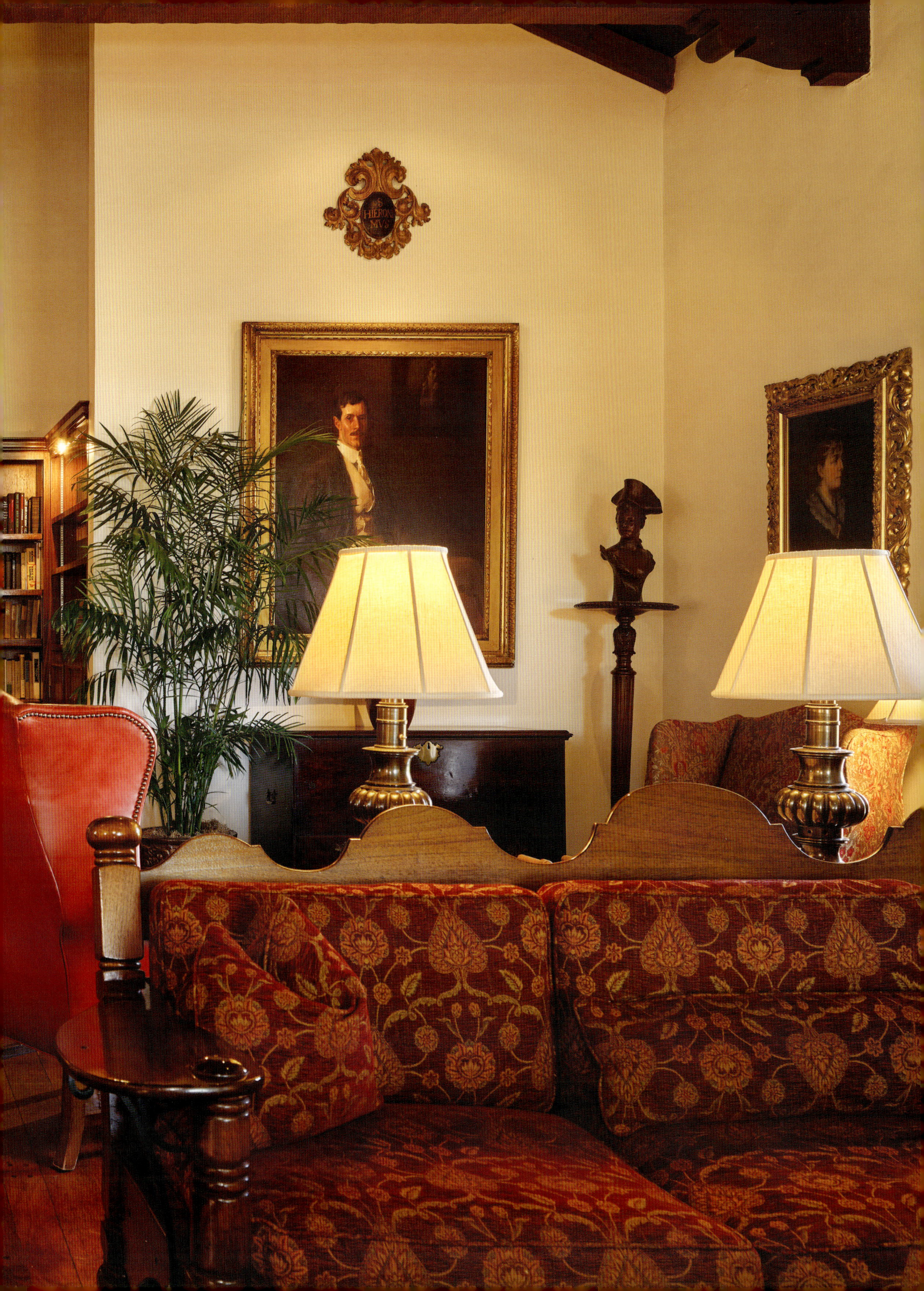

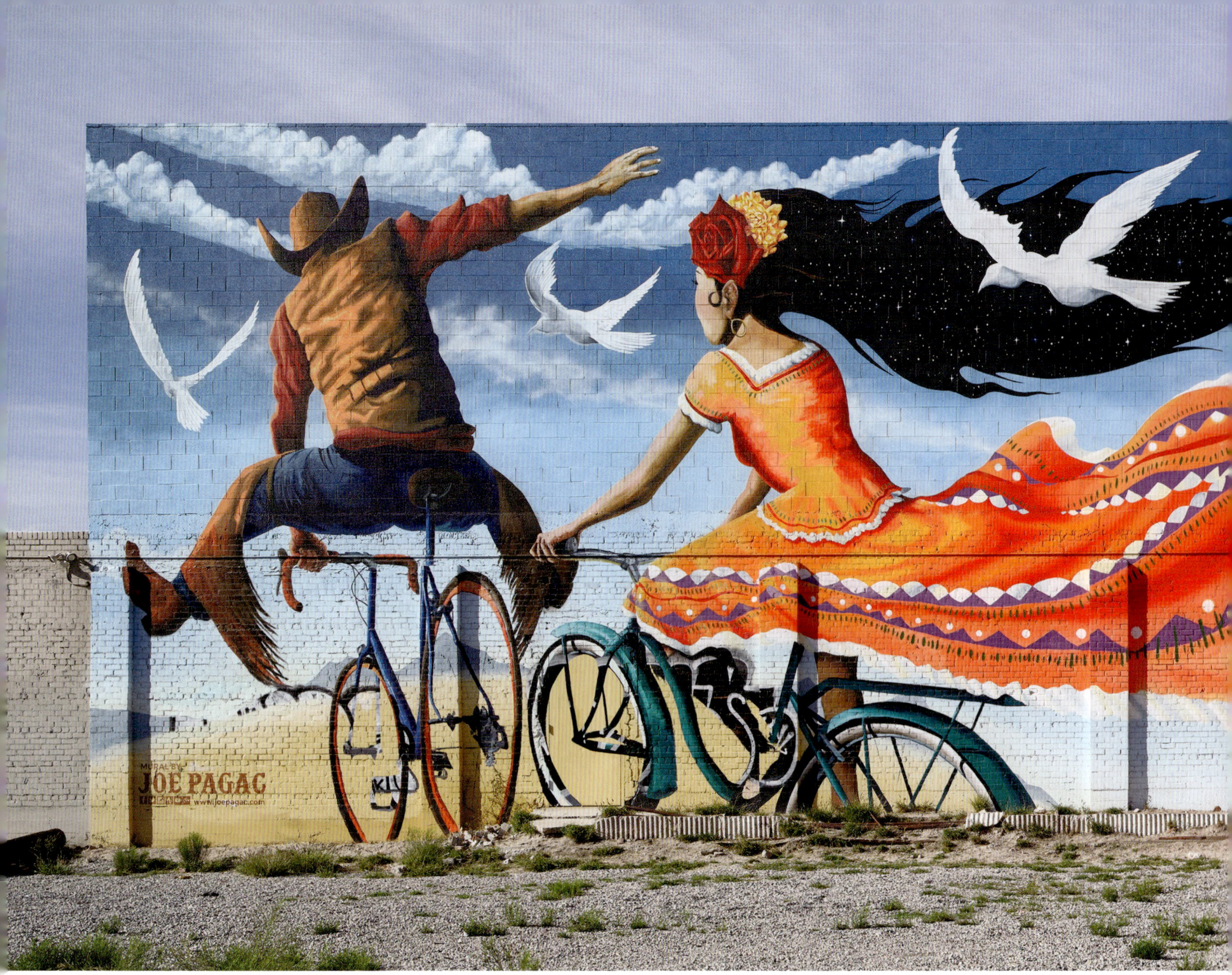
JOE PAGAC

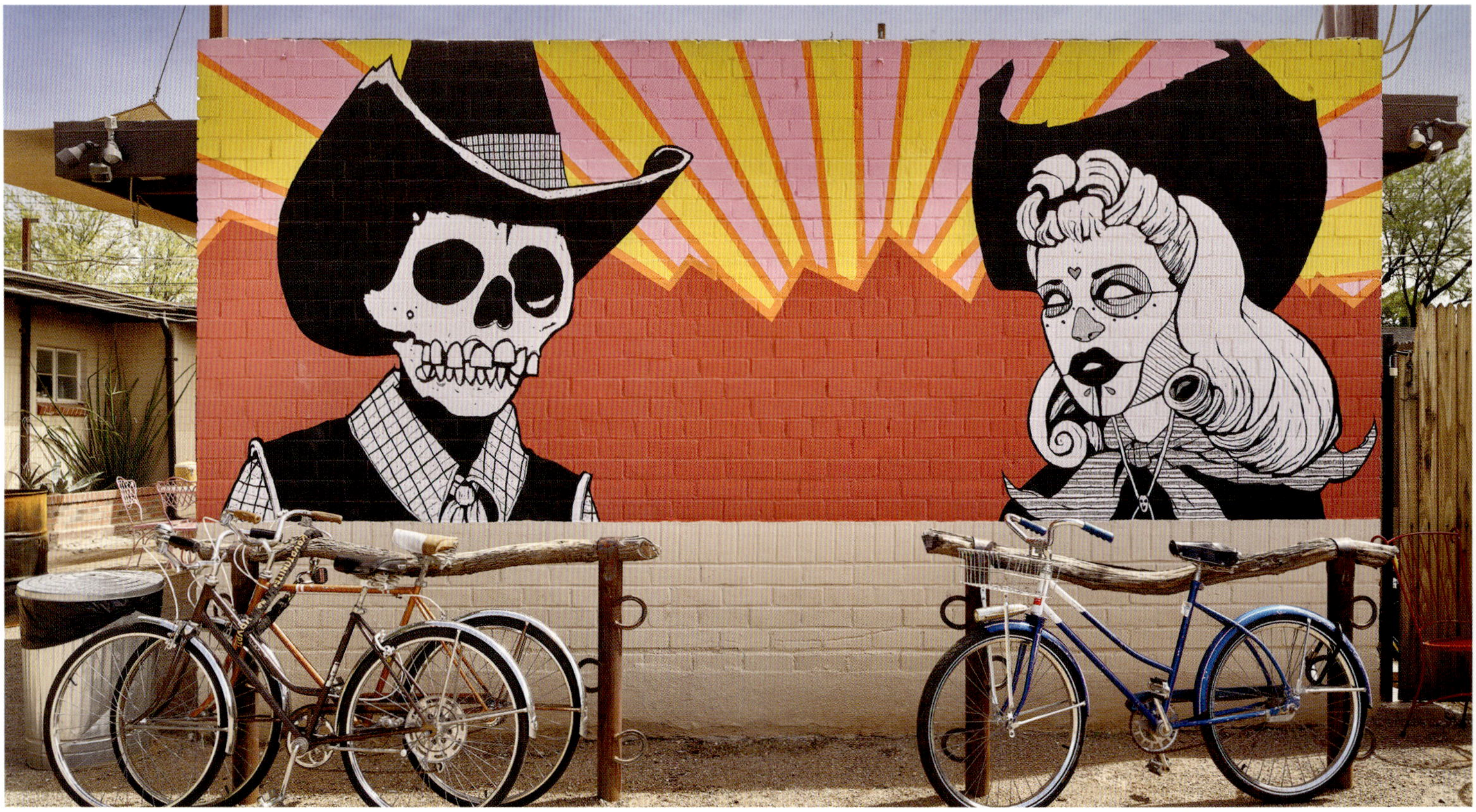

Above: Much of Tucson evokes a comfortable, even subdued ambience. And then there are its in-your-face murals. Joe Pagac's *Epic Rides*, for instance, somehow imagines a man, a woman, a javelina, a tortoise, and a jackalope on a desert bike ride. Opposite: Danny Martin drew this emaciated cowpuncher couple on a wall of the Clifton Hotel in the Barrio Viejo. Left: A flamboyant mural—as red as a vermilion flycatcher—identified the Flycatcher music club on Fourth Avenue before it closed in 2018. Overleaf: Pagac is back with his vivid conception of an anthropomorphic saguaro feeding a hovering hummingbird. Sort of.

Tucson · 197

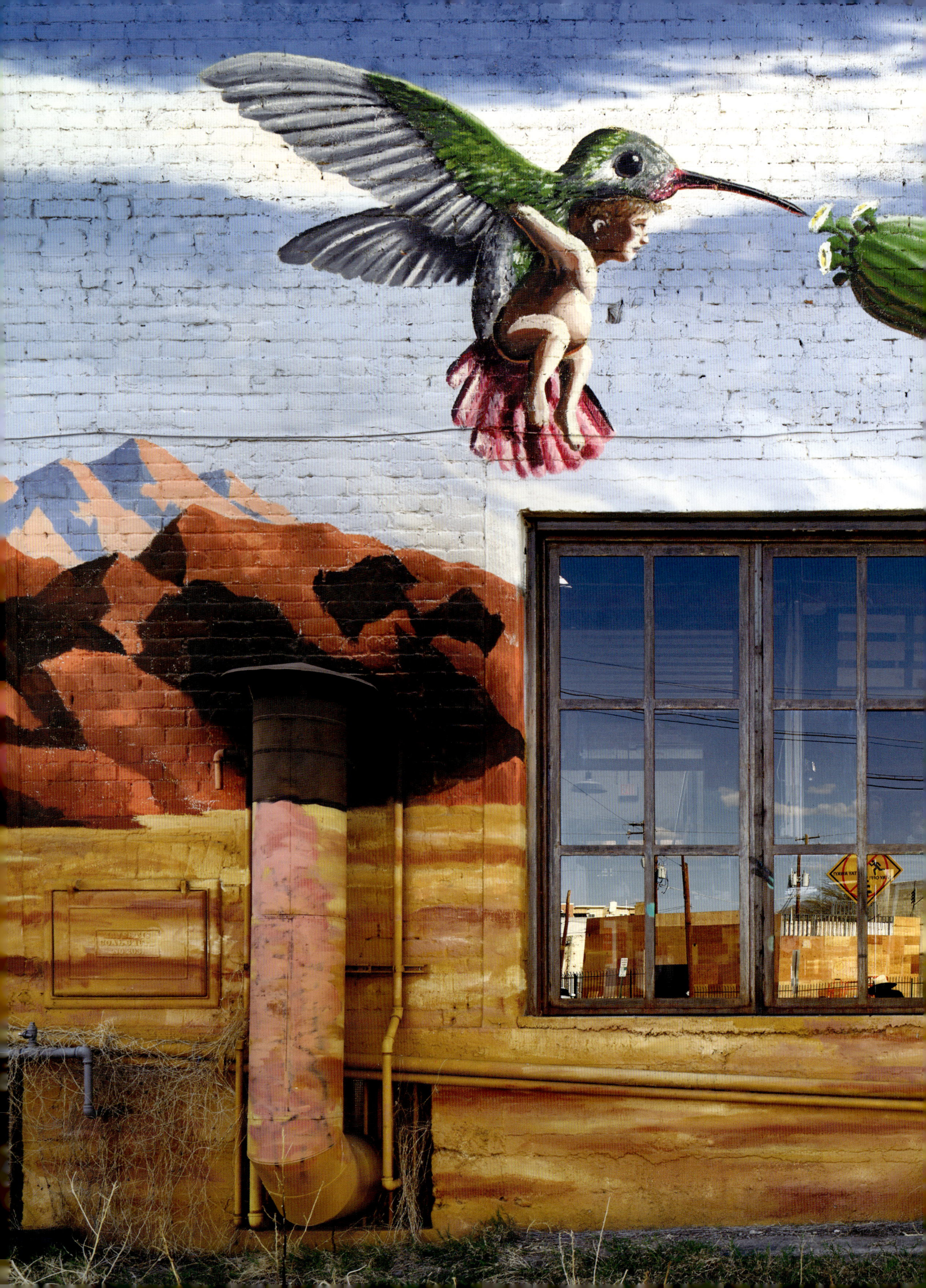

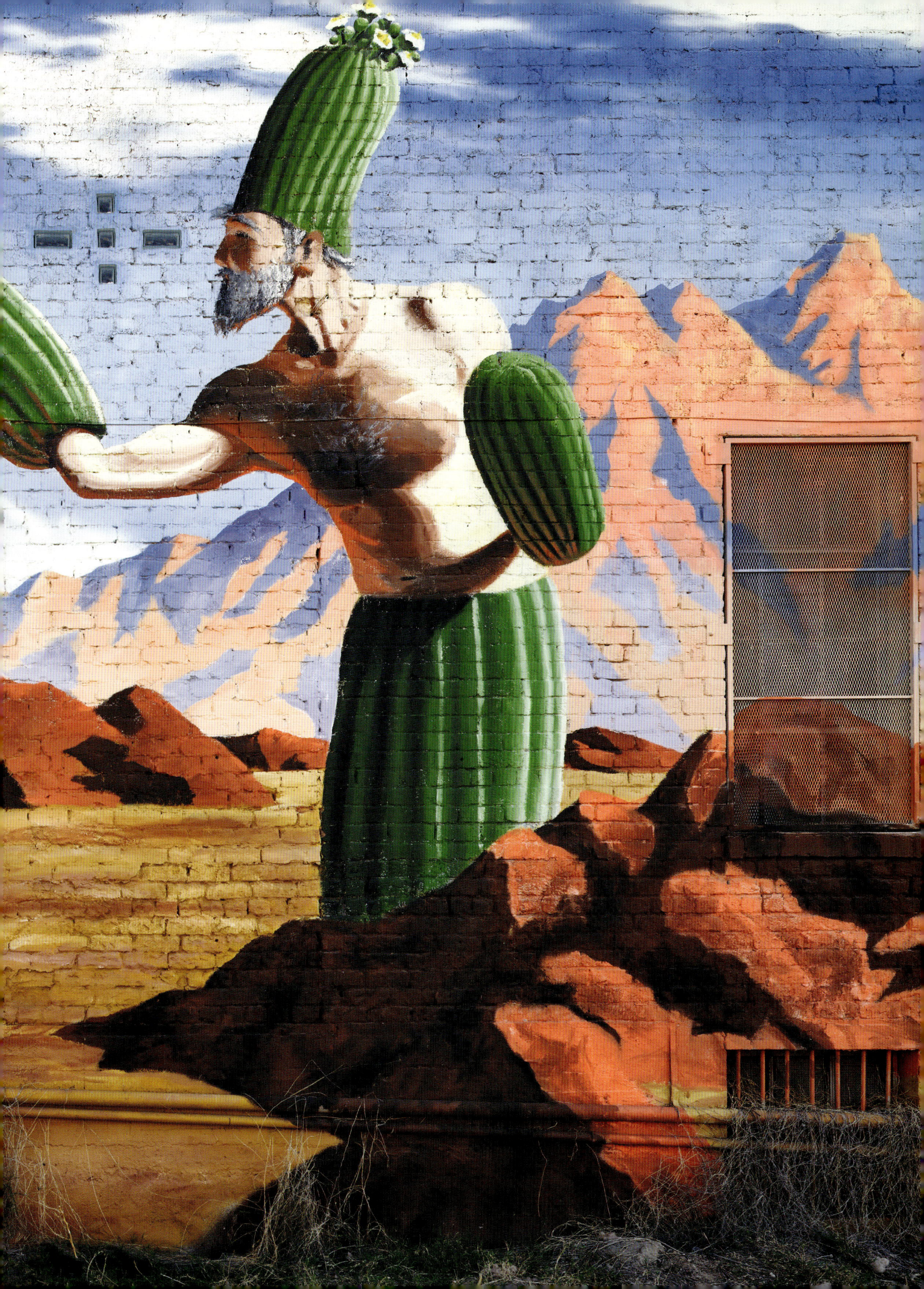

SWIMMING POOL
PICCARRETA DAVIS
PUEBLO HOTEL and APARTMENTS
VACANCY
HOTEL PARKING

Opposite: This evocative Diving Girl sign adorns the former Pueblo Hotel and Apartments, a World War II incarnation of the renowned southwestern architect Henry C. Trost's 1903 Willard Hotel. Abandoned in 1984, then used for law offices and such, it now houses a cosmetology school and salon. Above: Tucson's historic Hotel Congress is known not as much for its 1918 period decor as it is for being the place where the notorious bank robber John Dillinger was captured in January 1934. His end came later that year in Chicago.

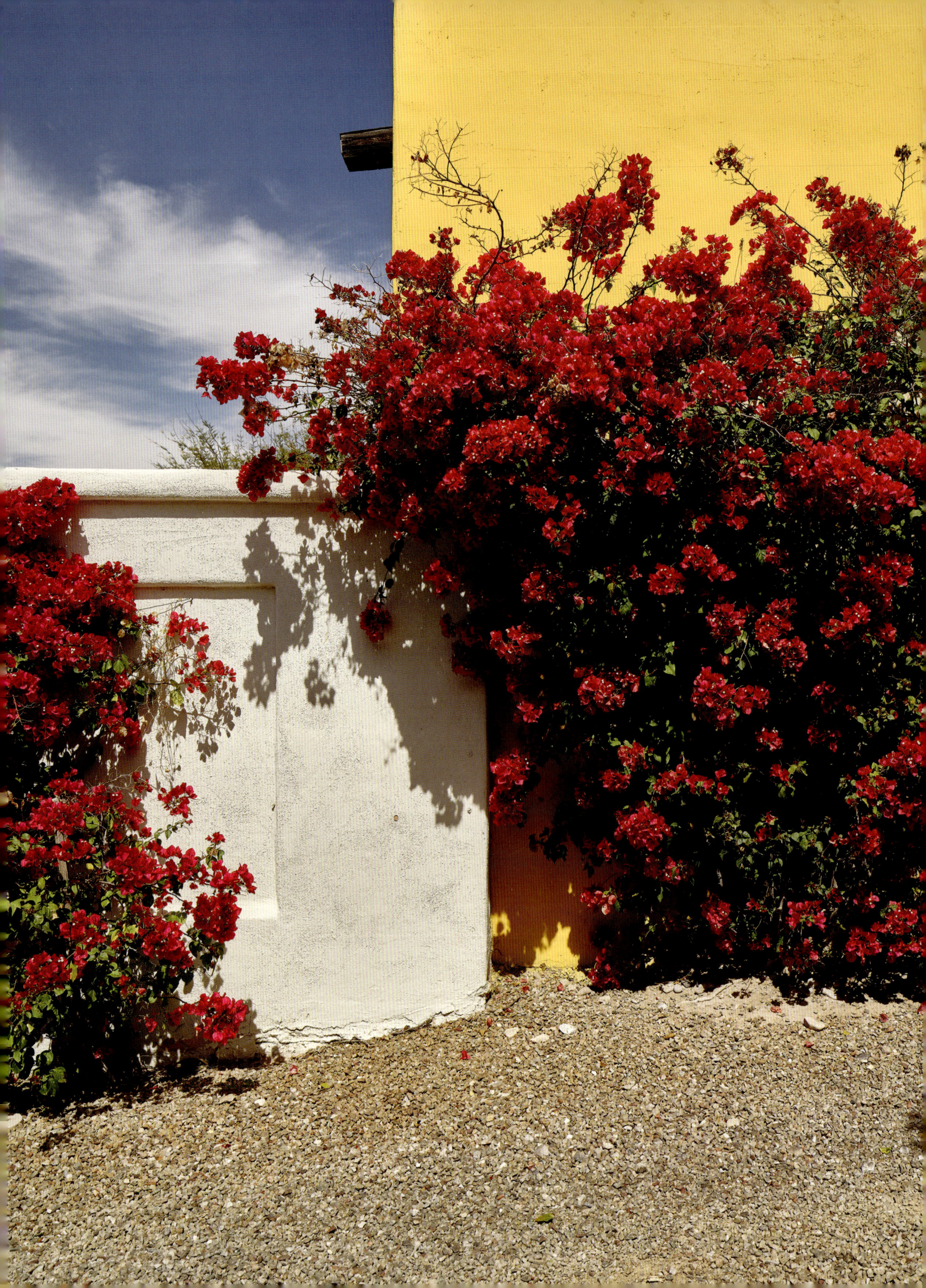

Left: Bougainvilleas explode with color outside this Tucson home in the Barrio Viejo. Below: An Ernest Hemingway lookalike, Vic Borg, is the longtime owner of the Stewart Boot Company, which has been making Western footwear of everything from mule hide to ostrich skin since the 1940s in South Tucson. Overleaf: This enormous "boneyard" of nearly forty-four hundred airplanes—the world's largest such aircraft final resting place—occupies twenty-six hundred acres of Davis-Monthan Air Force Base.

Tucson · 203

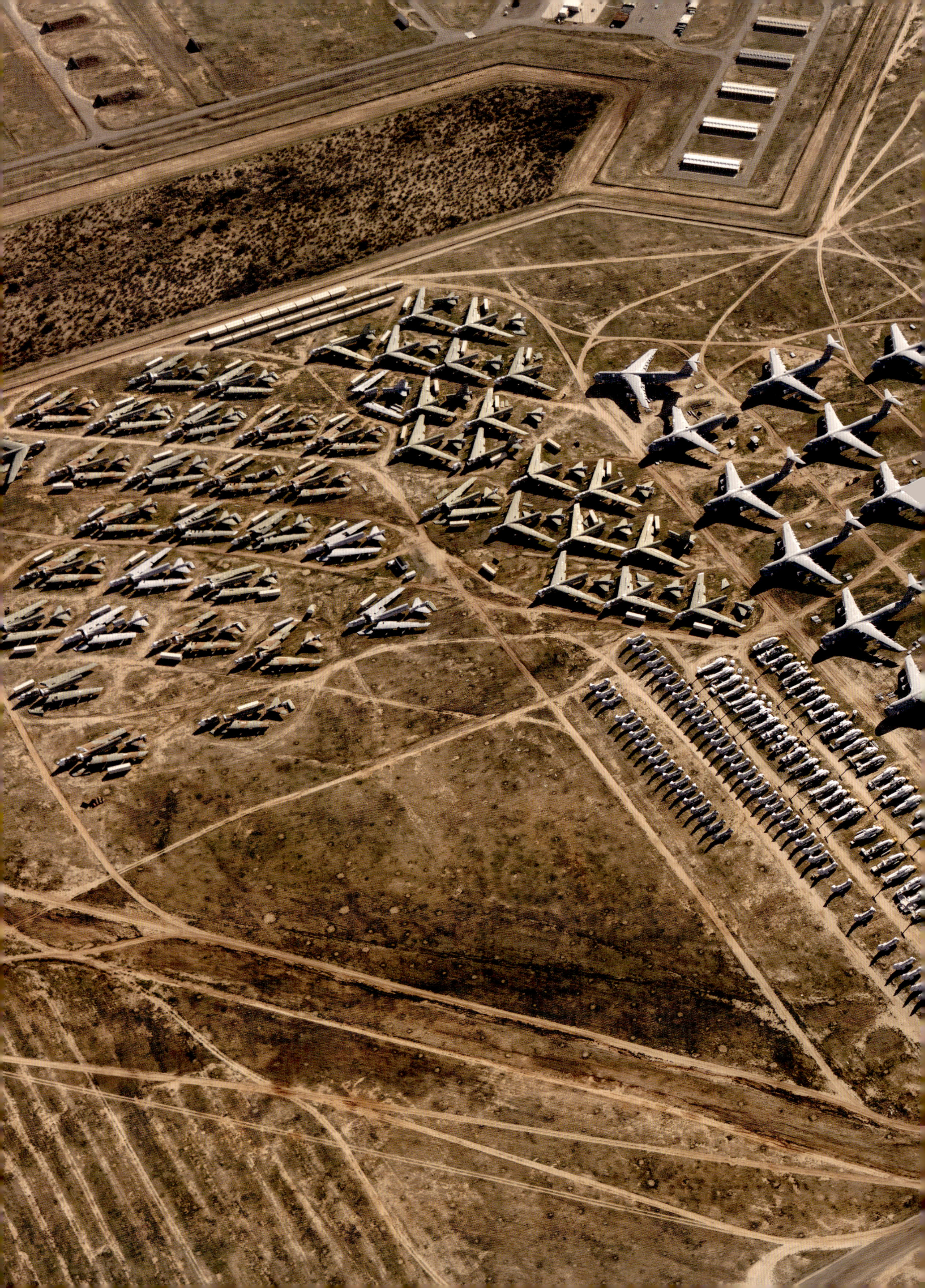

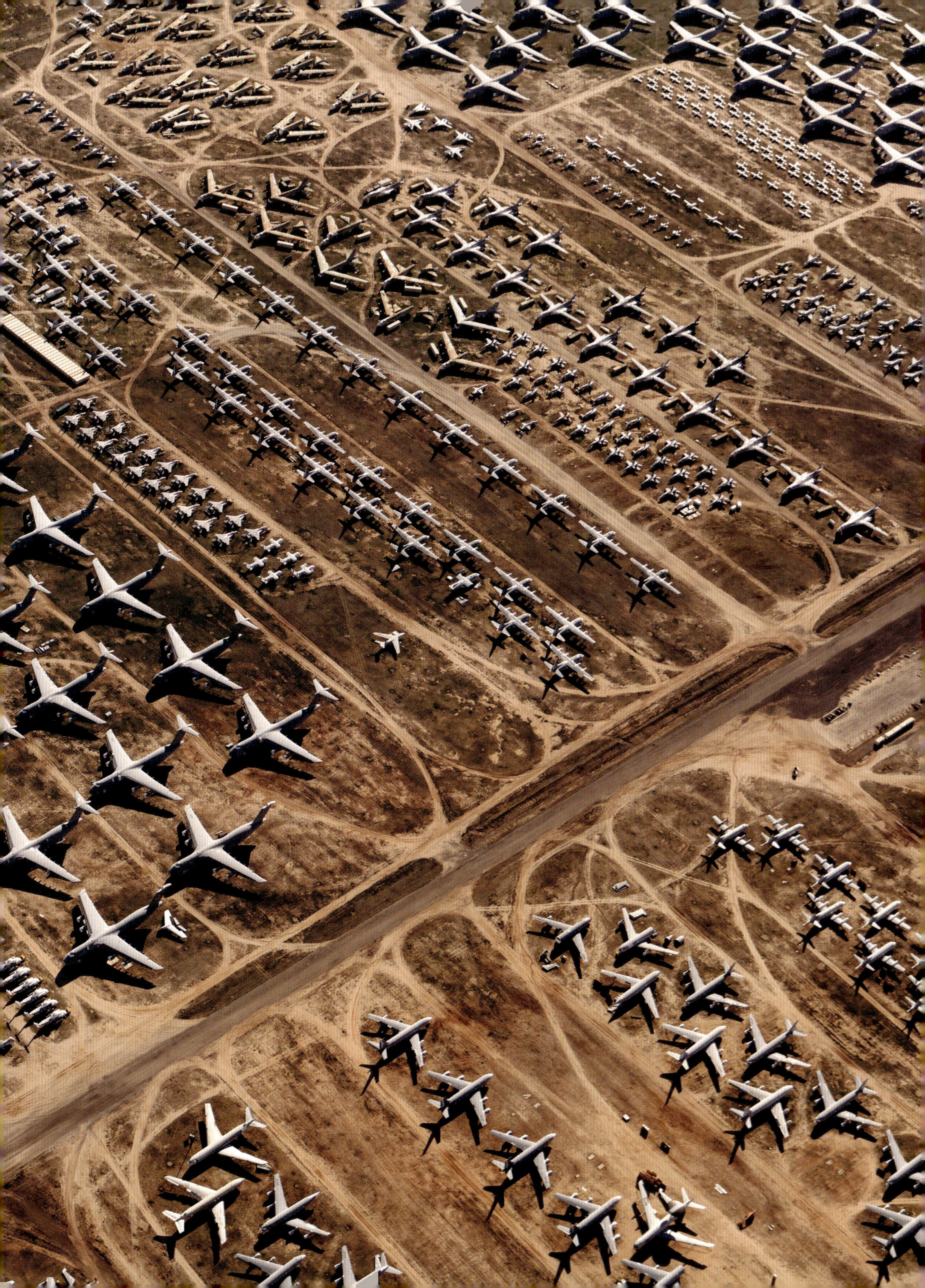

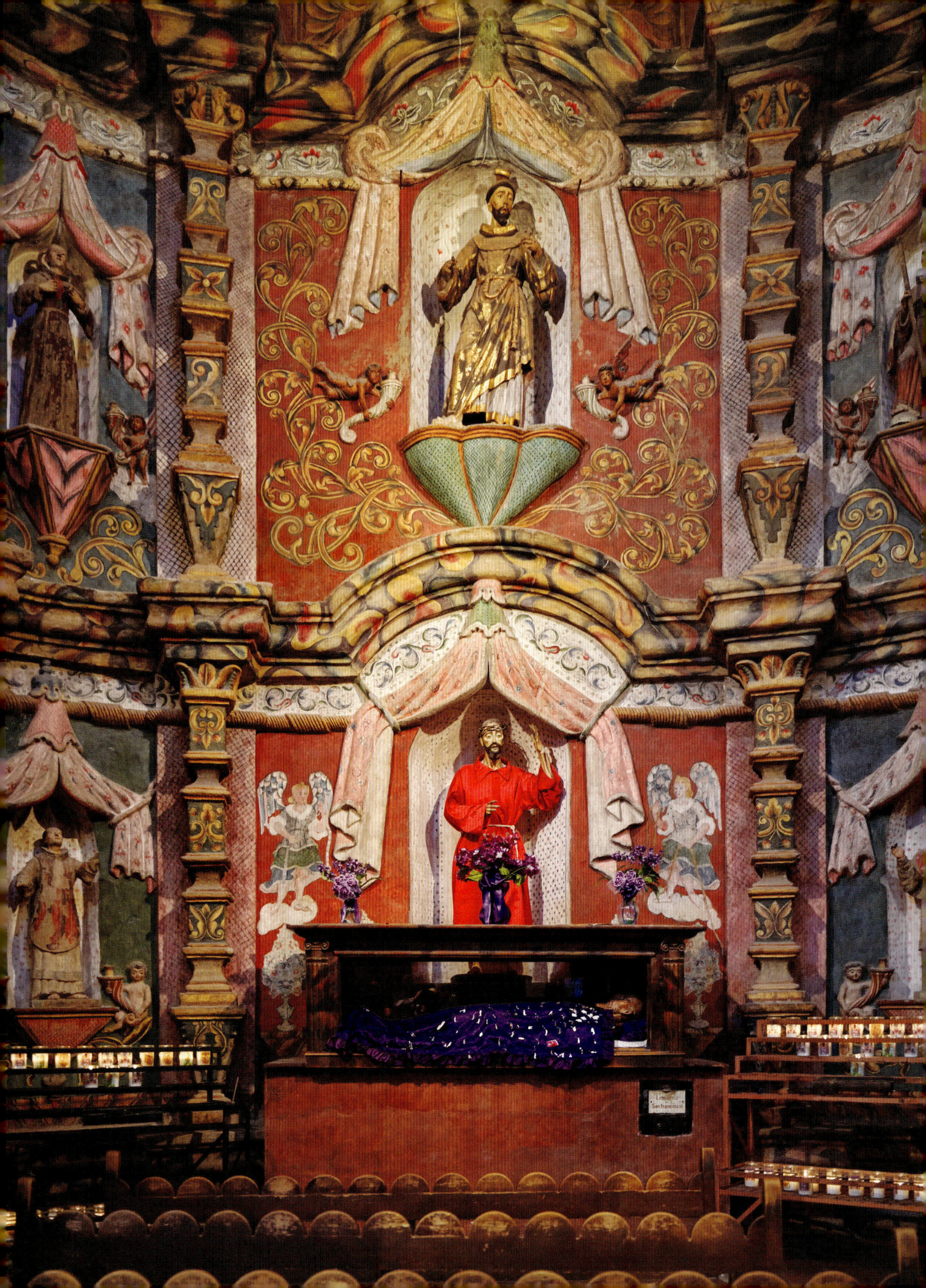
San Francisco

Now in its third century, the Mission San Xavier del Bac has survived earthquake, lightning, and water damage; witnessed the arrival, departure, and return of the Franciscans; and fallen under Spanish, Mexican, and American governance. The church, a notable example of Spanish colonial architecture, was built with local labor and completed in 1797. It is situated on the San Xavier Reservation south of Tucson, where it is part of the Tohono O'odham Nation.

Below: In the small settlement of Tumacacori, the remains of La Misión San José, which was never completed, date to 1828. The mission and its immediate surroundings are now a national historical park. Opposite: This undulating iron wall at the Morley Gate Border Station in Nogales, across from the larger Mexican city of the same name, has long been in place. According to some estimates, as many as ten thousand people a day enter the United States at this busy crossing.

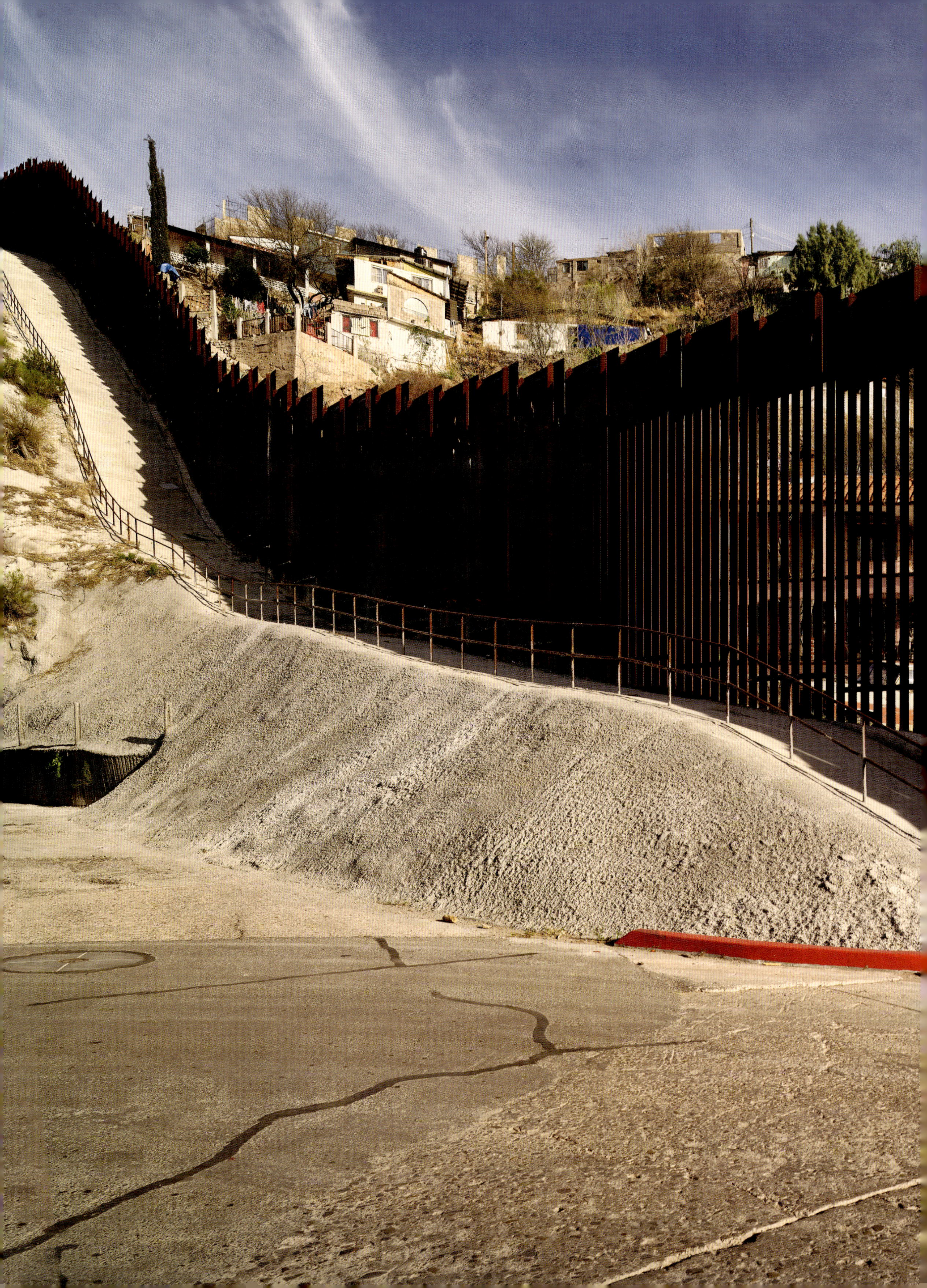

SANTA CRUZ COUNTY
HISTORIC
1904 COURTHOUSE
21 E. COURT STREET
MANUEL RUIZ
ROBERT DAMON
JOHN MAYNARD
MUSEUM

Both of these images capture the historic Santa Cruz County Courthouse in Nogales. One is the real thing, which towers on a hill high above downtown. The Trost and Rust firm's Classical Revival–style 1904 landmark features a frieze in the pediment depicting Justice. The other rendition is Isis Casorla and Alan Gonzalez's 2005 hands-across-the-border painting on the side of a simple stucco building blocks away. The sun rays of the Arizona state flag crown the top. The county borrowed its name (holy cross in Spanish) from the region's prominent river.

Nogales · 211

Above: The Avenue Hotel in Douglas, constructed in adjacent and architecturally diverse stages in 1901 and 1915 primarily as a place of rest for railroad workers, is now a bed-and-breakfast inn. Right: At the Gadsden Hotel, catty-corner across the street, the dramatic Italian-marble staircase is the showpiece. The 1907 five-story establishment was named after the Gadsden Purchase, an 1854 treaty negotiated by the American ambassador to Mexico James Gadsden, which added almost 192 million acres to the United States in what are now Arizona and New Mexico.

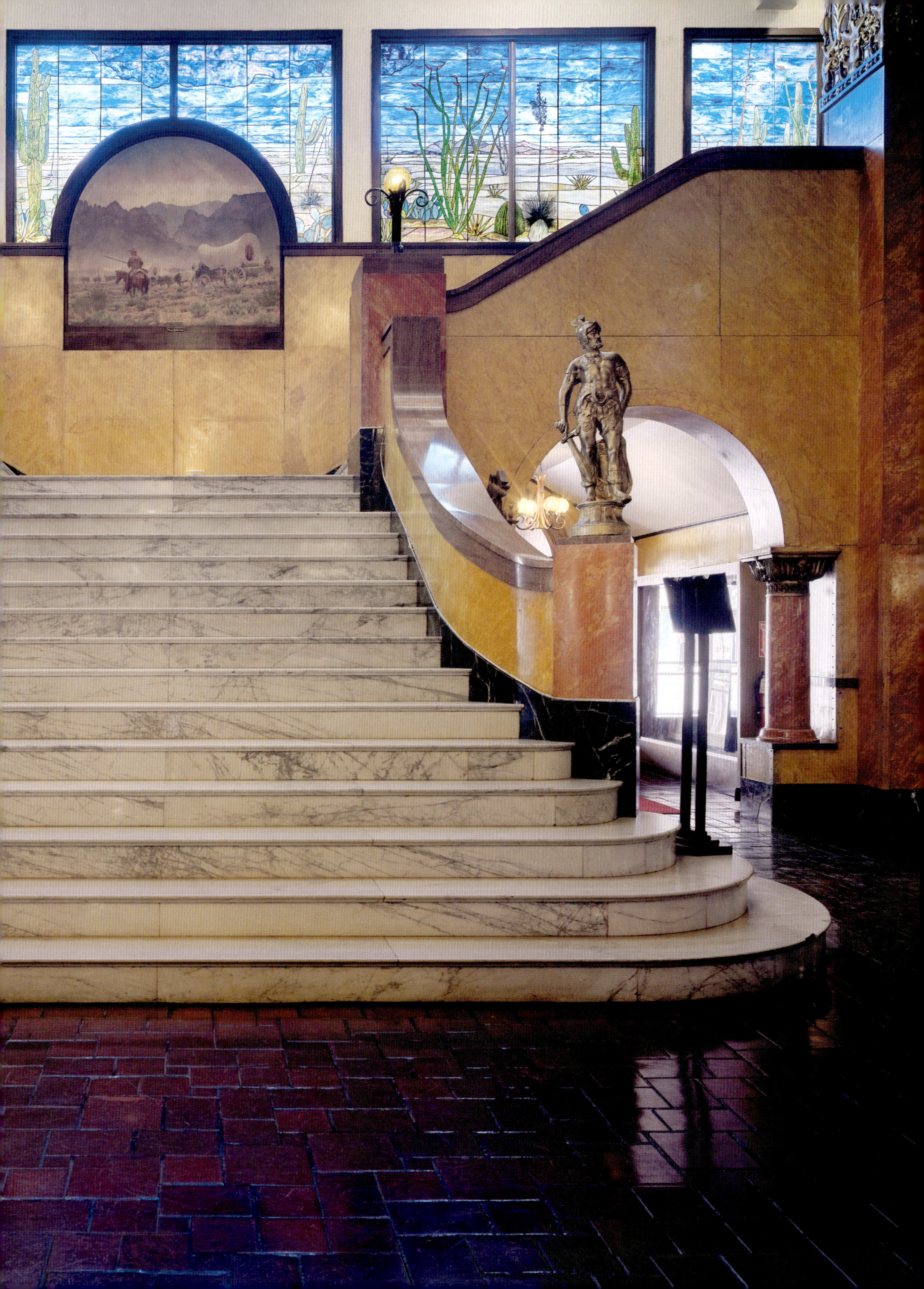

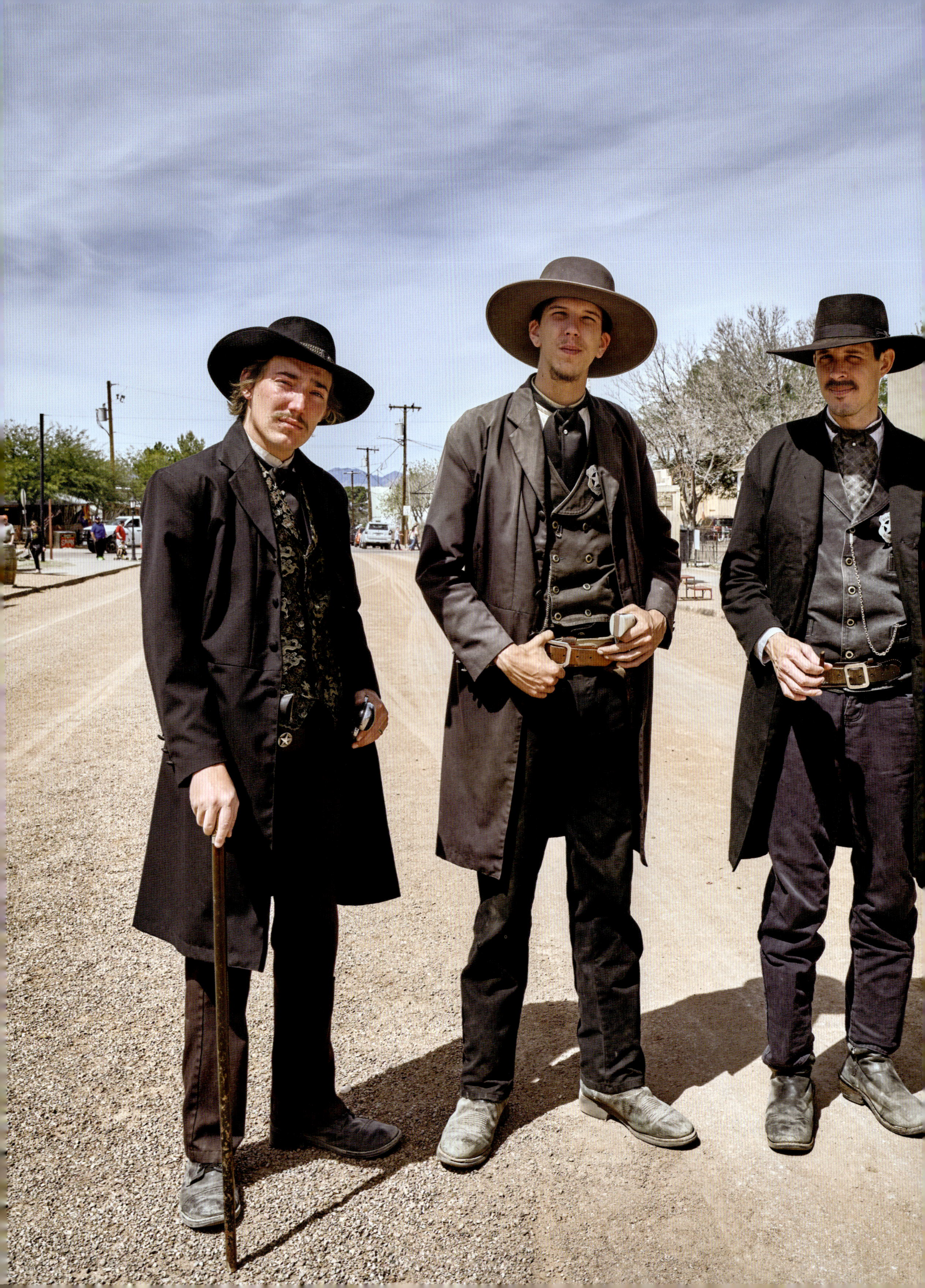

Left: At the O.K. Corral attraction in Tombstone, re-enactors relive the "Town Too Tough to Die" days of the 1880s, when Western legends such as "Doc" Holliday, Wyatt Earp, and Earp's brothers Virgil and Morgan walked the streets. They were on the peace officers' side of the infamous Gunfight at the O.K. Corral, a deadly, thirty-second blaze of bullets in 1881. Below and overleaf: Down the way at the Old Tombstone Wild West theme park, other costumed characters also give visitors a feel for the mining town's quarrelsome days.

Tombstone · 215

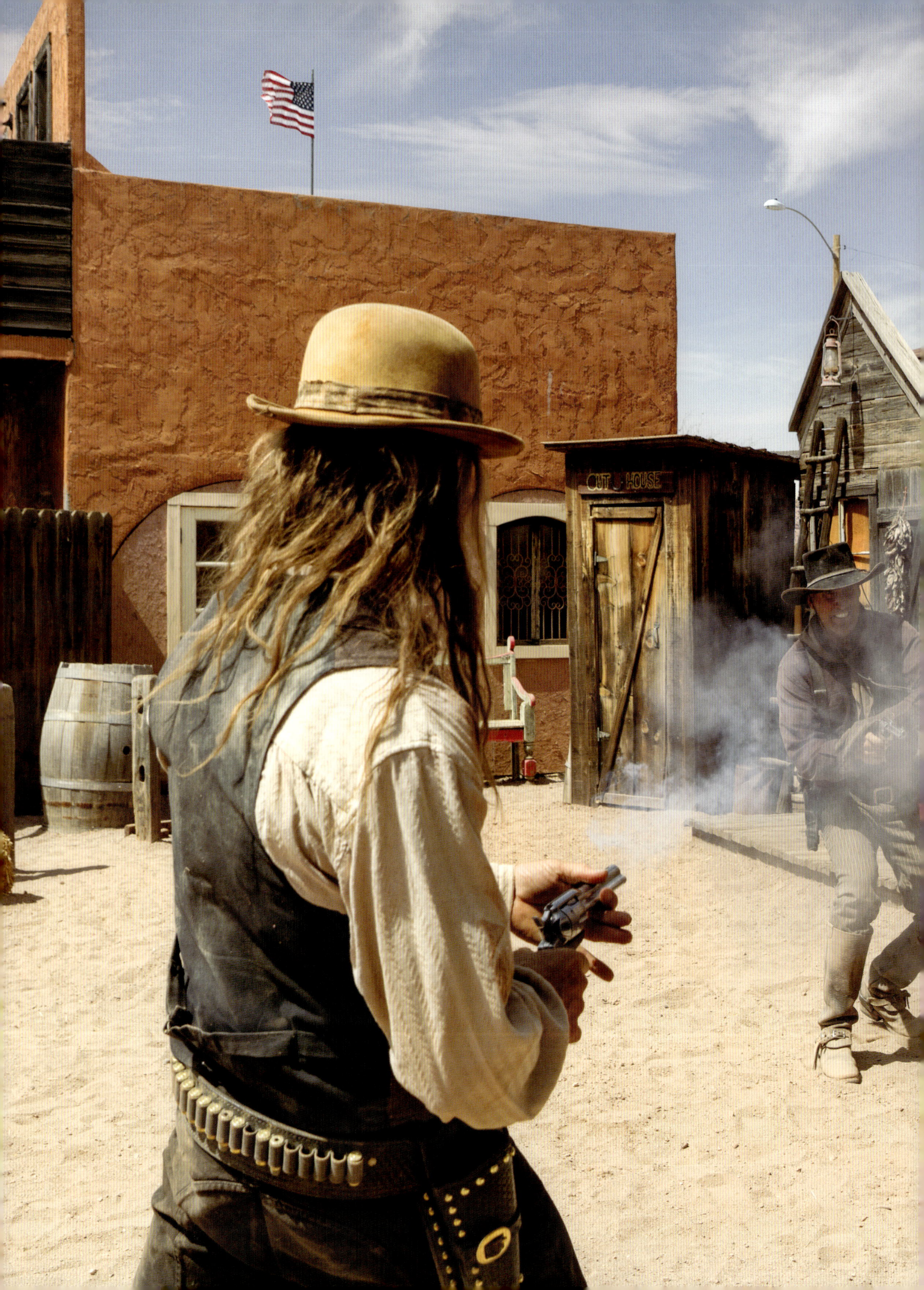
OUT HOUSE

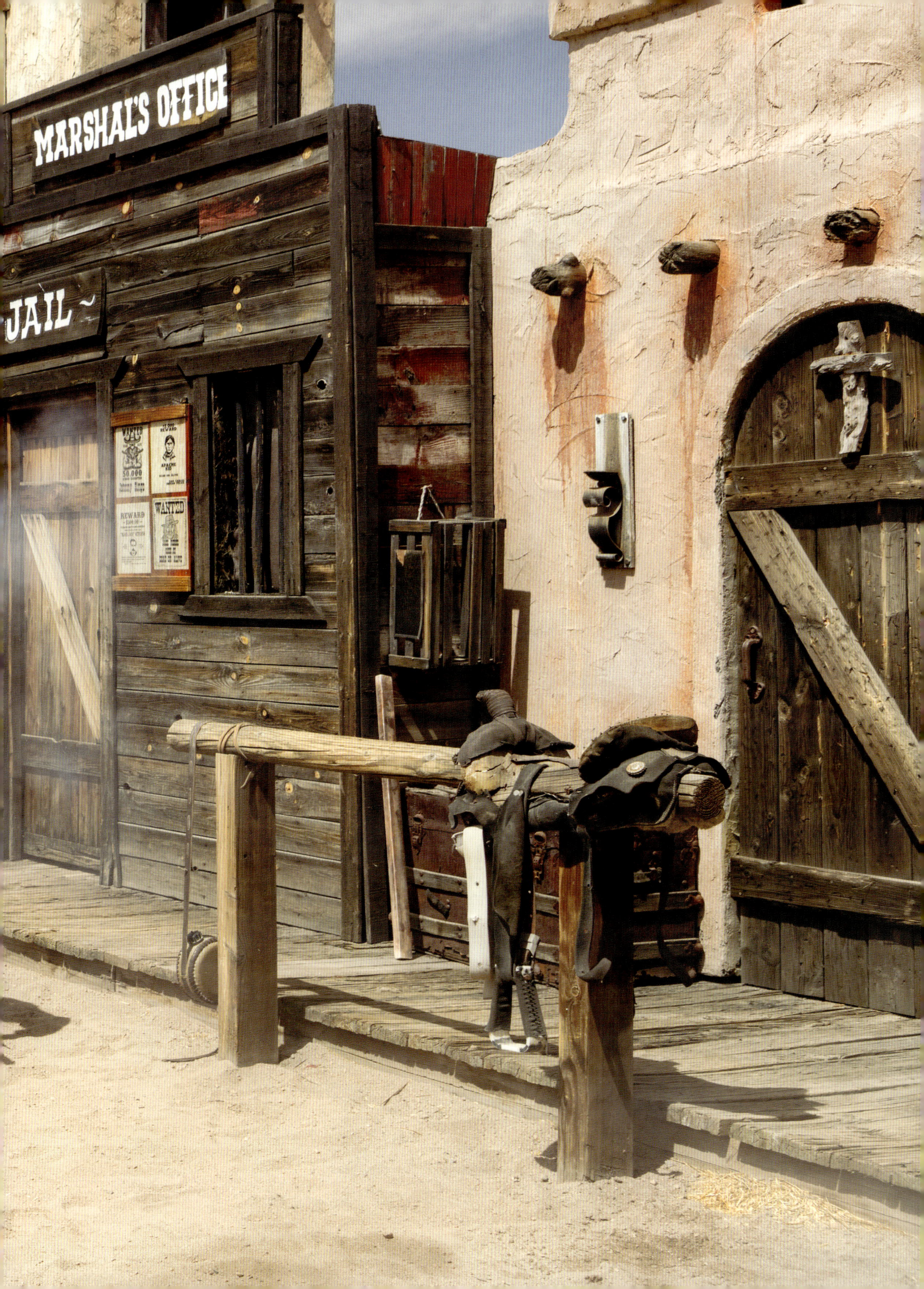
MARSHAL'S OFFICE
JAIL
REWARD
WANTED

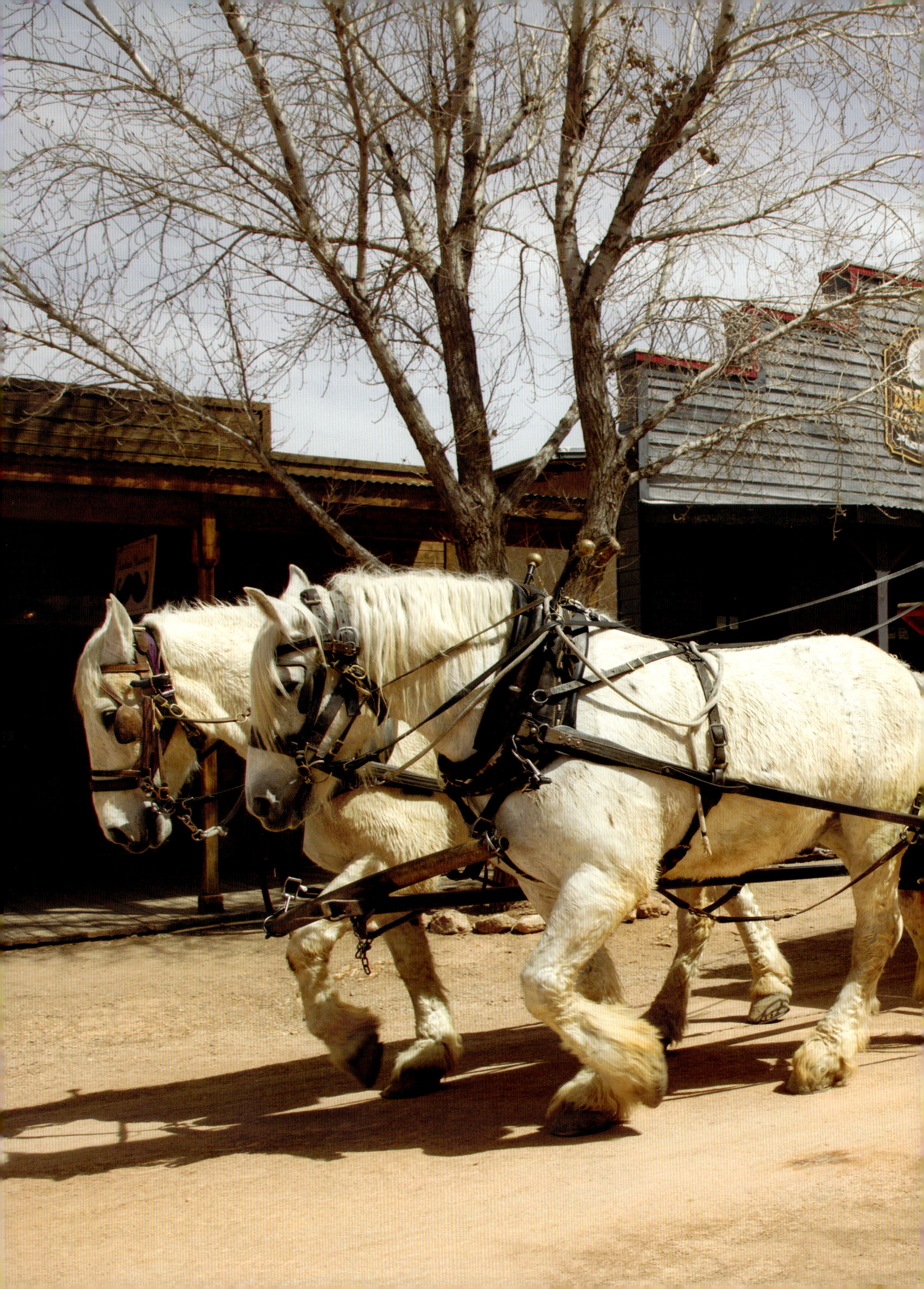

Left: In this corner of the Old Tombstone theme park, things are quiet away from the mock shootouts. Above: Dozens of movies and commercial shoots have been produced at Gammons Gulch, a re-created Old West town near Benson. It was built piece by piece by Jay Gammons, a onetime security man at a movie studio in Tucson, with the help of donations of vintage artifacts. Overleaf: The sun has fallen near the desolate Fort Bowie National Historic Site in Cochise County.

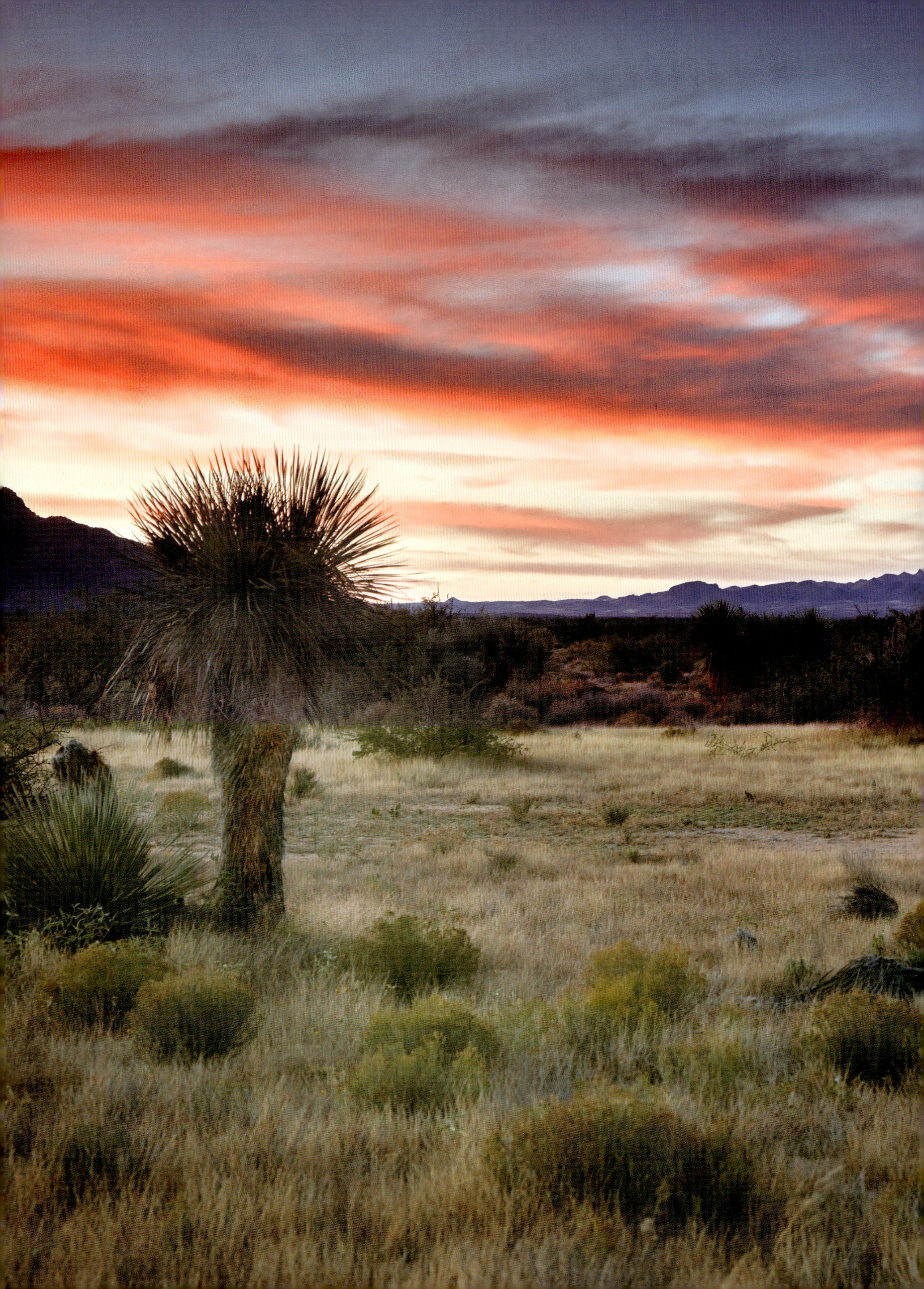

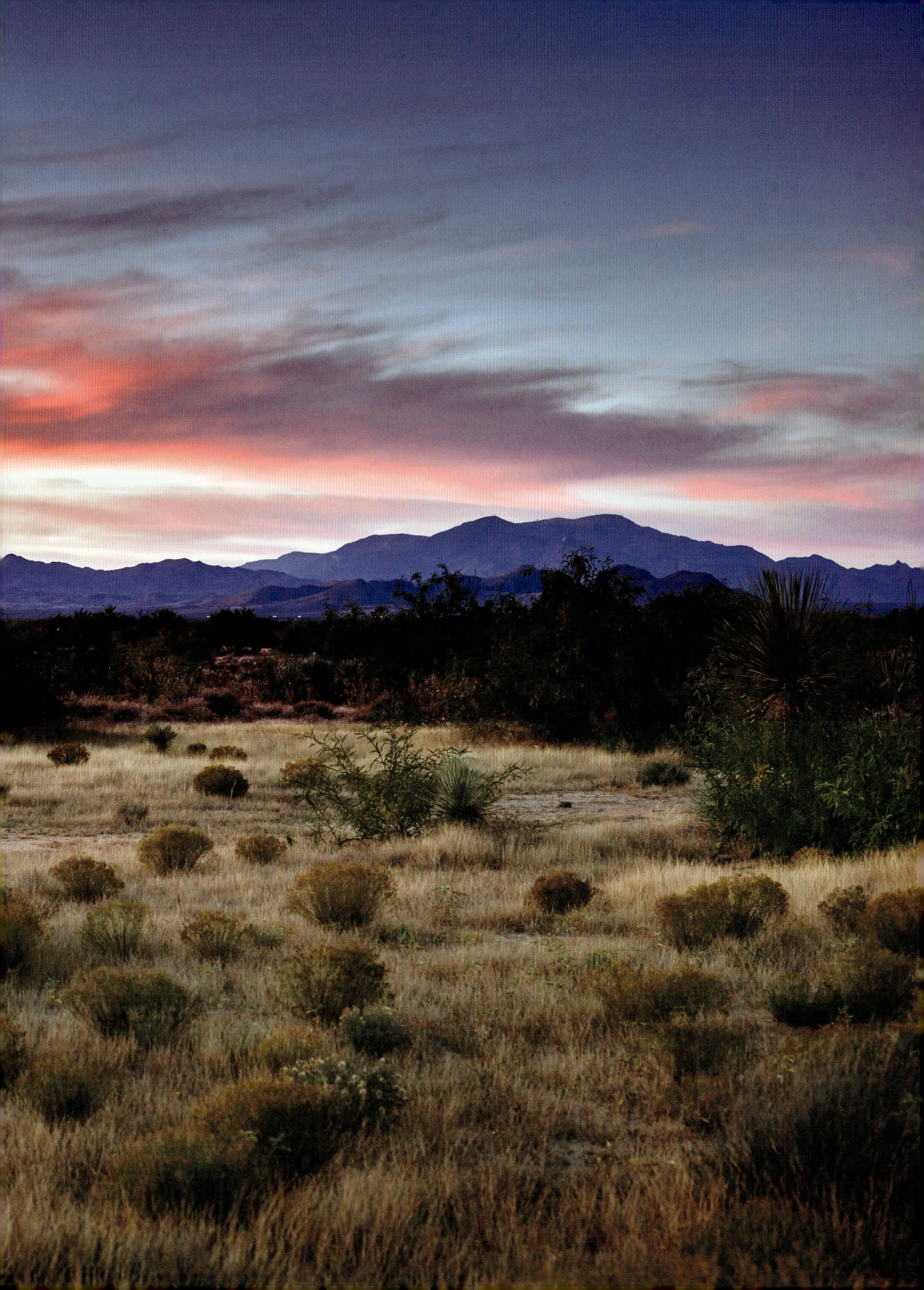

Above: Remnants of Fort Bowie remain far down a tricky trail in Cochise County. From here the U.S. Army directed decades-long efforts to rein in the Apaches and their chief, Geronimo. The fort was abandoned in 1894. Right and opposite: Chiricahua National Monument, thirty-seven miles from Willcox, is more of a canyonlike park. It protects balanced rocks and columnlike formations, called hoodoos, that proliferate in the winding gorge.

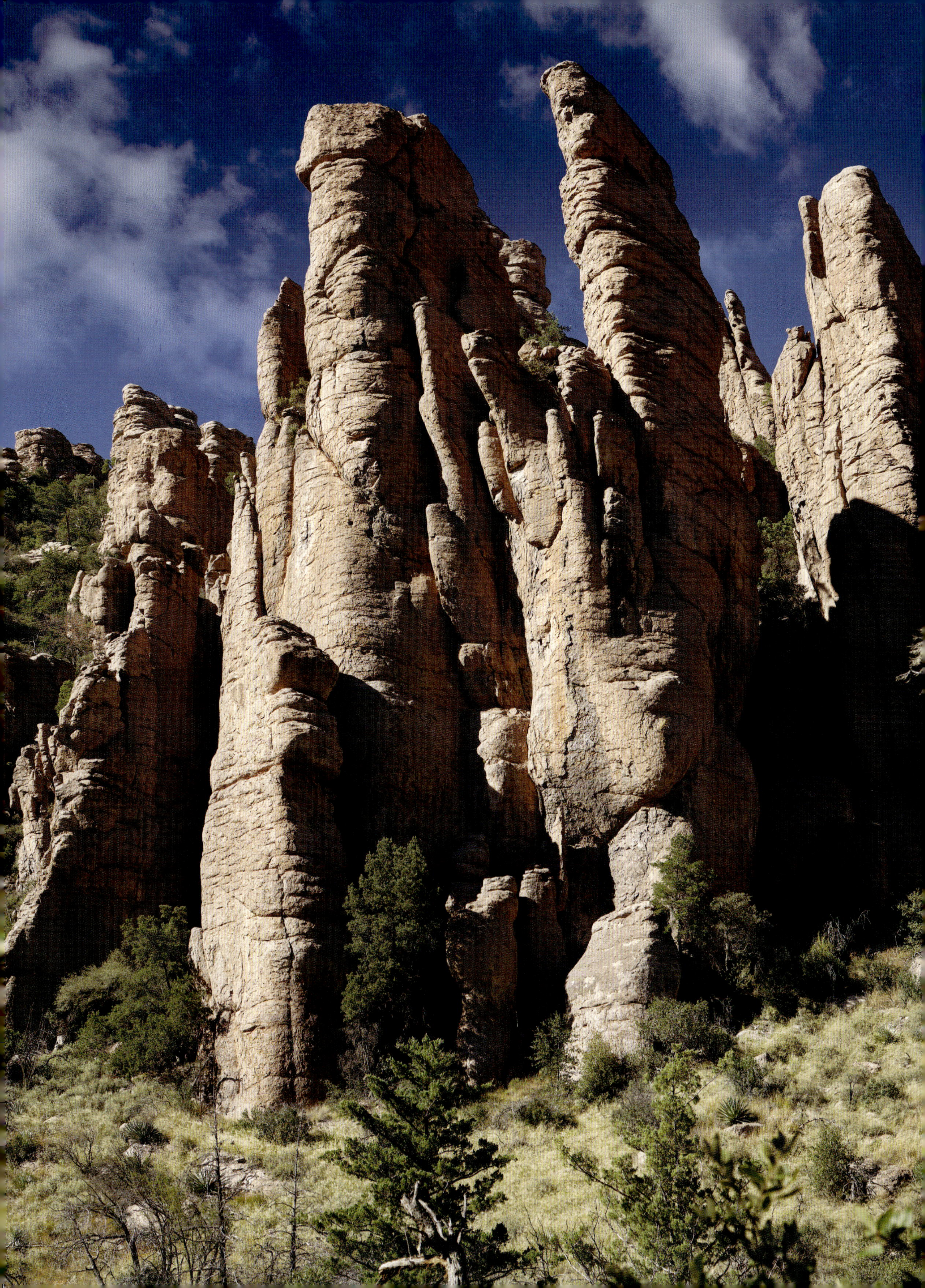

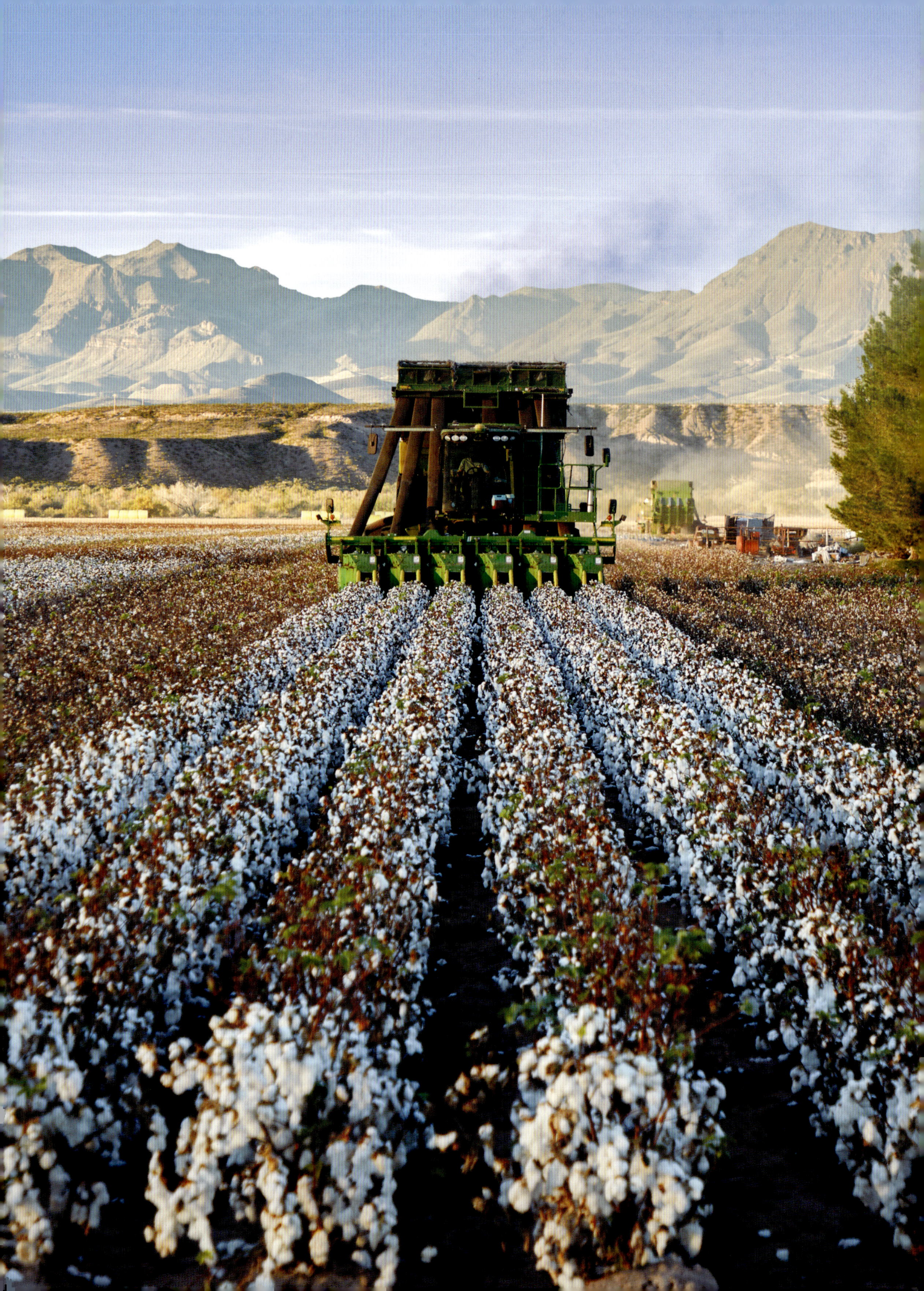

Opposite: A harvester gobbles up cotton bolls near Safford. Upland cotton is far and away Arizona's leading cash crop. Above and left: Duncan is a small southeastern town near the New Mexico border. Fittingly aligned along Railroad Avenue, local businesses face northeast, directly across tracks that run right through downtown. Overleaf: The Salt River Canyon Wilderness Area, near Globe, is called the Mini Grand Canyon by its devotees. The canyon road presents many challenging ascents, descents, and hairpin curves.

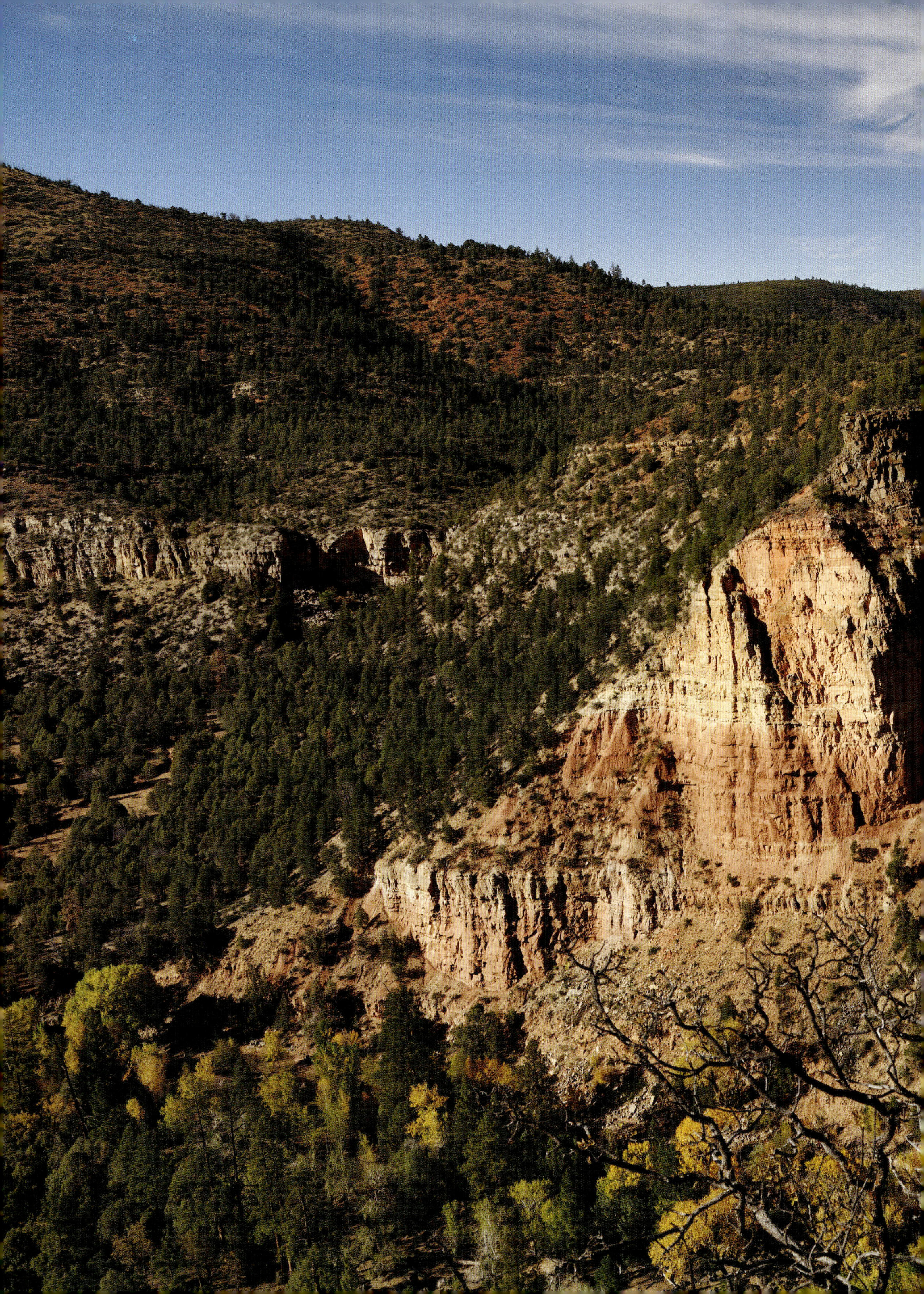

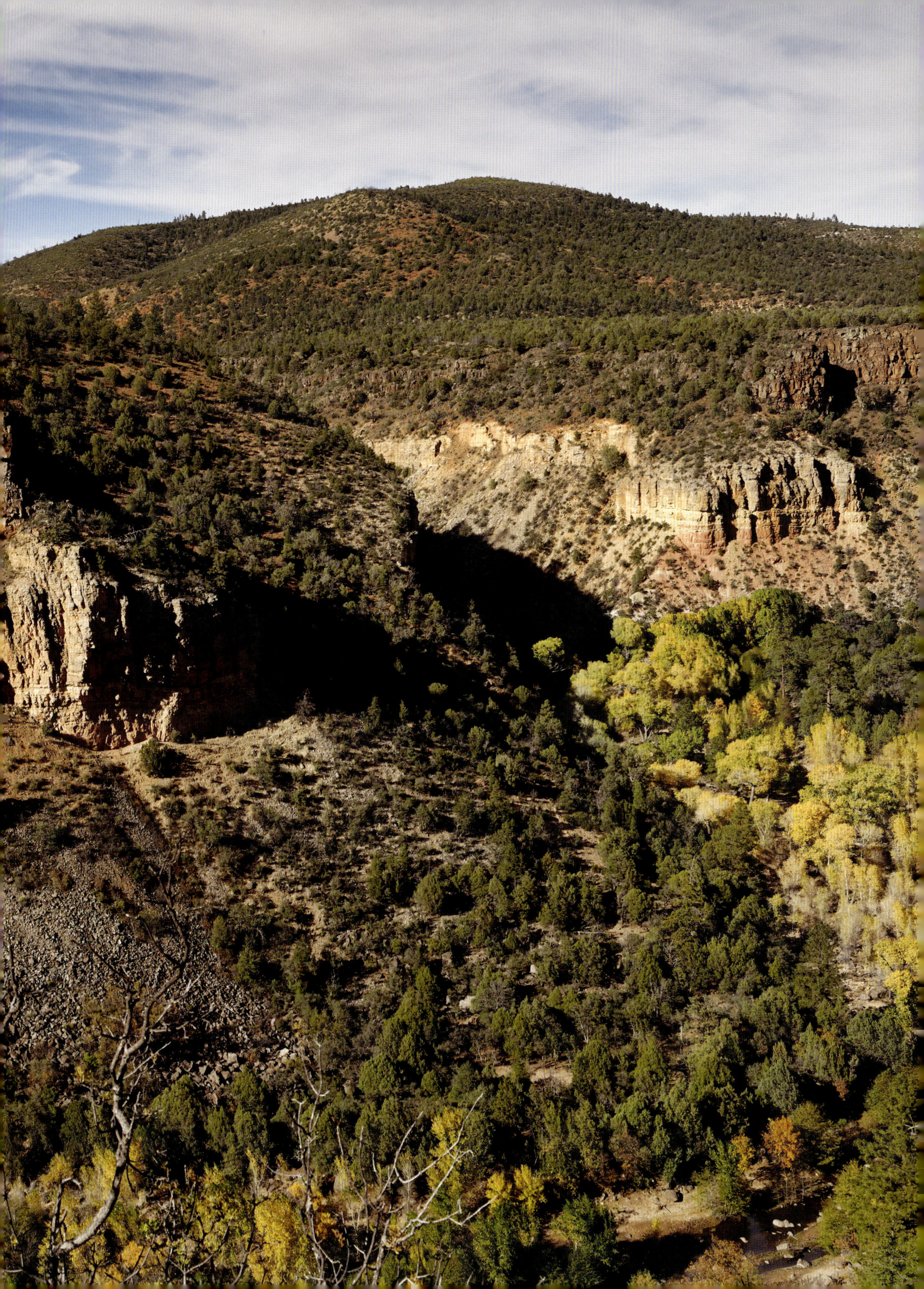

Right: A palm tree stands alone in Salt River Canyon, which bisects the length of a thirty-two-thousand-acre wilderness within Tonto National Forest. Opposite: The Tonto Natural Bridge rises more than 180 feet above Pine Creek and spans a four-hundred-foot-long tunnel below. Overleaf: Low remains of a former volcanic mountain capture one's attention down a long, decidedly unwinding road in the Round Valley.

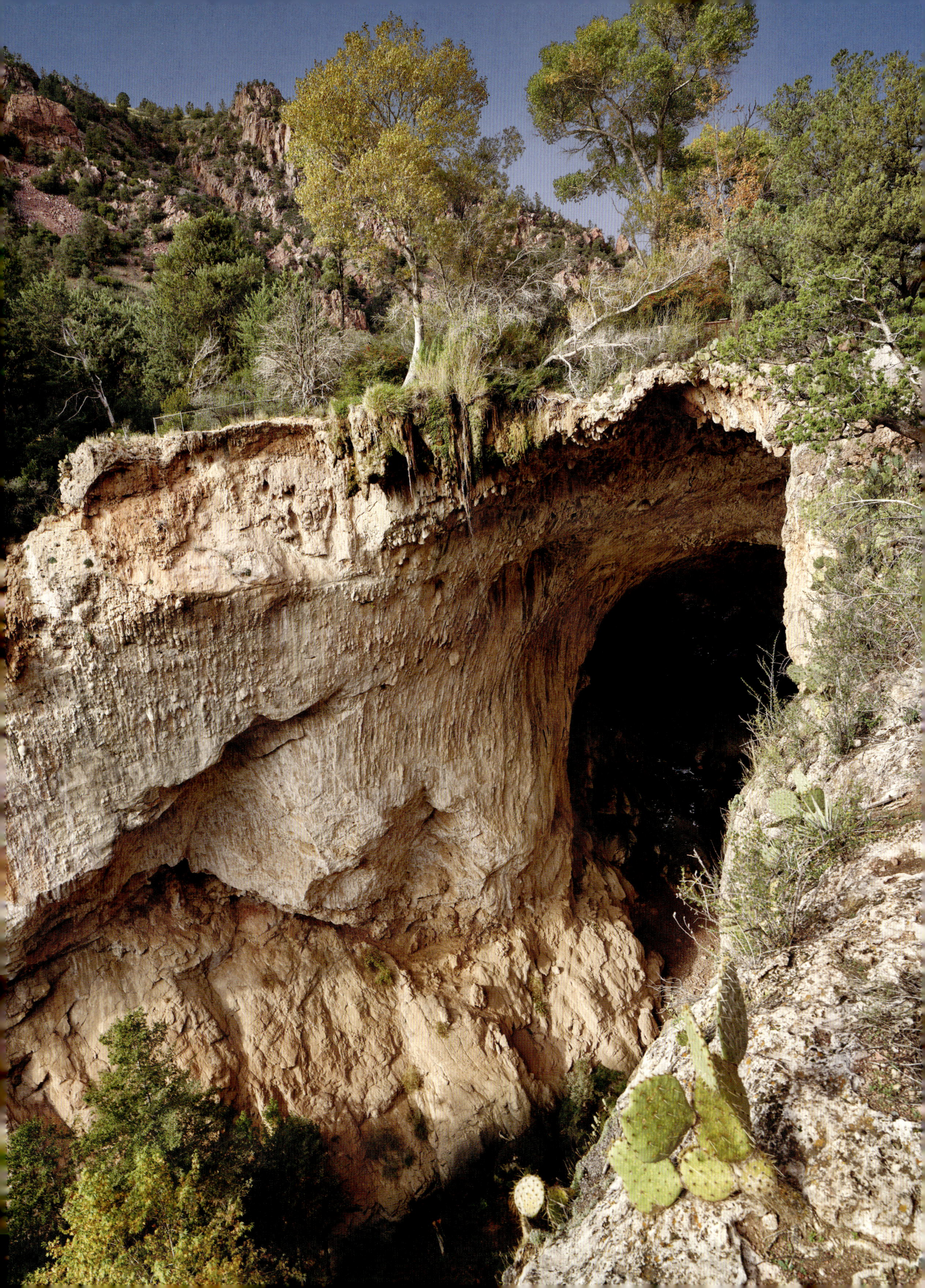

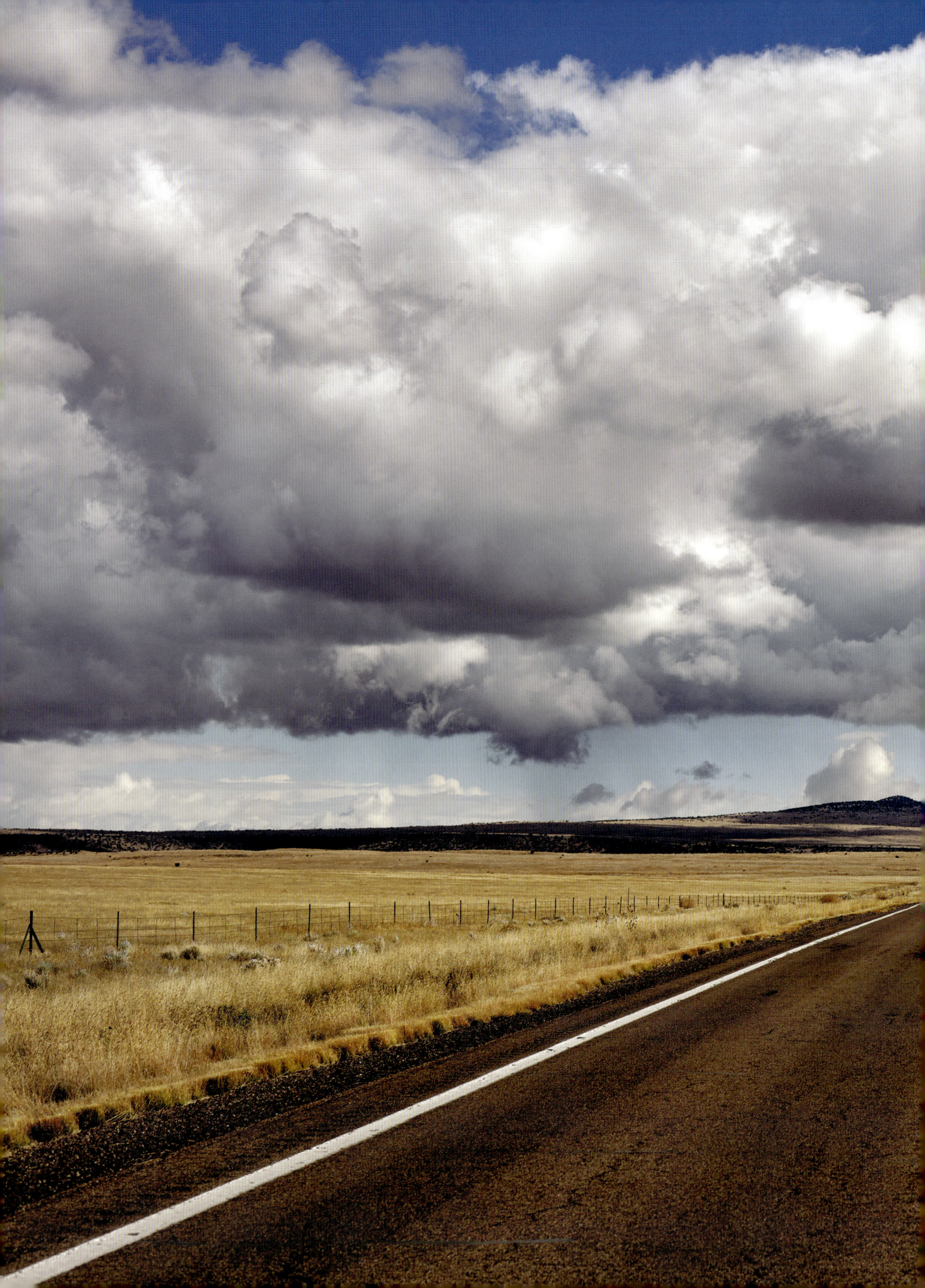

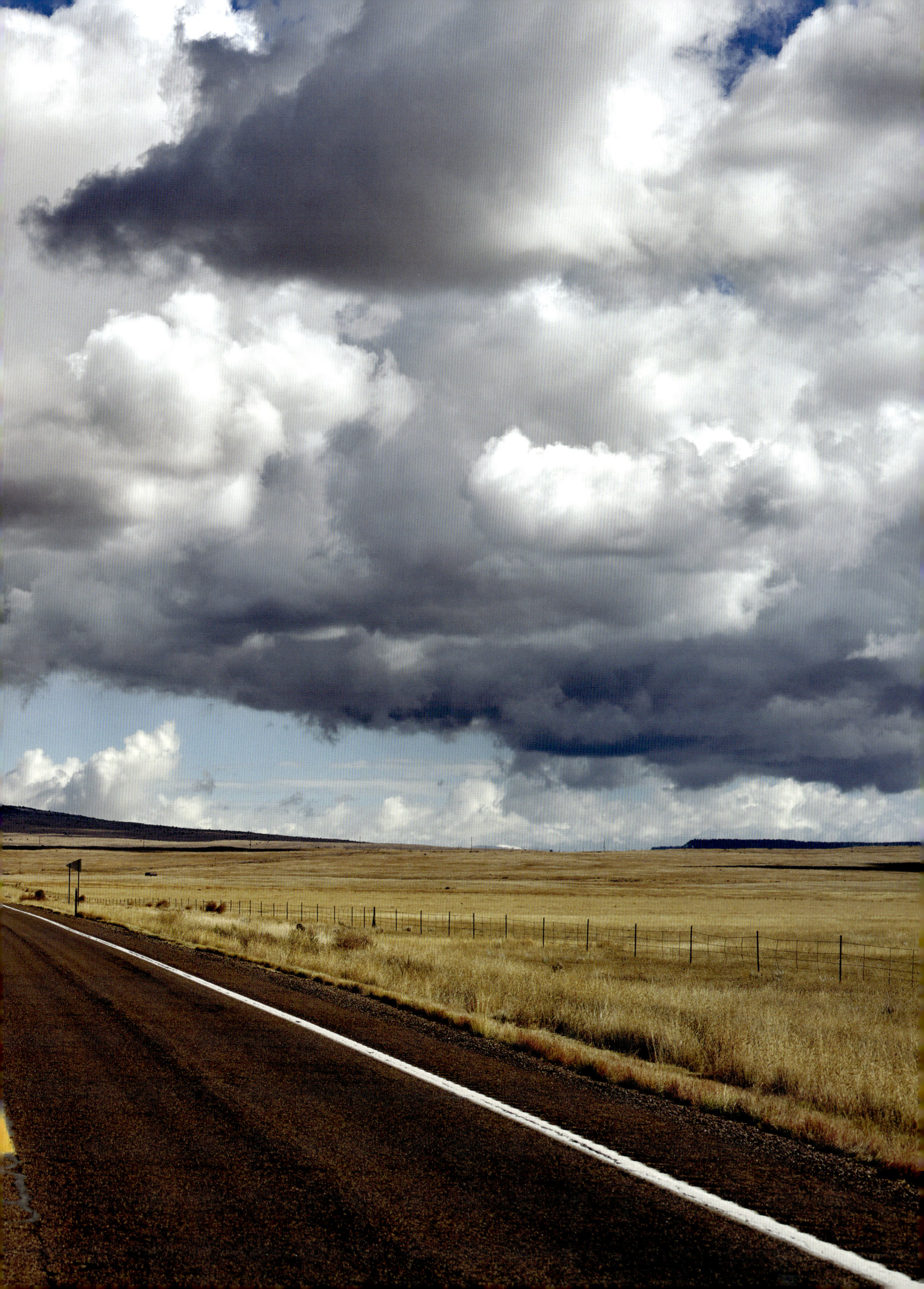

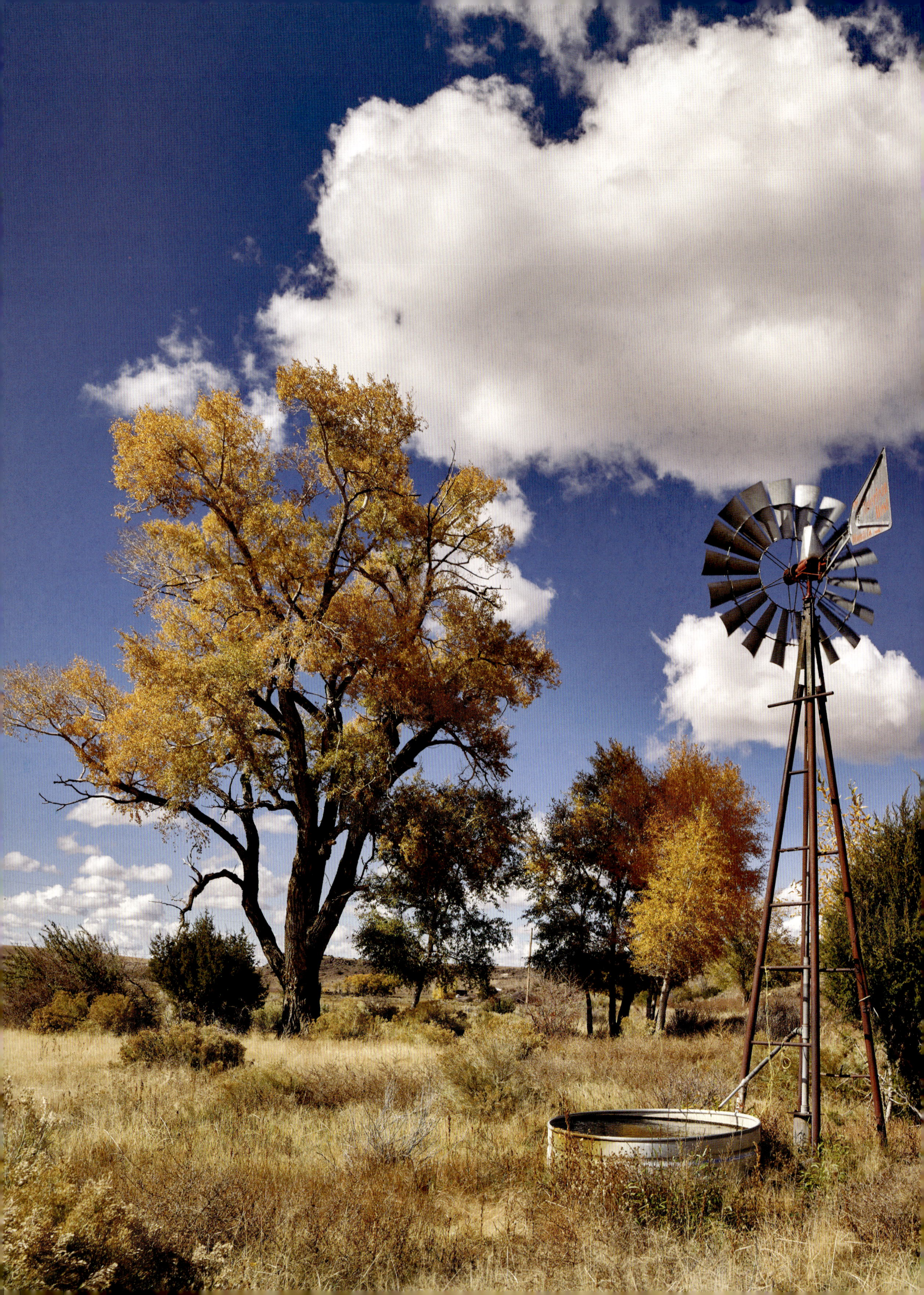

Left: Arizona offers picturesque autumns but only in its higher reaches, such as this one at 6,967 feet, outside Springerville. Below: Footprints of stone structures at the Casa Malpais archaeological site are hidden from easy view in the White Mountains. Its great kiva and ancient stone stairways were built, and rock art painted, around 1250 by Puebloan peoples. Bottom: So prolific and omnipresent are Arizona's ponderosa pines that this image, taken near Globe, could have been approximated below the Grand Canyon, 280 miles to the north.

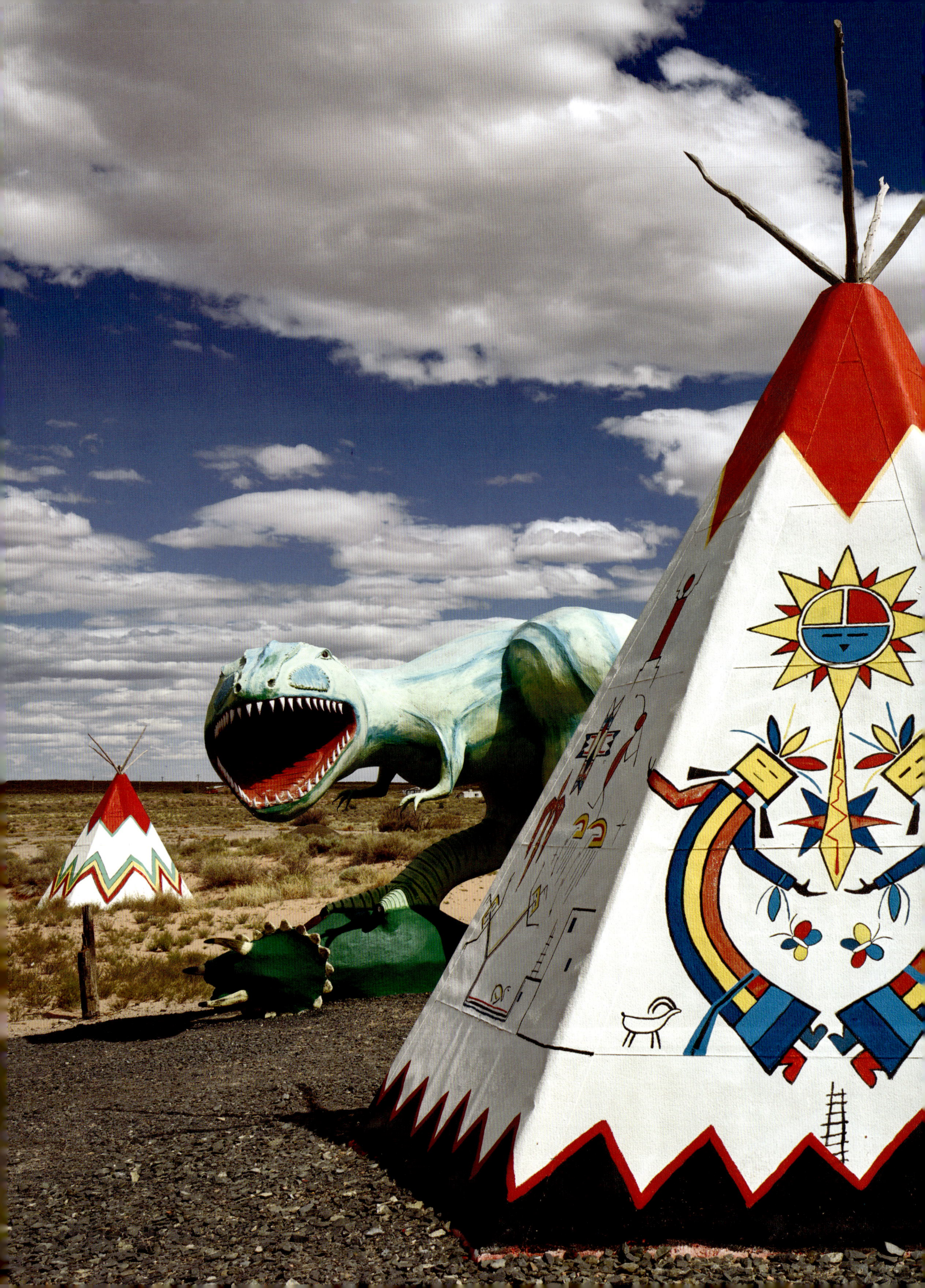

Left: A surprise is in store outside the Painted Desert Indian Center, a classic roadside attraction off the interstate along the old Route 66, east of Holbrook. Above: A welcoming committee awaits outside the Antler Attic shop in Pinetop-Lakeside, a woodsy Navajo County summer resort and second-home area for residents of Arizona's large desert cities. Overleaf: The old Wigwam Motel, a complex of units built in Holbrook to evoke Indian tipis, was once part of a 1930s and '40s Wigwam Villages chain built from here to Florida.

Holbrook · Pinetop-Lakeside · 235

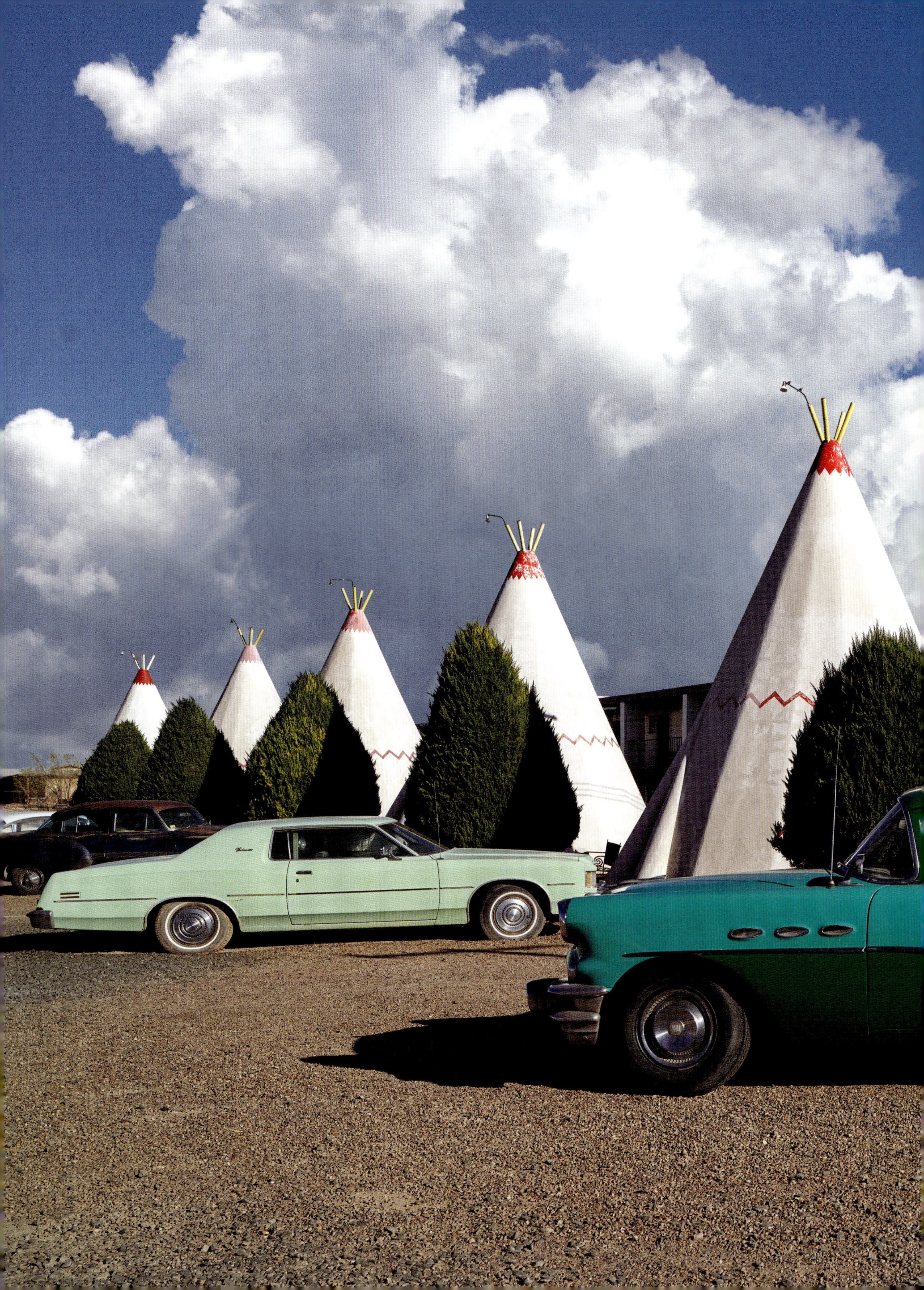

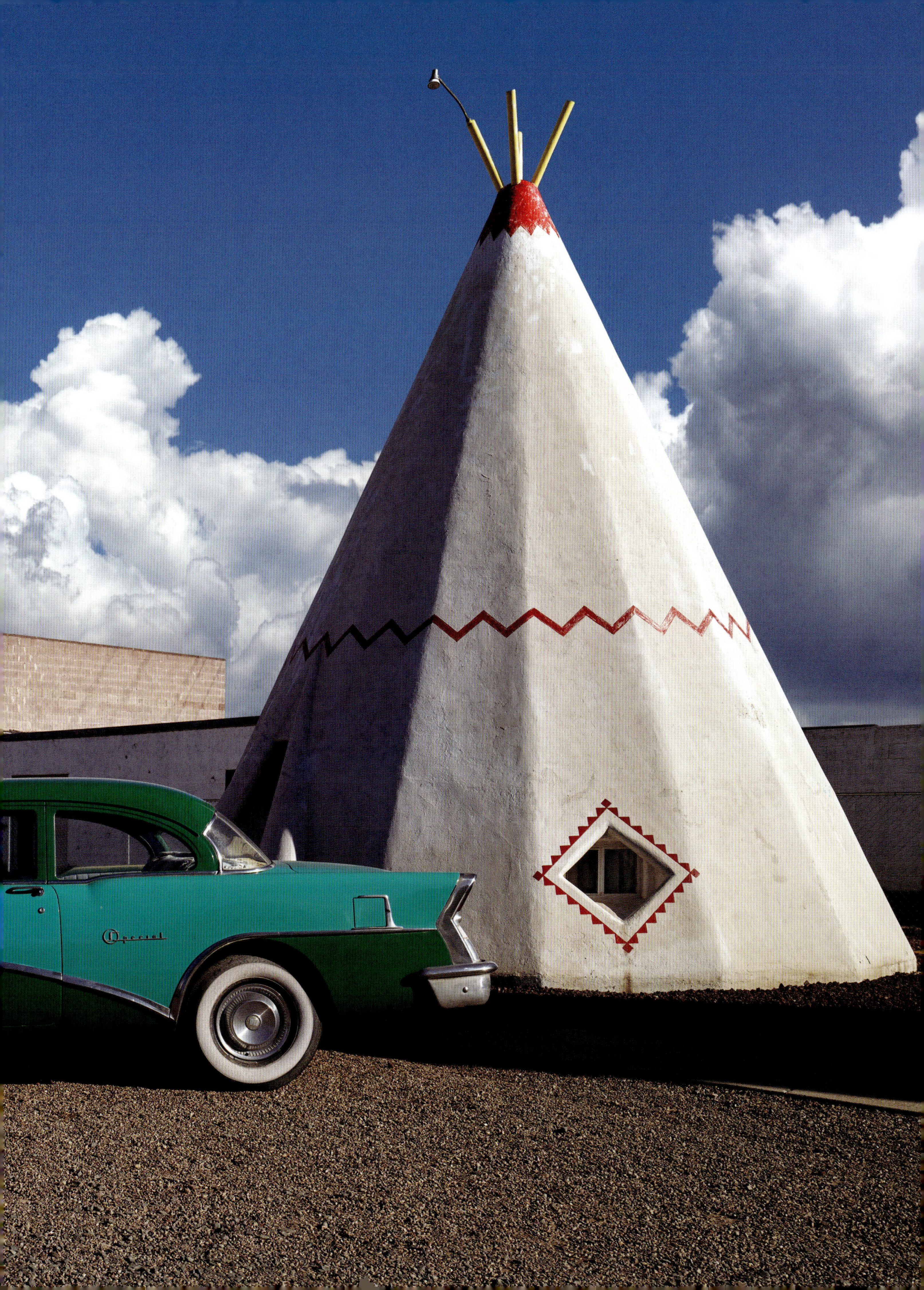
Special

Above and right: Chip Thomas's haunting art, made from his photographs of Navajo people, brightens the landscape of far-northeastern Arizona. Opposite: Recalling signs for Rock City and Ruby Falls back east, a billboard blitz touting the Jack Rabbit Trading Post once teased drivers along the old two-lane highway past Joseph City, near Winslow. Most of the bunny signs are gone, but the gift shop remains. In fact … here (actually next door) … it … is!

238 · Joseph City

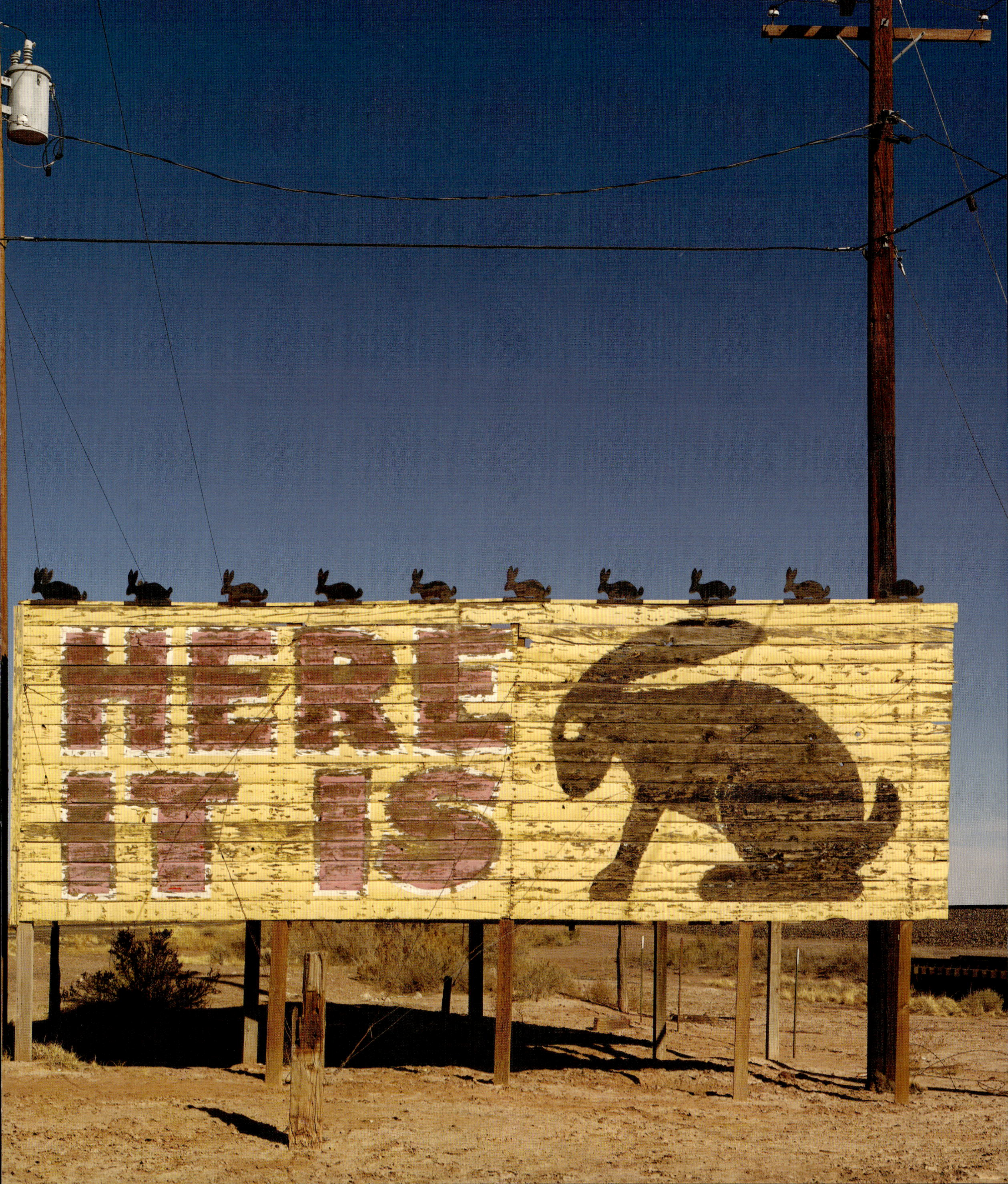
HERE
IT IS

Can a song revive a community? Consider this: After Interstate 40 bypassed Winslow in 1979—"bleeding it dry," in the words of the *Los Angeles Times*—the town tapped into the lasting mystique of Glenn Frey and the Eagles' line "I'm a-standin' on the corner in Winslow, Arizona," from their hit song "Take It Easy." To this day, tourists by the thousands snap selfies at Standin' on the Corner Park, right downtown, and spend bundles on food, drinks, and souvenirs.

240 · Winslow

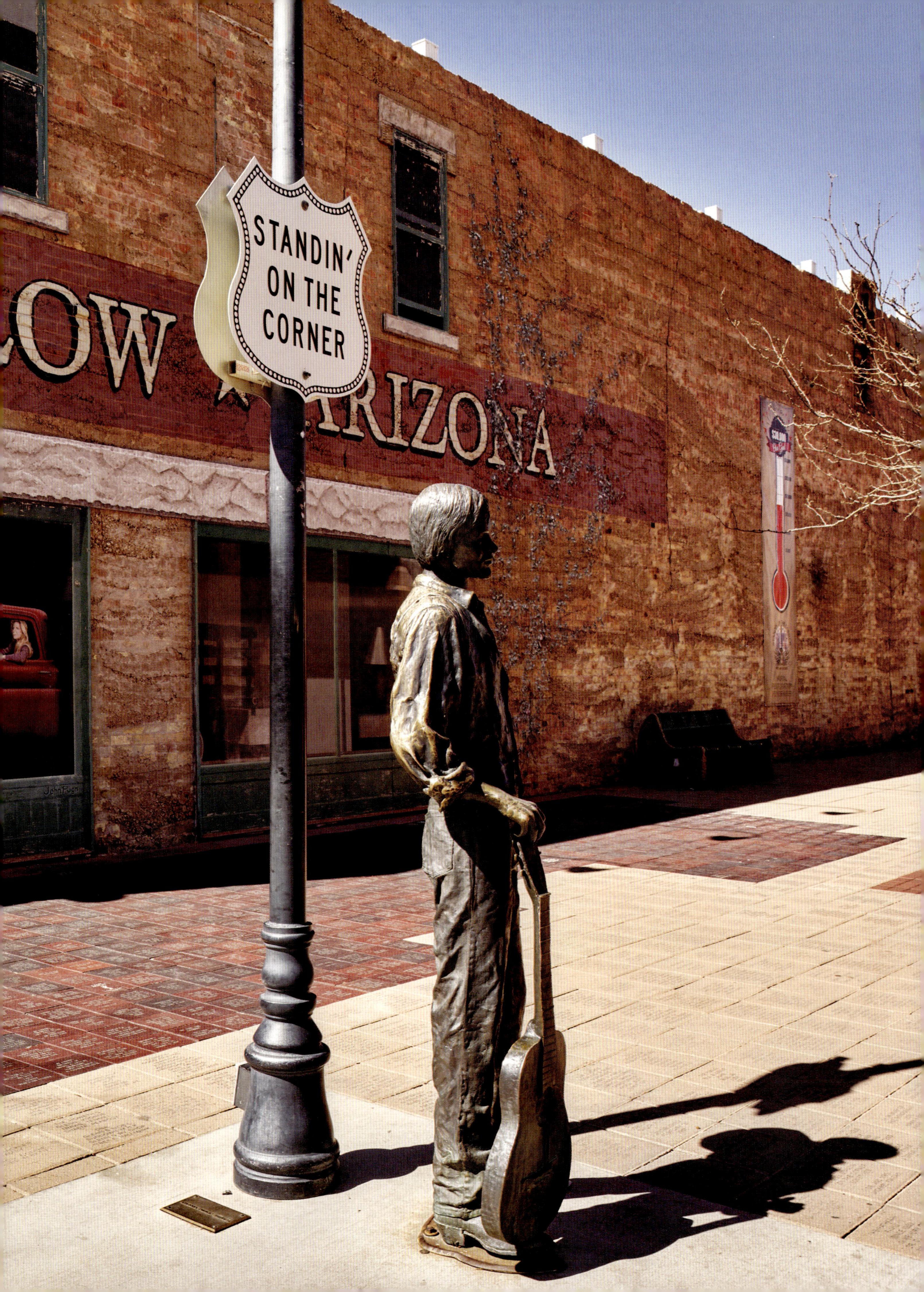
STANDIN'
ON THE
CORNER
LOW
ARIZONA

Below: In these days of animated movies, can looking at ancient dinosaur tracks be much of an attraction? Perhaps, if barely, on the barren plateau near Tuba City. Opposite: There will be no more paying customers, however, at what is left of a quirky 1920s zoo in the bleak ghost town of Two Guns, along the old Route 66 between Winona and Winslow. The stone attraction was the brainstorm of Harry "Two Guns" Miller, who took on the persona of "Chief Crazy Thunder" when he greeted visitors.

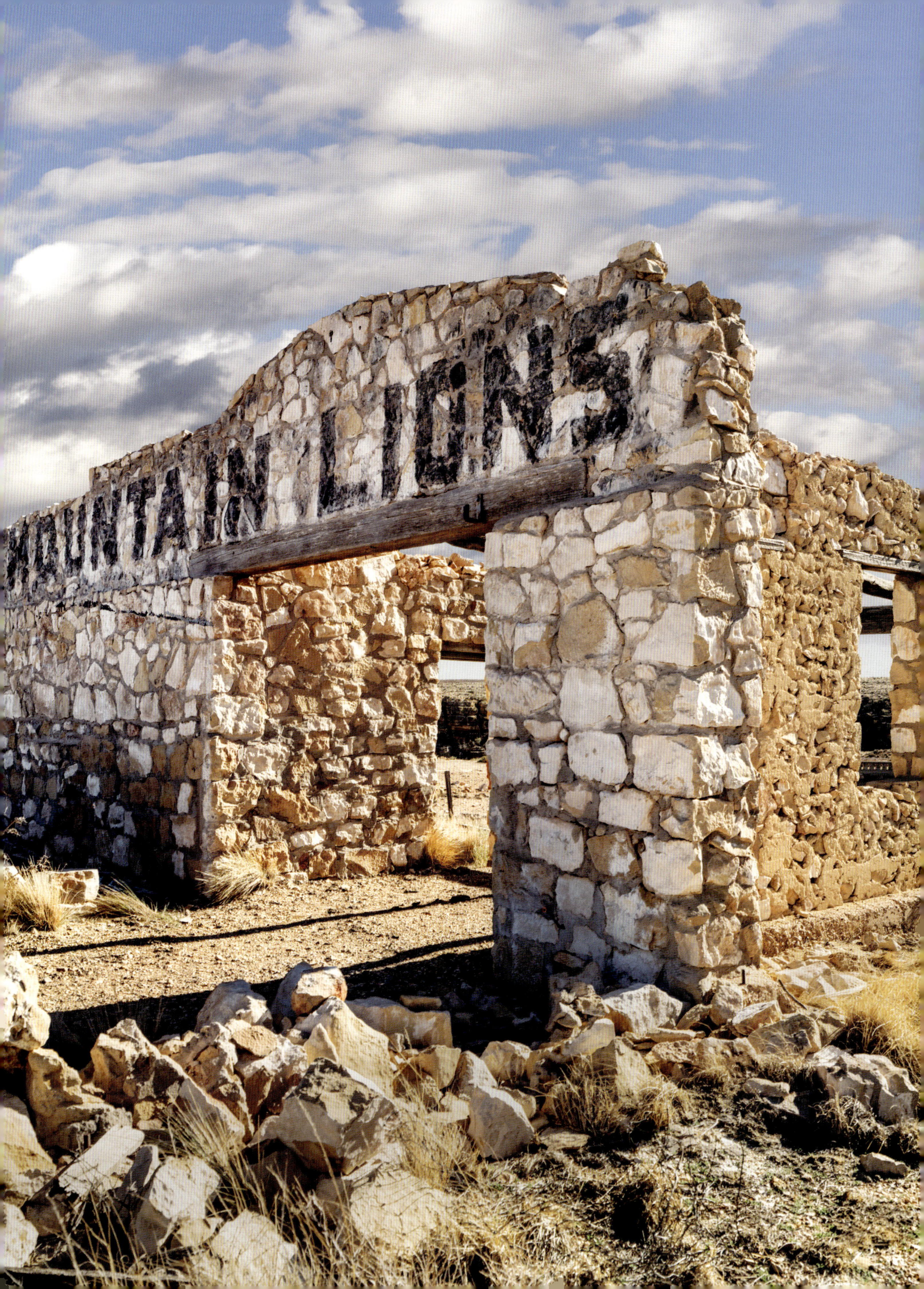
MOUNTAIN LIONS

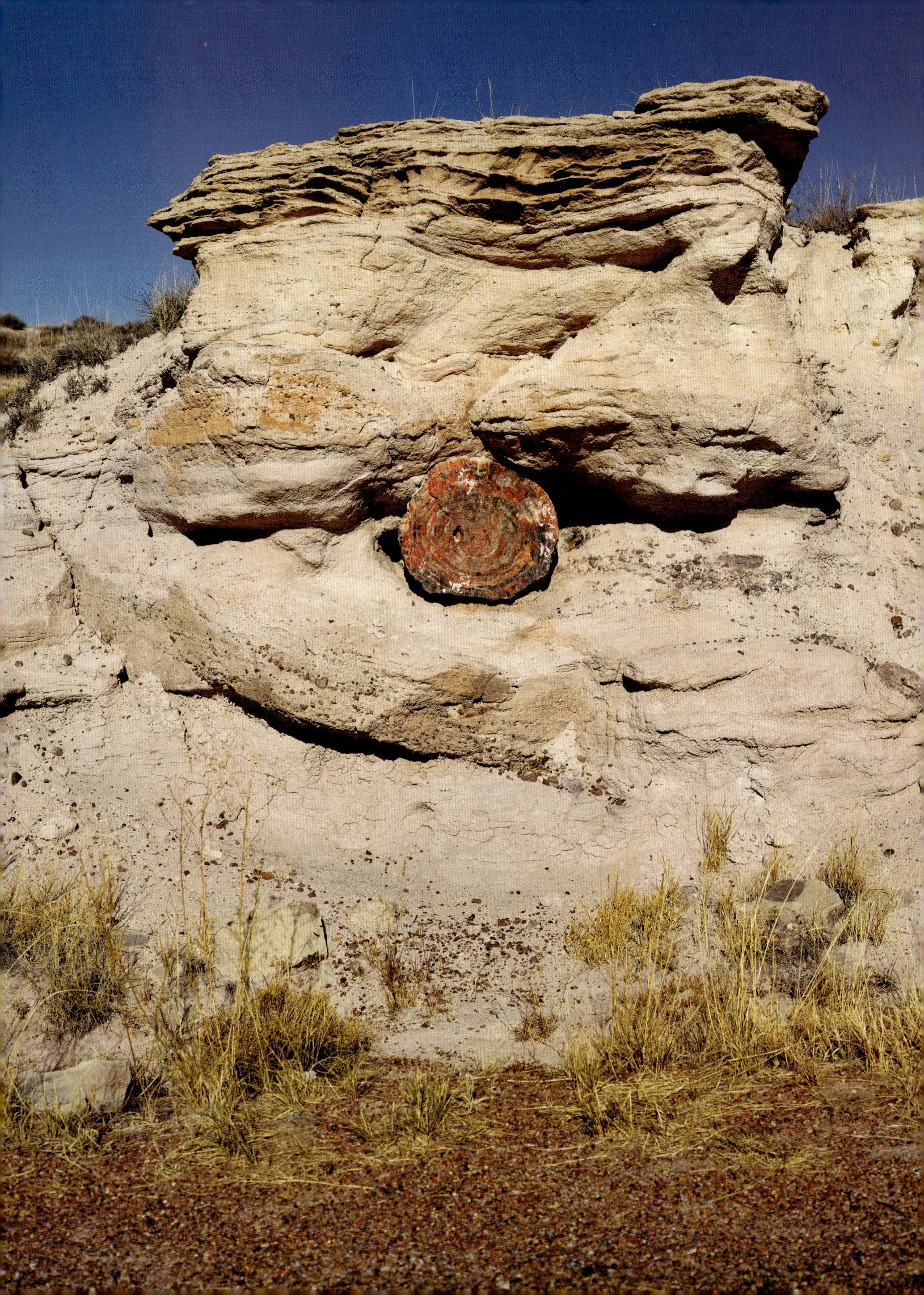

Fossilized specimens are still scattered about the Petrified Forest National Park, near Holbrook. They are hardened remains of trees, or parts of them, that fell in the Late Triassic Period, about 225 million years ago. The park's splendors so impressed early preservationists that it was the second-ever site designated a protected national monument in 1906. (Devils Tower in Wyoming was first.) Overleaf: These nearby colorful badlands were given the name Painted Desert by a Spanish expedition under Francisco Vázquez de Coronado in 1540.

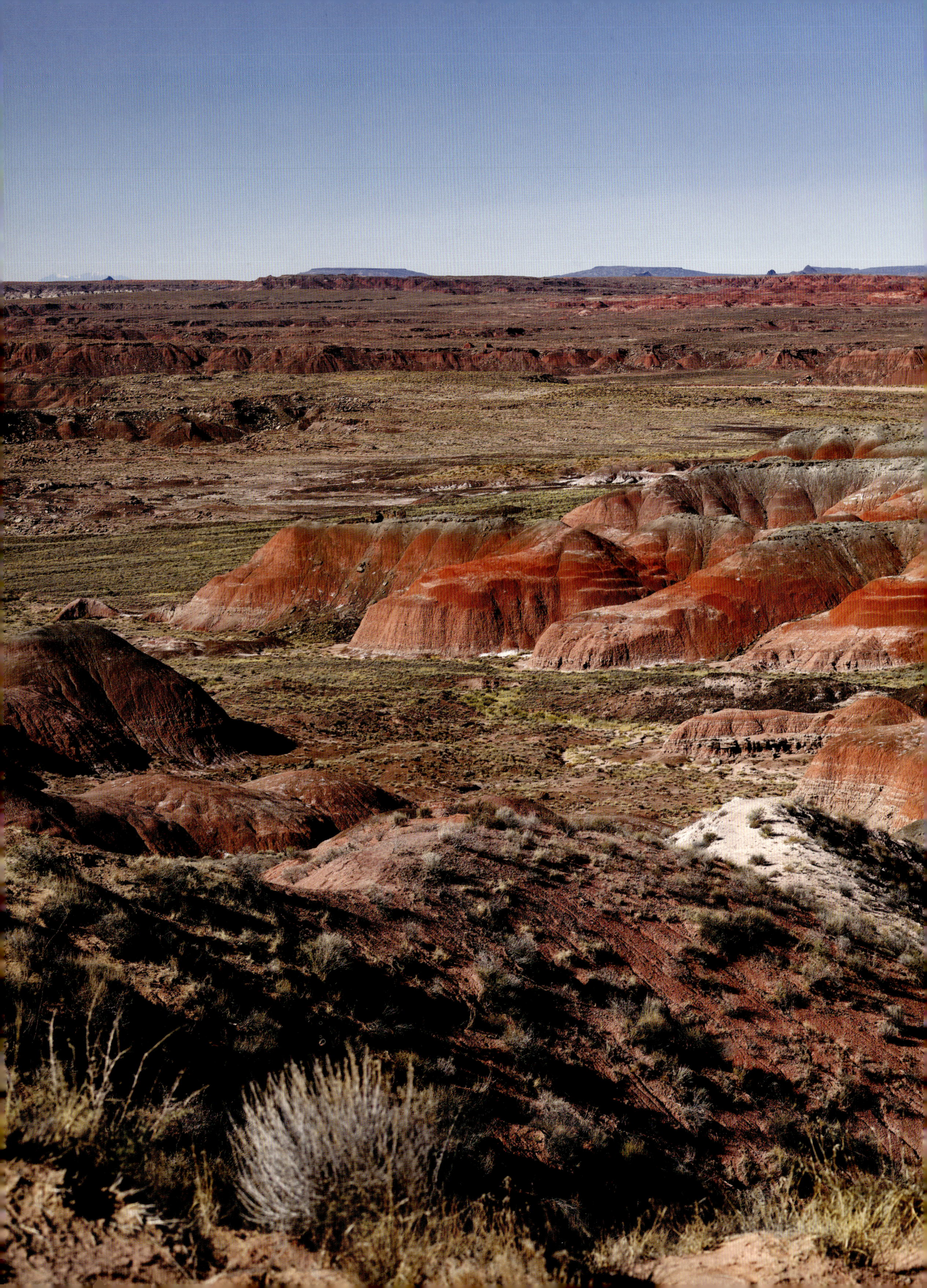

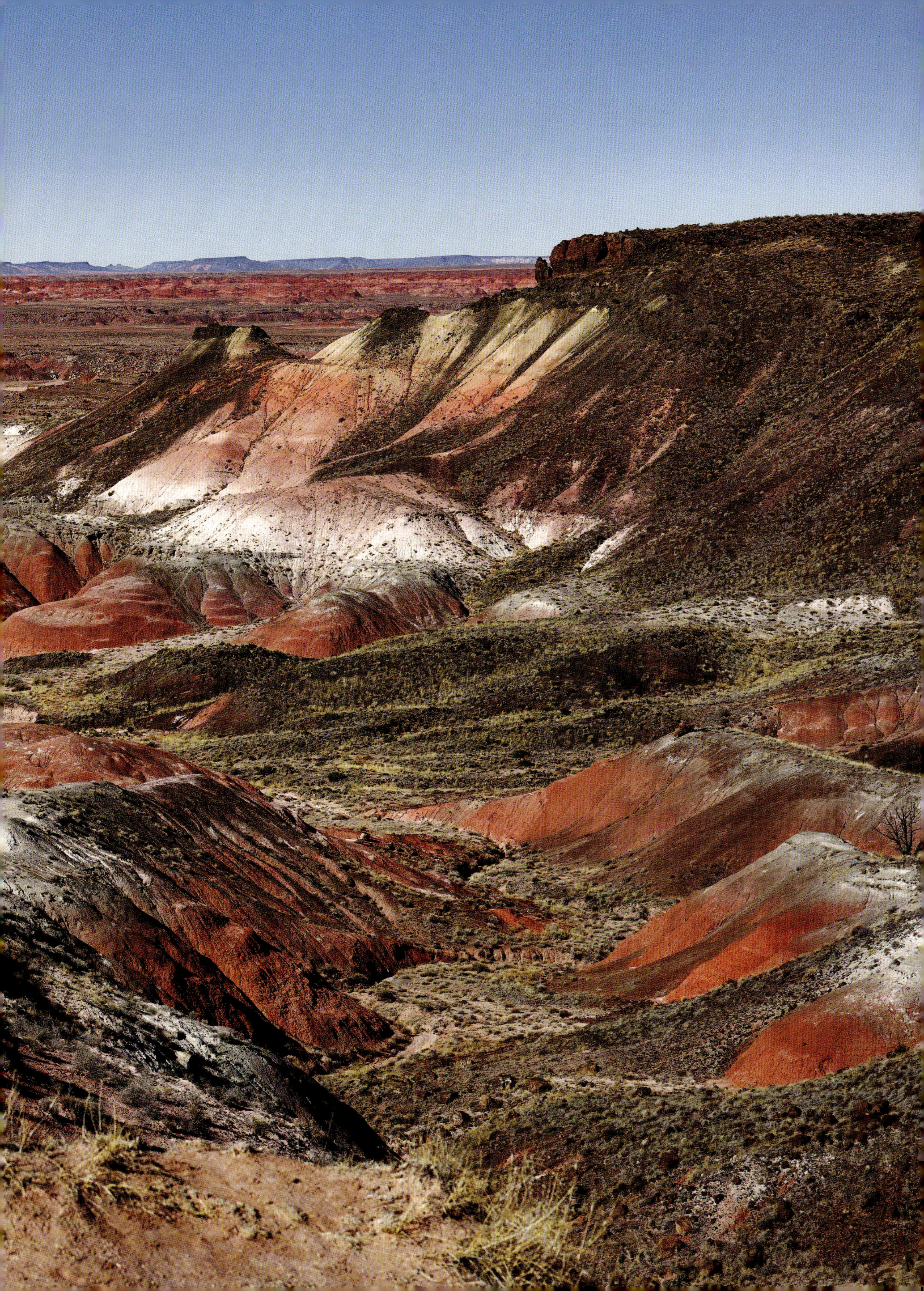

Below: One might call this incredible sunset, near Kayenta, outdoor art—*fleeting* outdoor art to be savored in the moment. Opposite: The Hubbell Trading Post, a national historic site near Ganado on the Navajo Nation, was long a bartering interface between Navajos and white settlers. John Hubbell bought the post in 1878, and his family continued to run it until the National Park Service purchased it in 1967.

**** PLEASE ****
Ask for assistance with Pottery.
Thank you
Please ask for assistance with Pottery

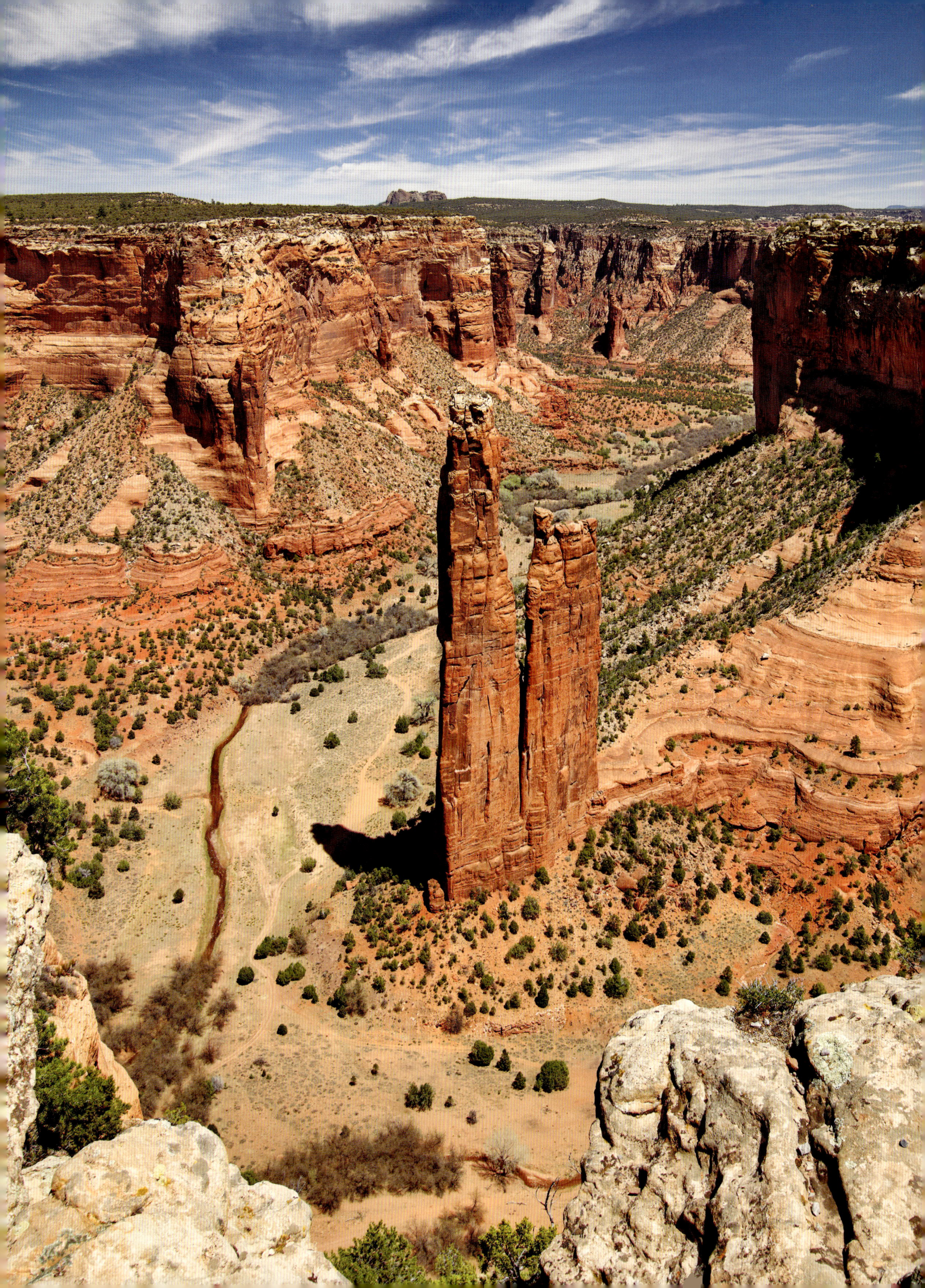

At Canyon de Chelly within Navajo lands, the best-known and most intriguing feature is a sandstone spire called Spider Rock, shown opposite. Located in the Four Corners region near Chinle, the national monument area has been continuously inhabited for some five thousand years.

Monument Valley is a ninety-two-thousand-acre Navajo Tribal Park that crosses from northeastern Arizona into Utah on the Colorado Plateau. It is far from any city, but its sweeping vistas of towering sandstone buttes have made it a must-see destination for visitors from around the world. The valley's steeply sloped Mitten Buttes, each with a distinctive narrow "thumb," can be viewed from several overlooks. Overleaf: Thanks to depictions in 1930s movies, Monument Valley is often employed as the quintessential representation of the American West.

252 · *Oljato-Monument Valley*

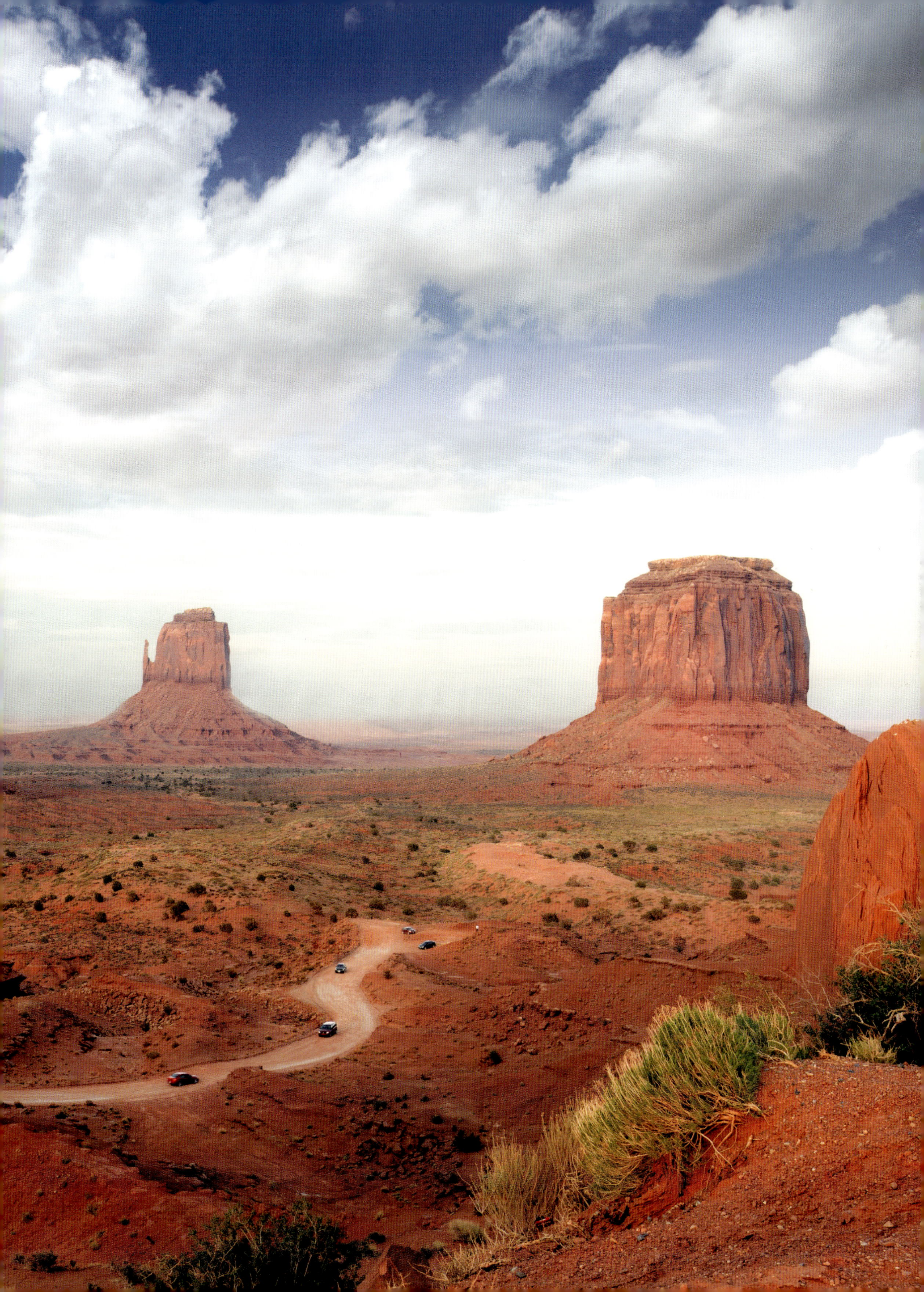

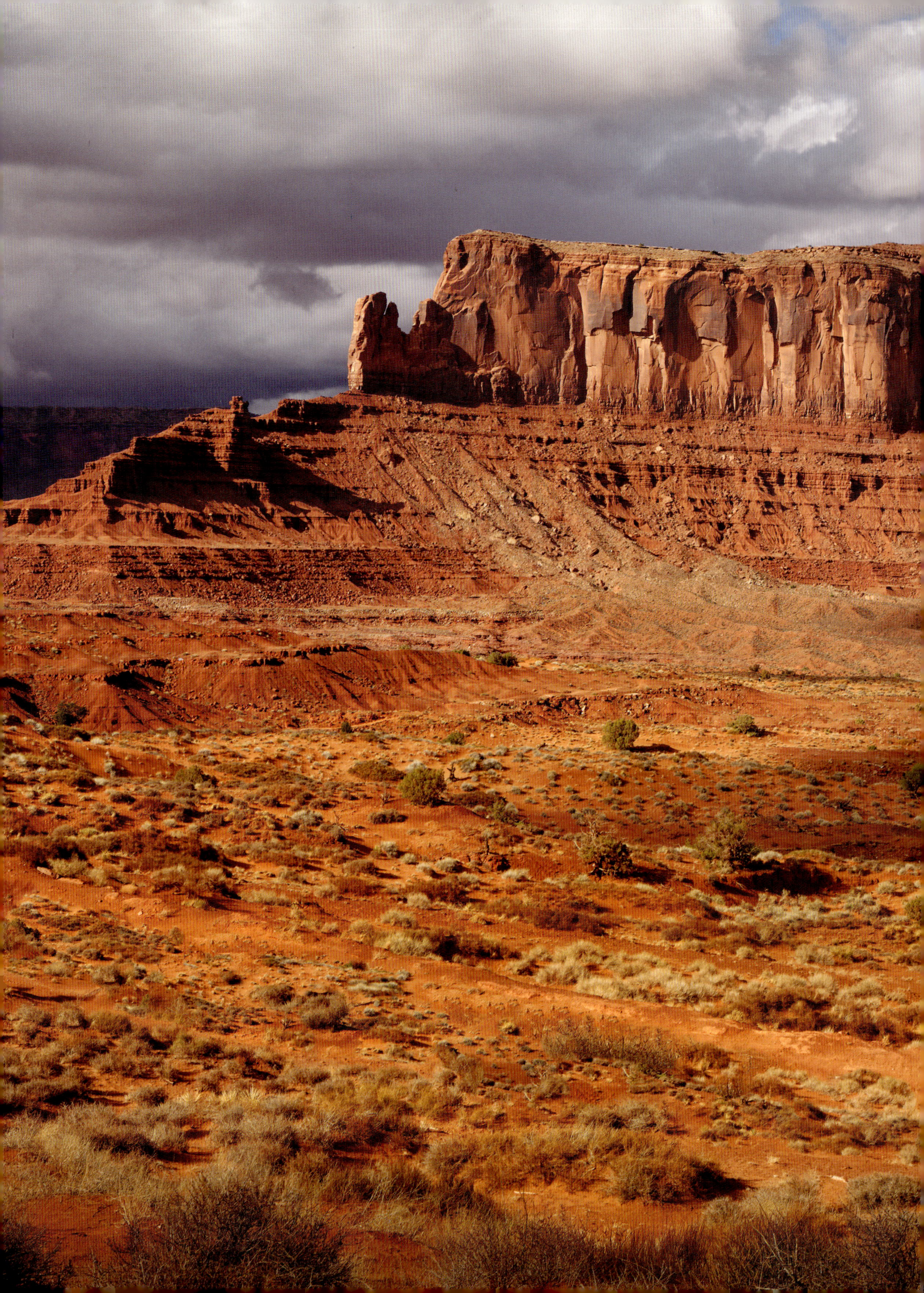

Copyright © 2019 by Chelsea Publishing, Inc.

Introduction copyright © 2019 by Lattie F. Coor

Lyrics to the chorus of the "Arizona March Song" by Margaret Rowe Clifford, adopted by the state legislature as the Arizona state anthem on February 28, 1919

All rights reserved.

No part of the contents of this book may be reproduced without the written permission of the publisher.

First edition published in 2019 by
Chelsea Publishing, Inc.
7501 Carroll Avenue, Takoma Park, Maryland 20912
800-847-6918

Publication made possible through the generous support of Craig and Barbara Barrett

Photographs from the Craig & Barbara Barrett Arizona Collection, Library of Congress

Photographs from the Carol M. Highsmith Archive, Library of Congress

www.CarolHighsmithAmerica.com
www.ThisIsAmericaFoundation.org

ISBN 978-1-7923-1802-3

Composed in Hoefler text and titling
Design and typography by Robert L. Wiser
Photograph captions by Ted Landphair
Production by Diane Maddex, Archetype Press
Printed by Tien Wah Press in Malaysia

Acknowledgments:

Carol M. Highsmith and Ted Landphair believe that no one has yet seized on "Amiable Arizona" as a slogan for the nation's forty-eighth state. Why would one, considering its natural wonders? But we came away just as impressed with Arizonans' friendliness, can-do spirit, and cheerful eye to the future—memorable though its past has been. We owe thanks to a host of kind and generous folks we encountered, including the following....

H. Alan Day, who took enormous time and trouble to get us to the Lazy B Ranch, a hundred miles from anywhere, then filled our visit with warm stories of his and his sisters Sandra and Ann's life-shaping experiences there.

Jeff Fisher, the genial docent who took Carol to nooks she would never have found high above Springerville at the Casa Malpais archaeological site. Then he gladly trudged all the way back up the mountain and miraculously found Carol's misplaced cellphone.

Jeff Goodman, vice president of the Frank Lloyd Wright Foundation for communication and partnerships, who masterfully conveyed the magic of both Taliesin West and its creator, the indomitable Frank Lloyd Wright.

Steve Hennig, who got us to places—from lead-mine shafts to a bridge with a humongous sign about oceans—we would never have dreamed existed in Yuma.

Dr. Ann Marshall, director of research at the Heard Museum, who astutely made it apparent why Hopi katsina dolls have captured Arizonans' imagination for a century.

Michael Sexton, historian extraordinaire at Lowell Observatory, who taught Carol just the right As, Bs, and Cs of astronomy to make sure that she left with stars in her eyes.

Mara Thill, Craig and Barbara Barrett's assistant, who, with unfailing aplomb, got us exactly what we needed, when and with whom we needed it, all across Arizona.

Sharon Tyson, our Titan of Tucson, who raised awareness— and a ruckus where called for—to spread the importance of our Library of Congress study of the Grand Canyon State.

Cory and Tiffany Unsworth, owners of the Kanab Touring Company in Utah, who, quite simply, did the impossible. They gave Carol and the Barretts the chance to experience the unforgettable Wave. Carol's images will show you why this was an experience of a lifetime.

And Susanne Walsh, who cheerfully got Carol everywhere but on a horse at the White Stallion Ranch.

Front Endpapers:

The Colorado River, which looks so small and benign from the rim, carved Arizona's breathtaking, iconic Grand Canyon six thousand feet below.

If there is a rival to the Grand Canyon as the symbol of Arizona's grandeur, the shimmering rocks below Sedona are a contender.

Back Endpapers:

The one place where four states—Arizona, New Mexico, Utah, and Colorado—meet is a distant, but much photographed, geographical oddity.

Behind hills near Antares, the sun relinquishes its dominion over the Arizona high desert and its wide assortment of plants and creatures.